1945

BOOKS BY KEN CUTHBERTSON

1945

THE YEAR THAT MADE MODERN CANADA

KEN CUTHBERTSON

PATRICK CREAN EDITIONS
An imprint of HarperCollins*Publishers*Ltd

1945

Published by Patrick Crean Editions, an imprint of HarperCollins Publishers Ltd

First edition

HarperCollins books may be purchased for educational, business,
or sales promotional use through our Special Markets Department.

HarperCollins Publishers Ltd
Bay Adelaide Centre, East Tower
22 Adelaide Street West, 41st Floor
Toronto, Ontario, Canada
M5H 4E3

www.harpercollins.ca

Library and Archives Canada Cataloguing in Publication

Title: 1945 : the year that made modern Canada / Ken Cuthbertson.
Other titles: Nineteen forty-five | Names: Cuthbertson, Ken, author.
Description: Includes bibliographical references and index.
Identifiers: Canadiana (print) 20200272489 | Canadiana (ebook) 2020027273x
ISBN 9781443459341 (hardcover) | ISBN 9781443459365 (ebook)
Subjects: LCSH: Canada—History—1945- | LCSH: Canadians—History—20th century.
CSH: Canada—History—1945-1963.
Classification: LCC FC580 .C88 2020 | DDC 971.063/2—dc23

Printed and bound in the United States of America

LSC/H 10 9 8 7 6 5 4 3 2 1

For
James T. Cuthbertson
(1914–1995),
a proud Royal Canadian Navy veteran of WWII,
and
Jocarol M. (née Minicola) Watson
(1945–2019)

CONTENTS

Opposite: The 8,000 soldiers who arrived in Halifax aboard the SS *Île de France* on June 21, 1945, were the first Canadians to be repatriated from Europe at war's end. (Library and Archives Canada [LAC], no. PA-192969)

1945

I'm thinking hard about the future.
[Canada] *may* be The Country.
—Benjamin Britten, English composer, 1939

INTRODUCTION

THERE HAS NEVER BEEN ANOTHER YEAR LIKE IT, AND IT SEEMS unlikely there ever will be again. Not for the world or for Canada. The year 1945 was a watershed in the life of this country. Oral historian Barry Broadfoot said it succinctly and well when he observed that "at war's end there was very little in Canada that was as it had been in [September] '39."[1]

Not only did 1945 mark the end of the catastrophic six-year global war that had scarred and forever changed Canada, it was also the moment—for that's what a year is in the grand sweep of history—that the light bulb went on. Suddenly, it all made sense.

It was in 1945 that Canadians began trying to sort out who they were as a people and decide where their home and native land was or *should be* headed in the post-war era. "Nineteen forty-five was the year when most Canadians began to learn that, for the first time, most of them could live comfortably."[2]

The potential for prosperity and greatness had been there from the beginning in 1867. It beckoned, as alluring as a wondrous unopened gift. In 1904, Prime Minister Wilfrid Laurier asserted that "the twentieth century belongs to Canada."[3] Others recognized the same potential; the American corporate titan Thomas Watson Sr. was among them. The chairman and chief executive officer of the mighty International

1

Business Machines (IBM), one of the world's most successful corporations, recognized Canada's potential, and he said as much.

In November 1938, Canada remained in the grips of the Great Depression, and yet where so many others saw only despair, America's "$1,000-a-day man"—as the media dubbed the sixty-four-year-old Watson in the days when $1,000 was still a lot of money—saw no end of economic potential and opportunities. On a visit to Toronto, Watson advised R.E. Knowles, the *Toronto Daily Star*'s ace "celebrity reporter" (and author of the book *Famous People Who Have Met Me*), that he was bullish on Canada's economic prospects. Said Watson, "I think this [of the] future: your country is eligible, in the next twenty-five years, for just about the greatest expansion of any country in the world." The reasons were obvious to him: "Canada's vast area . . . her illimitable resources, and the high average of her citizenship."[4]

Watson, who brimmed with Yankee-trader business smarts and a bustling can-do approach to life, recognized what too many Canadians in their characteristic reserve either overlooked or were too timid to seize upon and run with. The Canada of the 1930s was a vast, undeveloped land populated by just 11.5 million residents. Where others saw this as being problematic, Watson saw opportunity writ large—Canada was a blank canvas with unlimited development potential. As it turned out, the IBM chief's instincts were razor sharp. However, he was a tad off in his timing; his prediction came true a lot sooner than he or anyone else ever dreamed.

That happened not because of the foresight of business entrepreneurs. Nor was it thanks to the kind of government-backed jumpstart that helped the United States escape the ravages of the Great Depression; Canada had no President Franklin D. Roosevelt, and it had no New Deal. It was the September 1939 outbreak of war in Europe that was the catalyst.

At the time, the Dominion of Canada had a mere seventy-one years of history in its rear-view mirror. It was still a youngster as nations go. Incredibly, there were Canadians who were as old as the country itself; some of them had vivid memories of that July day in 1867 when Canada won its independence from Britain.

The British influence was still very strong and pervasive in Canada during the WWII era. (LAC, PA-1930077)

Toronto barrister James Roaf, who was eighty-eight years old in 1939, boasted to a newspaper interviewer that he had "many tales to tell of families of the Fathers of Confederation, many of whom he knew personally."[5] In a conversation with that same journalist, businessman Alexander Galt recalled that his father, Sir Alexander T. Galt—one of the thirty-six Fathers of Confederation—"was the soul of generosity and kindness. He never whipped me once." Those were very different times.

Had Roaf or Galt been asked, they doubtless also could have recounted how Canada had always been a sleepy economic and political backwater. The national economy was resource-driven, export-dependent, and cyclical. Canadians enjoyed good times, and they suffered through bad times. None were leaner or meaner than the decade of the 1930s. The protectionism that was rampant globally during the Great Depression stifled markets for the natural resources and agricultural produce that were the lifeblood of the Canadian economy. And so, no country suffered more in the 1930s.

Germany was the poster child for economic despair in those years, but consider this: while that nation's gross national product (GNP) fell by sixteen per cent from 1929 to 1933, Canada's GNP plummeted by almost *fifty* per cent—from $6.1 billion to $3.5.[6] An economic power-house Canada was not.

The nadir of the downturn came in 1933. That year, half of this country's wage earners were drawing some form of government assistance. The national unemployment rate soared to thirty per cent, and the average annual income was less than $500 at a time when the poverty line for a family of four was more than double that amount. Small wonder that hope and optimism, two of life's essentials, were in such short supply. Times were tough. Not "Honey, we're-a-little-short-for-a-Caribbean-cruise" tough, but rather "There's no-money-for-food-or-rent-this-month" tough.

Conditions had improved marginally as the decade wound down; however, by 1939 the world was on the slippery slope to the bloodiest, most costly war in the long history of bloody, costly wars. Sixty million people—a number so obscenely large that it boggles the mind—would die in the conflict. Yet Canada was fortunate. Geographically insulated from the carnage and generously endowed with natural resources, this country was one of the precious few that benefited from the conflict. The notion that "war is good for the economy" is a cliché for a reason. It's often true.

Canada's GNP leapt from $5.6 billion in 1939 to $11.9 billion in

1945. If the nation's economic possibilities suddenly seemed endless, it's because they were, and people realized it. By 1945, this country was wealthier, more robust, and more outward-looking than anyone had ever imagined at the onset of World War II (WWII) six years earlier. Today, Canada's GDP is more than $1.7 *trillion*, and this country is one of the most prosperous on the planet.[7]

The changes that transformed Canada during the war happened at warp speed. In retrospect, it's stunning to realize how many game-changing developments coalesced in 1945 and catapulted this country into the post-war era on a giddy, gloriously prosperous high that would endure for decades. As a year-end editorial in the *Regina Leader-Post* put it, 1945 had been "one of the great and historical years of our age, perhaps of all time."[8] One momentous development after another had dominated the headlines in Canada that year.

In April, Mackenzie King led a Canadian delegation to the founding conference of the United Nations in San Francisco. There, this country's representatives worked behind the scenes, quietly but effectively, to ensure that Canada and other middle powers and smaller nations would have their voices heard in the General Assembly of this new international organization. They did this despite the fact they were largely excluded when representatives from the United States, Britain, France, Russia, and China, the so-called major powers, sat down at the decision-making table. Canada had punched well above its weight economically and militarily during the war. Canadian troops had fought for the first time as a unified force under homegrown command and the Canadian flag, and the Royal Canadian Navy (RCN) had played a pivotal role in the Battle of the Atlantic and other nautical campaigns. As a result, several of the bright young men who were Mackenzie King's key advisors, a new breed of Ottawa mandarins, prodded the prime minister to press for a bigger role for Canada on the international stage. Their demands, reasonable though they may have been, were largely frustrated by the hardball geopolitical realities of the Cold War era.

In May, the First Canadian Army ousted a brutal German occupying force from the Netherlands and rescued the Dutch people from starvation. Canadian commanders then had the well-earned satisfaction of accepting the enemy's VE day surrender. Meanwhile, back home in Canada, jubilant sailors of the RCN celebrated the war's end by tearing apart the historic port city of Halifax in some of the worst rioting this country has ever seen. Their actions would unwittingly help bring an untimely, inglorious, and sudden end to the career of an admiral who was the only Canadian in two world wars to command an Allied theatre of action.

In July, the first federal government "baby bonus" cheques went into the mail—from $5 to $8 for each child sixteen or younger. At a time when the average annual income was less than $5,000 (ten times what it had been in 1933), families embraced this "free money." The idea of a monthly family allowance cheque was a winner. The era of universal social welfare programs had begun in Canada in earnest, and there was no turning back.

On August 6th, Canadian-mined and -refined uranium fuelled Little Boy, the atomic bomb that an American warplane dropped on the Japanese city of Hiroshima; 80,000 people died in a heartbeat. Three days later, a second bomb destroyed the city of Nagasaki. Suddenly, the nature of warfare and the realities of daily life were forever changed for everyone on this planet. As one cynical wag quipped, "The atomic age is here to stay, but are *we*?" The question was a valid one that merited serious consideration.

Hot on the heels of that stunning development, in early September, Canada unexpectedly found itself at the epicentre of a seismic political upheaval that history remembers as "the Gouzenko affair." The defection of a cipher clerk from the Soviet Union's embassy in Ottawa shattered the already frayed alliance between the Union of Soviet Socialist Republics (USSR) and the West, and it sparked the opening salvos of the Cold War. That protracted contest would cast an ominous shadow over the globe for more than four decades and would push the world to the brink of nuclear apocalypse on several occasions.

In the urbanized, peaceful, and prosperous Canada of today, it's all too easy to forget that this country is among the most blessed anywhere. The reasons are rooted in the epoch-defining events of 1945. That was the year in which Canada came of age. It was a remarkable time to be alive.

With each passing day, there are fewer and fewer Canadians—members of the "Greatest Generation"—who can bear witness to that truth. Even the youngest of the surviving Canadian military veterans who won the war and played such an integral role in the emergence of Canada as a modern, progressive, and prosperous nation are now frail nonagenarians. The American general Douglas MacArthur was wrong: old soldiers *do* die, and they *do* fade away. Just 33,000 Canadian veterans of WWII are still with us to take the commemorative salute or to remind us of what that is. That's a pity, for if history teaches us anything, it is that "stuff" doesn't *just happen*. It does so because of the actions of people, mostly those of ordinary men and women.

As I write these words, Canada—along with the rest of the world—is struggling to deal with challenges that potentially are as seismic as those that reshaped this country coming out of WWII. The COVID-19 pandemic has sparked an unprecedented flurry of public spending and government intervention in the everyday lives of ordinary people. There is rising tide of discussion about expanding the country's social safety net to include a national universal pharmacare program, or possibly even to reform the system entirely by implementing a guaranteed annual income, an initiative whose effects would be far-reaching and profound.

What is clear is that the relationship between citizens and the state is changing in some fundamental ways. It seems likely that for better or worse it will take years for the long-term effects of this to become clear. We can only hope and pray that when they finally do, those changes will be as beneficial as the ones that transformed this country going forward post-1945.

This book explores and explains some of the changes that reshaped Canada at war's end. It is a family album of a sort, a collection of narrative snapshots of some of those people—remarkable Canadians all—who endured and emerged triumphant from that by times wondrous, by times harrowing kaleidoscopic year that was 1945. This was the year that gave birth to the prosperous, peaceful Canada of today, a country that somehow often works despite itself. Modern Canada.

Kingston, Ontario
May 2020

PART I

ON THE EVE OF VICTORY

Private K.O. Earl, Perth Regiment, resting in the forest north of Arnhem, Netherlands, April 15, 1945. (LAC, MIKAN no. 3227364)

CHAPTER 1

"What a Way to Spend New Year's Eve"

A LONG WAY FROM HOME. LIKE A LOT OF CANADIAN MEN and women, on New Year's Eve 1944, that's where Captain Harold "Hal" MacDonald of the North Shore (New Brunswick) Regiment was. This twenty-seven-year-old native of Saint John, New Brunswick, could only dream of being back home in Canada, where family and friends were ringing in the new year, the sixth calendar year of the war. Hunkered down in a remote southeastern corner of the Netherlands as he was, MacDonald had little cause for celebration on this wintry Sunday night.

It had been snowing off and on for several days. Then suddenly, the temperature turned slushy mild. The thaw didn't last. On the final day of 1944, the mercury dipped again, and the inch or two of snow that covered the ground went crispy underfoot. Hal MacDonald stayed indoors, passing his evening in a battered old farmhouse that he and his compatriots had cleaned up for use as a temporary field headquarters. "The Stag Inn," they had dubbed it. Sitting there, MacDonald felt loneliness, despair, and anger bubbling inside him. He wasn't the only one who was experiencing these emotions.

A total of 1,040,126 Canadians served in the military during WWII; three-quarters of them were still in uniform on New Year's Day 1945.[1] Captain Hal MacDonald was among the 350,000 Canadian men and women who were overseas, most of them with the First Canadian Army, which was at the sharp end of the Allied stick in the fighting that raged in northwestern Europe. Every last member of Canada's all-volunteer military ached to return home sooner rather than later. But how much longer would the war drag on? That was the million-dollar question nobody could answer, although it seemed inevitable that the war in Europe was in its final days. The only ones who didn't understand that or wouldn't accept it were the most fanatical Nazis—in particular hardcore members of the *Schutzstaffel* (SS) and fuzzy-cheeked members of the Hitler Youth—many of whom seemed hell-bent on fighting to the death, or at least on continuing their struggles until the very final minutes of the war.

Hal MacDonald, like his comrades-in-arms, was increasingly dismayed to discover in his relentless advance toward Germany that many of the enemy soldiers were teenage boys or elderly men. These reluctant warriors had no choice but to take up arms; at least 20,000 Germans who refused to do so were summarily executed, shot dead, mostly in the last year of the war.[2] And so the Germans fought on, leaving the Allied troops no choice but to engage them in combat. It was kill or be killed.

The First Canadian Army, the largest military force this country has ever fielded—and in all likelihood *ever* will field—was under the command of fifty-seven-year-old Hamilton, Ontario, native General Henry "Harry" Crerar. The Canadians were clawing their way across the Dutch lowlands. Every mile of the way, they battled the rump of a reduced, desperate German *Wehrmacht* that had occupied the Netherlands since May 1940 and wasn't yet willing to admit defeat. The page one headline in the December 30 edition of the *Ottawa Citizen* served as a grim reminder of that fact when it trumpeted, "Canadian guns beat off bold Nazi forays." The ages of the German soldiers who were doing the shooting didn't much matter; their bullets killed. Hal MacDonald and every other Canadian soldier knew that all too well.

This country's troops were among the first Allied units to begin the liberation of Europe. They had stormed ashore on the beaches of Sicily in the summer of 1943 and again in the D-Day landings on June 6, 1944. Worth noting is that in the latter action the Canadians fought for the first time ever as a unified force under the Canadian flag.

Over the course of the long months of fighting that followed, through Italy and across France, Belgium, the Netherlands, and into Germany itself, thousands of Canadians died. In the five weeks between October 1 and November 8, 1944, 6,367 Canadians fell in the battles that ousted the German occupiers from the Scheldt River estuary and liberated the port of Antwerp. Infantry units, including Hal MacDonald's North Shore Regiment, suffered heavy losses in the fighting. That unit, like others under General Crerar's command, was critically short-handed and pleading for reinforcements who never came. There was a reason.

Back home, a bitter debate over conscription was raging. After the fall of France in the spring of 1940, the Liberal government of Prime Minister Mackenzie King had introduced conscription on a limited basis; the National Resources Mobilization Act (NRMA) allowed deployment of conscripts for military service in Canada only. However, as the country's involvement in the war deepened and the need for reinforcements grew, King had staged an April 1942 plebiscite in which he asked Canadians' permission to broaden the terms of conscription. The eight predominantly English-speaking provinces voted yes; French-speaking Quebec was the lone province to vote no. This had put the prime minister in a difficult spot.

His response had been what for him was a typical bit of political chicanery. King had amended the original NRMA legislation, removing a clause that restricted the geographical limitation on where conscripts could and would be required to serve. This had given the government leeway to equivocate, something at which King was a master. His new mantra became "Not necessarily conscription, but conscription if necessary," verbiage that had an absurdist ring to it. However, it served its purpose politically. The prime minister was desperate to avoid a repeat of the WWI conscription crisis, which had sparked civil unrest in Quebec and threatened to split the country in two. Pro-conscription English Canadians had railed against anti-conscription French, and vice versa. When five days of anti-conscription rioting had flared in the streets of Quebec City in the spring of 1918, it had taken almost 6,000 army troops to restore order.

King wanted no repeat of that turmoil, and so he was loath to deploy the so-called "zombies"—the derogatory epithet that Canadians hung on 60,000 NRMA conscripts—initially for thirty days, later for four months, and then for the duration of the war. Until the final weeks of the war, none of them were obliged to serve overseas. This was a source of much antagonism among the troops at the front. As one member of the Cape Breton Highlanders regiment put it, "We were hurting for men and losing heavily, far more than we could afford, and there was Mackenzie King, fat like a little toad, sitting in Ottawa and thinking of his political skin, his goddamned worthless skin, just so he wouldn't offend the French, in Quebec, who gave him his balance of power in Parliament."[3]

The January 1, 1945, editorial in the *Toronto Daily Star* expressed similar sentiments and said what a majority of English Canadians were feeling when it asserted that "Canada has made a notable effort, but more will probably have to be done to draw on the reserve power of the nation to wage war." Meanwhile, author Roger Duhamel, writing in *Maclean's* magazine (which during WWII published an overseas edition for Canadian men and women serving in the military), offered Quebec's dissenting perspective when he wrote, "[French Canadians] do not like to be reproached for our lukewarmness toward the war effort when our compatriots, even if they are brigaded mainly in English-speaking regiments, are being killed in every part of the world without hearing a command in their mother tongue and without the incentive of an Empire to defend."[4]

The prime minister remained sensitive to both sides in the conscription debate, and so his strategy was to dither in hopes the fighting in Europe would end before he had no other choice but to take action. But King's plans came perilously close to being derailed on November 1, 1944, when Defence Minister Colonel J.L. Ralston arrived at a Cabinet meeting intent on pushing his demand for full conscription. Ralston had recently visited the front and while there had met with Canada's senior military leaders. He'd seen firsthand the dire need for reinforcements. Despite this, Mackenzie King was unmoved by Ralston's pleas. Instead, the prime minister rose from his chair in the middle of the meeting and made a dramatic announcement: after much deliberation, he had decided that General Andrew McNaughton, a former head of the Canadian army, might be capable of finding a way forward without resorting to conscription. The implication of King's words was obvious. Ralston was out as defence minister.

The colonel rose from his chair without saying a word, shook King's hand, and then left the room. King got his way, but ironically just a few weeks later, McNaughton would feel compelled to appeal to the prime minister for a measure of conscription.

Hal MacDonald and other Canadian troops in the short-handed units battling Nazis in the Dutch lowlands grew angrier by the day as they followed the conscription debate. Small wonder. News of sit-down strikes and rioting by zombie conscripts back home in Canada was more than a little hard to stomach. "Latest reports give us a very bad taste in our mouths and our ire and disgust are at a high peak," MacDonald wrote in a December 1, 1944, letter home.[5]

A man of slight build with wavy hair, piercing eyes, and Van Heflin–like movie star good looks, MacDonald was as precise in his thinking as he was in his manner. If he had a motto, it surely would have been "Always do your best." Fittingly so, for in civilian life he had followed that credo in the accounting department of the Saint John business where he worked.

MacDonald was one of the 54,000 men who had volunteered to fight for king and country in September 1939. He enlisted for patriotic reasons. Many others did so simply because they wanted to work. With more than ten per cent of the workforce still unemployed, the prospect of suddenly having a full-time job that also provided free food, clothing, accommodation, and medical care was attractive to many recruits, even if being an army private paid only $1.30 a day.

Hal MacDonald soon got a pay raise. He would rise through the ranks to become the North Shore (New Brunswick) Regiment's adjutant. By war's end on May 8, 1945, he would be serving as North Shore's liaison officer with the 8th Brigade, of which the regiment was part. A lot had happened in the three years Hal MacDonald spent overseas.

On June 5, 1942, just ten days before the North Shore Regiment sailed out of Halifax bound for England, MacDonald had gotten married, taking as his bride Marjorie Taylor, a reporter on the now-defunct *Saint John Times-Globe* newspaper. Ironically, it may have been Hal who was the more prolific writer of the two. Write he did, and often. All told, MacDonald penned 463 letters to his wife. Read together these many years later, they provide a vivid and revealing account of his day-to-day life during the agonizing final months of the war in Europe.

Take, for example, MacDonald's letter written on Christmas Day 1944. He and the other men of the North Shore Regiment were marking time near the historic Dutch town of Nijmegen, barely twelve miles (twenty kilometres) from the German border. The city sits on a ridge that is a natural lookout from where you can survey the verdant countryside along the banks of the Maas. Spanning this great river was the Nijmegen Bridge, which carried the traffic from the town of Arnhem, eleven miles (seventeen kilometres) to the northwest.

Nijmegen, with roots going back two millennia to Roman times, is the Netherlands' oldest city. Among its many claims to fame is that it was the birthplace in 1788 of communist philosopher Karl Marx's mother, Henriette Pressburg. More than a century and a half later, in the post-WWII era, the town would also be where heavy metal rockers

Alex Van Halen (in 1953) and his brother, Eddie Van Halen (in 1955), entered the world.

While all of that is interesting, what's most noteworthy about Nijmegen for us is that because of its proximity to a strategically important river bridge, the town was the first Dutch city the invading German army seized in 1940. In late 1944, it was also the venue of one of the fiercest and bloodiest battles of WWII. When the Allies finally ousted the German occupiers, both sides hunkered down as they waited to see what would happen next. That's how and why Hal MacDonald found himself in Nijmegen during the 1944 holiday season. And what a sorry excuse for a holiday it was.

Canadian troops, like their American allies, were "dreaming of a white Christmas," as the popular holiday tune sung by American crooner Bing Crosby suggested, but the reality was markedly different. "Method of counting the days till Christmas was 'Three more Fighting Days till Christmas,'" MacDonald reported in a letter home. "Then the best one was one of the guys calling for fire & he says 'Peace on Earth, Goodwill towards Men—bring down fire on Target Ten.' And so it goes."[6]

MacDonald's woes were compounded by dental ailments. His gums had become infected after an army dentist removed an abscessed tooth on December 20, and so MacDonald remained in agony. His only available relief came in the form of pain-numbing shots of whisky. Small wonder MacDonald was feeling downcast and a tad numb on Christmas Day. "For us, it was just another day. Frankly, it was hard to realize it was Christmas."

The night before, on Christmas Eve, the Germans on the lines opposite the Canadians had staged a bit of Yuletide "entertainment." The scene was reminiscent of the ones that had sometimes played out on the battlefields of WWI. "A [German] bugler playing *Silent Night*," MacDonald told his wife. "Reply to that was a hell of a lot of fire. Then they set up a loudspeaker & started calling us friends & asking if carols made us lonely & they played carols. Ha—the b's got more than they expected."[7]

Captain Harold "Hal" MacDonald. (Catharine MacDonald)

It had been six months since the D-Day invasion, and Hal MacDonald and the other men of the North Shore Regiment—like just about every other soldier on both sides—were bone-tired, battle-weary, and dreaming of just one thing: going home. It didn't help that MacDonald's mouth was killing him. Being "completely fed up" with the war, he struggled not to show it and didn't always succeed. "One of the Sods who has never been out of [Brigade] since [June 6] mentioned about the tough time in the line. That finished me," MacDonald wrote. "I gave out & asked him what he knew about it. Honestly, I think the men who live in slit trenches should have a separate decoration. [As adjutant] I used to write up all OR [other ranks] citations and the CO [commanding officer] wrote up the Officers'. Necessitates the addition of a lot of baloney as the armchair heroes don't, or don't seem to, realize what action is."[8]

A week later, on New Year's Eve, MacDonald's mouth was still killing him. After "forcing down" as much dinner as he could handle, he continued to dull his pain with whisky and did his best to take his mind off his woes. He did so by passing a couple of hours playing cribbage. At ten o'clock, the soothing sounds of Canada's own Guy Lombardo orchestra were flowing from the radio. Awash in nostalgia and aching to be at home, MacDonald sat down to write yet another letter to his wife, Marjorie. His pencil-pushing was interrupted by a pal who convinced him to join a craps game that needed players. When the last dice were cast, MacDonald ended up two guilders to the good. "What a way to spend New Year's Eve," he mused in his letter home. "Shouldn't be too caustic, or rather, moody. Have so much to be thankful for."

SOME WELL-KNOWN CANADIANS WHO WERE BORN IN 1945

The year 1945 marked the start of the great post-war baby boom. Almost 289,000 babies were born in Canada that year. Among them are some well-known names:

- Roberta Bondar, astronaut
- Wayne Cashman, NHL player
- Bruce Cockburn, singer/songwriter
- Joy Fielding, novelist
- Robert Munsch, children's author
- Steve Smith (a.k.a. Red Green), comedian
- Steven Truscott, wrongly convicted of murder
- Rogie Vachon, NHL goalie
- Neil Young, singer/songwriter
- Sneezy Waters, singer/actor

Mackenzie King rules Canada because he himself is the
embodiment of Canada—cold and cautious on the outside,
dowdy and pussy in every overt action, but inside a mass
of intuition and dark intentions.
—Robertson Davies, *The Manticore* (1972)

CHAPTER 2

Alone Again . . . Naturally

I N OTTAWA, 3,500 MILES (5,700 KILOMETRES) TO THE WEST OF
Nijmegen, New Year's Eve 1945 was cold and serene. Here the war
seemed distant and even a tad unreal.

An inch of fresh snow that had fallen early on the morning of
December 31 for a few hours had given the nation's capital a pristine
winter-wonderland appearance. A coat of downy white had cloaked
the Peace Tower's soaring, majestic spire, the castle-like Gothic battle-
ments of the adjacent buildings of Parliament Hill, and the surrounding glacis of lawns and walkways.

On nearby streets, the snow had muffled the soundtrack of urban
life early on the Sunday morning. The city's rickety electric trollies
had rocked along slowly, most of them empty save for those subdued
riders who were on their way to church. The cars and trucks that
had crept along downtown streets had done so with all the speed of
cold molasses, their chained tires clattering as they trailed tracks in
the snow.

It was said that in winter Ottawa seemed "to shrink in size without
foliage and flowers—the smallness of the houses to each other, become
plain—so do the drabness and poverty of the architecture. Snow fills
up the spaces and seems to bring the buildings closer together."[1]

On a working day, many of the buildings in the nation's capital were abuzz with activity. The number of federal civil servants had increased almost threefold during the war years—from 46,000 in 1939 to 116,000 by 1945.[2] Many of these worker bees toiled within sight of Parliament Hill; the Ottawa workforce had grown from 11,000 in 1939 to more than 18,000 by early 1945.

The rapid expansion of the civil service posed major headaches for government nabobs and city officials. That reality was reflected in the downtown streetscapes. It was said there were two styles of architecture in Ottawa at that time: Empire and Emergency. "The government has mushroomed rows of temporary wooden buildings, especially along Wellington Street, to be used as office accommodation for new departments and the swollen staffs of old ones," a *Maclean's* reporter noted in 1941. "Nothing has been done, however, about finding places to live in for the people who have been brought into the capital city to work in these buildings."[3]

By 1945, Ottawa's population was still just 160,000. Even so—or perhaps because of it—rental accommodation remained scarcer than roses in January. Houses and apartments were in desperately short supply. So, too, were rooms in the city's boarding houses and even in its few hotels, the Château Laurier and the Lord Elgin the most prominent among them. A favourite joke that was making the rounds in Ottawa at this time—grim but funny because it had a ring of truth to it—was the one about a passerby who spotted a man drowning in the Rideau Canal and stopped to shout the question, "Where do you live?" When the puzzled man sputtered a reply, the passerby rushed away in hopes of getting to the drowning man's hotel before anyone else could rent the soon-to-be vacant room. Unfortunately for the passerby, the person who had pushed the victim into the river had gotten there before him.

While downtown Ottawa bustled on weekdays, it was a different place on weekends, especially on Sundays. Canada being a predominantly Christian country in the 1940s, most shops were closed on the

Sabbath. Public transit ran on a reduced schedule. Bars and pubs were shuttered, and worshipers filled the pews of city churches for morning services.

Despite its outsize status as the home of Canada's federal government and the nexus of the country's "all-in" war effort, Ottawa still had a small-town ambience to it, much as it had since its frontier beginnings in 1826. You could even say that Bytown—as it was originally called and continued to be known until 1855—was "run of the mill."

Queen Victoria, on the urging of advisors in 1867, had designated the town as the capital of the new Dominion of Canada. The reason was simple. Bytown was halfway between Montreal and Toronto, and—almost as important—it wasn't Kingston, the erstwhile first capital. Vested interests in Canada's two largest cities wanted a new capital, not that anyone in far-off London much cared. To eyes there, Canada was a mere splash of red on a global map of a British Empire that was at the height of its imperial glory and claimed sovereignty over four hundred million subjects. That was one of every five people on the planet.

No reigning British monarch had ever visited Canada, and none would do so until King George VI toured the country in 1939. However, Queen Victoria may well have been aware that Ottawa, the new capital of the new Dominion of Canada, was the hub of a thriving regional forestry industry. After all, the demand for red and white pine, initially for the squared timber that was used in British shipyards, and later for sawn lumber that fed building industries in the United Kingdom and areas of the United States, fuelled prosperity and population growth in communities up and down the Ottawa Valley. Regardless, owing to the area's geographical remoteness, even with the coming of the railway in December 1854, Ottawa remained a relatively out-of-the-way northern outpost. That insularity persisted until well into the twentieth century.

In 1950, the Canadian diplomat and diarist Charles Ritchie would observe that "Ottawa remains in its soul, a small town . . . a lumbering settlement in the Ottawa Valley. That spirit still pervades the place."[4] The very tweedy 1st Baron Tweedsmuir, who served as Governor General of Canada (1935–40), also picked up on the arboreal theme when he dismissed Ottawa as a "sub-Arctic lumber village."[5] Regardless, with its Victorian ambience and stolid demeanour, Ottawa was the perfect backdrop for the eventful life and political career of William Lyon Mackenzie King, Canada's longest-serving prime minister and its dominant political figure of the WWII era. If you accept the results of a 1997 *Maclean's* magazine survey of Canadian historians, King was also the "best" of the twenty-three people—twenty-two men and one woman—who have served as prime minister. He edged out Sir John A. Macdonald and Sir Wilfrid Laurier in the voting.

Mounted members of the RCMP patrolled Parliament Hill year-round in the 1940s.
(Jack Fletcher/National Geographic Creative)

Those pundits who took part in the *Maclean's* poll had little positive to say about King the man, even though they begrudgingly conceded that they were "impressed by his great political skills, his devotion to unity, his establishment of Canada's international persona, his crucial steps towards establishment of the social welfare safety net, and the brilliant way he ran Canada's enormous war effort."[6]

Despite this, most Canadians today who don't know the Mackenzie King story tend to think of him—if they know anything at all about the man—as being "the epitome of political dullness," as historian Jack Granatstein has so succinctly put it.[7] But where King is concerned, appearances were deceiving. He wasn't the man that most Canadians— even his political colleagues and supporters—assumed he was.

The most insightful and authoritative of the many King biographies to be found on library shelves is C.P. Stacey's 1976 book *A Very Double Life: The Private World of Mackenzie King*.[8] The suggestive title is apt, for behind King's pious, buttoned-down public persona, there lurked another, much more secretive and darker character. The "unbuttoned" Mr. King was one strange dude. "The heavy comfortable clothes cut in a spacious old-fashioned way, the high stiff collar, the pearl tie pin, the thick black cord that hangs from [King's] massive spectacles, the elaborate cane—all these, and an air of immovable dignity, suggest some contemporary of Sir Wilfrid [Laurier]," one of his former secretaries once wrote. "Looking at Mackenzie King, one is taken back to leisurely days in small Ontario cities, when the leading citizens passed the summer evenings bowling on the green and thought twice before they removed their vests in the company of ladies."[9]

William Lyon Mackenzie King was a nineteenth-century man, Victorian to the core. His maternal grandfather, William Lyon Mackenzie, was the political firebrand who led the failed rebellion of 1837 in Upper Canada, the ill-fated attempt to bring about political reform and responsible government. Mackenzie King grew up believing it was his destiny to finish the unfinished business of leading

Canada to greatness. That was an idea instilled in him and cultivated by his doting mother. The affection was mutual.

Mackenzie King worshipped the family matriarch with a devotion so enduring and intense it would have given Norman "Psycho" Bates goosebumps. And after Isabel (Mackenzie) King's 1917 death, her son struggled to contact her in the afterlife. He did so via seances, by consulting with mediums, gazing hopefully into a crystal ball, and reading tea leaves. It's fair to say that Mackenzie King, the man who guided Canada through WWII and more than anyone else played a pivotal role in shaping and defining the Canada of today, was our strangest and most enigmatic political leader.

I F HE HAD BEEN alive in the third decade of the twenty-first century, there's zero chance King would have ever won elected office. Not in this era of social media, the 24/7 cable news cycle, and rampant cynicism about politicians and all things political. Even in his day, this was a man who defied easy analysis. He was the most unlikely of politicians, not someone you'd ever think could become prime minister of Canada, let alone its longest-serving one.

Short and pudgy as a dumpling, King was bushy-browed and jowly, and he sported a "follicularly challenged" comb-over. It's not being unfair to point out that the camera wasn't Mackenzie King's friend. Whenever he posed for a photograph, he invariably was attired in a three-piece suit and tie that screamed, "Here's your archetypal old white guy"—one whose idea of a good time would be to spend an evening sorting his stamp collection, reading Tennyson, or reviewing a piece of draft legislation. One of King's left-leaning political opponents once commented that "the height of [King's] ambition was to pile a parliamentary committee on a royal commission."[10]

Despite his undistinguished physical appearance and what can fairly be described as a diffident public demeanour—"Parliament will have to decide" was his stock response whenever he was asked a question he didn't want to or couldn't answer—there is no doubt that King had what today we'd call "political smarts." He was crafty, cunningly ruthless in a Machiavellian way, with what many of his contemporaries recognized as a ceaseless itch for power. King was a master in the art of backroom wheeling and dealing. He won elections and was able to move the wheels of government. And after all, at the end of the day that's what counts in the Darwinian world of partisan politics. King's domestic political successes speak for themselves. So do his idiosyncrasies, which really were what set him apart from the crowd and make him such an intriguing historical figure.

King was hopelessly insecure, and yet he was a tactless bully who never hesitated to use his power to humiliate or humble those who got on his wrong side. Other Canadian politicians bludgeoned their political opponents, figuratively speaking for the most part (thankfully), while King preferred to wield a stiletto, which he used to skewer his enemies.

Mackenzie King and Franklin Roosevelt at the Quebec City conference, August 1943. (FDR Presidential Library, NPx 48223622-10)

His mercenary behaviour was justified, he believed, because he was certain that he had been divinely ordained to lead Canada to greatness. Never mind that Mackenzie King didn't look like central casting's idea of a leader. He was a recluse, a prude, and the archetypal "cold fish." One of the joys of King's life was "bask[ing] in the friendship of the great and near-great—a Franklin Roosevelt, a John D. Rockefeller, a Ramsay MacDonald, or a member of the British nobility."[11]

A S THE YEAR 1944 faded away, Canada's seventy-year-old prime minister—the man whom Hal MacDonald and so many of Canada's other men and women in uniform reviled—was almost a decade into his third and final term in office. That tenure spanned the period from 1935 to 1948, which was one of the most tumultuous in Canadian history.

On the morning of December 31, 1944, Mackenzie King had been alone, the norm for most Sunday mornings. In this quiet time, as usual, he had been content to lounge around at home. In the winter months, his refuge was Laurier House, a yellow-brick, slate-roofed Victorian mansion at 335 Laurier Avenue East, in the Sandy Hill neighbourhood of downtown Ottawa.

King loved living at Laurier House. The dwelling had been the home of Prime Minister Wilfrid Laurier and his wife, Zoé, who had lived there for twenty-two years, from 1897 until Sir Wilfrid died in 1919. Then, because the Lauriers had no children, when Mrs. Laurier shuffled off this mortal coil two years later, she bequeathed Laurier House to Mackenzie King, who was her dear late husband's protégé and one of his chief admirers. King would live there until 1948. A lifelong bachelor and, like the Lauriers, childless, he bequeathed the dwelling to the government and people of Canada. Today, it is a local landmark and national historic site.

Laurier House is open to public tours. Visitors can browse the overstuffed book-lined third-floor study, from which King governed

Canada for more than two decades. In a corner of that wood-panelled room, next to a window, sits the large portrait of King's mother that was among his most cherished possessions. A special lamp illuminated it day and night. It was also here on the top floor of Laurier House that King slept, in the same bedroom in which both Wilfrid and Zoé Laurier had drawn their last breaths. Creepy though that may sound, King felt very much at home in these surroundings. Such was the nature of the man. He had few close relatives, regarded social events as a waste of time, and entertained only when there was a political reason for doing so.

Mackenzie King kept the portrait of his late mother, which was the focal point of his study, illuminated day and night. (LAC, MIKAN no. 3334012)

In addition to his dog, Mackenzie King's most trusted and loved daily companions in Laurier House were the spirits of deceased friends and loved ones—his mother in particular. For a man who was political to his core, King had surprisingly few close contacts. Mostly they were restricted to those people he felt comfortable dealing with or having around. The Laurier House staff included a cook, a kitchen maid, two parlour maids, a chauffeur, and a valet/butler, all of whom were live-ins. But King wasn't an easy man to work for or even be around, and so "the records reveal . . . considerable turnover throughout the whole period of King's life in the house."[12]

One of the few exceptions was a man named John Nicol, whom King employed as his valet/butler from 1921 into the mid-1940s. On the rare occasions King mentioned Nicol in his conversations, he referred to him by his surname, and Nicol was noted on the staff list as being the prime minister's "confidential messenger," whatever that meant. While there has long been speculation about King's sexuality, there's no smoking gun that proves he was bisexual or gay. If he was, neither orientation would have been anything he or anyone else openly admitted to at that time. Of course, there were myriad reasons for this, social, vocational, political, and legal; by Section 178 of the Criminal Code of 1927 (which was still the law in 1945), sexual relations between males—"gross indecency"—was a crime that was punishable by life in prison.

Many of the details of King's adult private life will forever be shrouded in uncertainty, although his diaries do reveal some juicy details of his encounters with the street prostitutes whom he was supposedly intent on "saving from themselves" during his student days at the University of Toronto, when he was filled with religious fervour. Owing to King's self-admitted "frailty of . . . nature," his efforts repeatedly went awry, and he "wandered like a lost child at the biddings of passion."[13] King confided to his diary, "God only knows why I am so weak. He knows I fight hard."[14] Perhaps. But he couldn't help himself. Each time the devil got the better of him, he came away feeling racked with guilt and vowing never again to give in to lust. He was true to his word. At least until the next time. "There is no doubt that I lead a very double life," he wrote in his diary. "I strive to do right and continually do wrong."[15]

The older he got, the more guarded King was about the details of his private life. But many aspects of his workaday routines are an open book. His diary speaks volumes, literally. And the list of frequently dialed phone numbers that he kept on his nightstand speaks volumes about what was important to King during the war years.

Among the numbers he considered vital were those for his barber, his jeweller, and his country club. Also, the phone numbers for the Ottawa hospital, the offices of the Canadian Press and Canadian Pacific Telegraph, the front desks at the Château Laurier and Lord Elgin hotels, and the staff who looked after Kingsmere, his beloved summer retreat northeast of Ottawa.

King recorded his interactions with his inner circle, the minutiae of his daily life, and his thoughts in more than 50,000 pages of diaries. If you were ever to stack them one on top of the other, the diaries would tower more than twenty-three feet (seven metres) high. King wrote entries on most days from 1893, when he was nineteen years old, until just three days before his death in July 1950. In the early days, when he wrote each day's entry by hand—often using a stubby pencil because he had an aversion to using sharp pencils—the entries are more personal and candid. Later in life, when he dictated his daily entries to a secretary, they tended to be more circumspect, though still revealing. Consider his jottings for Sunday, December 31, 1944.

King reported having slept soundly the previous night while dreaming sweet dreams of attending a party aboard a yacht belonging to the Governor General, the Earl of Athlone, and his wife, Alice. These were the sort of nocturnal reveries that filled the head of Canada's prime minister in his later years.

Dreaming done for another night, Mackenzie King had risen from his bed at 8:30 a.m. on a snowy December 31, 1944. Then, as he did most days, he had sat down to a breakfast prepared for him by his housekeeper. As was his habit, King had dined solo, seated at an oval table in a room that formerly had been the housekeeper's bedroom. King seldom entertained formally, and the room where he ate meals when he was at home was adjacent to his sleeping quarters. Eating here in the morning was easier and more convenient than traipsing downstairs in his dressing gown to have his toast and morning tea while sitting alone in the dining room.

Today, he might well have watched television, used his smart phone to check his email, or dashed off a few tweets while sipping a second cup of breakfast tea. In 1944, like many Canadians, Mackenzie King listened to the radio. It was his habit to read the newspaper over breakfast and then tune in to the 9 a.m. newscast on the Dominion Network of the Canadian Broadcasting Corporation (CBC). This was something from which King derived no small measure of satisfaction. After all, the radio service was one of his creations.

King's predecessor as prime minister, Conservative R.B. Bennett, had created the Canadian Radio Broadcasting Commission (CRBC) in 1932 to oversee what he envisioned as a system of private broadcasting, such as existed in the United States. But King had other ideas. Most every breath Mackenzie King took and everything he did had a political rationale. In November 1936, he followed the British lead, making radio programming a public service when he established the CBC as a Crown corporation.

A million Canadian homes had a radio at the time, and that number grew by leaps and bounds after the outbreak of war in Europe. In the dark days that followed, the CBC radio service became a powerful weapon in the government's communication arsenal. Ironically, in many parts of the country, the public network's programming was transmitted by privately owned radio stations. During the war years, CBC brought the latest news from the front into the living rooms of Canadians from coast to coast; the eloquent voice of the network's senior war correspondent, Matthew Halton, and those of seasoned reporters Bob Bowman and Arthur Holmes were as familiar to many Canadians as the voices of family members.

The CBC news on the final day of 1944, as on most mornings around that time, was generally positive. The year had been a good one for the Allies. In the wake of the successful D-Day landing on the beaches of Normandy, the Allied armies were slowly, but surely, winning the fight against the Nazis. The tide of battle had also turned in the Pacific. There the Japanese were bloodied and in retreat but still unbowed, fanatical, and—the fear was—willing to fight to the last man, woman, and child.

At the dawn of 1945, the year that was destined to be the most eventful and transformative in human history, Canadians had every reason to feel optimistic. Most people had come to accept that the daily news reports they read or heard on radio were censored and therefore weren't always to be believed, but even so it was apparent that it was only a matter of time until war would end in an Allied victory. All signs pointed in that direction. Indeed, the dozen "experts" who contributed to a *Maclean's* article titled "Forecast for 1945" were unanimous in predicting that the war was in its final weeks. "Germany will be defeated before April 1," one writer assured his readers.[16] Close, but no cigar. His prediction would prove to be off by just one month.

The editors of the Canadian army's daily newspaper, the *Maple Leaf*, were no less confident that an Allied victory in Europe was imminent. Looking ahead to the post-war era, in December 1944 they invited readers to weigh in on the question "What is to be done to Germany to prevent another war?" The responses offered by Canada's fighting men and women, as reported by the *Toronto Daily Star*, were surprising.

The consensus of opinion was that it was education, not military might, that would ensure Germany honoured the terms of any surrender agreement. "Only when the German people are steeped in the democratic way of life and can look back on their attempts to conquer the world with the same detached view of civilized people looking at the barbarities of their ancestors will the world be safe from the peril of German aggression," wrote one soldier.[17]

I T IS DOUBTFUL THAT Mackenzie King read the *Maple Leaf* or that he knew or cared a whit about the results of the newspaper's reader poll. King wasn't military-minded, nor was he comfortable dealing with military matters. Not in the least. As mentioned earlier, his reluctance to impose compulsory overseas conscription as a means to relieve a shortage of Canadian troops on the battlefields of northwestern Europe had earned King the scorn of military brass and rank-and-file soldiers alike. In late 1944 and early 1945, some Canadian infantry units were so short of manpower that they were fighting at barely more than half strength. This sapped morale and cost lives, yet King refused to do anything to provide relief. As military historian Tim Cook has pointed out, "Conscription was a bridge too far for King."[18]

The prime minister's fears of anti-conscription civil unrest were well-founded. Knowing this, he and his most trusted advisors had displayed all the dispassionate resolve of insurance actuaries as they weighed the odds of the various options before them: "Basing their calculations on approximately three more months of heavy fighting in Europe, the government, in checking the number of volunteers still available [in early 1945] . . . came to the conclusion that the army could operate without overseas conscription."[19]

As Mackenzie King passed the time on the final night of 1944, he had pushed the war and the conscription controversy to the back recesses of his mind. He was preoccupied with personal concerns, many of which centred on delusions of his own importance on the world stage. King reflected on the possible meaning of the dreams he'd had the previous night about Princess Alice, the Governor General's wife, and King George V. He then wrote a few letters, mailed a photo of himself to an admiring supporter, and telephoned New Year's greetings to American industrialist John D. Rockefeller, who was his long-time friend and former employer, and to President Franklin D. Roosevelt. "At a quarter to five, I got FDR on the phone," King wrote in his diary. "It was a pleasant interlude and I was glad to have it before the present year was out."[20] As the telephone conversation with FDR was ending,

King noted the position of the hands of the clock; they were aligned at 4:55 p.m. In his mind, that was a highly favourable sign.

To say that Mackenzie King was superstitious is akin to saying that Donald Trump might have a touch of ego. It was another of King's personal quirks that as a believer in numerology—a belief in the divine or mystical relationship between a number and one or more real-life events—he was constantly taking note of the position and interplay of the hands of the clock. If they were overlapping or aligned when he was doing something he felt was important, he interpreted it as an indication fate was smiling upon him. Similarly, when King noted that the loose-leaf paper he used in his daily journal had three O-shaped holes, he was convinced it was significant that the three and the O equalled the number thirty. Exactly why this was worth noting, he never explained. However, in King's mind it was.

He was upbeat after taking a brief nap and having a cup of tea. He then ventured out into the still, snowy streets to attend the "watch night service"[21] at St. Andrew's, the Presbyterian church that King routinely attended. There he was intrigued by the evening's sermon, which dealt with the life of the prophet Moses. King weighed the parallels between his own situation and that of Moses, a solitary leader who was as one with his followers yet remained apart from them. That self-image appealed to King. It lingered in his mind as he made his way home after the church service and when he stopped off for "a little reading"—a session with one of the mediums he routinely consulted. All of this set the tone for the rest of King's night.

He spent the waning minutes of New Year's Eve, until midnight, praying and in quiet meditation. After reading some passages in a book he was convinced his late father had directed him to contemplate, King ended his solitary celebration by shaking the paw of his dog, Pat, and kissing the mutt good night. Canada's most powerful politician and wartime leader then sat staring "at the little case with dear mother's hair and ring, both of which I was able to touch before the old year was out," King confided to his diary. "Her hair continues to breathe vitality.

It was full of silvery loveliness by the light of the lamp at the close of the year."[22]

King ended his diary entry for December 31, 1944, expressing dismay that he hadn't heard the sound of bells ringing on this tranquil New Year's Eve. In fact, Dominion Carillonneur Robert Donnell had performed a concert, loudly ringing in the new year with the tolling of the Peace Tower's fifty-three bells. Doing so was an Ottawa tradition for thirty years, from 1940 to 1970. The pealing of sixty tons (about fifty-four tonnes) of bells would reverberate throughout the snowy downtown streets of Ottawa for several minutes. On this New Year's Eve, Mackenzie King had been so wrapped up in his own thoughts and personal reveries that he was aware of nothing else. He had no way of knowing—no one did—that for Canada, six years of conflict would soon come to an end, and that going forward this country would be forever changed.

More than a million Canadians were in uniform and everyone in Canada was involved in some way in the home war effort.

—Barry Broadfoot, *Six War Years, 1939–45*

CHAPTER 3

On the Home Front

ANY FOREIGN VISITOR TO CANADA IN 1945 WOULD HAVE noticed a couple of central things about everyday life in this country. Both were inescapable.

The first was the relative prosperity that Canadians enjoyed. Even with rationing in effect, a cornucopia of food and consumer goods was available in the shops. Most people had plenty to eat. "The government rationed butter, sugar, meat, and some other foods, but my dad had a full-time job, and so our family always had enough to eat," recalled Barbara (née Robson) Fitsell, a native of Cape Breton Island. In 1945, she was eighteen and living at home in Sydney with her parents and three siblings. "Fish was plentiful," Fitsell remembered, "and it was inexpensive. My dad kept a lobster trap in the water beside the dock at the steel mill where he worked—although he wasn't supposed to—and so we also enjoyed a lobster dinner from time to time."[1]

Thousands of "British guest children" who escaped the trauma of war by billeting with Canadian host families enjoyed a similar bounty. Many of them marvelled at the astounding variety of sweets they found available in this country. Typical was the fourteen-year-old British girl with a sweet tooth who giggled when she recounted to a Toronto newspaper reporter how delighted she was to have "sampled every flavour of soda, but two" at a corner drugstore.[2] To her and other visitors to Canada, such abundance was surprising and even shocking.

It certainly shocked a twenty-four-year-old Russian military officer who arrived in Canada in June 1943 to begin a posting as the cipher clerk at the embassy of the Soviet Union. Igor Gouzenko, who was destined to shed his obscurity in spectacular fashion and to change the course of history a couple of years later, could scarcely believe his eyes when he saw the variety and quantity of food and consumer goods available in stores in Edmonton, his point of entry when he arrived in Canada. Government propaganda in Stalinist Russia had it that Canadians, working people especially, were downtrodden and hungry. "We weren't prepared for the wealth of food in the . . . hotel where we stayed," Gouzenko would recall, "nor the abundance of clothing, candies, and luxuries of all kinds in such windows as those of the huge Hudson's Bay store on the main street."[3]

No less surprising was the fact that such goods were available at prices most ordinary people could afford. During WWII, when a skilled tradesman in Canada earned a dollar an hour, a dozen eggs cost thirty-seven cents. Bread was eight cents a loaf. Four dollars bought a new pair of men's shoes. And a moviegoer would spend twenty-five cents to see *Going My Way*, the Bing Crosby movie that won the year's Academy Award for Best Picture.

The cost of food and consumer goods had soared during WWI. Not so during WWII. The Liberal government had imposed wage and price controls on September 3, 1939, a week before Canada officially declared war on Nazi Germany. Initially, the Wartime Prices and Trade Board (WPTB) had slapped partial limits on rents and on the cost of coal, sugar, timber, steel, milk, and a few other consumer goods. By 1941, with the war intensifying and the demand for raw materials soaring, inflation was creeping upward, pulling prices with it. The Ottawa government responded by transferring responsibility for the WPTB from the Department of Labour to the Department of Finance and by broadening the list of foods and consumer goods that were subject to price controls. Scottish-born Donald Gordon, a gruff, tough-talking banker who in 1935 had been the founding head of the Bank of Canada, took over as WPTB chairman.

Gordon reportedly kept his brain box lubricated and turbocharged each day by downing a bottle of Scotch, yet he was one of the King government's most recognizable and powerful figures during the war years. The WPTB, with its thirteen regional offices and a hundred local offices, was "a giant agency that controlled the lives of businesspeople and ordinary citizens alike. Ration cards for scarce foods and for gasoline became the norm; tokens were necessary to purchase meats; car tires became scarce as hen's teeth; and every housewife was urged to grow vegetables in her backyard, to report waste, and to save money, edible fats, and even milkweed for life preservers."[4] Milkweed for life preservers? Strange, but true.

With war raging in the Pacific, the cotton-like fibrous material called kapok that once filled life preservers was unavailable; it comes from the kapok trees found on the Indonesian island of Java. Milkweed pods became the homegrown substitute.

Prime Minister Mackenzie King had surprisingly little interest or expertise in any of this or in economic policy matters. On principle, he disliked price controls as much as he frowned on the very idea of government intervention in the economy. King was also suspicious of those who touted such ideas, despite the fact they included two of the government's most powerful civil servants. Deputy Finance Minister Clifford Clark and Under-Secretary of State for External Affairs Oscar D. Skelton were outspoken champions of wage and price controls. Both men had taught at Queen's University before coming to Ottawa, and both had no fear of an activist social-service state. In fact, to Mackenzie King's dismay, they championed the idea. "I am beginning to see the wisdom of not taking into the government, men who have not had some political training, however able they may be," he told his diary. "The academic mind is not the best one to handle the problems of Government."[5]

King was a reluctant convert to the need for wartime wage and price controls. Advocates argued that such measures would provide Ottawa with a valuable tool with which to limit inflation and curb the growing union demands for higher wages and improved working conditions. When William Mackintosh, yet another Queen's University economist, who served as a key advisor to Finance Minister James Lorimer (J.L.) Ilsley, prepared a policy statement setting out the case for expanding wage and price controls, King listened politely to the lanky, balding academic. But anything King heard went in one ear and out the other. Having little interest in the document that Mackintosh had handed him, King "read two or three paragraphs, looked up, and said, 'This is important isn't it?'"[6]

Mackintosh had made such a compelling case in support of his views that King felt obliged to give in, and so he grudgingly accepted the economist's recommendations.

THE SECOND THING ANY foreign visitor to Canada in 1945 would have noticed about life here was how peaceful this country was. Canadians were fortunate beyond measure in that regard. Geography insulated this "peaceable kingdom," sparing it from the trauma and ravages of the war in Europe and the Pacific. In 1942, German submarines put ashore agents in Gaspé and near Saint John, New Brunswick. Both men were apprehended before they could do any harm. Then in 1943, a U-boat landing party came ashore on a remote beach in Labrador and set up an automatic weather transmitting station. These incidents were of little consequence. Canada's only meaningful exposure to the war was the U-boat attacks that happened off the east coast. In 1942, in particular, German U-boats enjoyed considerable successes attacking Allied ships in the North Atlantic and in the Gulf of St. Lawrence. The latter proved to be a rich hunting ground for enemy submarines; they attacked seven convoys, sinking twenty merchant vessels, a loaded troopship, and two RCN warships. The pièce de résistance, so far as domestic impact was concerned, was the October 14, 1942, sinking of the SS *Caribou*, the passenger ferry from Sydney to Port aux Basques. When it was torpedoed, it went down with the loss of 136 people, ten of them children.

In the wake of the December 1941 Japanese sneak attack on the American naval base at Pearl Harbor, residents of British Columbia were on the alert for similar strikes or even for an attempted Japanese invasion. We now know that for a variety of reasons any such fear was unwarranted. The logistics of a Japanese invasion would have been daunting to say the least; a 4,400-mile (7,100 kilometre) ocean expanse separates Japan from the coast of British Columbia.[7] However, there was no denying that the war in the Pacific was a grim affair. Nowadays, we tend to forget the conflict had all the elements of a modern-day holy war between Occident and Orient. Both sides viewed the other with the same bigotry and poisonous illogic that was reflected in the long, painful history of anti-Asian discrimination and racism that blighted Canada's west coast.

During the war years, eighty per cent of Canada's 11.5 million residents were white and Christian, predominantly of British or French heritage; just *three-tenths of one per cent* of the population were Chinese, and just *two-tenths of one per cent* were Japanese. The numbers were roughly ten times higher on the west coast, where immigrants of "Oriental heritage" usually settled. But even there, they were a tiny minority. Despite this, the war focused fresh animosity on the Japanese, and in late 1941 and into 1942, police and military officials rounded up and detained almost 22,000 Japanese Canadians. The injustice didn't stop there. The federal government seized personal and real property belonging to these "enemy aliens" while confining some and dispersing others, including whole families—exiling them, really—to remote areas of the British Columbia interior and the Prairie provinces. Among the displaced was a five-year-old boy named David Suzuki; as you may know, he would grow up to become a world-renowned scientist and environmental activist. "To the white community we looked different; we looked just like the enemy and thus deserved to be treated like the enemy," Suzuki has recalled.[8]

Thousands of Japanese Canadians were rounded up during WWII and relocated to internment camps in the BC interior. (LAC, MIKAN no. 3193859)

None of those many thousands of Japanese Canadians who were sent into internal exile in 1942 were ever charged with a crime. Nor were they afforded due legal process. Adding insult to injury, a January 18, 1943, order-in-council liquidated all real and personal property owned by Japanese Canadians whom the government had placed in "protective custody." The fire sale proceeds were used to offset the cost of the "social assistance" these people had received when they were forcibly relocated. So much for the rule of law in wartime.

A 1944 public opinion poll suggested that a whopping eighty-three per cent of Canadians supported the post-war deportation of all Japanese who weren't Canadian citizens. By today's sensibilities and with the luxury of hindsight, the discrimination Japanese found themselves subjected to by dint of their race alone and the widespread public support for such bigotry are indefensible and shameful.[9] Not so in 1945 when most Canadians felt the treatment of Japanese was justified and reasonable.

The fact Canadian society in the 1940s was unabashedly racist is a shameful reality that historians have chronicled in painful detail. Yet the truth seems to have been that while many Canadians held racist views, for the most part their prejudices weren't deep-seated; they were the product of ignorance and lack of contact with groups with whom they had little or no interaction on a daily basis, in particular Japanese, Chinese, East Indian, Black, and Jewish people.

Like the Japanese and Chinese, East Indians and Blacks made up a minuscule fraction of Canada's population. In the case of East Indians, it was less than one-tenth of a per cent, while only about two-tenths of one per cent of the Canadian population were "Negroes," as government data tables categorized them. That latter number is somewhat surprising, given the long history of Black presence in Canada.

The first person of African descent to *visit* territory that one day would become part of Canada was a linguistically gifted former Black slave—"freeman" Mathieu da Costa. He served as Samuel de Champlain's interpreter when the French explorer arrived here in 1603. "The first person of African descent to live in Canada was an anonymous man who died of scurvy in Port Royal during the winter of 1606–1607."[10] And, of course, there was an influx of Black people in the wake of Britain's 1833 abolition of slavery and another during the time of the American Civil War (1861–65), which ended slavery in that country. By 1867, there were 40,000 Black people in Canada. Most lived in southern Ontario and Nova Scotia, with a concentration of Black residents in the impoverished Halifax neighbourhood of Africville, which was a ghetto in all but name.

Jews in Canada were subject to the same kind of discrimination and "ghettoization"—especially in Montreal, where more than ninety per cent of Quebec's Jewish population lived. The first Jews had arrived there in the 1760s. As *The Canadian Encyclopedia* notes, the

Roman Catholic church in Quebec fanned the flames of anti-Semitism because it associated Jews with modernism, liberalism and a host of other "dangerous doctrines." However, if you think anti-Semitism was confined to Quebec, think again. It was so widespread in Canada as to be mainstream. Jews, like other non-Aryan races in the 1940s, found themselves subject to discriminatory immigration quotas.

Neither of Canada's two "founding peoples"—English and French —were adept at spotting the differences among non-Caucasian faces; that is, if they even took the time to try. David Suzuki has noted that in the 1940s there were prohibitions against First Nations people being in pubs. One of Suzuki's uncles, whose skin tone was dusky, was sitting in a watering hole one day enjoying a cold beer when another patron asked him what tribe he belonged to. "The Jap tribe," he replied.[11]

Overt discrimination against the one per cent of the Canadian population who were Aboriginal was widespread in the 1940s. The kind of comments made by *Globe and Mail* sports columnist Jim Coleman one day in October 1943 stand as a vivid reminder of that. Coleman reported that Chief Andrew Paull, a prominent Squamish leader, rights activist, lawyer, and lacrosse player of the day, had passed through Toronto en route to Ottawa. Paull was travelling to the capital to take part in a First Nations protest against what he felt were the paternalistic policies of the Department of Indian Affairs. "Chief Paull says that unless the Federal Government makes some compromise, the Indians will have no alternative but to raze the capital and scalp all Cabinet Ministers and Senators under the age of 80," Coleman wrote.[12]

That comment and others of a similar ilk were standard fare, made as a matter of course and with tongue firmly in cheek; however, they were also typical of the flippant and even dismissive tone of most media coverage of First Nations people and issues at that time. When leaders of the North American Indian Brotherhood gathered in Montreal in July 1945 to discuss their grievances against the Department of Indian Affairs, which insisted on holding in trust grant monies, oil royalties, and proceeds from sales of treaty lands, the same *Globe and Mail*—

Canada's self-proclaimed "National Newspaper"—headlined its news story "Indian Powwow to View Handling of $15 million."

Attitudes are changing today, no question. However, all these years later we are still wrestling with the bitter legacy of the racism that was once prevalent among Canadians. There can be no mistaking that First Nations peoples have long endured and been victimized by systemic discrimination at the hands of those who came here from Europe.

There is a standard of human behaviour that is timeless and that cuts across cultures, religions, demographic differences: what lawyers refer to as "equity"—what's right or wrong and what's *fair* in the mind of any right-thinking, moral person. Any way you cut it, the Aboriginal people of North America have gotten a raw deal. Where Canada is concerned, think residential schools, or even something as fundamental to our democracy and way of life as the right to vote. The puzzling question is why.

In the early 1940s, in a typical year, about 18,000 First Nations children found themselves in "Indian residential schools," most of which were operated by priests and nuns of the Roman Catholic or Anglican churches. To this day, Canadians struggle to come to grips with and atone for the terrible, tortured legacy of the emotional, physical, sexual, and cultural mistreatment of children who attended many of those schools. So, too, do those who were directly affected and, in far too many cases, abused.

Where voting is concerned, it's easy to forget—if ever we were even aware—that while First Nations people were given a conditional right to vote at the time of Confederation in 1867, few did so because there was a huge quid pro quo involved. In order to exercise their franchise, First Nations people were required to surrender their treaty rights and status (which, too often, the Crown failed to honour anyway). It wasn't until 1948 that a parliamentary committee recommended that all "status Indians" be given the unconditional right to vote. Despite this, it was another twelve years before Prime Minister John Diefenbaker made that happen in 1960. And don't forget: there was no Charter of

Rights and Freedoms at that time; it would be another twenty-two years before the Canadian Bill of Rights was adopted as part of the 1982 repatriation of the constitution by the government of Prime Minister Pierre Trudeau.

It's also worth noting that for the first eighty years of independence from Britain—until the Canadian Citizenship Act was enacted in 1947—the legal status of "Canadian citizen" didn't exist. Anyone born or naturalized in Canada was considered to be a British subject. Where First Nations people were concerned, that was a bad joke. Where others were concerned, it was meaningless. That was the case for Japanese Canadians during WWII, especially those who were born in Japan. They were deemed to be "enemy aliens." As for those young people who were born here of Japanese-Canadian parents, the government simply ignored any questions about their legal status as British subjects. There was no point in splitting hairs. After all, the wartime round-up of Japanese Canadians was perfectly "legal" because it was authorized by Order-in-Council PC 1486, which Prime Minister Mackenzie King had signed into law in February 1942. That order-in-council gave the Royal Canadian Mounted Police (RCMP) and other police authorities to remove and detain "any and all persons" from any "protective area" in the country, this case the province of British Columbia. If you're thinking that any such direction sounds fundamentally undemocratic and illegal, you'd be correct. However, it became "legal" under the terms of the War Measures Act. Extraordinary times sometimes call for extraordinary measures, or so the thinking went.

When Parliament passed that supposedly temporary law, upon the outbreak of WWI in August 1914, it enabled Prime Minister Robert Borden and his cabinet to rule by decree—something media reports of the day aptly described as having authorized "exceedingly wide authority to apply precautionary measures and broad powers."[13] The War Measures Act, which is sweeping in its mandate, allows for the censorship and suppression of communications; tight control of transportation, trade, and manufacturing; price controls; seizure of private property; and the arrest, detention, and deportation without charges or due process of any "enemy aliens"—those individuals who had roots in an enemy country. These latter two powers have proved to be especially problematic.

The War Measures Act was used to both good and bad effect during the two world wars of the last century. Astoundingly, during WWII, the government issued 6,414 orders under the act.[14] To say that some of them are now viewed as being controversial would be an understatement. The same can be said of the most high-profile post-WWII invocation of the War Measures Act, which happened during the October 1970 crisis in Quebec. Anyone old enough to have been around at the time will recall how Prime Minister Pierre Trudeau invoked emergency powers to deal with the threat of homegrown terrorism from the leftist Front de libération du Québec. Some historians now say he used a sledgehammer to kill a fly. Others insist he did what needed to be done.

As for the King government's wartime restrictions on civil liberties, they would remain in effect to the last calendar day of 1945. That was six months after any threat of enemy attack or sabotage was likely and they were all but forgotten by most Canadians (although as we shall see, Mr. King was to make liberal use—pun intended—of the restrictions in September 1945). By early 1945, the war in Europe was in its final stages, and it seemed an Allied victory was all but inevitable. However, Canadians continued to endure many of the restrictions of war—censorship, for one.

Thus in the early months of 1945, the government continued downplaying and even suppressing news about Allied military setbacks, although they were increasingly few and far between. Even news media reports of the Japanese fire balloons that were being aimed at the west coast of North America—with little to no effect—were forbidden. Yet Canadian newspapers routinely published lists of the names of war dead, and all families dreaded the knock on the front door when a telegram would arrive bearing grim news that a loved one had been killed or "was missing in action."

The late filmmaker Christopher Chapman recalled one cold January night in 1943 when he was sixteen and still living with his parents in Toronto. He and the other members of his family had just returned home from the movies and were laughing and enjoying hot chocolate when the doorbell rang. It was about eleven o'clock.

"We fell silent as my father went to the door followed by Mum," Chapman recalled. "In the silence we heard the door close and a moment later we heard Daddy say in a low tone, 'This is it.' These words, their meaning slowly realized . . . stayed with me a lifetime."[15] That was how the Chapman family learned that their second-oldest son, Bob, was one of the 42,042 Canadians who had made "the ultimate sacrifice" and would not be coming home from the war. "Regret to inform you advice has been received from the Royal Canadian Air Force Casualties Offices overseas that . . ."

After the war, I hope to get married, but even then, I'd much prefer to work rather than to stay at home. There's no reason why women should be forced back into the home if they're willing to work elsewhere.
—Elsie Harvey, eighteen-year-old riveter, Boeing Aircraft, Vancouver, 1944

CHAPTER 4

Splendid Work by Splendid Women

IT ALMOST GOES WITHOUT SAYING THAT CANADIAN SOCIETY in 1945—like most others at the time—was patriarchal. However, in some ways, this country was even more atavistic than some. That certainly was true when it came to accepting female volunteers who stepped forward for wartime military service; there was no tradition of this in Canada. In WWI, with the notable exception of the 3,141 nursing sisters who served as officers in the Canadian Medical Corps on the home front or overseas, there was little, if any, female presence in this country's military.[1] Initially, the situation was much the same during WWII.

Almost 4,500 women volunteered as nursing sisters, serving near the front lines and some even in harm's way, within the range of enemy guns or bombs.[2] The Royal Canadian Army Medical Corps women who served in London during the worst of the 1940 German bombing of the city were dubbed "the Blitz Sisters" by the British. The moniker was apt.

Eighty-eight of those fearless women who volunteered to serve as nurses in England and elsewhere overseas during WWII lost their lives. The first was twenty-eight-year-old Toronto native Lieutenant

(Nursing Sister) Marion E. Bell, who perished in a September 26, 1940, motoring accident that happened in England. The last was thirty-five-year-old Lieutenant (Nursing Sister) Gladys Fitzgerald, from Peterborough, Ontario, who succumbed to the lingering effects of her wartime injuries on December 30, 1945.

Of course, not all Canadian women who volunteered for wartime military duty were nurses. Some actually served in the army, navy, and air force. This came about because as the Canadian economy picked up steam in 1940 and fighting in Europe moved into its second year, the flow of male volunteer recruits slowed to a trickle. With no other choice, the leaders of Canada's armed forces began seriously considering the idea of allowing women into the military to fill non-combat roles; this was a step Britain had taken in 1939. Australia, New Zealand, and South Africa soon did the same, organizing homegrown female military auxiliaries; Canada lagged behind. "The plain truth of the matter is that there's a lot of masculine skepticism around, which has to be overcome as the groundwork is being laid," a Department of National Defence official in Ottawa explained.[3] No matter, the need for manpower—or "person power," to be more exact—trumped any gender-based prejudice.

Not surprisingly, it was the "junior service" of the Canadian military, the RCAF—which had been founded in 1924 and was less bound by fusty tradition and male chauvinism—that was first off the mark to begin accepting female volunteers. The Women's Division, Royal Canadian Air Force (WD) took flight in July 1940. The army followed the air force lead a month later. In August 1941, it announced the creation of the Canadian Women's Army Corps (CWAC), and Defence Minister James Ralston appointed fifty-seven-year-old nurse Elizabeth Smellie ("Miss Smellie," as most people called her) of the Royal Canadian Army Medical Corps to organize and head the new service. Although the new matron-in-chief carried the rank of colonel—the native of Port Arthur (now Thunder Bay) was the first woman to do so in the Canadian army—her official title spoke volumes about the military's attitude toward the CWAC and Smellie's own approach to her new job. When a little boy stopped short on the street one day and saluted the colonel, she asked him, "Why did you do that? Do I look like a soldier?" She had a point. In her dark-blue skirt and jacket, blue felt hat, and flying cape with its red lining, Smellie didn't look like a Canadian soldier.

"No, ma'am," came the boy's reply. "But my father told me always to salute the King's Uniform. I've never seen anything like [your uniform] before, but somehow I know you're in it."[4] Smellie was indeed "in it," as were the women in the auxiliary services of the other two branches of the Canadian military.

The last service to begin accepting female volunteers was the Royal Canadian Navy. The senior service had dithered for two years, until finally on July 31, 1942, it launched the Women's Royal Canadian Naval Service (WRCNS). The members of the service would become popularly known as "Wrens." Apart from the fact the name sounds feminine and homey, it seemed natural given that the WRCNS was modelled on the Women's Royal Navy Service (WRNS). The British nickname crossed the Atlantic along with the idea of a women's naval service.

The inaugural senior officers who commanded the Canadian Wrens were British "loaners," but Canadian women soon replaced them. The service's first native-born head (the only one, given that the Wrens disbanded at war's end) was thirty-five-year-old Halifax native Lieutenant-Commander Isabel Macneill. She took command in June 1943, after having graduated from HMCS *Conestoga*—the navy's dryland facility in what was then Galt, Ontario (now known as Cambridge), as one of the twenty-two members of the first class of female officer cadets. Because the Canadian navy, like the Royal Navy, designates its dryland bases as "stone frigates"—in effect, stone ships—Macneill technically was a ship captain. As such, that gave her a unique distinction: she was the first and *only* female commander of a ship in a navy of the British Commonwealth during WWII.[5] "'Aye, aye sir' is slightly changed to 'Yes, ma'am,' for the captain on the bridge is a woman," the *Globe and Mail* reported.[6]

A LTHOUGH THEY WERE BARRED from actual combat, almost 50,000 Canadian women between the ages of eighteen and forty-five volunteered for military duty. Initially, they received just two-thirds of the pay of a man in uniform, and the women had no fringe benefits. In response to public pressure, that eventually was changed. The pay of female members of the armed forces was raised to eighty per cent of what males were earning, and *some* benefits were provided. Department of National Defence officials continued to offer a variety of excuses for this inequity, none of them convincing. The talking point was that women's wages were kept low to ensure the military wasn't competing with war industries for labour. Regardless, the wage disparity persisted because that was how things were at the time, and it really didn't seem to matter to most women. They didn't sign up for the money.

When asked why they signed up, even though by the early 1940s there were lots of factory and clerical jobs available, most women who volunteered for the military said they did so for patriotic reasons; indeed, the motto of the CWAC was apt: "We serve that men may fight." Other women signed up for the adventure, "just for the heck of it," or because a male family member had done so. It's revealing and it's reflective of the ethos of the day that some women who didn't volunteer viewed those who did with suspicion and even hostility.

Public opinion was strongly opposed to allowing women to join the military. A 1942 poll showed that just seven per cent of Canadians were in favour. Opposition was strongest in Quebec, where support for Canadian involvement in the war was tepid and the Catholic church preached that a woman's place was in the home. One Wren reported "being pushed out of a store in Montreal by the owner because she was shopping in uniform and her friends were spat upon in the street."[7]

Shoulder to shoulder, a CWAC recruiting poster.
(Canadian War Museum, no. 19880069-865)

Members of the CWAC parade through the streets of Vancouver, circa 1945.
(Canadian Army photo)

Another young woman, who had joined the air force WD, found herself shouted at and insulted as she walked along an Ottawa street: "[Some women] didn't like us because there was a shortage of men ... and they thought that the WDs had the men that they figured they should have."[8]

Whatever the reasons Canadian women had for volunteering for military service, the vast majority of those who did so filled workaday clerical, administrative, communications, and other support roles. The duties they performed weren't always exciting or even challenging, but they were vital nonetheless. Take the contributions of Geraldine (Gorman) Bagnall, for example. Twenty years old when she volunteered, the Halifax resident was assigned to a Naval Aid detachment in her hometown. "We replaced the guys who went overseas and when we were called on, we did whatever jobs we were asked to do," she recalled proudly.[9]

Beatrice (Grant) Corbett, a twenty-two-year-old Queen's University graduate from Kingston, Ontario, joined the Women's Royal Canadian Naval Service in 1944. She then spent the duration of the war on the west coast—in Esquimalt, British Columbia—where she worked in top-secret naval intelligence, intercepting and decoding Japanese naval communications. "It was said that the work we did shortened the Pacific war by two years," Corbett said proudly.[10] She was probably right about that.

Although both Geraldine Gorman and Bea Grant were stationed in Canada, other Canadian women who served overseas were even closer to and more engaged in the action. That was certainly so for the handful of fearless Canadian women with lofty dreams who volunteered for the Air Transport Auxiliary (ATA). Their story is as little known as it is fascinating.

The ATA was a British-instigated wartime service that ferried military aircraft—mostly Hurricanes, Spitfires, and Mosquito bombers—between factories and storage facilities to squadrons on the front lines of the air war in Britain. It was challenging, demanding, and at times dangerous work.

Toronto-born Marion (Powell) Orr was one of just five Canadians among the 166 women from the Commonwealth, the United States, Holland, and Poland who served in the ATA. Orr was twenty-six years old in June 1942 when she and her friend Violet Milstead, a twenty-two-year-old Toronto native, signed up. The pair spent the last three years of the war overseas, logging hundreds of hours of flying time, making an invaluable contribution to the Allied war effort, and like all the women pilots who flew with the ATA, blazing a trail for today's female aviators.[11]

Post-war, both Marion Orr and Violet Milstead (who became Violet Milstead Warren when she married) went on to long and very distinguished civilian aviation careers. Orr became Canada's first female flight instructor, winning 1982 induction into the Canadian Aviation Hall of Fame and 1993 induction as a Member of the Order of Canada. Violet Milstead was Canada's first female bush pilot, and she, too, is a member of the Canadian Aviation Hall of Fame and a Member of the Order of Canada.

Marion Orr and Violet Milstead. (Cramahe Township Public Library)

WITH MORE THAN A million Canadians of both genders in uniform during the course of WWII, and with 750,000 of them serving at least some time overseas, the national economy soon faced a labour crunch. The onset of war in September 1939 abruptly ended the mass unemployment that had plagued the Canadian economy for almost a decade of economic depression.

A large percentage of the newly created war-industry jobs were filled by men who were too old to fight, deemed medically unfit, or employed in essential war work. Cynics pointed out that the veterans of WWI were now working in factories that turned out killing machines, weapons, and bullets for their sons to use in WWII. They were right about that.

Other wartime jobs were done by conscientious objectors and by POWs (prisoners of war), Germans mostly, with a sprinkling of Italians in the mix. There were nine POW camps in Canada—five in

Alberta and four in Ontario—and 46,000 POWs spent time "behind Canadian barbed wire."[12] The most trustworthy of them went to work on Canadian farms.

However, as had been the case during WWI, with so many able-bodied men in the military, the task of filling vacant jobs on the home front fell to Canadian women, who responded enthusiastically. Women played a sizeable and crucial role in this country's war effort. The federal government encouraged this engagement by offering tax breaks and providing daycare that was subsidized or even free. Such enticements proved effective. Women joined the workforce by the hundreds of thousands. As journalist and historian Barry Broadfoot noted, "They flowed into the factories in the thousands, into the shipyards, the aircraft factories, the textile plants and the foundries; they worked in lumber mills and in dairies, and they ran farms single-handed."[13]

Wartime employment in Canada reached its peak in the autumn of 1944. At that time, more than 4.5 million workers were "on the job," and the national unemployment rate fell to 1.4 per cent, down from 11.4 per cent in 1939. More than a million women were suddenly out of the home and working full time (and that number didn't include the many women who were working part time or who toiled on family farms to keep things going while the men of the family were away). More than 260,000 Canadian women were involved in the production of munitions, armaments, and equipment. Thirty per cent of the workers in the aircraft industry were female, as were almost half of the workforce in many war-related factories. All felt they were "doing their bit" in Canada's war effort. Poet Edna Jaques, who toiled on a munitions factory assembly line, wrote, "Deep down in your heart you enjoy it and are queerly satisfied to have a part in this gigantic struggle that embraces all mankind in its deadly grip."[14]

B Y DECEMBER 1941, WHEN the United States formally joined the war, Canada had already been at war for two years, and the idea of

Canadian women being involved in the economy and doing "their bit" on the home front had long since become old hat. It just seemed like the natural thing to do. There was no fanfare, no hoopla. Canadian women donned their coveralls and went to work. Things were a tad different south of the border.

There's nothing Americans excel at more than flag-waving and myth-making. And that never was truer than during WWII. When a female aircraft assembly line worker named Rose Will Monroe inspired songwriters Redd Evans and John J. Loeb, they wrote a song called "Rosie the Riveter." That tune, which became a huge hit in the United States and also here in Canada, prompted millions of American women to join the workforce.

In 1943, illustrator Norman Rockwell created an iconic *Saturday Evening Post* magazine cover that depicted a composite female character named Rosie the Riveter. And the following year, Hollywood made a movie with the same name. So not only did the idea of a spunky woman doing a job that a man would have done in the pre-war years become sexy, it also became a patriotic duty.

Canadian women found their own Rosie the Riveter in the person of Elizabeth "Elsie" MacGill, a bespectacled Vancouver native. In retrospect, Elsie seems so very Canadian, eh? Whereas America's Rosie the Riveter had "attitude" and wore her coveralls over a blue T-shirt that showed off burly arms that looked as if they could heft a beer keg, Elsie was much less brassy. She wore wire glasses, had a high forehead and fine porcelain-like features, and carried two university degrees in her back pocket. Today, we'd say she looked nerdy. However, appearances were deceiving. Anything that Elsie MacGill may have lacked in physical presence, she more than made up for in her brains and grit.

MacGill overcame polio in her twenties and persevered in her academic studies. When she earned a master of science degree in aeronautical engineering, she became the first woman in the world to be accredited in that lofty profession. MacGill put her advanced training to use in the early 1940s. As manager of the Canadian Car and Foundry company's Thunder Bay factory, she oversaw production of more than 2,000 Hawker Hurricanes, one of the workhorse Allied fighter planes of WWII. It was in this capacity that Elsie MacGill became a minor celebrity. "War effort is something, which is as microscopic in the unit as the individual, but as mighty in the sum total as an army," she once said.[15]

Ironically, it was the American publication *True Comics* that lionized Canadian Elsie MacGill. (True Comics)

Ironically (and tellingly), as was the case with Rosie the Riveter, it was an American publication that was responsible for MacGill's fame. She became known as "Queen of the Hurricanes" when an account of her exploits was featured in the January 1942 edition of a New York–based educational comic book called *True Comics*.

Post-war, MacGill continued to work as an aeronautical industry consultant, and in 1946, in her work as the first female technical advisor for the International Civil Aviation Organization (ICAO), she helped draft international regulations for the design and production of commercial airliners. MacGill would achieve another notable first the following year when she served as the first female chair of a United

Nations committee. Her accomplishments didn't end there.

Elsie MacGill was named to Canada's Royal Commission on the Status of Women in 1967, and she remained active in women's rights issues, including the fights for paid maternity leave and the liberalization of the laws governing women's reproductive rights. She died in 1980 at the age of seventy-five. Like so many of the Canadian women who were involved in this country's war effort, MacGill opened doors for those women who followed in her footsteps. By challenging the prevailing gender stereotypes of the day and proving that women could do most everything men could—and sometimes better—MacGill and her sisters provided a tantalizing foretaste of what the future might one day hold, if only the social, political, and economic shackles could be removed and the vast, mostly untapped potential of half of Canada's population could flourish.

Canadian women had won many property rights by the early years of the twentieth century. As of 1918, all *Caucasian* women were able to vote in federal elections, and in 1928, the Privy Council in London overruled the Supreme Court of Canada when it agreed with the arguments put forward by "the Famous Five"—Henrietta Muir Edwards, Louise McKinney, Nellie McClung, Emily Murphy, and Irene Parlby— when it ruled that women were "persons" for purposes of interpreting the British North America Act (BNA Act) of 1867.

Those legal victories apparently were enough for most Canadian women. Perhaps the pioneer American feminist Betty Friedan was onto something when she observed the real enemy of women "is women's denigration of themselves," in her groundbreaking 1963 book *The Feminine Mystique*. Much of the progress toward achieving gender equality that Canadian women—and those in the United States—made during WWII would be shelved or forgotten in the wash of post-war prosperity and the biological imperatives of the baby boom. Both developments added a disappointing and unexpected exclamation point to what unquestioningly marked feminism's first wave. The second, which was sparked by the turbulence of the 1960s and 1970s, was destined to leave in its wake a measure of complacency on the part of many younger women and a welter of disappointments in the minds of those among their elders who felt dismay over the unmet goals and unrealized potential of what they saw as being an unfinished revolution.

We can only wonder if future generations looking back will see the fury unleashed by the #MeToo movement at the tail end of the second decade of the twenty-first century as marking the start of a third wave of feminism. Perhaps, but only time will tell.

The thousands of Canadian women who joined the workforce kept factories humming during WWII. (Archives of Ontario, Canadian Car and Foundry Collection)

[Women] are the warriors of His Majesty's forces who fight
along the home front, working day and night.
—Poet Edna Jaques, 1942

CHAPTER 5

When the Boys Come Marching Home Again

N THE EARLY MONTHS OF 1945, AS THE WAR MOVED TOWARD
the Allied victory that now seemed all but inevitable, Canadians
were awash in uncertainty. While there was widespread and palpable
relief that the war was almost over and the "boys" (and "gals") would
soon come marching home again, there was also a growing unease
about what would happen to the economy when they did.

People feared that "normalcy" and reduced government spending
would also bring about a return of the hunger and unemployment of
the 1930s. A feature article in *Maclean's* magazine caught the essence of
the public mood when it asked the pivotal question that was in everyone's mind at war's end: "Can we all get jobs?"[1]

Government officials, corporate heads, religious leaders, labour
leaders, and even many members of the public—males and females
alike, surprisingly—figured the logical way to ensure the continuation
of full employment and prosperity was for Canadian women to stand
down and return to being mothers and housewives at war's end. After
all, they'd done so in 1918, and it was time to do so again. Simplistic
though that idea was, a lot of people bought into it. Never mind that
the Canadian economy had nosedived after WWI or that it made no
sense in terms of economic productivity for women, who were more
than half the population, to revert to being stay-at-home mothers and
homemakers.

Statistics gathered in the United States showed that in some industries—particularly ones in which precision was an essential element of job performance (such as in the production of electronic equipment, optical gear, and instruments)—females were thirty per cent more productive than their male co-workers.[2] There were no comparable Canadian numbers, but anecdotal evidence suggested the situation was similar in this country, and there's every reason to assume that was indeed the case.

What is beyond dispute is that across the board the productivity of Canada's wartime industries was nothing short of amazing. Overall, Canadian industry produced more than $9.5 billion worth of war materials; that's roughly equivalent to $135 billion in today's dollars. To get a sense of the impact this had on the Allied war effort, consider this: Canada produced forty per cent of the aluminum that went into Allied military aircraft, ninety-five per cent of the nickel used to make engines and machine parts, and fifteen per cent of the lead for bullets. All told, the automobile plants of General Motors, Ford, and Chrysler, "the Big Three" of yesteryear, produced 815,729 military vehicles during six years of war; that staggering total meant about 447 vehicles rolled off the assembly lines each and every day. Small wonder that Canada's "wartime production overall rank[ed] fourth among the Allies, behind only the United States, the United Kingdom, and the Soviet Union."[3]

Many war-industry plants operated on a forty-eight-hour work week. And while a typical assembly line worker earned sixty cents per hour (that would be about $8.50 in today's dollars), more often than not a woman took home less money than did a man working beside her. Private sector, public sector—it made no difference. The employment situation in the Department of External Affairs in Ottawa was typical of the latter.

In 1939, there were just fifty-five people working in the whole department; forty-three of them were clerical support staff. All were men. As the wartime need for staff grew and the department launched a recruiting drive, university-educated candidates were the prime targets. However, the pool of potential new employees was relatively small; at that time, few Canadians attended university. In 1940, the number who did so was only about half of one per cent of the entire population: 65,731 students, and just 13,500 of them were women. Given that the majority of young, able-bodied men were in the military or otherwise employed in the war effort, the focus of Department of External Affairs recruiting efforts by default turned to university-educated women. Those who joined the departmental staff signed on as grade 4 clerks with a starting annual salary of $1,620. Male recruits doing the same work were hired at grade 3 level. Their starting annual salary was $2,280. Female employees had no easy or politically acceptable way to protest. They were obliged to accept their lot and did, albeit reluctantly.

Despite the inequities of the male–female wage gap, many Canadian women wanted to continue working at war's end. A survey done at one Toronto plant in 1944 indicated that eighty per cent of female employees were eager to stay on the job.[4] To the relief of the owners of that business, when push came to shove, most didn't, and that opened up jobs for returning veterans. However, some strong-willed women refused to quit; they were the more determined or financially needy ones. The situation at this plant, which had made military aircraft during the war, was typical.

When the business resumed peacetime production of farming implements, the expectation was that the 2,000 female employees—a quarter of the workforce—would be laid off or would leave of their own accord. "The employment of women workers, to say the least, will be discouraged," the chairman of the company's post-war planning committee explained. His rationale was simple: "Women will not be strong enough to do this heavy work."[5]

When *Maclean's* journalist Janet Tupper wrote about Canadian women's post-war employment aspirations for an article that was provocatively titled "Little Women—What Now?" she found no shortage of men on the shop floors who shared that executive's chauvinistic opinion. "The average man employed in industry seems to share this view of his woman colleague. As far as he is concerned, women in post-war industry had better stick to the same kind of work they held before the war. The men don't want them in their blacksmith's shops or driving their trucks," Tupper wrote. "'Some of them are okay,' admitted one worker. 'But take them all around, they're a darned nuisance in heavy jobs. I guess they try to pull their weight all right, but I don't know. I just don't want to have women around my job. Let them stay home and bring up the kids.'"[6]

Public opinion during the war years was no quicker to warm to, much less accept, the idea of gender equality as a permanent workplace reality than it had been to the idea of accepting women in the military. The latter didn't fit with the traditional role of women as nurturers and homemakers. Unspoken was the underlying issue that most men did not want to see women in the workplace because they were competitors for jobs, and they would work for lower wages, even if doing so was something they neither wanted nor liked. A Canadian Institute of Public Opinion (CIPO) survey in October 1945 showed that sixty per cent of Canadians—of both genders—were of the opinion that employers should hire men before they hired women.[7]

L IKE MOST CANADIANS IN the early months of 1945, Prime Minister Mackenzie King was spending a lot of time musing about reconstruction and the return to normalcy. The results of CIPO polls and those being done on the hush-hush by the government's own Wartime Information Board confirmed that Canadians were anxious about what would happen when the war ended. If a million men and women, many of whom had served overseas and who had learned to shoot guns in anger, were demobilized and returned home expecting to be rewarded for the sacrifices they and their buddies had made during the war, it didn't take a genius to figure there might be trouble.

Mackenzie King was determined to see that didn't happen; if it did, he knew his Liberal party would lose the general election that was scheduled for the spring of 1945. What he wrestled with was the decision on how much the federal government could and should involve itself in post-war economic stimulation. There was little doubt that with the economy booming, Ottawa could afford to expand the scope and range of social programs. However, doing so was something that made King and other fiscal conservatives uneasy. Compounding the prime minister's uncertainties was the fact that the provincial premiers were outspoken in their opposition to some proposed federal initiatives, which they saw as intrusions on their constitutional turf. Federal–provincial squabbles are as old as Confederation and the British North America Act of 1867.

The landmark 1940 Royal Commission on Dominion–Provincial Relations, which the media referred to as the Rowell–Sirois Commission (because it was first headed by cleric-turned-lawyer Newton W. Rowell, who stepped aside after suffering a stroke, and then by lawyer Joseph Sirois), had provided a roadmap to the future. That three-volume document recommended the transfer of areas of authority between Ottawa and the provincial governments and the creation of a program of grants that would equalize provincial tax revenues. (Sounds familiar, doesn't it?) As *The Canadian Encyclopedia* explains, "The federal government was to assume responsibility for unemployment insurance and contributory pensions, and full control of personal and corporate income taxes and succession duties, while taking responsibility for provincial debts. A program of National Adjustment Grants [transfer payments] was to make payments to poorer provinces."[8]

Several key ministers in Mackenzie King's Cabinet had their own ideas about how the federal government should move forward at war's end. They were adamant in voicing opposition to any enhanced or large-scale government involvement in Canada's post-war economy. Most prominent among the naysayers was Clarence Decatur (C.D.) Howe, the "get-up-and-go engineering type," as business writer Peter C. Newman tabbed him. Howe's "personality dominated the Ottawa scene during the 1940s and 1950s."[9]

Few federal Cabinet ministers have ever enjoyed a higher public profile, wielded greater clout, or had a more enduring impact on
Canada than did this American-born dynamo.[10] Howe served for five
years as this country's wartime Minister of Munitions and Supply and
then, beginning in late 1944, as the Minister of Reconstruction. He has
been described as "an economic czar,"[11] and the descriptor fits. No one
did more to transform the Canadian economy from being reliant on
agriculture and raw materials to being industrially based. And no one
did more to pave the way for post-war prosperity in Canada.

C.D. Howe—"the Minister of Everything." (LAC, MIKAN no. 3615435)

In his more than two decades in Ottawa, C.D. Howe served two
prime ministers—first Mackenzie King and then his successor, Louis
St. Laurent—as "the Minister of Everything." A measure of the continuing impact of Howe's legacy is the fact that the C.D. Howe Institute, an
influential Toronto-based non-profit think tank, perpetuates his memory by promoting interest in sound public policy. Yet few Canadians
today recognize Howe's name ("Howe? Didn't he play hockey for the
Detroit Red Wings?") or can tell you anything about the man. That's a
pity because he's someone who served Canada well and unstintingly.
There's an anecdote about his dedication that nicely illustrates this.

In 1940, in the wake of the "miracle at Dunkirk"—the evacuation of more than 475,000 Allied troops from France with the loss of all their equipment—the British government alerted Canada that it could no longer provide planes for the British Commonwealth Air Training Plan. Howe, aware of how vital the initiative was to the Allied war effort, immediately travelled to Washington and New York looking for suitable American military aircraft to fill the gap. When he learned that such planes were available on a "cash-and-carry" basis only, without a moment's hesitation Howe wrote a *personal* cheque for $8 million to cover the cost. No one could ever say he was reluctant to "put his money where his mouth was." After writing that cheque, the "man of direct action [who] gets things done," as one newspaper columnist described him, flew back to Ottawa post-haste to make sure his cheque didn't bounce.[12]

It would be difficult to imagine Mackenzie King acting as C.D. Howe did. And unlike the prime minister, Howe was never shy about making a tough decision. He "was neither Liberal nor liberal in the manner of Mackenzie King and his friends . . . [yet] government interference in the economy, centralized power and drastic administrative solutions held no terror for him."[13] At least, that was his stance in wartime. Howe, a staunch proponent of capitalism and free enterprise, championed privately financed pipeline projects that would carry Alberta natural gas to eastern markets. (That, too, sounds hauntingly familiar these days.) Despite this, he also founded twenty-eight Crown corporations during his years in Ottawa. Howe's unofficial motto was "Full employment rather than handouts from the government."

When John Stirling, the head of the Canadian Construction Association, called upon Howe to lobby for large-scale public works projects in the post-war era, the minister was quick to shoot down the request. "John, when the war is over . . . this country is going to have the greatest era of prosperity it's ever seen,"[14] Howe predicted, not knowing that he was repeating an optimistic prophecy that IBM chairman Thomas Watson Sr. had offered back in November 1938 when he opined that Canada was ripe, as he had told a *Toronto Daily Star* interviewer in November 1938, for the "greatest expansion of any country in the world."[15]

It's not surprising that Howe's worldview jived with Watson's. Both men were self-made millionaires, and both were American. Watson hailed from a hardscrabble farming background in upstate New York, while Howe was of austere Puritan stock, having been born and bred in historic Waltham, Massachusetts (est. 1738), a town known for its watchmakers. That's ironic given Howe's temperament. The man was not a clock-watcher. "He stands about five feet ten. He has the bearing of an athlete, narrow hips and broad chest. His features are sharp; his chin juts out. His blue eyes are straight," one journalist wrote. "All over him is the stamp of aggressiveness."[16] Howe's biographers sounded a similar note. As one of them observed, "Friends and the public alike remarked on the baggy, rumpled, stained or shambling character of his clothing—all the more noticeable by contrast to the decisiveness of his gestures and the quick responses in that flat, clipped voice."[17]

C.D. Howe, with his craggy black eyebrows and perpetual scowl, was never easy to deal with. Some people regarded him as being down-right arrogant. He must have seemed that way for he had a short fuse and little patience for small talk or political give-and-take—he once famously dismissed House of Commons debates as "children's hour." Such was Howe's nature, but perhaps that was what enabled him to accomplish so much. He was born to be a high achiever.

C.D. HOWE WAS JUST twenty years old when he graduated from the Massachusetts Institute of Technology (MIT) in 1907. He did so having earned two things: an engineering degree and the reputation of being a young man who was destined for greatness. "At Tech we recognized that Howe was lucky," one of his classmates recalled. "No one who knew him would throw dice or play pitch-penny with him. He always won."[18]

Howe went north to Halifax, where he served a four-year stint as a professor of engineering before abandoning academia in 1913 to take a $5,000-per-year job with the Board of Grain Commissioners in Fort William, Ontario.[19] He then proceeded to make a name for himself building Great Lakes storage elevators, bridges, and other infrastructure that served Canada's booming prairie grain industry during WWI and afterward. Howe was so adept at this that he was able to leave the civil service and start his own business. He did well for himself, well enough that he survived the 1929 stock market crash relatively unscathed even though the grain business tanked. By 1934, Howe was ready for new challenges. And because he saw himself as "a builder," he decided to do whatever he could to help Canada get back on the right track economically. "To a man of Howe's ardent optimistic nature, depressions are no more than a challenge to think straighter and work harder,"[20] one observer noted.

Howe had become prominent in the Fort William community, and so the Liberals recruited him as the party's candidate in that riding in the 1935 election. When Howe won easily, Mackenzie King more than made good on his promise of a Cabinet appointment, rewarding him with two portfolios: Railways and Canals, and Marine. However, both soon were rolled into one, and Howe became Minister of Transport. This was a post he was well qualified for and that he handled with great aplomb and efficiency. He proved his mettle by shepherding some government initiatives that were destined to have long-term impact on the country. Three that merit mention are the creation of the Canadian Broadcasting Corporation, Canadian National Railways, and Trans-Canada Airlines (which became Air Canada in 1965).

Despite their differences in personality and temperament, Howe and King worked well as a team. They could never be friends, but their skills were complementary. King had recognized this, and so in April 1940 he named Howe to head the Department of Munitions and Supply, the all-powerful government agency that was tasked with managing all aspects of Canada's defence production and supply.

The job of mobilizing Canadian industry to meet the wartime needs of this country and its Allies was as enormous in scope as it was staggering in complexity. Howe pulled it off, doing so in no small measure because he was able to recruit more than a dozen of Canada's top business leaders to work under him, heading various wartime initiatives. These dollar-a-year men—"Howe's boys," as they were known—were "loaned" to the government by their corporate employers, which kept the men on the company payroll and paid their salaries.[21] Many of these executive volunteers weren't fans of Mackenzie King, nor were they Liberal supporters; however, they agreed to get involved because C.D. Howe had asked them to do so. Among them was Edward Plunket (E.P.) Taylor, who was one of Canada's most dynamic and influential business leaders and one of Mackenzie King's most implacable critics.

POPULAR FOODS DURING WORLD WAR II

With rationing of meat, butter, sugar, and many other dietary staples in effect, Canadians had to be creative in their cooking, and nothing went to waste—even the fat drippings from bacon and other meats. Some of the most frequently eaten foods of 1945—though not necessarily the most popular—included the following:

- Spam canned meat and other canned foods of all kinds
- Victory Garden vegetables
- Kraft macaroni and cheese
- cottage cheese
- meat loaves and casseroles—made from whatever type of meat was available
- apple brown Betty (a dessert made with apples, leftover bread, and no sugar)
- baked custard

Like Howe, Taylor was destined to play a lead role in reshaping the face of the Canadian economy and the country in 1945 and beyond. More on that later, but for now suffice it to say that Taylor merits mention here because of his involvement in an incident that very nearly cost C.D. Howe and Taylor their lives and that speaks volumes about Prime Minister Mackenzie King, the man who was Howe's boss. It happened on December 14, 1940.

On that day, Howe, Taylor, Vancouver department store owner Colonel William C. Woodward, and Montreal accountant and former Quebec Cabinet minister Gordon W. Scott were travelling together. The foursome was among 140 passengers and crew aboard the British passenger ship SS *Western Prince*. The Canadians were en route to England for a series of meetings on the British war effort, in which Canada played an integral support role. At age fifty-four, Howe was feeling exhausted and needed time away from the unrelenting demands of his then-work as Minister of Munitions and Supply. What he wanted was "a slow voyage, away from telephones, constant meetings, and the drain of tough decision making; away from the frustrations of the restraining net of bureaucracy."[22]

Howe was enjoying the voyage until about 6 a.m. on that Saturday morning. The *Western Prince* was 550 miles (885 kilometres) west of the Irish coast when it came under attack by a German U-boat. Howe, who was still dozing in his bed, heard the thud of a torpedo that slammed into the ship and exploded. Moments later, the ship began taking on water.

Despite the icy wind and the heaving waves, the passengers and crew had no choice but to abandon ship. Fortunately, the *Western Prince*'s radio operator had sent off an emergency SOS signal before the German submarine fired a second torpedo into the stricken ship, which sent it to the bottom in less than two minutes. C.D. Howe and the thirty other souls in his lifeboat found themselves adrift in the frigid North Atlantic. Given the weather and grim sea conditions, their survival chances seemed slim. Making a perilous situation even worse

was the inflexible standing order from the British Admiralty decreeing that unless specifically ordered to do so by an Allied warship, no
British merchant vessel should *ever* stop to rescue survivors of a sinking ship, not if a U-boat was known to be in the area.

When word reached Ottawa that the ship Howe was travelling
on had gone missing, Mackenzie King was distressed. "Ralston [the
Minister of Defence] and Howe are the two most valuable men in our
war effort," he wrote in his diary. Compounding the prime minister's
dread was the fear he might have been responsible in some measure
for Howe's misfortune. One of King's superstitions was "that it was
not well to say good-bye to a person with a glass between."[23] It was bad
luck to do so.

King had gone to the train station to see Howe off and had waved
farewell just as the glass door was swinging shut behind Howe. It was
too late to remedy the situation, and so King raced back to his office,
where he hurriedly looked up the address of the Howe family home in
Ottawa: 7 Crescent Drive. King was relieved, for he regarded seven as
his lucky number, and so in his mind, this happenstance likely would
cancel out the bad luck brought on by the botched farewell, or would
at least absolve him of any responsibility if Howe was lost. That feeling of reassurance was buttressed that evening when King studied the
leaves in his teacup. In doing so, he believed he saw three men in a
small boat, and "hoisted from the end of the boat was quite clearly the
letter 'H.'"[24]

Who can say whether or not the signs of ill luck and good fortune
King observed, or the tea leaves in his cup, played any role in deter-
mining the fate of C.D. Howe and his travelling companions? What
is for certain is that the captain of a westbound British merchant
ship, the SS *Baron Kinnaird*, defied that standing Admiralty order
(and obeyed the tea leaves?). He risked all when he altered course and
stopped to pluck the *Western Prince* passengers and crew from the
North Atlantic. C.D. Howe, E.P. Taylor, and William Woodward were
saved after seven harrowing, frigid hours in their lifeboat. Montreal

businessman Gordon Scott wasn't as fortunate. With the rescue under way, the huge waves dashed a lifeboat against the hull of the *Baron Kinnaird*, crushing him.

That experience had a profound, lasting impact on C.D. Howe. He later told a British interviewer that he "considered every hour that he lived from that day onwards to be borrowed time."[25] If that was true, it's no less true to say he used the remaining twenty years of his life to maximum advantage. Post-war, Howe would be in charge of reconstruction, and in the 1950s, he worked hard to strengthen Canada's steel industry, pipelines, and foreign trade. Howe's political career continued until 1957 when he and his Liberal colleagues were swept from office by the John Diefenbaker–led Conservatives. By that time, Howe's legacy was secure. "I've been called a socialist, also a conservative," Howe told journalist Peter C. Newman shortly before his 1960 death. "I always thought private industry could do anything better than public or government enterprise. But some things need to be done by the nation as a whole, and we did them the best we could."[26]

Maurice Richard was a catalyst for social change in Quebec, and, therefore, in Canada, and I don't think there's any other Canadian athlete you can say that about.
—Richard biographer Charles Foran

CHAPTER 6

Two Solitudes on and off the Ice

EVEN IN TIME OF WAR, LIFE GOES ON. In Canada, especially in the winter months, life includes hockey.

During WWII, the sport provided welcome diversion from the news of battles, death, and suffering that dominated headlines. Millions of Canadians from coast to coast, and even those who were in uniform overseas, continued to follow their favourite teams in the six-team National Hockey League (NHL). They did so with a passion that was tribal in its intensity.

Prior to the first NHL expansion in 1967 there really were only two teams for most Canadian hockey fans: English Canada rooted for the Toronto Maple Leafs and French Canada supported the Montreal Canadiens. The on-ice rivalry mirrored the competition between Canada's two largest cities. However, in the spring of 1945, an injury-prone twenty-three-year-old forward named Maurice Richard became the focus of attention for supporters of both teams.

To Leafs fans, Richard was a villain. To Canadiens fans, the unilingual Richard, a native-born Quebecker, was a hero who was uniquely theirs. In good measure, that was because he was the archetypal Everyman—"*Monsieur tout le monde*." In many ways, he was exactly that, yet there can be no doubt that from the day he laced on his first pair of skates, he was special.

Richard would achieve enduring fame in a stellar eighteen-year career in which he would set a single-season scoring record, establish a new NHL career scoring mark with 544 goals in total, and play on eight Stanley Cup–winning teams. This was more than enough to earn him a spot in the Hockey Hall of Fame and induction into the Order of Canada in 1967 as a charter member of that club. All of this was owing to the greatness Richard earned with his pluck, grit, and hockey talent. It was adoring fans, the media, and opportunistic hangers-on—Quebecois nationalist politicians and intellectuals, in particular—who heaped adulation upon Richard and in doing so turned him into an enduring symbol of pride in French Canada. He would come to be a larger-than-life figure who was "great" in every sense of the word; however, being shy and soft-spoken by nature, he was a reluctant hero, at least initially.

As 1944 faded to black, Richard was no different from any other young Canadian man with a wife and child to support. He was intent on just one thing: earning a regular pay cheque playing hockey for *les Canadiens*. The farthest thing from his mind was a desire—much less a willingness—to become a symbolic figure who skated along the nexus of the fault lines that separated Canada's "two solitudes," as author Hugh MacLennan would label them. No matter. That would be Richard's fate.

It was the cumulative weight of his otherworldly athletic talents, his fiery temperament, his Quebecois ethnicity, and the tenor of the times that thrust Richard into the spotlight and into Canada's national consciousness. Like Babe Ruth before him, Jackie Robinson (who also played in Montreal, albeit only at the start of his career in the mid-1940s), and Muhammad Ali afterward, Richard was destined to emerge as a cultural icon and secular saint in French Canada. And like those other larger-than-life heroes, Richard would transcend his sport in ways that are both culturally significant and enduring. It was in 1945, one of the most momentous and epochal years in this country's history, that the legend of Rocket Richard took flight.

Given his druthers and his initial doubts about his long-term prospects to earn a living playing hockey, Richard would have joined the military as so many other young men did during the war years, even in Quebec. That was not to be. Maurice Richard was twice rejected for military service because he was deemed to be medically unfit. Hockey injuries—two broken ankles and a broken wrist, all suffered before he was twenty-one—led to that designation. It seems ironic that a young man who wasn't capable of military service could endure the physical grind in the rough-and-tumble world of the NHL. But shooting pucks and shooting bullets are two very different skills. Richard had no say in his military deferment. So instead of suiting up in the stolid khaki of the Canadian military, he donned the *bleu, blanc, et rouge* of the Montreal Canadiens.

Richard would live with and eventually overcome his hockey injuries. While no one ever described his skating style as graceful, there can be no arguing that he "got the job done." He did that, and much more. Richard's searing, insatiable drive to win, his on-ice skills, and that intangible gutsiness—leadership ability—more than made up for any physical limitations he endured and had to learn to live with.

Richard, five-foot-ten tall and barrel-chested, tipped the scales at just 180 pounds (178 centimetres and 82 kilograms). By today's standards, that's modest at best; the average NHL player now checks in at six-foot-one and 205 pounds (185 centimetres and 93 kilograms). In 1945, Richard was average size for a professional hockey player, bang on. But the sport at that time was different, on the ice and off.

Unlike today's NHL players, who are well paid—$925,000 at the entry level and $2.4 million on average going forward—Richard and his teammates collected a relative pittance. His first contract with the Canadiens, for the 1942–43 season, paid him $3,500.[1] At the time, that was about twice as much as an average industrial worker making ninety cents an hour was taking home each year. NHL players weren't doing badly, you're probably thinking. Right? Well, not exactly.

Then, as now, most professional hockey careers were short, and the risk of permanent, debilitating injury was high. As a result, until the late 1970s, when player salaries rose dramatically following the launch of the World Hockey Association (WHA) as a rival to the NHL and when the players unionized, most professional hockey players had little choice but to work at other jobs during the off-season. In the 1940s, that annual downtime was five months, May through September. Maurice Richard was typical. Early in his hockey career, when he was a teenager, he spent the warm-weather months working as a machinist.

As challenging as it was for an NHL player to earn a living back then, it was no less different for the league itself. Today, the NHL is big business in every sense of the term. This thirty-one-team corporate entity (thirty-two teams starting in the 2021–22 season) reaps more than $6 billion in annual revenue. The players and most team owners now make piles of money. But for the first quarter century after the NHL's founding in 1917, the league skated on thin ice financially.

The Great Depression, in particular, dealt the NHL a hip check that sent it reeling. There were ten teams in 1930. When war began in September 1939, hockey—like North America's other professional sports leagues—drew heat for continuing to carry on business. However, the criticism gradually died down, giving way first to tolerance and finally to tepid approval on the part of the government, military, media, and public. American sportswriter-turned-war-correspondent Quentin Reynolds was one of those who argued the case for sports leagues continuing to play in wartime.

Speaking at a February 1943 media dinner in New York, Reynolds pointed out that while England's soccer leagues had shut down when war began, they soon resumed play in an effort to boost morale on the home front. Reynolds also noted how in Russia, 50,000 spectators reportedly had turned out in Moscow for a 1941 championship soccer match between teams from Moscow and Leningrad although the invading German army was only fifty miles (eighty kilometres) away. What's more, *Pravda*, the Soviet government's newspaper, gave page one placement to a story about the soccer game and printed a million extra copies of that day's newspaper for soldiers at the front.

Commenting on Reynolds's remarks, a sports columnist for the *Montreal Gazette* opined that in wartime a desire to escape prompted fans to continue following their favourite sports teams, even if it was only possible to do so by reading the sports pages of their local newspaper or by tuning in to the radio broadcasts of the games. "At a sporting event they can forget [the war] for a while and return to work refreshed," the columnist wrote.[2]

While that was true, there was no denying that the level of play in hockey and other professional sports during the war years was reduced. By the 1942–43 season, two-thirds of regular NHL players were in uniform.[3] Many of those who continued to play hockey for a living also were serving in the reserves or working part time in war-related industries. The NHL had withered to just six teams—what baby boomer fans now nostalgically remember as "the Original Six": Montreal, Toronto, Boston, New York, Detroit, and Chicago.

Teams in Ottawa, New York, Philadelphia, St. Louis, and Montreal (the Maroons in 1939) had all gone belly-up during the Great Depression. Even the Montreal Canadiens were going through a difficult stretch, especially in the late 1930s and early 1940s. The team was losing games almost as quickly as it was losing money.

The Canadiens had been one of the NHL's charter franchises, having been bankrolled in 1917 by Renfrew, Ontario–born businessman J. Ambrose O'Brien. A savvy entrepreneur, O'Brien started his own hockey league, the National Hockey Association. It soon rebranded itself as the NHL. O'Brien's original marketing plan called for the Canadiens to be the team of French-speaking Montrealers, while the rival Montreal Wanderers were to be the team of choice for Anglos.

But the Wanderers folded when on January 2, 1918, their arena burned to the ground in what some hockey historians remember as being the "most famous fire in hockey history."[4] The blaze happened just a few hours before a scheduled game between the Wanderers and the Canadiens. That match was never rescheduled, and Montreal had just one NHL team until the Montreal Maroons were established in 1924 as the new team of the city's English-speaking hockey fans.

Aside from the twenty-three seasons the Quebec Nordiques competed in the now-defunct WHA (1972–79) and then the NHL (1979–1995), after the Maroons folded, the Canadiens have been Quebec's team. And so many of the Canadiens' fans and members of the media affectionately took to calling the team "the Habs," short for *les Habitants*. The Habs moniker was born because some people incorrectly assumed—or perhaps wished—that the *H* in the middle of the Canadiens' iconic logo stood for *les Habitants*, the early French settlers of Quebec. The letter actually stands for *Hockey*, the word being part of the team's official business name: Club de Hockey Canadien Incorporated.

By 1931, although that corporate entity could boast of having won four Stanley Cups, it continued to struggle financially. In the latter half of the decade, the Canadiens repeatedly finished at or near the bottom of league standings, and then just when it seemed things couldn't get any worse, they did.

In August of 1939, two weeks before the Nazi blitzkrieg began rolling across Europe, the team's newly appointed coach, Charles "Babe" Siebert, drowned in a swimming accident. With a hastily hired replacement coach behind the bench and an aging roster on the ice, the Canadiens weren't expected to do much in the 1939–40 season. They didn't disappoint. The team finished last, winning just ten of forty-eight games. Fans stayed away in droves. Attendance plummeted to just 3,000 fans per game in the 9,300-seat Montreal Forum.

In those days, chicken wire separated the arena's three-dollar prime seats from the cheap bench-type seating higher up in the tiers. Admission there cost sixty-five cents, and some of the sightlines were obstructed. In retrospect, it might have made sense to have the pricier seats screened off with chicken wire. The only protective netting around the ice surface at that time was atop the boards behind each net. If they weren't watching the play carefully, the well-heeled ladies and gentlemen who sat rinkside, where they could see and be seen, risked losing their teeth or worse. It's a good thing there were no cell phones back then and that injury lawyers were less enterprising than they are today.

The Montreal Forum, home of the Montreal Canadiens, circa 1945.
(City of Montreal Archives, Wikimedia Commons)

Spectators getting dinged with pucks were the least of the Canadiens' woes during the early war years. With the team in dire financial straits, management considered suspending operations for the duration of the war. Then they hit upon a better solution; they sold the franchise to the Canadian Arena Company, owner of the Montreal Forum. Not long after that, an unlikely saviour arrived on the scene to help the team's new owners turn things around.

Conn Smythe, the irascible owner of the Maple Leafs, archrival of *les Canadiens* as English Canada's hockey team, was in no hurry to see the lucrative Toronto–Montreal rivalry end. In hopes of rekindling flagging hockey interest in Montreal, he suggested the Canadiens hire former Maple Leafs coach James Dickenson "Dick" Irvin to run the team. The forty-eight-year-old Hamilton, Ontario, native was a veteran of thirteen seasons as a player, most of them in the Western Canada Hockey League. Irvin was also a knowledgeable hockey man, and today he is better remembered for his work behind the bench than on the ice. A gruff no-nonsense coach with a proven track record, he'd led the Leafs to seven league finals and one Stanley Cup in his nine seasons with the blue-and-white. However, by 1940, he'd worn out his welcome in Toronto.

Montreal's French-language media howled at the idea of a unilingual anglophone guiding the Canadiens. However, the jeers turned to cheers in Irvin's first two seasons in Montreal, for under his leadership the team made the playoffs in both seasons, albeit still with a losing record. More important from a business perspective, game attendance began to increase. Things were starting to look up.

It was around this time that Maurice Richard donned a Canadiens sweater, and the team's fortunes took a dramatic turn for the better. Not that it was all Richard's doing, not initially. Many hockey people doubted that this slim, soft-spoken kid from Montreal's working-class north end even had what it took to survive in the NHL, much less to become a star. Injuries threatened to derail a promising hockey career before it really got started.

JOSEPH HENRI MAURICE RICHARD rose from humble beginnings. Banal though that may sound, it's true. He was born August 4, 1921, in Montreal's blue-collar Bordeaux neighbourhood, the eldest son of Onésime and Alice (née Laramée) Richard. Both hailed from the hardscrabble Gaspé region of Quebec, and both had migrated to Montreal hoping to find work. At the time, the city was Canada's largest, with a population of about 618,000. The couple met in Montreal and married in 1920. Onésime hammered out a living as a carpenter at the Canadian Pacific Railway yards; Alice kept the home fire burning and had babies.

It's not surprising that the Richard family were devout Roman Catholics; it would be surprising if they hadn't been. The Church exerted a powerful, pervasive influence over life in the Richard household and in the province of Quebec—so much so that when the American humourist Mark Twain visited Montreal in 1881, he described it as "the city of a hundred bell towers." He then whimsically observed, "This is the first time that I was ever in a city where you couldn't throw a brick without breaking a church window."⁵ While it's not known how many bricks Twain was accustomed to throwing when he visited a city, he evidently refrained from throwing any in Montreal.

One of the recurring messages preached by parish priests in Quebec in the early decades of the last century was the need for *la revanche des berceaux*, the "revenge of the cradles." That phrase, the mantra of Quebec nationalists in the early years of the twentieth century, promoted the idea that by pumping out babies, French Canadians would be able to retain majority status in the province. Doing so might enable them to avenge—and perhaps even roll back—the British conquest of New France. The Richards did their part in this noble cause, producing eight children—five sons and three daughters.

As the couple's eldest son, young Maurice seemed destined to follow in his father's footsteps in every regard. That is, as soon as he was old enough, he'd get a job and do whatever he could to help support the family until he married. In that sense, the blueprint for his life was drawn early: once he'd learned a trade and married a good French-speaking Catholic girl, he'd rear his own brood of little Richards and settle into a blue-collar job. His existence would be as predictable as the days of the week. Ah, but as the rapper Eminem has said, "Life is a crazy ride, and nothing is guaranteed." Life often does take an unexpected turn, sometimes several of them. That was so for Maurice Richard.

Onésime Richard was a sports fan. For some unknown reason, baseball was his first love. But when the Canadiens won the Stanley

Cup in 1924, he found himself swept up in the excitement, and he became a hockey fan. The following year, he bought his eldest son a pair of skates. It would prove to be a worthwhile and life-changing investment. Young Maurice took to the ice the way a politician takes to an expense account. In the winter, he wore the skates everywhere—on city streets, in neighbourhood parks, on ponds, and on the frozen St. Lawrence River. It's said the only time the boy took off his skates was to go to school or bed. (If you've ever worn your skates to school or bed, you'll understand why he did that.)

It wasn't long before young Maurice was playing shinny hockey and "hog," a game in which the puck carrier tries to keep it from other players. He excelled at both games, so much so that he was invited to play for the Bordeaux parish's hockey team. By age fifteen, Richard had sprouted to adult height, although he was yet to fill out physically and so was as lean as his hockey stick. Regardless, whatever he may have lacked in physical presence, he more than made up for with his intensity and passion to win. Opponents found both qualities intimidating. A natural athlete, Richard also excelled on the baseball field and in the boxing ring. When a schoolteacher gave him some boxing lessons, Richard entered Montreal's annual Golden Gloves tournament. He didn't win, but he more than held his own. "Some of his neighbourhood chums suspected that Maurice could make a better boxer than either a baseball or hockey player," one observer reported.[6]

Boxing would be just a passing fancy, though. Hockey was and always would be Richard's first sporting love, his *raison d'être*. In his teens, he became fanatic about the sport, tuning in to Canadiens games on the radio and suiting up for three different teams, getting around the rules against doing so by playing under assumed names—"Maurice Rochon" was one. Richard was playing as many as six games a week and skating on his own whenever he had the time.

Unfortunately for his family, Onésime Richard lost his job in 1932 and would remain unemployed for four long, trying years. At age eleven, Maurice began caddying at a local golf course to make money to help feed the family. It wasn't enough, and so the Richards relied on government aid to make ends meet. The embarrassing experience of being obliged to use government vouchers to buy food seared itself into Maurice Richard's memory. Vowing never to find himself in that position, he quit regular school at age sixteen to enroll at a technical college. Richard hoped that by acquiring a trade, he'd always be able to find a steady job. Things didn't work out as planned, but learning to operate a metal lathe did provide him with summer employment during the uncertain early years of his hockey career.

Richard was about sixteen when he began to play juvenile hockey, competing against young men up to nineteen years of age.[7] Still, he dominated play, while winning a reputation for having a short fuse, quick fists—those boxing lessons came in handy—and an uncanny knack for putting the puck in the net. In 1938–39, Richard's third and final year of juvenile hockey, he scored 133 of his team's 144 goals. Despite this, the idea of earning a living playing the game still seemed a crazy dream at best.

FOLLOWING THE SEPTEMBER 1939 onset of war in Europe, a job was a job, and so young men began rushing off to join the military. Prime hockey talent was in short supply. The Montreal Canadiens' top point getter at the time was Hector "Toe" Blake, a thirty-year-old native of the rock-ribbed hard northern Ontario town of Victoria Mines. Blake already had seventeen seasons of hockey experience on his stats sheet, and he wasn't getting any younger. The Canadiens understandably were on the lookout for fresh talent, and so the team's scouts were beating the bushes in search of young players in Quebec's many minor hockey leagues.

One of the three minor hockey teams Maurice Richard was playing for that season had a gas station as its sponsor. It was while wearing the sweater of the Paquette team that Richard caught the eye of Aurèle

Joliat, the retired Canadiens star, five-foot-seven and a pint-sized 135 pounds (170 centimetres and 61 kilograms), who was renowned during his own NHL playing days for both his goal-scoring abilities and the trademark black cap he had worn on the ice—helmets were almost as rare as one-legged players.[8] Joliat, who had retired in 1938 after a sixteen-year Hall of Fame career, did some bird-dogging for his old team, scouting minor hockey games and recommending young players to the Canadiens.

Prior to the seismic changes that would reshape the NHL in the wake of the league's 1967 expansion to twelve teams, each club operated its own network of junior and minor professional affiliates. With no central scouting or annual amateur draft then, team scouts could and did woo and sign to contracts players who were as young as fifteen. The competition for the top hockey prospects in the mid-1950s was so intense that the Canadiens operated thirteen junior affiliates in cities and towns across Quebec and Ontario. All NHL teams had an insatiable appetite for young talent, but the Canadiens outdid the competition. That was especially true when it came to unearthing French-speaking hockey talent in Quebec. And so it was that Aurèle Joliat recommended that the Canadiens sign Richard for their Verdun Maple Leafs junior team.

Apart from Richard's goal scoring, one thing that intrigued Joliat was the novelty of the fact the kid was a left-hand shot, yet he played right wing—on his "wrong" side—with marked success. Richard's shot, both forehand and backhand, was hard, and he fired pucks with laser-like accuracy at a time when lasers were still the stuff of Flash Gordon science fiction.

One of Richard's juvenile hockey coaches was Canadiens player Paul Haynes—a future Hockey Hall of Famer whose career ended in 1941 when he was cut from the team after skipping a practice in New York to attend an opera. It was Haynes who started Richard playing on right wing, to take advantage of the young man's quick acceleration. Haynes had noticed that when Richard carried the puck down the right side of the ice, he could use his skating speed and explosiveness to button-hook around most defencemen. Doing so often yielded him a clear shot on the net.

Richard would eventually fill out and bulk up physically. His skating strength and speed were two of his greatest assets; however, there was another that was even more important to his success. Look at any photo of Richard in his prime, and his most noticeable feature is the legendary fire in his eyes—the Rocket's red glare. Those famous, fiery orbs glared like the headlights on a steam engine. Richard in full flight would not—could not—be deterred, let alone stopped. Even as an eighteen-year-old, in full stride he skated like a man possessed.

Strangely enough, one of the most intriguing and poetic descriptions of Richard was offered by American writer William Faulkner, the 1949 winner of the Nobel Prize for Literature. Being a Mississippi native, Faulkner had experienced ice only as the crushed variety found in the mint juleps that were his favourite cocktail. In 1955, *Sports Illustrated*, a new magazine created by American publisher Henry Luce—the man who was also behind *Life* and *Time*—asked Faulkner to attend a New York Rangers game and write about his impressions. Faulkner did that in a brief article titled "An Innocent at Rinkside."

The Canadiens were the Rangers' opponent on the night Faulkner attended a game. Not surprisingly, his eyes were drawn to Maurice Richard, whose on-ice presence reminded Faulkner of the "glittering fatal alien quality of snakes."[9] The analogy, as odd as it was memorable, caught the primal essence of Richard's relentless, lethal intensity. This was something he was born with and that empowered him. Paul Haynes had sensed as much. "The thought occurred to me that if [he] was used regularly on the right wing, he'd have more opportunity to use his particular skills," Haynes recalled many years later, "especially since, if he did get ridden off-angle, he still had that sizzling backhander as a threat."[10]

The wrinkle that Haynes added to Richard's game created opportunities for what became the trademark move that would set him apart from the crowd. In 1939, Richard was still a gangly eighteen-year-old who received no special treatment when he reported to the Verdun Maple Leafs (while continuing to play for a team in the Parc Lafontaine League). Being an unknown entity in Verdun, young Maurice had limited ice time. He appeared in just ten regular-season games but still managed to score four goals. For good measure, he added six more in four playoff games. Such a promising performance and the fact Richard was French-speaking were enough to earn him a promotion within the Canadiens' system.

He started the 1940–41 season with a farm team in the Quebec Senior Hockey League. It was here, playing against grown men, that Richard suffered the first serious injury of his hockey career. He collected an assist in the first game of the season before breaking an ankle when an opponent slammed him into the boards. That finished his season and his luck didn't improve the following year.

Richard appeared in just thirty-one games in the 1941–42 campaign, scoring eight goals before falling victim to another serious injury. This time he slid headfirst into a goalpost. In those days, nets had no give; they sat on pegs that anchored them to the ice. Richard managed to get his arm up in time to protect his head when he collided with the goalpost, but he broke his left wrist in the process. The injury healed quickly, or perhaps he rushed to get back on the ice. Either way, he returned in time for the playoffs, scoring two goals in the six games.

Having suffered two serious injuries in two seasons of senior play raised grave doubts in Richard's mind that he was tough enough for a career in professional hockey. To at least consider another line of work seemed like the sensible thing to do; he and his girlfriend were getting serious about the possibilities of a life together. Maurice had met a blue-eyed redhead, Lucille Norchet, when he was sixteen and playing for the Paquette Club of the Park Lafontaine Juvenile League. Lucille's older brother, Georges, was the team's playing captain and coach. Although Lucille was three years younger than Maurice, it was love at first sight when they met. If it's true that opposites attract, theirs was an ideal match. He was shy and soft-spoken, at least when he wasn't playing hockey. She was gregarious, enjoyed being with and around people, and was never shy about making decisions.

One day not long after they became a couple, Lucille advised Maurice that she didn't approve of how he wore his hair. He'd been combing his thick mop of dark hair slicked straight back, in a style popular at the time. Lucille had concluded that her beau would look better, more dashing, if he styled his hair differently. So, she took out her comb and went to work, installing a well-positioned part on the left side of his noggin. If Maurice objected and said so, he evidently lost the argument. He would comb his hair with a part from then on, a permanent reminder of Lucille's place in his life.

In 1942, Maurice was about to turn twenty-one, while Lucille was seventeen. Over the objections of her father, the couple announced their intention to marry. With that in mind, Richard decided to join the military, thinking that doing so would provide him with a steady job and reliable income. But the hockey gods had decreed otherwise. To his dismay, when Richard visited the Canadian army recruitment bureau, the assessors rejected him on medical grounds. As it turned out, the injuries Richard had suffered playing hockey were among the luckiest breaks—if you'll excuse that groan-worthy pun—he ever experienced.

Although Richard's two seasons with the Canadiens' farm team had been cut short by injuries, the flashes of brilliance he'd shown were enough to earn him an invitation to the big club's training camp in the autumn of 1942. Richard made the most of the opportunity, and on October 29, he signed a contract with the Canadiens that paid him $3,500. That was a small fortune to a young man from Montreal's working-class north end. "I still can't figure what the Canadiens saw in me to offer that first pro contract," Richard would later say.[11]

He was a better hockey player than a scout, at least where his own abilities were concerned. The Canadiens' general manager had concluded it was worth taking a chance on him. Tommy Gorman recognized that Richard had a special talent, and it didn't hurt that French was his first language. There were just two other francophones on the Montreal Canadiens' roster in 1942–43.

Maurice Richard was twenty-two in 1942–43, his rookie season with the Montreal Canadiens. (Bibliothèque et Archives nationales du Québec, no. 06M, P48, S1, P12158)

That season was destined to be the first of eighteen Richard would play for the team in a storied career that would see him reluctantly become, in the words of biographer Charles Foran, "Saint Maurice, defender and exemplar of the downtrodden French Canadian through both his brilliant play and the righteous violence of his fists."[12]

J OYOUS SUPPORTERS OF THE Montreal Canadiens would have ample reasons to celebrate, even deify Maurice "the Rocket" Richard in 1945.

He overcame more than his fair share of grief early in his NHL career, and his scoring prowess stoked the passions of fans as the skills of no hockey player had, perhaps ever. What's more, his on-ice prowess put hockey on the radar as a sporting spectacle even to non-fans in distant places. Remarkably, a 1945 poll of readers of the *Los Angeles Times* celebrated Richard as hockey's greatest player.[13] Remember, this was long before NHL expansion, long before Wayne Gretzky's 1988 arrival in Los Angeles stirred interest in ice hockey among sports fans in southern California, and among Americans generally. The name of Rocket Richard had become synonymous with hockey, yet in many ways the man's legend soared above the sport.

He had been just twenty-two when he joined the Canadiens for the 1942–43 season. At the time, the team had a surplus of veteran right wingers, and because Richard was a left-hand shot, Coach Irvin slotted him in to play left wing. That was the orthodox thing to do. Rookies, no matter how highly touted or talented, had to prove they deserved to play in the six-team NHL, let alone to snatch a roster spot from a veteran. In 1942, more than 80,000 men and boys—no, there were no female leagues at the time—were playing organized hockey in Canada; only about 120 of those players were earning a living playing in the NHL. War or no war, and even with the talent pool shallower than usual, the league was still hockey's top tier. Competition for jobs remained intense.

Richard was understandably thrilled just to have a contract, and he was determined to make the best of his opportunity. He began doing so when he scored the first goal of his NHL career in the Canadiens' second game of the season, a 10–4 blowout of the New York Rangers. Richard would tally five more times before falling victim to injury once again. That happened in a December 27 game when veteran Boston Bruin defenceman Jack Crawford rode Richard into the boards, snapping his right ankle.

People inevitably began to wonder if the Canadiens' rookie was star-crossed or simply wasn't physically tough enough to play in the NHL. Canadiens coach Dick Irvin suspected that was the case. He was overheard telling a hockey colleague that he didn't think Richard was going to "make it."

Now, more than ever, Richard wrestled with the same self-doubts. "It seemed I was always on my ass or in the hospital," he said.[14] He was right. Small wonder that Richard seriously thought about finding a more secure, less punishing, line of work. Newly married and with his wife, Lucille, expecting their first child, Richard again tried to enlist. Once again, the army rejected him for medical reasons. X-rays of his broken ankle showed the bones hadn't healed properly; he would forever have a misshapen foot.

Richard had a choice—he could go to work full time in the machine shop where he toiled each summer, or he could stick with hockey and try to learn to skate on a wonky ankle. Some dreams die hard, and Richard's desire to play for the Montreal Canadiens was one of them. Fortunately, Lady Luck cut him some slack for once when he began training feverishly in hopes of making a successful return to the team for the 1943–44 season.

The first of the Richards' seven children, daughter Huguette, was born prior to the start of that season. The media and hockey fans knew Maurice Richard as a fearless, fiery competitor who never backed down. He would do whatever he had to do in order to score goals and help the Canadiens win. But there was another side to Richard: the devoted family man. "He's supposed to be so hard," Lucille Richard once told an interviewer. "But wait till you see him at home. He's so gentle and kind, so good to the kids. Too good, I tell him."[15]

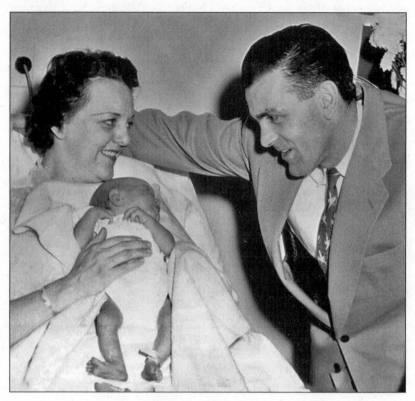

Maurice Richard, a doting father, was at wife Lucille's side for the birth of each of the couple's seven children. (LAC, MIKAN no. 3612868)

Whenever Lucille gave birth, her husband waited at her side, no matter how long it took for the baby to arrive. And when the child did come into the world, Richard cried tears of joy. His children meant everything to him. The evidence: when Huguette, his first child, weighed a hefty nine pounds (four kilograms) at birth, Maurice Richard switched his uniform number from fifteen to nine. Lucky number nine. The number he would make his own in Montreal; it would retire with him. At the same time, Richard benefited from Coach Irvin's decision to try playing him on the right wing alongside veteran left-winger Toe Blake and centre Elmer Lach. The combination clicked immediately because of the trio's complementary hockey skills and because the fluently bilingual Blake was able to serve as the linguistic go-between for his linemates. Richard spoke little English, while Lach, a chirpy Saskatchewan native, knew only a few words of French. Lingual obstacles aside, "the Punch Line" was destined to become one of the legendary lines in NHL history; all three members of the line were Hall of Fame bound.

It was also around this time that Richard picked up his signature nickname: "the Rocket." Earlier, teammates had dubbed him "Bones" for the obvious reason that he seemed frail and injury-prone. Irreverent though such a nickname was, it fit. But no longer. Richard picked up his famous nickname one day into the 1942–43 season. Healthy now, he was starting to live up to his potential.

For much of the last century, professional athletes carried nicknames, colourful ones—think boxers Joe "the Brown Bomber" Louis and Jack "the Manassa Mauler" Dempsey, baseball players "Shoeless Joe" Jackson, Lou "Iron Horse" Gehrig, and Herman "Babe" Ruth. Some names were funny, some ironic, some simply fit the athlete and his playing style. That was certainly the case with Richard's nickname. It stuck because of his gift for surprising opponents with his lightning speed. He could shift gears in the wink of an eye, turn on the afterburners, and blow by opposing defencemen in his rush to the net. It was one of Richard's teammates, a plucky third-line winger with the Canadiens named Ray Getliffe, who dubbed Richard "the Rocket" after watching him perform one day at a team practice.

"I was sitting on the bench with [teammates] Murph Chamberlain and Phil Watson. . . . Elmer Lach was on the ice with Maurice Richard and fed him a lovely pass. Richard got the puck and took off," Getliffe recalled many years later. "I leaned over to Murph and said, 'Wow, Richard took off like a rocket!'"[16]

As it happened, *Montreal Gazette* sportswriter Austin "Dink" Carroll was standing nearby and chanced to overhear the comment. When in one of his columns not long afterward Carroll referred to Richard as "the Rocket," the name stuck, and a legend was born.

Richard and his fleet-footed Canadiens teammates, "the flying Frenchmen," were the class of the NHL in the 1943–44 season. The team won forty-five of fifty regular-season games and breezed to a Stanley Cup win, the team's first in thirteen long years. Although the Rocket finished third in the NHL scoring race behind linemates Elmer Lach and Toe Blake, he led the Montreal team with thirty-two regular-season goals and then added twelve more in the post-season.

Other NHL teams took notice of Richard's emergence as a big-time goal scorer and a budding star; both the New York Rangers and the Toronto Maple Leafs approached the Canadiens to gauge the team's willingness to trade Richard or sell his contract. Toronto owner Conn Smythe offered the Canadiens $25,000 for Richard's services. Canada's hockey history would have been much different if Montreal general manager Tommy Gorman had accepted Smythe's money. He wisely didn't, and that autumn the reigning Stanley Cup champion Canadiens picked up in the 1944–45 season where they had left off in April.

By the end of December 1944, the Canadiens had breezed to a record of sixteen wins, four losses, and two ties. That was good enough for first place in the league standings. As for Richard, he had set an NHL single-game scoring record, counting five goals and adding three assists in a 9–1 blowout of the Detroit Red Wings on December 28. Richard scored twenty-four goals in the Canadiens' first twenty-two games, and he didn't slack off as the calendars turned to 1945. The year would be one of the most memorable—and defining—ones in the history of Canada, the NHL, and the life of Maurice "the Rocket" Richard.

IDWAY THROUGH JANUARY 1945, the Canadiens were still flying high, with just five losses in thirty games. Richard's goal total had reached thirty, and he was still scoring at a remarkable pace. As Quebec writer Roch Carrier would recall, in Quebec, in much of the Maritime provinces, and in other areas of Canada where the Canadiens were the team of choice, "Richard's goals [were] recounted like the exploits of long-ago heroes."[17]

For his part, Richard simply shrugged. He professed not to care about individual records; all he wanted to do, he insisted, was play hockey and help the Canadiens win another Stanley Cup. The media and fans had other ideas.

The excitement grew as it became clear that Richard was on pace to equal or perhaps even break the NHL's single-season goal-scoring record. That distinction was held by a Canadiens' star of yesteryear: shifty centre "Phantom" Joe Malone had counted forty-four goals in the twenty-two-game schedule that teams played in 1917–18, the NHL's very first season.

As would be the case today, when Richard continued to score and to chase Malone's goal-scoring record, pressure on him ramped up. So, too, did controversy surrounding his efforts. Critics pointed out that Malone had set his goal-scoring record in a twenty-two-game season, and at a time when Canada was also at war. Most "real" men—the top-tier NHL players—were supposedly in the military, fighting for king and country. Skeptics pointed out that because Richard found himself in the same no-win situation that Malone had been in, any goal-scoring record the Rocket might set would be of dubious merit. What was left unsaid, the proverbial elephant in the room, was that in early 1945, other dynamics were also fuelling anti-Richard sentiments.

Although the war in Europe was drawing to a close, there lingered much bitterness about the federal government's reluctance to introduce compulsory overseas conscription. Prime Minister King was so fearful of a recurrence of the violence that had threatened to tear Canada apart during the conscription crisis of WWI that he preferred to do nothing, as was his habit. By dithering, King hoped to "rag the puck," to borrow a hockey analogy, until the war in Europe was over. His conscription problem would then resolve itself.

Opposition to King's inaction ran deep in English Canada, where pro-conscription sentiments were strong; demands were growing to send more reservists—the zombies, as they had been derisively dubbed in English Canada—overseas. In January 1945, the first conscripts among the 15,000 who had been called up were ordered onto Europe-bound ships. However, 4,000 of these men deserted; 2,500 of them were Quebeckers.

In French Canada, where many people were adamantly opposed to compulsory overseas military service, the zombies received sympathetic treatment and safe harbour even when the authorities threatened grave consequences. Roch Carrier would remember how as a boy he "admired those men who refused to go to the Old Countries and get killed. I felt a natural sympathy for them," he wrote.[18] The mood in Quebec was defiant, and it was tense.

After five years in opposition, Union Nationale leader Maurice Duplessis, a staunch opponent of conscription and a sworn enemy of Mackenzie King, returned to power as Quebec's premier. He did so on the strength of a 1944 election platform that promised an inward-looking "back-to-the future" plan of economic and social development. In Duplessis's mind, Quebeckers were victims; they were "small people" who were besieged and in danger of being swamped by English language and culture. The foundation of this parochial worldview was built upon bedrock Roman Catholic family values and a restive opposition to anglophone domination of the Quebec economy, leftist politics, unions, feminism, and many of the other principles that would bubble to the surface in Quebec during the Quiet Revolution of the 1960s.

The tensions that were roiling Quebec and dividing Canadians were symptoms of the changes that were transforming Canada into a modern industrialized, urbanized nation, one that would stroll onto the world stage in the post-war era. Not surprisingly, the intellectual, economic, and political ferment that was underway set Canadians thinking about who they were as a people and where their country was headed. Out of the asperity of the French–English divide of the war years, there emerged two of the twentieth century's most culturally important and enduring Canadian novels: Hugh MacLennan's *Two Solitudes* and Gabrielle Roy's *Bonheur d'occasion*, which roughly translated means "secondhand happiness." The English version is known as *The Tin Flute*. Both books were very much products of the time.

The former is a novel whose title has come to symbolize one of Canada's most enduring and problematic dilemmas: the love–hate relationship between English and French. Ironically, the idea of two separate and distinct nations within a nation isn't at all what MacLennan had in mind when he chose the title for his novel. He derived that now iconic "two solitudes" phrase from a line in a 1904 letter written by the Austrian poet Rainer Maria Rilke (1875–1926).

Poor Herr Rilke, beset by marital problems, had mused in a letter to a friend that "love cannot exist in mutual assimilation or in subordination of one party to another, but it ought to consist in a mutual respect and protection of each other's inalienable identity and solitude."[19]

Who can say where artistic inspiration comes from? No matter. When MacLennan read that pensive passage in Rilke's letter, the phrase "two solitudes" lodged in his mind. It was MacLennan biographer Elspeth Cameron who pointed out that "as Rilke meant it and as MacLennan understood it, [this] was not simply a definition of two isolated entities; it was a definition of love."[20] Readers of MacLennan's writing failed to grasp the subtle essence of the phrase, and so "two solitudes" has come to stand as one of those unique Canadianisms that has become a cultural touchstone, as much a part of our collective DNA as "He shoots, he scores," "loonie," "two-four," or "double-double," eh?

At least in terms of its cultural significance, *The Tin Flute* has achieved a similar status in the literature of French Canada, albeit for different reasons. That book—the first and most widely read of Gabrielle Roy's fifteen novels—began life as a short story. It took on a life of its own, and then some. The original manuscript was eight hundred pages until Roy trimmed it down to five hundred. What made *Bonheur d'occasion* so compelling and unique was that it presented a realistic and heartbreakingly honest portrait of a struggling francophone working-class family in Montreal's Saint-Henri neighbourhood. In the words of one Roy biographer, the book was "a dark tale that leaves little hope for its protagonists."[21]

MOST POPULAR POP SONGS OF 1945

It was no accident that the songs most Canadians listened to, danced to, and were singing in 1945 were all by American artists. Most homes had a radio, and American stations were widely listened to; even the CBC played a lot of American tunes. Here are the year's most popular songs:

- Les Brown and Doris Day: "Sentimental Journey"
- Andrews Sisters: "Rum and Coca-Cola"
- Perry Como: "Till the End of Time"
- Les Brown: "My Dreams Are Getting Better All the Time"
- Johnny Mercer: "On the Atchison, Topeka and the Santa Fe"
- Harry James: "It's Been a Long, Long Time"
- Bing Crosby and Carmen Cavallaro: "I Can't Begin to Tell You"
- Sammy Kaye: "Chickery Chick"
- Johnny Mercer: "Ac-cent-tchu-ate the Positive"
- Vaughn Monroe: "There! I've Said It Again"

Critics have hailed *Bonheur d'occasion* as the first major novel to delve into the lives and travails of the many ordinary Canadians who were struggling to cope in an urban environment that to them still seemed strange and inhospitable. This was especially significant and resonant in Quebec during the war years. Roy would recall how her lawyer and friend Henri Girard, who did more than anyone to advance her career, had pointed out that "in [francophone] literature, writing about city life is anathema, unless it's done to denounce it. The [Roman Catholic] clergy has done everything in their power to keep French Canadians on the farm. Their efforts were wasted, in any case: over the last hundred years, we've never stopped crowding into the cities."[22]

Gabrielle Roy's perspective reflected that reality. While *Bonheur d'occasion* was set in Montreal and was primarily concerned with the plight of an impoverished francophone family, the themes of angst, rootlessness, and income disparity were ones that Canadians from coast to coast very much could identify with. Between 1940 and 1945, as more and more people migrated to the cities to work in war industries, the percentage of the Canadian population that lived in rural areas dropped from about forty-five per cent to thirty-eight per cent. That migration would continue post-war; today, only about nineteen per cent of Canadians live in rural areas.[23]

Gabrielle Roy, author of *The Tin Flute*. (LAC, MIKAN no. 4325087)

MacLennan's novel appeared in January of 1945, Roy's in June of the same year, although it didn't find a mass audience outside Quebec until 1947. That is when publishers in the United States and in English Canada marketed it under the title *The Tin Flute*. Critical praise for both books was widespread.

Two Solitudes captured a Governor General's Award for Literary Merit for fiction in 1945, while *The Tin Flute* won both the prestigious French literary award the Prix Femina and a Governor General's award in 1947. Both books became bestsellers, although curiously— for a novel written in French and that dealt with characters and situations so unique to Montreal and to Canada—it was *The Tin Flute* that enjoyed greater commercial success. MacLennan banked only about $12,000 in royalties in the first few years after *Two Solitudes* was published. Meanwhile, Roy fared considerably better.

The $100 advance cheque she received from her French publisher bounced. However, Roy did much better financially, banking more than $100,000 after the book was published in English, and Universal Studios scooped up movie rights for $75,000. *The Tin Flute* would rack up sales of more than 750,000 copies in the United States alone, in large measure because the Literary Guild of America made the novel a Feature Selection of the Month for May 1947. The 1940s were the heyday of the Book of the Month Club and the Literary Guild; they were powerful marketing juggernauts that overnight could make a book a mass-market bestseller.

What is especially interesting is that both *Two Solitudes* and *The Tin Flute* were unabashedly Canadian novels that were written by Montreal-based authors who were born elsewhere in Canada, who came of age while living abroad, and who then settled in Canada's most vibrant and exciting city in the 1940s. At that time, Montreal "was the only Canadian city comparable to New York," Margaret Atwood has observed. "It was the financial capital of Canada—bustling, cosmopolitan, multilingual and sophisticated, with impressive architecture both ancient and Victorian, and a lively nightclub scene frequented by A-list jazz musicians. It was also Sin City, known for its freely flowing liquor, its many prostitutes, and its civic corruption."[24]

Hugh MacLennan, author of *Two Solitudes*. (Hugh MacLennan Collection, Rare Books and Special Collections, McGill University Library)

Small wonder that writers such as Hugh MacLennan and Gabrielle Roy found themselves drawn to Montreal. MacLennan, who hailed from Glace Bay, Nova Scotia, had lived and studied in England and the United States; Roy, a francophone from St. Boniface, Manitoba, had lived in France and England prior to returning to Canada.

MacLennan's perspective and sensibilities were those of an anglophone, Roy's those of a francophone. In that regard, the two writers couldn't have been more different; yet in other ways, they had more in common than you might think. Both rebelled against the parochiality that confined them in their early lives, and both came to view the world through the lens of a class consciousness and collectivity that—for many smart people who should have known better—had a *flavour du jour* trendiness to it in the 1930s and in the latter years of WWII when smiling Uncle Joseph Stalin was an ally of convenience for Canada.

N OT SURPRISINGLY, MAURICE RICHARD neither knew of nor cared about any of this. It's highly unlikely he ever read *Two Solitudes* or *Bonheur d'occasion*. The Rocket was a hockey player, not a reader, and he had little interest in politics. He had other far more pressing and immediate concerns. For one, he was dismayed to find himself becoming a target for the hostile zealots in English Canada and a symbol of nationalistic pride for their francophone counterparts.

The legend of Rocket Richard really began to soar on that night in February 1945 when he tied Joe Malone's NHL single-season goal-scoring record. Fate had decreed this history-making feat would occur in a game against who else but the Toronto Maple Leafs— English Canada's team. A standing-room-only crowd, one of the largest of the 1944–45 season in Toronto, packed Maple Leaf Gardens that night, while countless thousands of fans across Canada, parts of the northern United States, and Newfoundland gathered around their radios to tune in to the play-by-play of the game.

The Saturday night radio broadcast of NHL games was the programming highlight of the week on both the French and English networks of the Canadian Broadcasting Corporation (CBC), and no games drew larger audiences than did Leafs–Canadiens games. Those radio broadcasts were integral to the growth of the rivalry between the two teams and would become a unique part of the national culture— tuning in became a Saturday night ritual for Canadians from coast to coast. In Quebec, French-speaking Michel Normandin was the radio voice of the Montreal Canadiens beginning in 1936, three years after the first games were broadcast on the CRBC's French-language service. Roch Carrier, who listened to games on radio during his youthful days in the 1940s, remembers how in his breathless play-by-play Normandin rolled his "r's." It was "Maurice RRRichard," scoring goals against the hated "Torrronto Maple Leafs."[25]

Normandin's English-language peer was Foster Hewitt, "the quintessential Anglo in all of hockey."[26] Blue-eyed, with curly brown hair, a pale complexion, and full, jowly cheeks, he wasn't someone who stood out in a crowd. The Toronto-born Hewitt stood only about five-foot-seven (170 centimetres) and weighed about 140 pounds (64 kilograms) soaking wet. However, as biographer Scott Young (the father of rock musician Neil Young) pointed out, Hewitt became a giant of Canadian broadcasting history and a legend in his own right. Magic happened whenever he sat behind a microphone to call a hockey game in that distinctive, high-pitched nasal voice; it gushed breathless excitement even during lulls in the game. Saturday night had forever been "bath night" in homes across Canada, in town and country. Now it was also the night when entire families gathered around their radios to hear Hewitt's weekly hockey broadcast. Today, with the fragmenting of audiences and the proliferation of hockey coverage on radio, television, and the internet, the same sort of communal event seldom, if ever, happens. In the 1940s, Saturday nights were special.

When Hewitt's Saturday night hockey broadcasts from Maple Leaf Gardens began, they aired on a network of radio stations belonging to Canadian National Railways. The games moved over to Toronto station CFRB the following year, and in 1934 Imperial Oil took over as advertising sponsor, replacing General Motors. At that time, Hewitt's broadcast started at 9 p.m., about halfway through the second period (in order not to harm ticket sales at the rink). That practice continued when Prime Minister Mackenzie King's newly created Crown corporation, the CBC, began delivering to a national audience the Saturday night hockey broadcasts, which already were informally known as "Hockey Night in Canada"—another term that was coined by the inventive Mr. Hewitt. He and colour man Percy LeSueur, a former Ottawa Senators goalkeeper in the pre-NHL era (1906–1914), developed a devoted following of English-language listeners Canada-wide. In fact, *Hockey Night in Canada* radio broadcasts were so popular that Hewitt and LeSueur received as many as 250 fan letters each day.

When Hall of Fame hockey star Bobby Hull, who had grown up listening to *Hockey Night in Canada* radio broadcasts, met Hewitt, he gushed, "It was like meeting God."[27]

During the war, the CBC provided the Empire Service of the British Broadcasting Corporation with the audio tape of a half-hour condensed version of *Hockey Night in Canada* broadcasts. The program, a reminder of home and hearth, was a powerful morale booster for Canadian military personnel overseas.

The voice of hockey in English Canada in 1945 was play-by-play announcer Foster Hewitt. (City of Toronto Archives, item 1653, series 975, file 218, no. 11436-6)

The radio broadcast of the historic game in which Rocket Richard tied Joe Malone's single-season goal-scoring record was one of the most memorable ever for Foster Hewitt and for his audience. On the night of February 17, 1945, Hewitt was perched in his lofty gondola, exactly fifty-six feet (seventeen metres) above the Maple Leaf Gardens ice surface. (Hewitt had measured the distance to determine the perfect height from which to view a game.) From here, he described all the on-ice action between the Canadiens and Leafs. As usual, the contest was hard-fought, with "Rugged Robert" Davidson, the left-winger the Leafs had assigned to keep the Rocket in check, getting the job done for most of the game. But he couldn't do so for the full sixty minutes.

The score was tied 3–3 late in the third period, as the acrid fog of cigarette smoke that filled arenas on game nights back then descended to hover several feet above the ice surface. Everyone smoked in hockey arenas in 1945—even the players, before and after games, and sometimes between periods.

On this particular Saturday night, fans in the nosebleed sections of Maple Leaf Gardens strained their eyes peering through the haze to see Richard suddenly break free of his shadow. The Rocket was in full flight as he snared an Elmer Lach pass at centre ice and scooted around Toronto defenceman Reg Hamilton. From ten feet in front of the Toronto net, Richard feigned a deke, and then he let fly a wrist shot. At exactly that moment, Maple Leafs goalie Frank McCool threw himself to the ice and, fully extended, came sliding out of his net. Richard crashed into him and went airborne. McCool somehow managed to get one of his leg pads in front of the Rocket's shot, but he couldn't stop it. The puck rolled behind him and into the net at 15:19 of the third period. "He shoots; he scores!" Foster Hewitt shouted, while 15,000 Toronto fans groaned as one, and on the ice Richard's teammates mobbed him, offering congratulatory backslaps. The record-tying goal was extra special because it was Richard's first against Toronto that season.

Globe and Mail sports columnist Jim Coleman, like other members of the Toronto media, wasn't ready to praise any Maple Leafs opponent, especially not someone whom Coleman insisted wasn't even the Canadiens' best player; that honour fell to Elmer Lach. And what's more, in Coleman's estimation, while Maurice Richard may have been an exciting talent, he lacked former Canadiens' great Howie Morenz's "gift for lifting the customers out of their seats." Even so, Coleman begrudgingly saluted Richard's achievement, allowing that "it wouldn't have been amiss for the officials, the Gardens' announcer and other hands to make a little more fuss about Richard's goal, which won the game. After all, he was making modern hockey history."[28]

MAURICE RICHARD MADE HISTORY once again when the Maple Leafs travelled to Montreal for a February 27 rematch. As had been the case ten days earlier in Toronto, an overflow crowd jammed the Forum. The time when the Canadiens averaged just 3,000 fans a game was long gone. Because the team was now an NHL powerhouse, fans were flocking to the rink and marvelling at the Maurice Richard's scoring abilities. Everybody loves a winner, so much so that the Canadiens' management responded to the growing interest by adding seats to the Forum and sprucing up the building.

Joe Malone was among the crowd that came out that night hoping to see Richard set a new single-season goal-scoring record. Malone had reached out to Richard a few days earlier, sending him a note of encouragement and support. To his surprise, Richard hadn't replied; the Rocket figured the missive was a joke being played on him by his teammates—Elmer Lach was always full of such mischief. Malone was forgiving, and so on the eve of his fifty-fifth birthday, he watched the Leafs–Canadiens game from an ice-level vantage point in the penalty box. Incredibly, in those days, this was a common area shared by players from both teams.

Play in this evening's game was fast, and spirited. Because the action was punctuated by a half-dozen fights, two misconduct penalties, and a slew of lesser infractions, a steady parade of players occupied the penalty box. Joe Malone had no shortage of company for much of the game. At one point, Tommy "Windy" O'Neill of the Leafs and Leo Lamoureux of the Canadiens pushed Malone aside so they could square off. As they were doing so, a Montreal fan slugged another Toronto player who was also sitting in the penalty box. The Forum ushers "gave this intruder the bum's rush," *Globe and Mail* sportswriter Jim Coleman reported, while "referee [King] Clancy stood on the rail screaming imprecations at [the fan's] effrontery."[29] Such violence and outbursts on and off the ice weren't unusual at the time.

Today's casual hockey fans and some sports commentators are fond of rhapsodizing about the "good old days" of NHL hockey, when fighting supposedly was rare, and skating and stickhandling were on display each game. These self-anointed hockey "purists" would be shocked to have watched this game—or any other NHL contest—in the pre-expansion era. With only six teams, rivalries were intense; players knew their opponents all too well. Familiarity really does breed contempt, especially in a fast body-contact sport such as hockey. Fisticuffs and intimidation were as much a part of the game as were stickhandling, skating, and body checking. "If you can't lick 'em in the alley, you can't beat 'em on the ice" was an oft-quoted bit of hockey wisdom uttered in 1952 by Conn Smythe, the irascible long-time owner of the Toronto Maple Leafs.

True to that philosophy, as had been the case in the game in Toronto when Richard had equalled Malone's goal-scoring mark, the Maple Leafs checked, hooked, and held the Rocket off the score sheet until late in that game on February 27. It wasn't until 17:12 of the final period that he broke free to notch his record-setting forty-fifth goal of the season, doing so in typical Richard fashion.

Ever the opportunist, he stole the puck away from a Leafs defender, then bulled his way toward the net. With all six blue shirts on the ice converging on him, there was a wild scramble. In the midst of it all, Richard managed to fire a backhand shot that somehow made its way past skates, sticks, and a body or two before glancing off Toronto goalie McCool's left skate and into the net. That goal wasn't the prettiest one Richard ever scored, but it counted. The crowd erupted in a deafening roar.

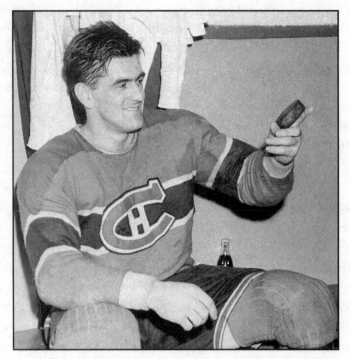

The Rocket holds the puck he fired to score goal number forty-five, setting a new NHL single-season goal-scoring record. (LAC, MIKAN no. 3612870)

Unlike the scene in Toronto when Richard had tied Malone's record, play in this game was halted for eleven minutes while Joe Malone presented Richard with his record-setting puck. It was a case of champion from yesterday honouring one from today. Fans continued to cheer, and flashbulbs popped as newspaper photographers snapped photos. "Joe, a modest man, had successfully fended off requests from most of the sports editors in town these past two weeks to have his picture taken with the Rocket. Joe thought too much publicity might make Maurice tighten up," *Montreal Gazette* sports columnist Dink Carroll reported.

After the game, the celebration of Richard's feat continued in the Canadiens' dressing room and in homes and pubs all across Quebec. "The French Canadians are no longer condemned to be hewers of wood and drawers of water, to be servants, employees," Roch Carrier would recall. "We're the champions of the world."[30]

THE ROCKET HAD SCORED his forty-fifth goal in the Canadiens' forty-second game of the 1944–45 season. It was a wondrous feat. But the team still had eight more regular-season games left to play. There was still plenty of time for the media and fans to speculate about how many more goals Richard might score that season. The big question now on most people's minds was, could he score the five more goals needed to bring his total to fifty in fifty games? Even Richard found himself being swept up in the excitement. His competitive juices were flowing in torrents.

The possibility of scoring "fifty in fifty" had a neat, pleasing symmetry to it for Richard and his Canadiens teammates, the Montreal media, and Quebec hockey fans. Not surprisingly, players on opposing teams—especially those who were English speakers—were of a different mind. Richard continued to find himself the target of special on-ice attention. Goals became ever more difficult for him to score.

Maurice Richard had always maintained that body checking wasn't a big part of his game ("If they leave me alone, I will leave them alone," he explained), nor was fighting. However, there was no doubting that he had a quick temper or that he was handy with his fists. When challenged, Richard never backed down. He couldn't afford to. Doing so would have made him more of a target than he already was. Each game, the opposition assigned a checker to hound and harass the Rocket. The standard routine was to slash, hook, elbow, jostle, and "trash-talk" him in hopes he could be goaded into retaliatory penalties. Sometimes this harassment worked, and when it did, Richard would go bananas.

In one especially notable incident in mid-December 1944, Richard got into it with New York Ranger enforcer Bob "Killer" Dill, who had boasted to the press that he was going "to get Richard." That Dill failed to do so wasn't for lack of effort. When Richard finally had enough of being goaded, the two dropped their gloves and exchanged greetings. Richard knocked Dill out cold. He did this not once but twice. The first time happened when the pair slugged it out on the ice. The fisticuffs continued when Richard and Dill adjourned to the penalty box. The Rangers tough guy had not learned his lesson, and so Richard decked him again. ("Dill Pickled" read a headline in the sports pages of the next day's edition of the *New York Mirror*.)

Just as happens today, such incidents stirred controversy and prompted some sportswriters and critics of the game to condemn the rising level of violence in hockey. There were even demands that the NHL suspend Richard or ban him from playing in the league. Canadiens' general manager Tommy Gorman scoffed at any such notion and decried what he called "the Wreck Richard Club."

Richard also had no shortage of tormentors in the stands. Fans in rinks around the league, nowhere more so than in Toronto, delighted in taunting him, accusing him of cowardice for not joining the military ("You slacker! Why haven't you joined up, Richard?"), and hurling hateful anti-French epithets his way. Richard scowled and glared as he struggled to force himself to turn the other cheek. Most of the time, he did so; at other times, he lashed out in anger and frustration.

Putting all the hostility he faced out of mind, Richard remained intent on trying to score fifty goals in fifty games. He tried desperately to do so in the Canadiens' last home game of the 1944–45 regular season, a Saturday night match against Chicago.

His best scoring chance came in the third period when referee

King Clancy awarded him a penalty shot. A hush fell over the standing-room-only crowd that had jammed the Forum in anticipation of seeing hockey history made. All eyes were on Richard as he skated in from centre ice, deking this way and that before firing a shot that the Chicago goalie—a journeyman named Doug Stevenson (whose NHL career total amounted to just eight games)—turned aside. The crowd groaned in unison.

The Canadiens hung on to win the game by a 4–3 score, but Montreal fans, the media, and the Canadiens were disappointed. With the team travelling to Boston the next night for the final game of the regular season, Richard's goal total remained stalled at forty-nine.

Both the fourth-place Bruins and the first-place Canadiens had locked up playoff spots, and so everyone knew the March 18 game would have no impact on the final standings. That didn't matter to the Bruins players. They were loath to be the ones to surrender a record-setting goal, especially to as bitter a rival as the Montreal Canadiens. Then as now, there was no love lost between Montreal and Boston.

Action in the game was wide open, and there were few penalties. Surprisingly, as the second period ended, the score was knotted at a goal for each team; Kenny Smith, a speedy Boston rookie who was shadowing the Rocket this night, gave him little skating room. As the third period wound down and the clouds of cigarette smoke in the arena thickened, it looked as if the Canadiens' star would fall short in his quest to score goal number fifty. But everything changed in a flash as quick as a rocket burst.

Shortly after the Bruins grabbed a 2–1 lead at 15:51 of the third period, the Canadiens rallied. Elmer Lach gained control of the puck behind the Boston net and darted toward the goal crease. There, Lach collided with Bruins goalie Harvey Bennett, and when the pair crashed to the ice, Richard pounced on the loose puck. His quick wrist shot found the wide-open net. Richard's fiftieth goal of the season tied the score at 2–2, rattled the Bruins, and—most importantly from Richard's perspective—earned him a $500 bonus that Canadiens general manager

Tommy Gorman had promised if he scored fifty goals that season. It also gave birth to a Canadian sporting legend.

Hockey fans in Montreal and across Quebec greeted news of Richard's record-setting goal with joy. Elsewhere in Canada and in those American cities where people followed hockey, Richard's feat received some press coverage, but there was minimal fanfare. At the time, the media and most hockey fans regarded the fact Richard had broken Joe Malone's single-season goal-scoring record as being more significant and noteworthy than the fact he had scored fifty goals in fifty games. Big deal. Even NHL officials felt that way. There was a lot of discussion about including an asterisk in the record book next to Richard's goal total for the 1944–45 season; after all, it had been set during the war years, when the quality of play was diluted.

In the end, wiser minds prevailed, and the NHL record keepers allowed Richard's record to stand. That decision pleased the Rocket, his teammates, Canadiens management, fans, the Montreal media, and many hockey people. Surprisingly Toronto hockey broadcaster Foster Hewitt was among them. "Records don't last forever," he pointed out. That blunt assessment was correct, of course. Records *are* made to be broken.

Maurice Richard's scoring record would stand for the next twenty-one years—until Chicago Black Hawks star Bobby Hull notched fifty-four goals in the sixty-five games he played in the 1965–66 season. Richard's fifty-in-fifty record proved somewhat more difficult to equal. No one did so until 1981 when Mike Bossy of the New York Islanders equalled Richard's feat. Of course, the same has been done numerous times in the years since then, by the likes of Wayne Gretzky, Brett Hull, and Mario Lemieux. Hockey's greatest players, all.

The sport of hockey has changed dramatically and immeasurably in the three-quarters of a century since Maurice Richard's wondrous record-setting 1944–45 season. The fifty goals he scored were destined to stand as his personal best in an eighteen-year career (even so, it wasn't enough to lead the Canadiens to a Stanley Cup in the spring of '45; they would fall to the Maple Leafs in a hard-fought six-game semi-final).

This whimsical *Maclean's* cover (February 1, 1949) by artist Franklin Arbuckle highlighted the Rocket's central role in the Leafs–Canadiens rivalry. (Thomas Fisher Rare Book Library, University of Toronto)

The following season, 1945–46, when the NHL returned to full strength and the pre-war talent level was restored, the Canadiens won their second Stanley Cup in three years. But Richard managed just twenty-seven goals and finished fifth in the league scoring race. When fans and the media criticized him for his relatively mediocre production, Richard lamented, "The worst thing I ever did was to score fifty goals last year."[31]

Many observers also insisted that Richard's 1945–46 goal total proved the record he had set was tainted. That's debatable, but what isn't is that in the 1946–47 season, Richard caught fire again. He scored a league-leading forty-five goals, although he did so in an expanded sixty-game season. Curiously, once again Montreal failed to win the Stanley Cup, losing to Toronto in a bitterly contested six-game final series.

Throughout most of his career, until he was in his late thirties and in the twilight of his time with *les Canadiens*, Richard remained among the NHL's leading scorers and one of hockey's brightest stars. He also won iconic status as the champion of French-Canadian pride. It was a mantle he grew increasingly willing to wear, even if he never became entirely comfortable in the role. Richard remained unassuming, soft-spoken, and at times even humble. That's what made him so enduringly popular with the media and fans in Montreal.

Richard was a blue-collar guy who never forgot where he came from or who he was. Here was a hockey star who, on the night before one of the biggest games of his career, had moved his family to a new house, lugging furniture and boxes himself. Why not? Richard never regarded himself as being "special." Canadiens management were content to see to it that he continued to regard himself that way. Thus, in the autumn of 1947, when Richard and team captain Emile Bouchard boycotted training camp and pre-season games in hopes of having their pay increased, their demands fell flat. General manager Frank Selke refused Richard's $20,000 contract request.

In the end, both Richard and Bouchard had no choice but to return to the team at their old salaries—in Richard's case, about $5,000 per season. That was a comfortable wage at the time, but given how much money and publicity the Rocket was helping to generate for the Canadiens and for the NHL, it was hardly fair. Incredibly, his annual salary topped out at $26,075, which he earned in 1959–60, the final season of an eighteen-year career in which he took home less than $100,000 all totalled.[32] The player who did as much as anyone to popularize hockey and the NHL was never adequately compensated.

The Rocket's post-1945 career featured numerous scoring records, seven more Stanley Cup victories, many more injuries, and periodic outbursts of rage, which were incited by the violent tactics opposing teams employed in their efforts to stymie Richard or goad him into penalties. He struck back, giving "as good as he got," and this sometimes landed him in trouble with NHL officials. That was the case in 1955 when NHL president Clarence Campbell suspended Richard for the last few games of the season and all of the playoffs. Campbell imposed the punishment after the Rocket engaged in a vicious stick-swinging brawl with Hal Laycoe of the Boston Bruins. Furious Montreal fans caused nearly a million dollars in damages in the infamous Richard riot, which would roil the streets of Montreal on the night of March 17, 1955. Order was restored only when Richard himself went on the radio the next day to appeal for calm. He did so reluctantly, for he was never at ease making public appearances or appearing on behalf of others who sought to cash in on his name recognition.

When Richard hung up his skates after the 1959–60 season, the Canadiens retired his number nine, and the Hockey Hall of Fame waived its then-customary five-year waiting period for eligibility so he could enter hockey's shrine in 1961. However, Richard would find his life after hockey was anything but easy or satisfying.

He briefly served as a Canadiens' goodwill ambassador before being named a vice-president of the team. But Richard wasn't cut out for front-office work, and in 1965, after just three years in suit and tie, he quit. As differences between Richard and the Canadiens piled up, his resentments festered, so much so that for the next sixteen years he refused to have anything to do with the team, even though his younger brother Henri was one of its on-ice stars.

The Rocket found that being a living legend wasn't easy. He struggled both to find new ways to earn a living and to keep himself in the public eye. He tried his hand at a variety of business ventures. He lent his name to a hockey magazine. He ran the 544/9 tavern in Montreal—so named because he had scored 544 career goals in his number nine jersey. He served as an advertising pitchman for various products ("Hey, Richard, two minutes for looking so good!" the referee called out as Richard skated to the penalty box in a television commercial for a men's hair dye product). At one point, he even sold fly fishing lures he had hand-tied. He also tried to return to hockey in the 1971–72 season as coach of the WHA's Quebec Nordiques, but that lasted just two games—a win and a loss—before he quit.

Richard and his wife, Lucille, continued to live in Montreal, near their seven children and fourteen grandchildren. The Rocket finally reconciled with the Canadiens in 1981, and after that his life was somewhat less stressful. Sadly, when Lucille Richard died in 1994, the Rocket was alone after fifty-two years of marriage. Four years later, doctors discovered he was suffering from abdominal cancer. He endured until May 27, 2000, when he succumbed to respiratory failure.

Happily, Richard lived long enough to see Teemu Selänne of the Anaheim Mighty Ducks become the inaugural winner of the Maurice "Rocket" Richard Trophy. The Montreal Canadiens in 1999 had donated the award to the NHL to honour the league's leading goal scorer each season.

It was a measure of Richard's enduring fame and his significance as a cultural icon that although it had been forty years since he hung up his skates, Quebec honoured him with a state funeral; he was the first non-politician to be honoured in this way. Richard's body lay in state at the Molson Centre, the Canadiens' home rink, and tens of thousands of mourners filed past the open casket to pay their respects. Afterward, a massive crowd converged on old Montreal, with many of them weeping as the funeral cortège wound its way to Notre Dame Basilica for Richard's funeral, which was aired live on both of Canada's national television networks of the day—CBC and CTV. Prime Minister Jean Chrétien attended, as did Quebec premier Lucien Bouchard and scores of other politicians and dignitaries, a Who's Who of hockey greats, and hundreds of ordinary hockey fans who came from far and wide.

The Richard funeral was an extraordinary event, unique for a Canadian sports figure. Is there a hockey star or another athlete today who in death would be venerated to such a degree or honoured in this way? That is highly unlikely.

Richard played his entire career with one team. That, too, is rare enough. But what most endeared the man to fans was his Everyman persona. "Mr. Richard didn't know anything about gold chains, substance abuse, or girlfriends in every city, and he didn't want to know," a *Montreal Gazette* writer noted.[33]

The legend of the Rocket as one of Canada's cultural icons—and French Canada's greatest—took flight in that glorious, momentous year that was 1945, and it endures.

PART II

VE DAY

Gleeful CWAC members joined Canadian servicemen for VE day celebrations on the streets of London, May 7, 1945. (Galt Museum & Archives, no. 19891053019)

CHAPTER 7

"Canadian Military History's Most Famous Nobody"

I T WAS MAY 3, 1945, AND GENERAL HAROLD "HARRY" CRERAR, the commander of the First Canadian Army, had a lot to feel good about.

Three days earlier, he had rejoiced after learning of the April 30 suicide of Nazi dictator Adolf Hitler, and then again on May 2 when German forces in Italy had surrendered. It was clear that WWII was in its final hours. What's more, Crerar himself had his own reasons to smile. He was on the mend physically, recovering from assorted health ailments, and he believed he'd soon be going home.

In a letter to his daughter back in Ottawa, the general mused, "Before this reaches you, the war in Europe may be officially declared as finished."[1] Happily, those words weren't just wishful thinking on Crerar's part. In his mind, the outcome of the war had been a foregone conclusion for almost a year, ever since the successful June 6, 1944, D-Day landings in Normandy had tipped the balance in the Allies' favour.

In the run-up to the invasion, on June 1 British field marshal Bernard Montgomery had held a final planning meeting at his headquarters near Portsmouth, on England's south coast. Afterward, he pulled out a betting ledger and invited the other Allied commanders— Crerar among them—to place a few "friendly wagers." One called for a prediction on how long Germany would continue the fight once the Allies opened a second front in Europe. In addition, Montgomery challenged American general George S. Patton—"Ol' Blood and Guts," as he called himself—to a bet on whether or not England would be back at war ten years after the current conflict. "He bet that she would not," Patton recalled. "To be a sport, I had to bet she would."[2] And the next war, Patton was convinced, would pit the Western allies against Russia, which he regarded as a nation of "Mongolian savages." Patton was never shy about speaking his mind.

Crerar, who by nature wasn't a braggart or a gambler, reserved his bet on how much longer the war would last. It wasn't until June 24, almost three weeks *after* D-Day, that he finally anted up. In an uncharacteristic fit of optimism, Crerar predicted that Germany would seek an armistice by September 1, 1944.[3] It is a good thing for the general's wallet that he wasn't in the habit of wagering. The war was still raging eight months later, and the First Canadian Army was slogging its way northwest through the Dutch lowlands. To the southeast, the British First Army was doing the same in Belgium, while in Luxembourg and France, three powerful American armies—the Ninth, Third, and Seventh—with the First French Army on their southern flank, were pushing east toward Germany.

The Allies advanced relentlessly along a 300-mile (480 kilometre) front that stretched across western Europe. By mid-April, more than 317,000 German soldiers had thrown down their weapons and become prisoners of war, preferring to be captured by the Allies rather than by the waves of Red Army troops that were surging westward out of the steppes, mercilessly murdering, raping, looting, and burning everything in their path. Many of the Germans who surrendered to the Allies were a sorry-looking lot. "Their officers were always smart as a whip, surrendering their side arms with a little ceremony and that kind of crap, but the men—how could they lose their boots, or their jackets?" one Canadian soldier wondered. "They'd surrender in bare feet, or with no pants on. Only the kids, and there were quite a few around fourteen, but the men looked like wild men of the mountains. Unshaven. Dirty. Some drunk."[4]

With each passing day, General Crerar feared that some of that same battle fatigue might be creeping into the soldiers of the First Canadian Army. For that reason, he expressed concerns about what he felt was deteriorating discipline, "slovenly turnout," and "poor saluting" on the part of the men in the ranks. You have to wonder if the general wasn't guilty of forgetting that not all soldiers served at headquarters, miles removed from the mayhem and carnage that were still happening on the front lines each day. The fighting was brutal. As Hal MacDonald of the North Shore (New Brunswick) Regiment noted in one of his many letters home, "We drove the Hun ahead of us till he hit the sea & stopped to fight. Rather like cornering an animal, & from what I've seen of a [concentration] camp near here, the word 'animal' applies."[5]

By the last week of April, the First Canadian Army had battled its way deep into the Netherlands and was striking inside the German border. The Canadians, along with the contingents of Dutch, Polish, and Highland troops who were included among their ranks, paused to regroup along a defensive line that ran between the IJsselmeer[6] and the Rhine; a loose, temporary truce had come into effect on April 19, when Montgomery had ordered Crerar to hold off on any further offensive actions.

Crerar had taken advantage of the lull in the fighting to fly to London. There he visited the Canadian Military Headquarters (CMHQ) for a briefing on the King government's tentative plans to demobilize and bring home the more than 300,000 military personnel who were overseas, at bases in England and on the battlefields of Europe. While in London, Crerar had also seized the opportunity to visit his son Peter, who was in a military hospital recovering from war wounds. The general himself then spent three days in sick bay, undergoing treatment for a stiff and painful shoulder. The condition was one Crerar was convinced he had developed after repeated exposure to frigid temperatures on the aerial reconnaissance flights that he some-times insisted on taking. His shoulder was causing problems, but the evidence also suggests the general was a hypochondriac.

Crerar was in the habit of repeatedly clearing his throat whenever he was concentrating. When someone pointed this out, he took steps to alleviate it—while ignoring or denying that his chain smoking might have had anything to do with the affliction. When he was working at military headquarters in Ottawa a few years earlier, Crerar always kept a box of cough drops at hand. "One night, with his eyes glued on the papers he was reading, he groped for them in a drawer and a mouse ran up his sleeve. Hearing a startled bellow, the General's military sec-retary ran in to find him open-mouthed and shaking. Crerar sent the secretary out for more cough drops to replace those which the mouse had contaminated."[7]

Such incidents aside, in 1945 Crerar was fifty-seven years old and starting to show his age physically. His climb through the ranks of the Canadian high command had taken him almost twenty-five years, and Crerar was determined to maintain his hard-won position. With that in mind, he strove to retain the support of Prime Minister King in Ottawa and Field Marshal Sir Alan Brooke, his military patron in London; throughout his career, Crerar went out of his way to main-tain good relations with his friends and contacts in the British military establishment. He understood how the army worked.

HARRY CRERAR WAS SOMEONE whose name your grandparents and parents probably would have been familiar with. Or maybe not. He has been described, not unfairly, as "Canadian military his-tory's most famous nobody."[8] Today, few Canadians know much, if anything, about the man who made such a huge contribution to this country's war effort. For eighteen months, Crerar commanded the 300,000-strong First Canadian Army and then played an important senior role in the country's post-war military demobilization.

Crerar had become this country's top soldier in late 1943, when his predecessor, General Andrew McNaughton, retired for "health reasons." That was correct, in a way; the reality was that James Ralston, the Minister of National Defence, was sick of dealing with McNaughton and gave him the boot. Generals and politicians tend not to get along well, especially when those with strong wills and big egos are butting heads.

General Harry Crerar liked it when the men of the First Canadian Army
referred to him as "Uncle Harry." (LAC, MIKAN no. 4232320)

During WWII, the Americans celebrated the battlefield successes of high-profile generals such as Dwight D. Eisenhower, George S. Patton, and Omar Bradley. The British venerated Bernard Montgomery; the Russians did likewise with Georgy Zhukov. The Germans applauded Generals Erich von Manstein and Erwin Rommel (at least until 1944, when he committed suicide after being implicated in the failed July 20 plot to kill Hitler). As in politics, in the military personality matters.

Canada's most famous military leader—at least in 1939 when war began—was the aforementioned Andrew McNaughton. The fifty-two-year-old native of the big-sky prairie hamlet of Moosomin, Saskatchewan, was a much-decorated WWI commander who was widely regarded as being "the father of the Canadian army." Surprisingly, he was also an outspoken opponent of conscription, and he championed the idea of Canadian troops staying together as a fighting force rather than being deployed in the field as units within the Allied forces.

Prime Minister Mackenzie King distrusted military men as a breed, but he liked "Andy" McNaughton's ideas and his low-key style. Unfortunately for the general, he didn't get along with Defence Minister James Ralston, who was his civilian boss. It also didn't help build a case for McNaughton's job security that he wasn't much of a battlefield leader or that his tactical judgment was questionable. It was McNaughton who, on Canada's behalf, had endorsed the disastrous 1942 Dieppe raid in which more than 900 Canadian soldiers lost their lives for no good reason. The fact that the general's judgment on some other occasions had been only slightly less troubling was the icing on the proverbial cake.

Harry Crerar and Andrew McNaughton had worked together in the 1920s. The two were friends. Both were progressive in their military thinking, and both trended conservative in their personal views. Crerar was opposed to the idea of universal suffrage, and he railed against the 1910 political reform that introduced payment for Members of Parliament; in Crerar's mind, that had "led to a lowering in the standard of outlook expected of [them]."[9]

Crerar and McNaughton were different in at least one significant regard: their personalities. McNaughton was outgoing and personable, so much so that Mackenzie King considered recommending him as the first Canadian-born Governor General. That was a role Harry Crerar would not have enjoyed had he been asked to play it. He didn't have the personality for pomp and ceremony or for glad-handing. As military historian Jack Granatstein once noted, "Crerar had the charisma of a turnip, was completely cold, and almost useless in a discussion."[10]

Canada's top general in WWII didn't have the inflated ego that many other top Allied commanders displayed, even after his photo appeared on the cover of a September 1944 edition of *Time* magazine. "Publicity-hating General Crerar was almost unknown to the Canadian people and since many Canadians do not think being colorful is good form, Ottawa war councillors made no effort to color him up," the American news magazine reported.[11]

That wasn't entirely true. As biographer Paul Dickson has noted, "There was a tepid campaign designed to ease concerns over the change of command that included abortive attempts to portray him as the 'Hamilton Tiger'—a reference to his hometown—but Crerar was not comfortable with the public side of his appointment."[12] In that regard, his low-key, no-nonsense approach to his work was typically Canadian, to a fault. While he was a competent staff officer, he wasn't a born leader. One officer who served under him quipped that as he saw it, Crerar "stood for shining buttons and all that chickenshit."[13]

Born April 28, 1888, into a "pure Scottish-Canadian" upper-middle-class family, Crerar attended Upper Canada College (UCC) in Toronto. He then enrolled at Royal Military College (RMC), graduating in 1909, thirteenth in a class of thirty. He was soft-spoken, of average height—about five-foot-eight (173 centimetres)—and of slim build. He wasn't someone who stood out in a crowd or felt comfortable doing so despite being immaculate in his dress and grooming. During the war years, the general sported one of those pencil-thin moustaches that were in vogue at the time; it lent him a touch of panache, like Clark Gable in *Gone with the Wind* or the swashbuckling Errol Flynn. However, Crerar was no dashing man of action. He loved sports and outdoor activities, but he was a bit of a klutz and was injury-prone.

It was his work habits that made Crerar a good soldier. He was diligent, conscientious, and detail-oriented. This was a man who took his life and his work seriously. Sometimes too much so. On occasion, he struggled to keep his emotions and temper in check, especially when he encountered ditherers and those who cut corners. Not that he ever encountered any such people in the military.

Something else about Crerar that merits at least passing mention is his reputation for being a penny pincher. Some said he was a "cheapskate." Yet in early 1945, in the final days of the war in Europe, the general saw to it that "A" Mess, where he, his top aides, and important visitors dined whenever possible, was outfitted with tablecloths and silver cutlery, and a string quartet provided ambient music.[14] There's nothing like a little Vivaldi or Mozart to brighten a hard day on the battlefield.

Historian C.P. Stacey, who was given the rank of major when he was appointed the official historian of the Canadian army, recalled dining with Crerar one evening in April 1945, near the town of Delden, three hours west of the German border. "I ate a meal in a mess tent pitched in really idyllic surroundings in a lovely Dutch park, while a band played soft music nearby," said Stacey. "The food and drink, while not sybaritic, were good. It was very pleasant, but several of us remarked that it was definitely not warlike."[15]

At the outset of the war in September 1939, Crerar had been cooling his heels as commandant at RMC; however, a self-promotional letter-writing campaign won Crerar a position at military headquarters in Ottawa. There he helped organize mobilization of the Canadian military and in 1940 copped appointment as Chief of the General Staff. It was a job he wanted and for which he was well suited. Crerar's notion of the First Canadian Army as "a national institution to promote Canadian unity and the army's profile" found favour with Prime Minister King.[16] This also proved pivotal in 1943 when Ralston, the defence minister, pushed Crerar's friend General McNaughton out as head of the First Canadian Army. Crerar succeeded him.

The general's nationalistic inclinations proved to be his salvation when at a May 1944 meeting with Mackenzie King, British general Bernard Montgomery lobbied the prime minister to ditch Crerar as

Canada's top general in Europe and replace him with Lieutenant-General Guy Simonds, a Montgomery protégé who, in Monty's none-too-humble opinion, was Canada's best tactical and operational commander. King wavered, but after dithering for a while, he stuck with Crerar. As usual, King was slow and deliberate in his decision making; however, in this case, as in many others, it turned out for the best.

J UST A DAY AFTER Crerar wrote home to report that he expected the war might soon be over, suddenly it was. At about 12:55 p.m. on the afternoon of May 4, one of Field Marshal Montgomery's chief aides telephoned Crerar to share some joyous news: Montgomery was meeting with German military officers representing Admiral Karl Dönitz, who had succeeded Hitler as head of the German state. Montgomery and his visitors were negotiating the broad terms of surrender for all remaining German forces in northwestern Europe. The rumours of secret talks that had been swirling for several months were now confirmed.

German emissaries initially had sounded out the Western Allies on the possibility of a peace plan that didn't include Russia; however, Churchill and Roosevelt rejected those overtures, even though American, British, and German representatives in neutral Switzerland spent several weeks secretly discussing various issues involved in the surrender of German forces in Italy. When Soviet dictator Joseph Stalin heard about these talks, code-named "Operation Sunrise," he threw a hissy fit—or pretended to—and demanded quid pro quo concessions from his Allied "friends."

The Russians played only a minor role in the negotiations leading to the May 4 final agreement that ended the war in Europe. That evening, Crerar and his senior officers had finished their dinner and were listening to the radio when a few minutes after eight o'clock, a British Broadcasting Corporation announcer interrupted regular programming to read a news bulletin—"This is London calling! Here is a news flash . . ." There followed a brief announcement that the German armies in Europe had surrendered unconditionally.

Within minutes, an official message from Field Marshal Montgomery confirmed that a peace agreement had indeed been reached. All offensive operations were to cease immediately, with a ceasefire set to go into effect as of eight o'clock the next morning, May 5. The war was over. Jubilant radio operators in the various divisions and brigades of the First Canadian Army sent out the order "Fire only if attacked by the enemy."

All of this seemed too good to be true, especially when total Canadian losses for the eleven months of fighting since D-Day were tallied up: 11,336 dead and 33,003 wounded. On May 4 alone, twenty more Canadian soldiers had died on the battlefield while forty others suffered wounds; on May 5, another three died, and seven more were wounded. It was exactly as Crerar had feared: when the end of the war finally came, it wouldn't be "as tidy as we could all wish." He had intimated this two weeks earlier in a letter to his brother: "With fanatic and crazy men, reason certainly does not prevail, and, for the good of the future, the more [Germans] that are killed off, the better."[17]

Although Crerar had a begrudging respect for his enemy, he had no sympathy for individual Germans. His bitter experiences in two world wars, the memories of friends and colleagues he had lost, and the suffering and destruction he had witnessed had left a bitter taste in his mouth. Harry Crerar had a hate-on for Germans, as did so many of the men and women serving under him. Despite the lingering rancor, once the initial shock and disbelief had passed, the announcement that the war was finally over came as something of an anti-climax for Crerar and his troops. On the last day of fighting, a clerk wrote in the unit diary of the battle-hardened Queen's Own Rifles of Canada: "When it became evident that it was really true, [the Canadian troops] felt not so much exultation as intense relief. . . . There is no celebration, but everybody is happy."[18]

STANLEY CUP CHAMPIONS

The Toronto Maple Leafs won the Stanley Cup in 1945, defeating the Detroit Red Wings by a score of 2–1 in the seventh and deciding game of the final. The Leafs won despite blowing a three-games-to-none lead in the series. Toronto had advanced to the final by ousting the defending-champion Montreal Canadiens in a six-game semi-final, while Detroit outlasted the Boston Bruins in a seven-game series. The 1945 Stanley Cup Final was the first in NHL history in which both teams started rookie goaltenders. Harry Lumley, who had become the youngest goaltender to play in the league the previous year, was in goal for the Red Wings, while Frank McCool substituted for regular Maple Leafs netminder Turk Broda, who—like many NHL players—was serving overseas with the Canadian army.

THE ALLIES' "CRUSHING AND complete victory over the German enemy," as General Crerar termed it in the message he sent to the members of the First Canadian Army on the evening of May 4, gave rise to a plethora of challenges when it came to negotiating the terms of the peace agreement. As the saying goes, the devil was in the details. What came next were the specifics of the surrender of German forces all along the Western Front.[19] In the Netherlands, this was the 117,000 troops in the German Fifteenth Army, who were led by Colonel-General Johannes Blaskowitz. This sixty-two-year-old tank specialist was the archetypal German officer: aristocratic in bearing, coolly efficient, and patriotic, though not a Nazi.

Crerar, ever emotional, refused to meet with or even have anything to do with Blaskowitz or any other Germans. "I saw no purpose in meeting any German generals, I have had them in adjoining fields," said Crerar. "That was enough."[20] Instead, he assigned two of his corps commanders, General Charles Foulkes and Lieutenant-General Guy Simonds, to accept the formal German surrender and to iron out the specifics. That happened in a May 5 meeting held in the reception area of the battered Hotel de Wereld in Wageningen, a Dutch town nine miles (fifteen kilometres) east of Arnhem. Foulkes chose this venue because of its location near the front line, the absence of civilians in the area, and the metaphorical nature of the name: *de Wereld*, which in English is "the World."

Lieutenant-General Charles Foulkes (*left centre*) accepted the surrender of German forces in the Netherlands, May 5, 1945. (LAC, MIKAN no. 3194859)

Journalists from the Allied nations looked on as a five-man Canadian delegation led by Foulkes and Prince Bernhard of the Netherlands, all of whom were unarmed, sat down across from Blaskowitz and five of his senior officers. The Germans gave the

Nazi salute when they arrived. All of them had Luger pistols in their right-thigh holsters and defiance in their eyes; defeat didn't sit easily or well with these men. *Globe and Mail* war correspondent Ralph Allen reported that Blaskowitz "showed no emotion, except possibly a steady, smouldering indignation," when Foulkes dictated the terms of surrender. "For the most part, [Blaskowitz's] hard little blue eyes looked down his nose and seemed to consign the whole proceedings to an abyss of absurdity from which they were rescued and sustained only by his sorely strained forbearance."[21]

The forty-five-minute meeting was conducted in a restrained, businesslike manner. Despite his hauteur, Blaskowitz spent considerable time asking the Canadians for assurances that he and his men would be protected from reprisals by Dutch resistance fighters, who understandably were eager to seek revenge on an enemy that had occupied the country, flooded large areas of it, and starved, terrorized, and murdered tens of thousands—including 104,000 Jews and more than 150,000 other people. Foulkes gave Blaskowitz his word that as "the only authority who will issue orders in Holland," he would "stand for no more nonsense from the Dutch resistance than from the Germans."[22] In the next breath, Foulkes rejected Blaskowitz's request that he and his men be treated as prisoners of war who would be protected and fed by the Allies. With food in short supply, the Germans were left to fend for themselves. The one sop that Foulkes offered Blaskowitz as a gesture of good faith was a willingness to allow the Germans to keep their "personal weapons" for protection. All of this and other specifics would be spelled out in a formal surrender document, which would be drawn up that evening. There was no typewriter available at the hotel or in the town to prepare it on the spot.

The most pressing issues having been tentatively settled, the meeting adjourned with both sides promising to return the next day, Sunday, May 6. Then, amid another flurry of Nazi salutes, Blaskowitz and his party departed. As they were doing so, an alert German orderly raced a car up from behind the vehicle Foulkes was riding in, blocking the way. "*Entschuldigung!*" (Excuse me!) The Canadian commander was forced to wait until the two staff cars carrying Blaskowitz and his aides had disappeared down the road. After having watched this scene play out, Ralph Allen wrote, "It was difficult to restrain the urge to tap your neighbour on the shoulder and ask: 'Hey brother, who won?'"[23]

Some of that German arrogance had dissipated when the Canadian and German representatives sat down to sign typed copies of the surrender agreement. With the help of a few suitably ironic reminders from the Canadians, the reality of the situation was finally beginning to sink in for the Germans. The war was over, and they had lost.

The two Canadian army officers who met with their German counterparts to sort out logistical details of the surrender were Jewish; it was no accident that Crerar gave them the assignment. And when another Canadian, Brigadier-General Jim Roberts—accompanied by Captain Harold "Hal" MacDonald of the North Shore (New Brunswick) Regiment—was escorting German general Erich von Straube and his aide to a meeting at a Canadian divisional headquarters, the German casually asked Roberts if he was a career soldier. Roberts shook his head. "I replied that I was never a professional soldier, but like most Canadian soldiers, I was a civilian volunteer and that, in my . . . pre-war life I'd been an ice cream maker."[24] That could not have been what von Straube was expecting to hear.

Surrendering to "common civilians" was a humbling experience for the professional officers of the *Wehrmacht*. So was having Lieutenant-General Guy Simonds read aloud the terms of surrender in a cool, confident, and no-nonsense voice when he met with German officers. Simonds was less accommodating than was General Foulkes. As a result, when Blaskowitz and his contingent of officers signed the final surrender document on May 6, they "looked like men in a dream, dazed, stupefied, and unable to realize that for them their world was utterly finished," as Crerar wrote in a report that he sent to Ottawa.[25]

═══

NCE THE OFFICIAL GERMAN surrender had been signed, and the war was officially over, General Crerar shifted his focus. Having delegated responsibility for the relief and clean-up operations in the Netherlands to General Foulkes, he now turned his attention to the paperwork and lobbying efforts involved in two matters he felt were pivotal. One was post-war repatriation and demobilization of the First Canadian Army. Where repatriation was concerned, Crerar was at odds with the rank and file serving under him. He felt it made for a more efficient and orderly process if soldiers returned home with their units, not as individuals whose priority was based on the number of service points accumulated.

As for demobilization itself, Crerar hoped the entire process would be viewed "not as the final chapter of wartime service, but as a transition, a life of peacetime civic service."[26] He was intent on doing whatever he could to make sure the best and brightest talent in the army remained in the ranks as part of the Allied occupation force in Europe and in the Canadian contingent that would soon be headed to the Pacific to help finish off Japan. These measures would help ensure there was no return to the neglect and stagnation of the army as had happened in the years between the wars; Crerar remembered how in 1939 Canada's full-time army had been reduced to just 10,500 men.

The other matter on Crerar's mind was much more personal. After more than five years abroad, he was weary of the war and weary of the ego-driven conflicts in the ranks of the Allied high command and among the officer corps of the First Canadian Army. Crerar had developed a personal dislike for the ambitious Lieutenant-General Guy Simonds, and with the animosity being mutual, Crerar was eager to go home. The general breathed a huge sigh of relief when he did so on July 21. After waving a fond farewell to his staff at his field headquarters in the Netherlands, he made his way to London for what would be a hectic ten-day stay, one of the highlights of which was a visit to Buckingham Palace, where King George VI invested him as an honorary member in the Order of the Companions of Honour. He also received a Distinguished Service Medal from the hands of visiting United States president Harry Truman.

On July 30, Crerar travelled by train to Glasgow, where he boarded the passenger liner SS *Île de France* for the voyage to Halifax. "With characteristic humility, General Crerar declined a speedy trip home by private air transport. He sailed aboard a troopship crammed with 9,000 Canadian soldiers, airmen, and sailors," *Maclean's* war correspondent L.S.B. Shapiro reported. "A 30-yard stretch of the boat deck shared with his 17 travelling companions was the only privilege of privacy approved by [Crerar]. He had his meals at the third sitting in the dining room used by 2,000 other officers on board"[27] and took off his shirt to sunbathe alongside hundreds of other pale-skinned men who lounged on the ship's deck. As Crerar biographer Paul Dickson noted, the general "was at his best: relaxed, humble, thoughtful, and open."[28]

Mackenzie King welcomed Crerar home by giving him a hero's welcome at an August 7 ceremony on Parliament Hill. Although the event was upstaged by news that the American air force had dropped a new kind of super bomb that had annihilated the Japanese city of Hiroshima, the media paid attention as the general praised the government's demobilization plans. They were "well thought out" and "the best devised by any country,"[29] he said.

For a few months after that grand homecoming, Crerar remained an object of curiosity by the media and public. He went on a six-week cross-Canada "farewell tour," and 20,000 people turned out to cheer him at an October rally in his hometown of Hamilton. There was talk of a Senate appointment for Crerar, a diplomatic posting, or some other government appointment. However, in the end he wasn't interested. He preferred to spend his retirement out of the public eye, at home with his wife in Ottawa.

By the time of his death on April 1, 1965, at age seventy-seven, Crerar would be a forgotten figure. Today, not one Canadian in a hundred could identify this "quiet Canadian," as a *Toronto Daily Star* editorial described him,[30] as being the man who commanded the largest

Canadian army ever and liberated Holland from Nazi oppression. In retrospect, his anonymity isn't surprising. "The people of Canada do not know Harry Crerar well," *Maclean's* war correspondent L.S.B. Shapiro reported in a 1945 CBC radio broadcast. "He was always loath to fill the spotlight and as a result no sharp facets of his character sparkled on the home front."[31] In both regards, you could say that Crerar was a typical Canadian soldier. He had a difficult, trying, and at times unpleasant job to do. He did it quietly, and he did it well. Then he went home and carried on with his life.

Ten million men pinch themselves and feel that they are still
alive and will soon be lying on their lawns and listening to
their wives and babies.
—Matthew Halton, CBC war correspondent, May 6, 1945

CHAPTER 8

It All Seemed So Simple, So Undramatic

IT WAS SEVEN O'CLOCK ON THE MORNING OF MAY 7, 1945, WHEN
he heard the wonderful news that had set giddy Canadians celebrating from coast to coast. Ironically, Mackenzie King would be among
the last Canadians to hear it.

Just moments before that happened, Canada's seventy-one-year-old prime minister had been sound asleep and lost in strange dreams,
as he so often was. On this occasion, he was a passenger aboard a speeding train that consisted of just two cars. His deceased parents were riding in one; he and two white rabbits, which he was chasing around and
around, were on the other. King had just grabbed hold of one of them
when his dream ended abruptly. Someone was calling his name.

"Mr. King . . . are you awake?"

The voice was that of the prime minister's valet. John Nicol had
tiptoed into the darkened bedroom of the San Francisco hotel suite in
which King had been staying for the last month, while attending the
founding conference of the United Nations.

Summoned back to reality, still groggy and uncomprehending,
King rolled over in bed and stared up at his valet.

"Sir, I have an important message for you," said Nicol. He then
proceeded to announce that the message was from Norman Robertson,
the Under-Secretary of State for External Affairs. He was also in San

Francisco, attending the United Nations conference as a member of the Canadian delegation that King was heading.

"Mr. Robertson would have called you when he heard from Ottawa, but it was 4 a.m. and he didn't want to wake you at such an early hour," said Nicol. "He's asked me to tell you that he has received word that the war in Europe is over. The Germans have surrendered."

"That's good news. Thank God," said King.

Now that he was awake, a thousand thoughts were already rushing through his mind. King knew he would have much to do on this historic day, but first things first. He rolled onto his side, turning away from Nicol. Then, as he later told his diary, he "uttered a prayer of thanksgiving and of rededication to the service of my fellow men."[1]

When Nicol left the room, King knelt at his bedside for another prayer. Later, he would record in his diary, "This has been a good day—a happy day . . . one in which the burden has been greatly lightened from the knowledge that Nazi militarism has, at last, been destroyed." Canadians clearly shared those sentiments, and understandably so.

Celebrating VE day on the streets of Toronto.
(City of Toronto Archives, fonds 1266, item 98390)

After 2,074 days of war in Europe, after all of the fighting, tears, pain, and sorrow, it was as if a great emotional dam had burst on that joyous spring morning. All Canadians had known for months that this day was coming, but when it finally arrived, it was still something of a surprise. Strange though it may seem, the farther away from the front lines Canadians were, the wilder and more joyous were their celebrations.

The reaction to the war's end among the Canadian troops, especially in the Netherlands, was one of relief that the killing was done, and so they would soon be going home. This was in marked contrast to the emotional response of the throngs of wildly cheering Dutch crowds who greeted the Canadians as liberators to be jubilantly hugged and kissed. To the soldiers of the First Canadian Army who had been putting their lives on the line each and every day, all of this seemed slightly surreal. "Death has walked at their side," the CBC war correspondent Matthew Halton reported. "It's hard to believe, for a day or two, that the nightmare is over and they can drink the wine of life."[2]

Jubilant Dutch civilians celebrating their liberation surround soldiers of the West Nova Scotia Regiment. (LAC, MIKAN no. 3203845)

That was a typical reaction among Canadian servicemen and servicewomen. It certainly was for the men of the RCAF 419 Squadron, which was part of the Sixth Bomber Group based at Middleton St. George, in England's Durham County. "We were expecting it, so when it finally came it was no surprise," said Flying Officer Stuart Crawford.

The then-twenty-eight-year-old native of Kingston, Ontario, a self-described "news junkie," lounged in the mess hall in his off hours, listening to the radio or reading any newspaper he could find. That was his way of relaxing and winding down from the stress of nighttime bombing raids over Germany. By early May of 1945, those perilous missions had all but stopped. It was evident the Germans were beaten.

"Our VE day celebrations were simple. I remember them very well," Crawford said. "Some of us talked about going into London, but it was 250 miles (400 kilometres) south, and we knew it would be jammed full of people by the time we could get there. We didn't have a place to stay in London, and none of the guys I chummed with were drinkers or big partiers, so we said to heck with it. We stayed at the airfield. Our VE day was quiet, a little anticlimactic. But we didn't care. We were alive and we were happy."[3]

Those Canadian servicemen and servicewomen who were lucky enough to find themselves in London joined the crowds that packed Trafalgar Square and the nearby Beaver Club, that wee touch of home-away-from-home for Canadians in the British capital. Across the English Channel in Paris, Canadians partied with crowds that thronged the Avenue des Champs-Élysées.

However, even with the sense of relief and accomplishment on VE day, in the back corners of the mind of every Canadian who was far from home there lurked personal hopes, dreams, uncertainties, and fears of what might lie ahead when they returned to Canada. The war had simplified life for the past six years. For better and worse, there had been a simple dichotomy to this struggle. It had been a clash of good and evil. Canadians had responded to the challenge by pulling together collectively to fight for the common cause.

Now that the guns had fallen silent once more and the "good guys" had somehow eked out a hard-fought, all-too-narrow victory, it was time to return to the mundane realities of workaday life in a post-war world. It was not easy to do so without forgetting the 42,000 friends and comrades who had fallen in the war and would not be returning home to Canada, or the 55,000 others who were wounded.

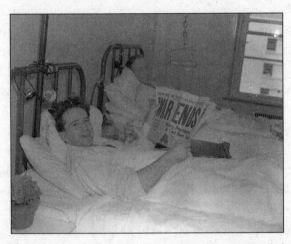

Many of the more than 55,000 Canadians wounded in WWII, including these wounded veterans in a Vancouver hospital, celebrated VE day from their hospital beds. (City of Vancouver Archives, AM1545-S3:CVA586-3831)

For some veterans, the future brimmed with possibilities. For others, life was suddenly filled with uncertainty and even a measure of dread. A Canadian soldier in France gave voice to the apprehension he and many other veterans were feeling when he confided to the CBC's Matthew Halton: "I'm afraid to go home. I have the feeling I'll never be able to tell what I've seen. . . . I feel I'll never be the same."[4]

Captain Frank "Bud" Lynch of the Essex Regiment, who had recently returned home to Toronto after having served overseas and been in combat, shared that uncertainty. As he told another radio news reporter, he felt "all mixed up" when he heard the news that the war was over. Lynch went out into the downtown streets and wandered aimlessly among the happy crowds. He wasn't sure how to react or where to go. "I wanted to be over there with my battalion," he said. "But I also wanted to be home with my loved ones. Inwardly, I had a feeling that I wanted to do something, and I was glad the war was over. I said this to myself many times . . . 'Yes, the war in Europe is over. But now what?'"[5] Bud Lynch was hardly alone in that regard. But if Canadians across the country were feeling the same way, it wasn't apparent, at least not today.

The first reports that the war was over had reached Canada early in the pre-dawn hours of this Monday morning. The moment they did, word spread with lightning speed by way of the "social media" of the time: the telephone grapevine, radio news bulletins, and special editions of newspapers.

"Unconditional Surrender" trumpeted the page one headlines of the *Toronto Daily Star*.

"Nazis Quit" read the banner wording above a charcoal sketch of a surrendering German soldier that filled the front page of the *Winnipeg Free Press*.

Winnipeg Free Press, May 7, 1945. (NewspaperArchive.com)

"*Fin de la guerre*," declared Montreal's *La Presse*. At long last, with the German surrender now official and the war ended, Canadians welcomed the return of peace.

In Ottawa, Acting Prime Minister J.L. Ilsley, the finance minister, addressed the nation via CBC radio on the afternoon of May 7. When Ilsley spoke, he decreed that the next day, May 8, would be VE day. It would be an official holiday, with festivities on Parliament Hill, and Prime Minister Mackenzie King would have something to say. When he did so, King delivered a surprisingly sombre radio address to English Canadians, cautioning that while they had "helped to rid the world of a great scourge," this was no time for "exultation." The war with Japan continued. (Justice Minister Louis St. Laurent, who was also in San Francisco, repeated the broadcast in French.)

Thousands attended Parliament Hill VE day celebrations on May 8, 1945. (LAC, MIKAN no. 3191733)

Canadians understood what King was saying, but they were in a mood to party, and many were already doing so. They had been since yesterday. As the sun rose across the country on the morning of May 7, spontaneous unrestrained celebrations had erupted in the streets of cities and towns from the Atlantic to the Pacific. Revellers spilled into the streets from their homes, schools, and workplaces. Men, women, and children of all ages rejoiced.

In some areas, school officials cancelled classes for the day. That was so in Wilton, Ontario, a sleepy rural hamlet twelve miles (twenty kilometres) west of the old army town of Kingston. There, nine-year-old George Henderson was about to set off on his daily one-and-a-quarter-mile (two kilometre) walk to the village school when a CBC announcer interrupted regular programming with a news bulletin: the war in Europe was over. "It was as if all our prayers had finally been answered," Henderson recalled. "Next day, my mother took me into Kingston to watch the huge Victory Parade that made its way up Princess Street. There were flags and bunting and thousands of people cheering. I'll never forget it."[6]

It seemed as if a Union Jack or a Red Ensign flew from a window of every home on every street in Canada. Special church services were held. Bells rang. Car horns blared. Fireworks flew. Businesses closed their doors when employees ignored pleas from government officials and raced off to join in the fun. Alcohol flowed like water.

In stodgy "Toronto the Good," Mayor Robert Saunders, fearful that celebrations could get out of hand, announced that all taverns would be closed for the day. That didn't stop tens of thousands of people from jamming downtown streets. Nor did it keep city residents from becoming swept up in the excitement of the moment. The parents of the first baby born in Toronto in the wee hours of the morning of May 8 named their new son "Victor," while the parents of the first baby girl to arrive dubbed her "Victoria."

Many other Canadians found themselves feeling no less giddy. Some behaved foolishly or irresponsibly. They did silly things they later regretted. (Yes, there were reports in early 1946 of a spike in births.)

In Quebec City, touring high school students invaded the provincial assembly when staff there left their posts and went off to celebrate. With opportunity knocking, the young people "ran wild." They rode their bicycles in the hallways and cavorted in the vacant legislative chamber, where they tore up and scattered papers they snatched from the members' desks. When they left, they made off with some souvenirs of the moment—two dozen cuspidors, "of which there is one for each member."[7] Speeches in the Quebec assembly in those days evidently were impassioned.

Just down the road in Montreal, large crowds of rowdy, drunken celebrants smashed scores of store windows in the downtown area, damaged thirty streetcars, and lit a huge bonfire that blocked traffic on Peel and Sainte-Catherine Streets.

In Niagara Falls, George Mackey and his wife were so preoccupied with the day's momentous events that they forgot how fast they were driving. The car of the two residents of nearby Chippawa missed a hairpin turn on a narrow road near the *Maid of the Mist* landing. They had a sinking feeling as their car shot into the blackness, turned end over end three times, and plummeted 130 feet (forty metres), landing on rocks at the bottom of the Niagara gorge. Miraculously, sans air bags and seatbelts, the Mackeys survived the ordeal with only minor injuries. "When I think of how far we plunged over that bank, I shudder and wonder why I'm alive," Mrs. Mackey told a newspaper reporter.[8] They don't make cars like they used to.

In Edmonton on May 8, police felt obliged "to take into custody" an effigy of Adolf Hitler, which was found hanging from a lamppost at a downtown intersection. "Some juveniles had covered it with kerosene and planned to set it on fire," the *Edmonton Journal* reported.[9]

In Vancouver, all of the city's sixty-three air raid sirens began wailing in unison at 7:04 a.m., just moments after the joyous news reached the west coast and four minutes after Mackenzie King heard it down the coast in San Francisco. Many of the Vancouver residents who poured into the streets were still in their sleepwear, "too excited to think of dressing,"[10] according to a story that appeared later that day in the *Vancouver Sun*.

A two-block-long conga line of office workers, service industry personnel, students, and other dancers snaked its way along Hastings Street. A newspaper reporter overheard two "grimy workmen" chatting. One man asked the other if he was going to work that morning. "'Hell no,' was the reply. 'I'm going to get good and drunk. I've been saving up for six months.'"[11]

Dick Halhed of the CBC described Vancouver as being "gaily hung with flags of the united nations; bunting and paper streamers hung from all the buildings." Tempering the joy was the sight of "a goodly number of middle-aged women . . . some were weeping." These were, he assumed, "mothers of boys who would not be returning."[12]

VE day celebrations on the streets of Vancouver.
(City of Vancouver Archives, AM1545-S3:CVA586-3852)

While Vancouver residents partied on VE day, they also remained painfully aware, much more so than did other Canadians, that the war in the Pacific was still raging. The next morning's edition of the *Vancouver Daily Province* reminded readers of that. The page one headline, "Germans Lay Down Their Arms," was anchored by a subhead that cautioned, "Churchill, Truman Proclaim Victory: Allied Leader [*sic*] Warns of Stern Task in Pacific War."

On and on the celebrations went, all across the country. For the most part, even when the revelries got out of hand, any damage done was relatively minor. The streets were soon swept clean, and life carried on as usual. That was so most everywhere. But not in Halifax. There, thousands of rioters ravaged large areas of the city's downtown business area, sullied the reputation of the Royal Canadian Navy, and helped bring the career of one of Canada's most accomplished naval commanders to an abrupt and ignominious end. The infamous Halifax riot was not an event of which any Canadian could be proud.

Fires burned tonight in the heart of Halifax as civilian and service police strove to enforce a curfew and clear the streets of thousands of victory rioters who have smashed and looted virtually every store in the downtown business section.
—*Globe and Mail*, May 9, 1945

CHAPTER 9

Wasn't That *a Party?*

ON THE MORNING OF MONDAY, MAY 7, 1945, REAR-ADMIRAL Leonard W. Murray was feeling good about the prospects for the day ahead in Halifax. A secret message he had received at five o'clock confirmed the accuracy of the intelligence reports that had been crossing his desk at Allied operational headquarters in recent days: the Germans were beaten, and the official announcement of their formal surrender could come at any moment.

With any luck, Murray hoped, that might even be today. Indeed, the page one headline of that morning's edition of the *Halifax Herald* proclaimed, "German Surrender Is Forecast for Today; Leaders at Posts." If that report proved to be accurate and this was the day peace finally returned, nothing would be happier news for Murray, the thousands of men and women under his command, or Halifax's 68,000 residents.

Nowhere in Canada were people closer to or more engaged in the war's ebb and flow than here in this historic port city, Canada's chief east coast seaport. As it had been during WWI—"the Warden of the North" as Rudyard Kipling dubbed it—Halifax was the hub of much of the Allied naval activity in the North Atlantic. And just as in that earlier conflict, during WWII the port was the embarkation point for hundreds of thousands of Europe-bound Allied sailors, soldiers, and airmen. They passed through Halifax or paused here to train for a few weeks before shipping out. Almost as many of those same men and women had returned home or would do so via Halifax sadder but wiser; thousands of them would come back battle-scarred.

It was in Bedford Basin, Halifax harbour's bustling catchment area, where cargo ships gathered to form into convoys for the hazardous voyages to Britain and Europe with essential shipments of troops, food, and munitions. It was also here, in the naval dockyard, that Allied ships were refitted and repaired.

In 1945, to the dismay of many locals, Halifax's "official" population was swollen with the more than 18,000 Allied military personnel who were stationed here, most of whom were naval reservists. Almost ninety per cent of the men and women in Canada's navy—"the people's navy"—were volunteer reservists.[1] Although they were eager to do their part in the war effort, the unfortunate reality was that many of them were poorly trained and had little appreciation for naval traditions or discipline.

Canadian sailors had a deserved reputation for being hard-drinking and argumentative. Many of the young men stationed in Halifax were away from home for the first time, and they were restive. They resented the high cost of living in the city and were angered by what they perceived as the locals' "snobbishness," by the lack of recreational activities, and by the dearth of young, unattached female company. There was a reason for the latter, mind you: "After the first great rash of teenage pregnancies, parents kept their daughters under unrelenting vigil."[2]

Sailors found little to do on nights off. The only affordable options for those who were out for a good time were to go to the movies or to prowl the streets looking for fun or trouble, or both. And yes, the sailors also drank. This was a chronic problem in a city where, despite a long history of bootlegging and alcohol smuggling, the prevailing ethos was one of prune-faced puritanism. Halifax's vocal and adamant temperance lobby routinely trumpeted its views and exerted pressure on local politicians and military officials to curb drinking. But sailors are known to enjoy an occasional beverage, to sometimes overindulge, and to take part in robust debates on the meaning of life. They have been known to engage in fisticuffs and break things, including one another. This little truism was especially problematic in wartime Halifax.

Because the city was hopelessly overcrowded, decent rental housing was as scarce as feathers on fish. The housing that was available tended to be of poor quality and overpriced. The thousands of servicemen and servicewomen who were stationed in the city but not housed in military facilities scrambled to find decent accommodation, as did the civilian workers who flocked to Halifax seeking employment. The federal government did nothing to help resolve the situation.

The inadequate facilities at His Majesty's Canadian Dockyard only compounded Halifax's problems and shortcomings. At the outset of war in 1939, the naval facilities were dilapidated, having remained pretty much as they had been when the Royal Navy abandoned them in 1905. The dockyard itself occupied a narrow, impossibly congested strip on the western shore of the harbour, roughly three-quarters of a mile (1.2 kilometres) long by 500 feet (150 metres) wide.

Given the grim experiences of WWI, the devastation wrought by the December 1917 Halifax explosion, and the RCN's repeated appeals for the money to make improvements, you well might wonder why Ottawa hadn't bothered to invest at least something on dockyard upgrades, to build new facilities across the harbour in Dartmouth, or even to learn the lessons of 1917.[3] None of that had happened (and weighty academic chronicles have been written to explain why). Suffice it to say that Mackenzie King, who was prime minister for thirteen of the nineteen years between the two world wars of the last century, was no friend of the military. What's more, Canada's financial crunch in the lean years of the run-up to the 1939 outbreak of war nixed any major spending on military infrastructure. The upshot was that Halifax was unprepared for the critical role it was called on to play in Canada's war effort, especially in light of the RCN's dramatic and unprecedented growth.

In 1939, Canada's naval "fleet" consisted of six old destroyers, three minesweepers, and fewer than 3,000 men. By June of 1944, at its wartime peak, almost 90,000 men and women were wearing RCN uniforms, and the senior service could boast of having 385 fighting ships at its command. Canada's navy in WWII was the third (or fourth, depending on the source you believe) largest in the world and was active in every theatre of the war. The RCN did whatever it was asked to do and made a significant contribution to the Allied victory. None was greater than its role in providing safe escort to thousands of merchant vessels that ferried vital war supplies to Britain. The RCN emerged as a national institution during the war, and Admiral Leonard W. Murray played a lead role in making that happen.

As commander-in-chief, Canadian Northwest Atlantic, during the last two years of the war (1943–45), Murray was in charge of all the Allied air and naval forces engaged in convoy protection in that cruel 2,500-mile-wide (4,000 kilometre) expanse of ocean that lies between Nova Scotia and the British Isles. This was a singular honour. Murray was the *only* Canadian military officer to be in charge of an Allied theatre of operations during either world war. He did his job conscientiously and well. So it was on the morning of May 7, 1945, that Admiral Murray had a smile on his face and an inkling in his mind that this would be a day for the history books. In fact, it would be. But not in a way that Murray ever could have imagined or wished.

The events that were about to unfold in Halifax would besmirch the RCN's reputation, result in millions of dollars in property damage in downtown Halifax, lead to three deaths, and bring Admiral Murray's distinguished thirty-three-year naval career to a sudden and ignoble end.

Of course, on this sunlit morning that was so brimming with hope and promise, Murray could not know any of this. He was blissfully unaware as he gave his wife, Jean, a goodbye peck on the cheek and headed out the door for yet another hectic day at the office.

The admiral's home at Lorne Terrace, the big old weather-beaten white house on the grounds of the naval dockyard, was almost two miles (three kilometres) from the navy's operational headquarters downtown. A sprinkling of rain had fallen overnight, but the morning dawned bright, clear, and dry over Halifax. The air that fluttered the two small flags on the front fenders of the admiral's staff car and came in the windows as the vehicle sped southeast along Barrington Street was cool and fresh; the briny Atlantic tang was perfume to the nose of a career navy man such as Leonard Murray.

T HE ALLIED NAVAL COMMAND's operational headquarters (HQ) in Halifax was a nondescript four-storey WWI-vintage structure. Located in the city's downtown business district, at the northwest corner of South and Barrington Streets, the building stood kitty-corner to Cornwallis Park. In the months prior to the war, the Royal Canadian Air Force (RCAF) had set up its east coast command centre here. At that time, Canada was rushing to prepare for wartime mobilization. With no time or money for a proper navy, the Liberal government prioritized strengthening the RCAF and launching maritime air patrols. That had all changed by 1943. The volume of naval activity in Halifax had mushroomed, as had the need for improved administration and command facilities.

In addition to the thousands of men on active sea duty and toiling in the naval dockyard, hundreds more men and women were involved in on-shore support roles and in processing the huge volume of top-secret naval intelligence information that arrived daily. The Allies had broken the Nazis' top-secret Enigma code and were intercepting, decoding, and reading the radio communications that flowed back and forth between the enemy's Atlantic U-boat fleet and its bases in Germany.

On October 1, 1944, the RCN had taken over part of the air force's South Street HQ, commissioning the floors of the facility it occupied as HMCS *Peregrine*. Murray's office was located in this beehive of activity. Typewriters and teletype machines clattered away 24/7, and a steady parade of Canadian, American, and British naval personnel came and went all day long. Murray had been reluctant to relocate here. He was content with his office space at the naval dockyard; however, there simply wasn't enough room there for him and for the scores of Allied naval staff now working under his command. Operational HQ had moved, and Murray was making the best of the situation.

As was his habit whenever he arrived at operational HQ, on the morning of May 7, 1945, the admiral greeted the two uniformed naval sentries who stood unblinking and at crisp attention outside the doors of the main entrance. Murray, a genial man, was known to go out of his way to say hello to the men and women under his command. His reputation for being approachable and open was well earned. He often made time to visit naval ships, where he met and talked with the men to whom he awarded service medals. "Admiral Murray was very personable. He was soft-spoken and kind. A true gentleman," said one navy man who met the admiral in 1944. "Those who served under him really liked and admired him."[4]

Wide-eyed with a round chin and Churchill-like ruddy cheeks, Leonard Murray was a big man physically, a teddy bear. He was "bulky," as another navy man who served under him put it.[5] Murray was forty-nine years old, and his six-foot (183-centimetre) frame was beginning to show the pudginess of middle age. If the admiral wasn't as active in 1945 as he had been in his younger years, there was a good reason. He was far too busy, often frantically so. "My war work was a solid slog, mostly at a desk, averaging fifteen hours a day with frequently a full twenty-four," he would later recall. "My job was to obtain the greatest possible result from relatively inexperienced personnel."[6] He did that and did it well. As a veteran military man, Murray was used to giving and taking orders and to leading. At heart, he was a navy man long before he had ever donned a uniform.

Admiral Leonard Murray. (LAC, MIKAN no. 141630)

Murray's family roots were deep in the soil of Nova Scotia's North Shore. His Scottish ancestors had settled in Pictou County in 1773; it was there that Murray was born June 22, 1896, in the hamlet of Granton. He was a gangling fourteen-year-old in January 1911 when he left home to enroll in the first class at the newly established (but ultimately short-lived) Royal Naval College of Canada in Halifax.

Murray excelled in his studies, graduating in 1913, third in a class of nineteen naval cadets. Worth noting is that one of Murray's classmates was Halifax-born George C. Jones, a navy man who even in his youth was politically astute, humourless, intolerant, and ruthlessly ambitious. For reasons only he could explain, Jones took a dislike to Murray, "possibly because he recognized in the younger Murray a rival in his quest to one day head the RCN," one naval historian has speculated.[7] In the small, insular world of the Canadian navy's senior command, this petty animosity would prove to be important to the careers of both men, as Murray would learn the hard way.

After WWI, the RCN had faced cutbacks and serious financial woes. Like many of his fellow RCN officers, Murray mused about retiring from the navy to pursue another career. He might well have done so had his application for a transfer to the Royal Navy not been approved. He spent most of the 1920s serving on British warships, working at the Royal Naval College, and living in England. Murray returned to Canada in early 1929 having achieved the rank of commander. Despite the ongoing ill will of his nemesis, George Jones—who technically was Murray's "superior" by virtue of the fact he had won promotion to captain on August 1, 1938, a day *before* Murray did—Murray's rise through the ranks of the RCN's command structure continued. Murray and Jones had duelling friends in high places. Another reminder of that came in December 1941 when Murray began wearing the bar, single stripe, and loop of the rear-admiral on his uniform sleeves; once again, his promotion was effective a day *after* George Jones also became a rear-admiral.

No matter. During this period, Murray was taking on ever more responsibility for North Atlantic convoy operations until finally, on April 30, 1943, he was named commander-in-chief, Canadian Northwest Atlantic. This was his rank on the morning of May 7, 1945. As the top RCN officer in Halifax, Rear-Admiral Leonard W. Murray knew that the proverbial buck stopped with him.

I T WAS SHORTLY AFTER 10 a.m. when the first reports of the German surrender in Europe reached Halifax. Local private radio stations and the CBC interrupted regular programming to deliver the news. These unofficial reports spread quickly. People began pouring onto city streets ready to let loose six years of pent-up hopes, fears, frustrations, and anticipation. Car horns sounded. Whistles at factories and on ships in the harbour tooted. Church bells rang. Celebrations began in earnest and with a vengeance.

Civic officials and their military counterparts had been meeting and planning for this moment for months. What initially had been called "Victory day" morphed into "Victory in Europe day"—VE day. The realization that the end of the war was coming was widespread, and the morning editions of Halifax newspapers were ready for it. They published a proclamation by Halifax mayor Allan M. Butler announcing the official VE day program that was "to be followed when the Government announces the day."

The list of planned activities included a parade of military bands, commemorative ceremonies on the Garrison Grounds at Citadel Hill, church services, and a gala evening fireworks display. In theory, all that sounded fine and decorous. But theory is one thing; reality is quite another. That much seemed self-evident, especially when it was common knowledge that servicemen, whose list of Halifax-related grievances was longer than Barrington Street, routinely threatened to "take this bum town apart" whenever the opportunity to do so presented itself. "For months running into years there had grown up the belief that [trouble] would happen if measures were not taken to head it off and prevent it," the *Halifax Herald* reported.[8]

Those words would prove to be prophetic. It didn't help that a series of occurrences—some happenstance, others that in retrospect were jaw-droppingly dumb—stoked the smouldering fires of discontent and anger that in turn sparked what *Maclean's* magazine would call "The $3-million 'party' that wrecked Halifax."[9]

For one thing, as word spread that the war was over, the employees of many shops, offices, movie theatres, and restaurants in Halifax and across the harbour in Dartmouth ran off to join the celebrations, despite requests from government officials that they stay on the job. When they did not do so, the businesses for which they worked closed for the day. Those owners who sensed trouble brewing battened down the hatches, boarding up doors and windows.

Meanwhile, Halifax police chief Judson Conrad was fearful that his eighty-three-man force would never be able to keep the peace if trouble started, much less control mobs of drunken sailors. Dealing with the unrest that routinely flared on weekends and service pay-days was challenging enough. So Conrad figured it would curb any drunkenness and rowdyism by soldiers and sailors if on VE day all Halifax liquor stores and pubs were closed, as they sometimes were over the Christmas holiday season when it seemed sailors might cause trouble. The police chief also asked military officials to close their "wet canteens"—those messes where dances were held and alcohol was served.

Admiral Murray was of a different mind. He advised the police chief that after discussing the matter with other senior military commanders, he'd concluded it would be best to allow the canteens at HMCS *Stadacona* naval barracks and at other military facilities in the Halifax area to stay open "under proper control," albeit with limited quantities of alcohol on hand. As Murray saw it, these precautions would help keep crowds of sailors off the streets and out of trouble. "This combined with an organization to set up sing-songs and entertainments should go a long way to relieve the impact of large numbers of joyful service personnel upon the city," Murray explained in a letter to Halifax's mayor.[10] That being so, the admiral reasoned, city police should be able to handle any trouble involving civilians; military police would be held in reserve, available to intervene if men and women in uniform got into the act.

Now normally, as everyone knows, there is nothing that sailors with free time love more than engaging in a lively singalong or watching entertainments; however, circumstances and the prevailing mood were a wee bit different in Halifax on May 7, 1945, and also on the following day, which Ottawa officially proclaimed as VE day.

The city officials who were in charge of the Halifax fireworks display scheduled for VE day held the event on May 7. That was a great success. A crowd of about 15,000 people gathered on the eastern slope of Citadel Hill that evening to watch the pyrotechnics. Afterward, the good citizens of Halifax and many of the military personnel who were among the spectators went home. But thousands of sailors weren't ready to call it a night. With open gangways in effect, those who were entitled to enjoy leave were free to come and go as they pleased from five o'clock in the afternoon until 7 a.m. the next morning. These guys and gals were in a mood to party.

Discipline was forgotten when VE day rioting erupted on the streets of Halifax.
(LAC, MIKAN no. 3363772)

Not surprisingly, all 6,000 bottles of beer at HMCS *Stadacona* and other military wet canteens were gone by 9 p.m., as were many of the mickeys of liquor that sailors and soldiers had squirrelled away or purchased from bootleggers. When the last bottles ran dry, the revellers streamed out of the naval dockyard. They headed south along Barrington Street, one of the city's main thoroughfares. The men and a sprinkling of women—members of the Women's Royal Canadian Naval Service (WRCNS)—were looking for more to drink and for a good time. Downtown, they were joined by army militia men and hundreds of seamen from ships in the harbour who'd raced ashore eager to eat, drink, make merry, and blow off steam. With the bars and restaurants shuttered tight, it did not take long for the lighthearted mood on the streets to turn ugly. "The boys got mad," recalled one Wren who was on the streets that night.[11] The time had come for men in uniform to give Halifax "payback" for six years of simmering resentments.

It was about 10 p.m. when a thirsty young sailor, name unknown, shouted it was time to "open a liquor store." That idea seemed like a good one. The milling crowd acted on it, smashing open the front door of one liquor store, then another, and finally the central provincial liquor store on nearby Sackville Street. The party was on.

"It wasn't long before hundreds of guys and gals . . . were coming out [of the liquor stores] with arms full of booze," another Wren recalled. "I had thirteen mickeys of rye stashed around me, in my uniform. Even about four in my bloomers, in my jacket and in my purse. . . . wherever you looked on [Citadel Hill] there was [sic] people drinking. Twos, fours, eights. Big parties, and let me say, more than a usual quota of screwing."[12]

An ill-fated city tram, the Number 126, happened to come creaking along Barrington Street just as the crowd was getting rowdy. The now well-lubricated mob of revellers surrounded the vehicle and began rocking it, good-naturedly at first. When a passing group of navy shore patrol officers intervened, the revellers backed off. However, as soon as the shore patrol officers moved along, the fun resumed. Only this time, the mood was darker and more menacing. Drunken sailors hijacked the tram and somehow managed to drive it off the tracks and into a shattered storefront. There it was set ablaze. A shore patrol vehicle that attempted to reach the scene was turned back by a hail of bottles and stones.

The situation was rapidly spinning out of control. That reality was underscored when a city fire engine arrived at the burning tram. Drunken yahoos repeatedly disconnected hoses from fire hydrants, thwarting firefighters' efforts to douse the flames. Halifax police who tried to arrest drunken sailors were harassed, and their paddy wagon was overturned and torched.

The looting, vandalism, violence, and drunken partying continued into the early hours of May 8. Roving mobs set fires, smashed windows, ransacked a second tram car, tore down utility poles and wiring, and scattered paper and other debris everywhere. The madness didn't end until rain began falling in the pre-dawn. Sailors who were still sober enough to do so staggered back to their barracks or their ships. Those whose legs wouldn't carry them slept it off wherever they passed out. The streets of the downtown business district were an ugly sight as the sun rose the next morning. But all was relatively quiet again, for now.

W ITH THE FEDERAL GOVERNMENT having declared May 8 to be the official VE day, a national holiday, and with the downtown looking like a battlefield, Halifax was all but shut down. Holiday or no holiday, the city's mayor, the police and fire chiefs, and the citizenry were outraged and disgusted by the destruction and violence of the previous night. Admiral Murray and other military brass also were taken aback; however, their view of events was more benign. As they saw it, the men and women of the navy had simply let off some steam.

Murray also assumed the news reports he'd heard of the devastation were exaggerated. If things had gotten a bit out of hand, that was regrettable. What's more, Murray naively believed any looting that had happened was mostly the doing of civilian troublemakers; it was up to the city police and the civilian courts to deal with them. At the same time, longstanding Royal Navy tradition—in which Murray was steeped—held that the navy had little responsibility for the behaviour or activities of its men when they were off duty and on shore. "Men were men," and as such they were responsible for their own actions. That being so, Murray condoned the approach adopted by the commanders of the unarmed navy shore patrol, who were under orders to stop any damage that sailors were doing only "if possible," but to back off if the troublemakers persisted or became violent. "The intention was to lead, as with a child, instead of saying 'Don't do that,'" the admiral would later explain.[13]

This was part and parcel of his rationale for not taking a stronger stand in the wake of the events of the night of Monday, May 7, and for his "full speed ahead, damn the torpedoes" approach on VE day, May 8. Murray felt the men and women under his command were entitled to celebrate the war's end. With that in mind, he announced that the open gangways would continue on Tuesday. All who were scheduled to have leave that day were good to go; that included everyone, even those who'd been off the previous day. Murray ordered that the traditional Royal Navy signal flag—"Splice the main brace"—be flown from the admiral's yardarm at the naval dockyard. That meant sailors were entitled to drink and party on with the commanding officer's blessing. In this case, the blessing of Admiral Murray.

Rioting on the streets of downtown Halifax on May 7–8 was alcohol fuelled. (Nova Scotia Archives, David Hall, NSARM/1981-412 10)

That decision, generous and well intentioned though it was, proved to be tone deaf and ill-advised—to the point of being bone-headed. It would prove costly for all concerned, no one more so than Leonard W. Murray himself.

A NOTHER IDEA TO FILE under "it seemed to make sense at the time": as a thank you to the men and women of the navy, on May 8 Colonel Sidney Oland, owner of Oland's Brewery, gave out free cases of beer to sailors until stock ran out. Meanwhile, the wet canteen at HMCS *Stadacona* reopened for business, even as small contingents of men from the army, navy, and air force marched through the streets of Halifax to take part in 9 a.m. civic ceremonies at the Garrison Grounds near Citadel Hill. Afterward, churches throughout the city held services of thanksgiving.

Admiral Murray had just returned home from one such ceremony when an aide appeared at his door with a request that he immediately call the mayor. Upon doing so, Murray learned city police were reporting that throngs of drunken sailors were again filling downtown streets; it was evident that more trouble was brewing. Butler suggested Murray take a drive downtown to see for himself. The admiral's presence, he suggested, would have a calming effect. Murray wasn't convinced; he feared the rioters might turn on him and attack his car. "I would have been the commander who was unable to control his troops," he would later explain.[14]

Murray ignored the mayor's suggestion, although he did issue orders that more shore patrol officers be put onto the streets. He also called the duty officer at HMCS *Stadacona* to ask about the situation there. "All quiet," he was advised. There was a good reason for that—the wet canteen's beer supply was gone, along with the looted booze from the previous night. A throng of frustrated and tipsy sailors had pelted the canteen with empty bottles and stones before heading downtown, intent on a repeat of last night's "fun." They soon found it.

The looting, vandalism, drinking, and violence resumed with a vengeance in Halifax and across the harbour in Dartmouth. Cheered on and aided by civilians who were eager to share in the spoils, the mob of men in uniforms overturned and burned cars, smashed windows, and looted stores and businesses. Keith's Brewery and other establishments that had escaped damage the night before were attacked. Woolworths, Birks jewellers, Colwell's menswear shop, and Mitchell Furs were among the favourite targets.

One of the few downtown windows not smashed on this night belonged to a barber shop in a building owned by one Emma Mackay. The little grey-haired woman positioned herself on the sidewalk in front of her building. For fifteen hours, she stood there pleading with rioters not to trash the place. "This store has been here for 56 years, and [the window] wasn't even broken in the Halifax explosion in 1917," she said.[15]

Mrs. Mackay was finally able to return home at 10 p.m. that night. By that time, the turmoil had ended, and her shop was still intact. Admiral Murray and Mayor Allan Butler had driven through the downtown in an RCAF sound truck late in the afternoon warning those rioters who were still on streets to immediately leave the area. Not long afterward, the first contingent of a thousand soldiers who were armed with rifles and fixed bayonets appeared on city streets and set about restoring the peace. Their presence was reinforced by thirty-five army provost officers who'd flown in from Camp Borden, an hour north of Toronto.

Fires were still smouldering and the cleanup was barely under way in downtown Halifax when the blame game began. A total of 211 people—117 civilians and 94 military people—had been charged with various riot-related offences. Three men died—two reportedly drank themselves to death, and one man, a naval lieutenant-commander, died from injuries suffered when he was attacked by unknown assailants. Property damage in downtown Halifax was pegged at as much as $5 million. That would be about $71 million today.

What is now generally forgotten is that the rioting that occurred in Halifax wasn't unique. Unrest occurred in other port cities, although certainly not on the scale of what happened in Halifax. In Sydney, the Cape Breton port located 250 miles (400 kilometres) to the north, sailors at HMCS *Protector* (the Point Edward Naval Base) reacted in much the same way their mates in Halifax did. They took to the streets, whooping, breaking windows, and playing "Ring Around the Rosie" after looting a liquor store. However, local police soon quelled the disturbance, and a nine o'clock curfew curtailed any further trouble. Since the Sydney naval base was small, the morale there was much better than in Halifax, and the well of animus was much less deep.

"To celebrate VE day, my buddies and I ordered a mickey of rye from a local bootlegger. We were all supposed to chip in to pay for it," recalled Bill Fitsell, a Barrie, Ontario, native whose navy rank was "writer"—a scribe who was responsible for all correspondence aboard his ship, HMCS *St. Francis*; even in wartime, there is paperwork to be done. "I always had money because I wasn't a heavy drinker, and so I paid the cabbie $10 when he delivered the bottle. Everybody had a good time, but of course I never got repaid."[16]

As was the case in Halifax, locals from Sydney and surrounding areas joined in the rioting, snatching up looted goods. Two young wannabe bootleggers from New Waterford carted home a carload of stolen booze, which they hastily stashed in a shed behind their house. When the lads raced off to retrieve a second load, neighbours who had been watching from afar went into action. "My brothers went over and collected the booze, and they hid it in the crawl space under our house," recalled Dominic ("Don") Petrie, who was eight at the time.[17] There is no honour among thieves.

THE VE DAY SHENANIGANS in Sydney; Saint John, New Brunswick; Gaspé, Quebec; and St. John's, Newfoundland, were small potatoes. The turmoil in Halifax was a different matter entirely. News of the trouble made headlines across Canada. The rioting was widely regarded as an embarrassment to Halifax, a black mark against the Royal Canadian Navy, and a damning indictment of the man who was supposed to be in charge of the navy: Admiral Leonard Murray. The local newspapers, civic leaders, the business community, and citizens were unanimous in blaming sailors for the trouble. They demanded that those responsible "be held accountable." And there was no doubt who that was.

Admiral Murray was having none of it. He remained adamant that it was civilians, not navy people, who had been responsible for most of the damage, especially the looting. In a letter to the Halifax newspapers, the admiral insisted that any role sailors had played in the rioting "was dictated more by drunkenness and excitement than by any desire for loot, and the major portion of such looting as did take place was perpetrated by the civil population."[18]

Murray believed that; others didn't. An editorial in the *Evening Mail* newspaper opined that while members of all three services were involved in the rioting, looting, and destruction, "the members of one service—the navy—were most prominent."[19] The *Halifax Herald* adopted an equally angry tone, demanding, "When duty and any failure in duty has been assessed, no considerations of rank, station, or degree can be permitted to stand in the way of adequate condign action on the part of the governing authorities."[20]

The concerns being voiced in Halifax were echoed in Ottawa. With a federal election campaign under way and the June 11 voting day just a month off, officials in Mackenzie King's Liberal government were concerned about the impact the rioting in Halifax would have on voters, on veterans in particular. A similar crisis had arisen in 1917 in the wake of the disastrous Halifax explosion, which killed more than 2,000 people. With a pivotal federal election campaign in full swing at that time, the Conservative government of Robert Borden had called a public inquiry. Now, twenty-eight years later, the King government adopted the same strategy.

Acting Prime Minister James L. Ilsley—a native Nova Scotian—announced that a public inquiry into the Halifax VE day rioting would be held as soon as possible. He made the announcement on May 10, hoping to shift attention from any talk of government responsibility for what happened in Halifax. Ilsley tabbed Justice Roy L. Kellock of the Supreme Court of Canada to oversee proceedings.

None of this was good news for Admiral Murray, who knew he'd already been tried and found guilty in the court of public opinion. If that wasn't bad enough, there came the news that his long-time nemesis, George Jones, now a vice-admiral and chief of the naval staff (having succeeded Murray's mentor, Vice-Admiral Percy Nelles, in January 1944), was taking charge of the navy's investigation into the background and circumstances of the riots.

Jones flew to Halifax on May 12 for a private meeting with Murray, where the events of May 7 and 8 were discussed in blunt terms. Afterward, no formal announcement was made on what had been said or decided, and Jones returned to Ottawa. Murray remained in Halifax, supposedly on leave. What had transpired at that May 12 meeting came out only during the eighteen days of testimony at the Kellock Commission, held between May 17 and June 18. When Murray was called to the witness stand, he was peppered with questions. Throughout the proceedings, the admiral stuck to his guns, insisting that while he'd been busy with his commander-in-chief duties, he'd done all he could to head off and deal with the rioting in Halifax. Furthermore, he insisted he'd done the right thing in allowing the men and women under his command to celebrate on May 7 and 8; the looting that had occurred was the work of civilians, not sailors.

While another witness was answering questions about the rioting and Admiral Murray's role in the days that followed it, Justice Kellock interrupted him to say, "The Court realizes that Admiral Murray has not been in command since May 12."[21] That news came as a revelation to most everyone in the courtroom. Murray must have known that Jones had relieved him of his command and had replaced him, but the admiral declined to offer any public comments about that or about the Jones-appointed board of inquiry headed by Rear-Admiral Victor Brodeur. Two of the three judges to assist Brodeur as he sat in judgment of Murray were officers who were junior to Murray.

Adding insult to injury, the result of their deliberations was never announced. If they ever did write a report, it never saw the light of day. "A finding in favour of Murray would exonerate him—and perhaps be seen as a whitewash," naval historian Marc Milner has explained. "To find against him would have given [Murray] grounds for demanding a court martial, something Jones could not allow."[22]

Murray had no option but to await the ruling of the Kellock Commission. When it was handed down in late July, it affixed the lion's share of the blame for the Halifax VE day riots on the failure of naval command—namely Admiral Leonard Murray.

The admiral was disappointed, and he felt betrayed by what he thought was a lack of support from the navy and from the federal government. In the post-war world and in an RCN in which Vice-Admiral George Jones was the chief of naval staff, Murray knew he was *persona non grata*, about as welcome as Mackenzie King at a veterans' reunion.

Murray chose not to fight his dismissal. To do so, he felt, would split the RCN into two openly hostile camps—those who supported him and those who sided with George Jones. Instead of delivering a broadside at his old nemesis, Murray quietly disappeared. He resigned his commission in March 1946 and opted for a kind of self-imposed exile. He and his wife, Jean, sailed for England, where Murray became a law student and was called to the bar in November 1949. He practised maritime law in London for a few years; however, when his wife fell ill, the couple relocated to a small town in Sussex, where Jean Murray died a few years later. Leonard Murray would eventually remarry, become active in local politics, and in 1965 run unsuccessfully for office. He would die six years later, on November 25, 1971, at the age of seventy-five. The following year, his ashes would come home, to be interred in the Naval Vault at St. Paul's Church in Halifax.

In 1970, on one of his rare post-war visits to Canada, Murray sat down for a lengthy interview with naval historian Alec Douglas in which he talked about his career, the Halifax VE day riots, and the abrupt end of his naval career. As always, the admiral was soft-spoken but direct. "Murray wasn't one to carry a grudge," Douglas recalled, "but he was resentful about how on various occasions his seniority had been adjusted by days, so technically George Jones was always his superior."[23]

Murray had ample reason to feel the treatment he'd received in 1945 and the accusations he faced were unfair. It's true, as some naval historians have argued, that the admiral deserved better. Many of the circumstances of his quick fall from grace were beyond his control. It was the federal government that failed to ensure Halifax was ready and able to absorb the huge influx of military personnel and civilian workers who suddenly began descending upon the city in 1939; however, with the benefit of hindsight, it's clear that Murray wasn't blameless for the VE day riots in Halifax.

At the very least, the admiral was guilty of poor decision making. He placed far too much blind faith in the goodness and decency of the volunteer sailors under his command. For them, the war was over. They'd done their bit and were going home, but before they did so, they had a score to settle with Halifax, a city for which they had no love. Murray should have recognized this and taken steps to see to it that the open gangways policy was reversed and sailors confined to base, particularly those who had enjoyed shore leave on May 7, the first day of rioting.

Naval historian Marc Milner was correct when he wrote, "By any measure, Rear Admiral Leonard Warren Murray was the most important commander in the Canadian navy's first century."[24] It's also true that by resigning and exiting as quietly as he did, Murray helped the RCN move forward into the post-war era with its proud record of wartime accomplishments largely intact. In that sense, he did the right and honourable thing. However, the evidence suggests that the same kind of political infighting, personality conflicts, and petty rivalries that brought Murray's career to such a sudden end may well continue to persist in the cloistered upper echelons of the Canadian military's command. The controversy, political posturing, and legal manoeuvrings that were the murky backdrop for the 2018 dismissal of Vice-Admiral Mark Norman stand as a recent example of that reality.

Norman was charged with breach of trust in connection with allegations that he had released sensitive government information to effect a procurement of naval supply ships, but the Crown ultimately dropped the charge because it was deemed there was "no reasonable chance of a conviction." Rumours about the possible reasons for the charge against Norman continued to swirl. However, the speculation died down when the vice-admiral and the federal government reached a "mutually agreeable" settlement. Like Leonard Murray's, the career of Mark Norman ended abruptly amid clouds of controversy.

The worst days to me are holidays, Saturdays, and Sundays, because I'm the only one who wants to work. Every day is the same to me.
—E.P. Taylor

CHAPTER 10

A New Way of Doing Business

WILLIAM LYON MACKENZIE KING WAS A MAN OF MANY vices, and yet, given the tenor of his times, it's surprising that a fondness for alcohol was not one of them. Canada's longest-serving prime minister was a teetotaller, and like many dyed-in-the-wool moralists, he was certain the world would be a better place if only everyone behaved as he did. However, even though he was an aging sexagenarian who was in the twilight of his political career (and knew it), King remained addicted to power. Partisan dictates continued to shape his decision making. That's why a December 1942 initiative he announced in what the media dubbed his "armour of God speech" was a surprise to many people.

Three months earlier, King had met with a delegation of United Church of Canada pro-temperance lobbyists. The clergymen explained they were appalled and alarmed that in the two years since the 1939 outbreak of war, alcohol consumption in Canada had doubled; they implored the prime minister to do something about it. Turning off the taps was the simplest solution. Their appeal worked. King had never had much use for what he derisively referred to as "the liquor interests."

Invoking emergency powers that were available to him in the War Measures Act, Mackenzie King had imposed a series of wide-ranging regulations that slapped limits on the production, sale, and consumption of alcohol in Canada. Regardless of your attitude toward prohibition, King had argued, the move made sense in time of war. Supporters of the temperance lobby, church leaders, and some provincial premiers were overjoyed. Other premiers joined the millions of ordinary Canadians—a majority of the population, especially men and women in uniform—when they emitted a collective groan. They were of a much different mind. So, too, were the owners of breweries, distilleries, and taverns, all of whom protested the measures. By early 1944, Ottawa would be obliged to roll back the restrictions. One of the leaders of the brewing-industry campaign against the temperance restrictions was the owner of Canadian Breweries, Canada's largest beer maker.

Edward Plunket (E.P.) Taylor was a Liberal supporter, at least nominally, but he was no fan of Mackenzie King or of "Big Government." Despite this, until mid-1942 Taylor had been the youngest Minister of Munitions and Supply, and one of the most high-profile of C.D. Howe's celebrated "dollar-a-year" boys. These half-dozen business leaders had volunteered their time, energies, and managerial talents to help ensure that Canada's wartime economy ran like a well-oiled machine, and it did.

Taylor normally shunned the spotlight. He wasn't someone who would step forward to sound off about government policy or draw attention to himself. A big, balding man, he was an inveterate pipe smoker with twinkling blue eyes, a deep voice, and a rumbling laugh. In casual conversation, Taylor tended to use the editorial "we" when talking about himself. The carefully crafted public persona was that of an Everyman who was "just one of the boys"—a beer-drinking golfer and horse-racing enthusiast whose idea of real luxury was having the money to be able to sit in the barber's chair for two shaves each day. At first blush, Taylor—"Eddie" as friends called him—was a model of easygoing amiability. However, appearances were deceiving.

Beneath that benign, laid-back exterior, this forty-one-year-old

Ottawa-born beer baron was an indefatigable "master of the capitalist theology."[1] Those on the left of the political spectrum scorned him as a rapacious corporate predator, a fast-buck artist who devoured small companies, closed plants, and laid off workers to cut costs and boost profits. There was no denying that Taylor did all those things, for his eye was always fixed firmly on the bottom line of his corporate balance sheet. Yet at the same time, he was also one of Canada's most generous philanthropists, giving to a wide variety of causes he felt were worthwhile. Talk about a paradox.

Many of Taylor's peers distrusted him and disapproved of what they regarded as his predatory ways. "Others point out that he . . . pumped more than $60 million into postwar Canadian business through expansion programs and new developments and that he indirectly provide[d] jobs for more than 30,000 Canadians," journalist Pierre Berton once noted.[2]

To editorial page cartoonists and many ordinary Canadians, Taylor would unwillingly come to be the quintessential face of "the Establishment" in the post-war era. He was Canada's "symbolic big shot." That image, too, was misleading.

Taylor was nowhere close to being one of this country's wealthiest men. Compared with such people as department store owner John Eaton, mining magnate Norman Urquhart, or industrialist K.C. Irving, Taylor was a relative pauper. Many of Canada's economic elite, especially those who were "old money," regarded him as an upstart, a parvenu. By 1963, when he was at the pinnacle of his success and fame, *Maclean's* magazine journalist Barbara Moon canvassed the mavens of Toronto's investment community for their opinions on E.P. Taylor. "The only superlative anyone in these precincts will pin on Taylor," Moon reported, "is that he commands 'more of the influence of wealth than any man in Canada,' whatever that means."[3]

While other corporate heads were far richer than E.P. Taylor, few— if any—had more power over the nation's economy. That he did was no accident, for he had a nimble business mind and a steely sense of resolve. "'Eddie can read a balance sheet like a poem and tell you where it doesn't scan,' they used to say along Bay Street,"[4] reported journalist Barbara Moon. That was true.

Recruiting E.P. Taylor to serve the government in wartime had been a coup for C.D. Howe, albeit a surprising and somewhat controversial one. The prime minister's right-hand man had appealed to the beer baron's patriotism in order to persuade him to volunteer his time and managerial talents in support of the war effort. Taylor's vanity also made the challenge irresistible. "What people don't understand is that [my] principal motivation isn't money," he often said. "I do something that is constructive. There are people who like to paint or garden. I like to create things."[5]

That goes a long way toward explaining why in June 1940 Taylor had put his Toronto-based business interests and family life on hold while he went to work for the federal government. After settling into a suite at Ottawa's Château Laurier hotel, he'd taken on two pivotal responsibilities in his new role as Director General of Munitions Production. One was seeing to it that Canadian industry ramped up to achieve maximum wartime production; the other was arranging contracts for all the guns, bombs, and equipment the Canadian and British militaries needed to wage war. These were big challenges, but they were ones for which E.P. Taylor was well suited. "A big, strapping man, [he] specialized in straightening out muddles," Gordon Sinclair of the *Toronto Daily Star* observed, "and from the time he joined the supply department soon after its organization, he had one difficult assignment after another."[6]

In marked contrast to Prime Minister Mackenzie King, whose management style was circuitous, cautious as a cat, and conciliatory when it suited his purposes, Taylor's manner was hard-driving and uncompromising. He seldom took a day off and was known to toil long hours, seven days a week, whatever it took to get a job done. Taylor expected and demanded that same dedication from others. It was typical of him that he shrugged off that December 1940 near-death experience in which he spent twelve hours in a lifeboat bobbing around on the icy North Atlantic after a German U-boat sank the ship on which he, C.D. Howe, and a couple of companions were passengers. Taylor credited his survival to his own resolve and to the Abercrombie & Fitch duck-hunting suit, a gift from his daughter, he had carried on the trip for use in just such an emergency.

Back at his desk in Ottawa afterward, Taylor had plunged into his wartime duties with renewed vigour. C.D. Howe relied on him to work with Deputy Finance Minister Clifford Clark and John Carswell, the Canadian government's purchasing representative in Washington, to draft the now-famous Hyde Park Declaration.[7] That agreement, which Mackenzie King and Franklin Roosevelt had signed after a seven-hour meeting on April 20, 1941, was a game changer for Canada and for the Allied war effort. Without it, Britain likely would have been unable to fend off the Nazi onslaught, and Canada's wartime economy likely would not have boomed as it did. As the *New York Times* reported, the pact provided for "a virtual merging of the economies of the United States and Canada for production of war materials for Great Britain and for hemisphere defence."[8]

In many people's eyes, E.P. Taylor was the post-war face of the Canadian Establishment. (City of Toronto Archives, fonds 1653, series 975, file 280)

Taylor's contribution to Britain's survival hadn't ended there. Four months later, at the request of Lord Beaverbrook—the Canadian-born businessman who was the Minister of Supply in British prime minister Winston Churchill's wartime Cabinet—Taylor had added to his already punishing workload when he took on the job of coordinating the efforts of the myriad British government and military agencies in Washington that were buying American-made munitions and armaments.

The pace and the pressure of the work had proven to be more onerous than anyone could handle, even a dynamo such as E.P. Taylor. By late 1942, after more than two years of relentless toil, he felt burned out. And he was also tired of the frustrations that sprang from dealing with the politics and the prickly personalities he faced daily in three capital Allied cities—Ottawa, Washington, and London. Taylor was a businessman, not a bureaucrat, a diplomat, or a soldier. By October 1942, impatient to resume a more proactive role in managing his own business interests, he had resigned from his government duties.

DURING THE WAR YEARS, Canadian Breweries was one of the country's largest beer makers, yet its business operations were among the least efficient. Rival Labatt, which sold less brew, enjoyed a profit margin three times higher than did Canadian Breweries. E.P. Taylor had been wrestling with that shortcoming and with a slew of other pressing business concerns when in December 1942, Mackenzie King introduced those annoying temperance initiatives. In a fit of pique—and doubtless feeling slighted after having voluntarily devoted two years of his time and acumen to the war effort—Taylor dashed off a plaintive letter to the prime minister. Taylor could have saved his time, ink, and paper. His appeal fell on deaf ears.

Mackenzie King's response to Taylor's protest was a perfunctory form letter. ("Dear Mr. Taylor . . .") If the frustrated beer baron suspected the prime minister was scarcely aware of Taylor's existence, let alone the service he had rendered the country, he was correct. In the more than 50,000 pages of King's diaries, there is just one passing mention of E.P. Taylor. The two men had once sat at the same breakfast table at the Harvard Club in New York; that had happened the day before King travelled to Hyde Park for that historic April 1941 meeting with Roosevelt. King's diary entry for that day commented that the Director General of Munitions Production was "a fine looking and really splendid fellow."[9] That seems to have been the extent of King's awareness of Eddie Taylor, who for two years was one of the most important officials in wartime Ottawa and who for more than forty years afterward would stand as one of Canada's foremost business leaders and as the face of the Canadian Establishment.

Taylor could only speculate about King's apparent indifference toward him and his service to the country, and it irked him. He was a man who was used to being listened to and to getting his own way. When that didn't happen, Taylor wasn't inclined to quietly cry in his beer; he vented. In this case, he did so in a stinging letter to the editor he sent to the *Ottawa Journal* in early February 1943. In addition to criticizing the specifics of the government's latest temperance measures, Taylor had offered a blunt assessment of what in his mind was the inappropriateness of Mackenzie King's decision to introduce them in the first place. "With all due respect to the outstanding accomplishments of our prime minister," Taylor wrote, "it should be obvious to all that he was about the most poorly qualified member of the Government to make a recommendation to the Cabinet as the amount of beer the hard-working people of Canada should be given under wartime conditions. There was no careful or long study of this matter. It was almost entirely a one-man job."[10]

Taylor's critical darts scored a bull's-eye. King read the morning paper each day as he ate breakfast, and when he spotted Taylor's criticism, he reacted angrily. In his mind, everything in life was about politics, and the letter marked Taylor as a political enemy.[11] At age sixty-eight, the prime minister was a grumpy old man. An unflattering, brutally frank profile of him that appeared in the January 1943 edition of the influential American magazine *Harper's* had touched a raw nerve when it made that abundantly clear. The truth can hurt.

Edward K. Brown, a Toronto-born academic who headed the English department at Cornell University in Ithaca, New York, penned the article after serving a six-month stint as King's secretary in 1942.[12] Brown's literary portrait painted King as an old man who was unhappy, hopelessly hidebound, superstitious as a sailor, and a slave to habits that were quirky to the point of being downright bizarre. "This man, devoted to Church and [House of Commons] is one of the loneliest beings alive," Brown wrote.[13]

While there is no record of King's reaction to Brown's article (he made no mention of it in his diary or publicly), it's safe to assume the prime minister wasn't happy with it; he was notoriously thin-skinned. The same could be said of his response to E.P. Taylor's letter to the editor. Not that anything King might have said would have mattered to Taylor or given him reason to pause, mind you. He was too busy formulating an ambitious plan that he hoped would expand his business empire, improve its efficiencies, and boost profits. As biographer Richard Rohmer would note: "The years at the close of the Second World War saw the emergence of a new E.P. Taylor. Now he was ready to use his solid Canadian Breweries base as a secure financial platform from which he could expand and diversify."[14]

Taylor was about to launch a new business venture called Argus Corporation, which was destined to emerge as an archetypal business conglomerate. It would be hugely profitable and powerful, growing through what stock market watchers call "unrelated diversification"— that is, gobbling up and then disassembling smaller, vulnerable companies. This particular business strategy cast a long shadow over the Canadian corporate landscape in the heady, freewheeling days of the post-1945 economic boom. At the same time that it made millions for Taylor and his associates, it did nothing to grow or strengthen the Canadian stock market.

The drive to acquire and build Hydra-like conglomerates would influence and shape Canada's boardroom ethos well into the 1970s. And E.P. Taylor would come to be the poster boy for this impetus. It was a role in which he revelled, for it was also one he almost seemed predestined to play. "Contrary to myth, Taylor was not born with a silver spoon in his mouth," Richard Rohmer would write. "Rather it was a silver tongue."[15] Taylor would use his eloquence to full advantage.

IT WAS WITH GOOD reason that one of E.P. Taylor's nicknames was "the optimist entrepreneur." With the war in Europe winding down in the spring of 1945 and an Allied victory all but inevitable, many Canadians feared that the return of peace would bring with it a return to the grim economic conditions of the 1930s. Taylor wasn't among them. To the contrary, he felt certain a post-war economic boom was coming.

Taylor increased Canadian Breweries' beer production and placed orders for expensive new tanks and bottling equipment that were to be delivered to the company's plants in Toronto, Waterloo, and Ottawa as soon as the war ended. The move paid off handsomely because by VE day, Canadian Breweries was positioned to prosper in the post-war world. The *Canadian Encyclopedia* explains how: "Interprovincial trade barriers, along with the provincial jurisdiction over the retail sale and distribution of alcoholic drinks, local sensitivities, and the federal government's permissive policy towards takeovers, all combined to make the acquisition of small- and medium-sized firms the main route toward market consolidation in Canada."[16]

The business plans of Canadian Breweries and of its two main rivals, Labatt and Molson—the so-called Big Three of the Canadian beer industry—all dictated the need to have plants in each region of the country. By 1962, the Big Three would come to swallow up a majority of the sixty-one breweries that had been in business in Canada in 1945, and the national brands they produced—Labatt Blue, Molson

Canadian, and Canadian Breweries' flagship brand, Carling Black Label—dominated the marketplace. These post-war acquisitions would fundamentally change and reshape for half a century the market structure of Canada's brewing industry. In 1945, all that was all in the future, of course.

When Taylor's father, Plunket Taylor, died in January 1944, he had left E.P. in full control of the family's brewing empire. The challenge of running the business was one Eddie Taylor relished. At age forty-three, he was intent on taking Canadian Breweries in a bold new direction. That gamble was one Taylor was convinced would pay handsomely.

With the cost of borrowed money being a deductible business expense and with interest rates hovering around 4.5 per cent—which seems staggeringly high and risky in today's marketplace but was par for the course in 1945—Taylor felt confident in moving ahead with his plan to start a closed-end investment holding company.[17] Forget starting a new business that would make widgets or provide services. This new corporate entity would purchase and hold enough shares in a select group of existing companies to enable Taylor to gain leverage over or even control of their boards of directors.

According to biographer Richard Rohmer, Taylor's inspiration for "the creation of an investment company had come from an American, Floyd Odlum, and a company he had put together in the United States called Atlas Corporation."[18] Odlum's initiative, which he had launched in 1928, was hugely successful. Atlas was the controlling shareholder in a holding company that had a diverse portfolio, including interests in utility companies, retail stores, mining operations, banks, and aviation-related industries. Odlum had had the foresight and business smarts to see the Great Depression coming and had sold off most of his holdings, and so he was sitting on millions of dollars in cash when the stock market crashed in October 1929. During the lean days of the Great Depression, he could buy stocks and take advantage of other investment opportunities at fire-sale prices. Floyd Odlum was said to be one of the few people in America who made money, a lot of it, in the 1930s. "Taylor and Odlum are much alike. Neither has paid great attention to the financial wiseacres," writer Pierre Berton would note.

The two men were friends, and one day Odlum jokingly suggested to Taylor that they team up to hire "the best goddamm financial expert money can buy. We'll pay him $100,000 a year if necessary. We'll ask his advice on every deal we make. And when he says 'buy,' we'll sell. When he says 'sell,' we'll buy."[19]

Taylor laughed, but he dreamed of emulating the irreverent Mr. Odlum's success. He was certain he could duplicate in Canada what Odlum had done in the United States. However, in order to do so, Taylor needed deep-pocketed minority partners he could trust. Taylor found them among the ranks of his former fellow "dollar-a-year" men from wartime government service.

Toronto industrialist Colonel Eric Phillips and lawyer Wallace McCutcheon, both of whom were in Taylor's social circle, agreed to buy into his venture—"the two princes to the Taylor throne," Pierre Berton would dub them.[20] Investment banker John A. "Bud" McDougald, "dark, and squarely built, a rich man's son with an Upper Canada College and private tutor background and a liking for Savile Row suits, monogrammed pocket handkerchiefs and Rolls-Royce cars,"[21] declined the invitation to do so. However, McDougald did agree to partner with Taylor in sundry business ventures, and together the two men formed their own investment company. The core business of Taylor, McDougald & Company was scouting out and developing potential investment opportunities for the Taylor–Phillips–McCutcheon partnership.

That latter entity, Argus Corporation, was born on September 24, 1945. At a time when Canada was drifting to the left politically, Taylor was swimming against the tide. In effect, he was betting that flush with post-war prosperity, Canadians would revert to the individualist outlook that had prevailed prior to the 1939 outbreak of war. Cynical though that idea may have been, it proved to be correct. Revelling in a prosperity the likes of which this country had never experienced, Canadians were intent on forgetting the hardships and deprivations of the Great Depression. Suddenly, life was all about home, hearth, and family. The economy was booming, and so was the stock market. E.P. Taylor had chosen the ideal time to launch his new business venture.

The precise financial details of Argus Corporation's initial $12.5 million in capitalization ($178 million in today's dollars) were complex, but it's enough to note here that the venture was launched with $4 million in preferred shares and $8.5 million in cash—about $6 million of which Taylor and his partners anted up. By the time Argus was officially incorporated, the value of its shareholdings had already started to increase. "Taylor retained his initial controlling interest by folding in his [Canadian] Breweries stock in return for a majority control of Argus," business journalist Peter C. Newman would note. "He described the Argus approach as searching for companies 'that will grow not only with the country, but faster than the country; companies where no large shareholder exists, so that we can acquire enough stock to give us an important voice in the policy decisions.'"[22]

Taylor succeeded in gaining meaningful control over companies that were profitable, but undervalued. The beauty of this business plan from Taylor's perspective was that he was able to do so without tying up the huge amounts of money that would have been required to buy a majority of shares. At the same time, Argus's cumulative equity could be and was used to leverage fresh investments in other companies.

Initially, the strategy behind this vision was a natural extension of tactics Taylor had used to grow Canadian Breweries during the 1930s; however, as Argus's holdings multiplied and its earnings grew, the company's investment focus broadened. Whereas Taylor had expanded Canadian Breweries by buying other companies that were in brewing or related businesses, Argus's long-term growth and prosperity were the product of buying significant or controlling interests in any companies whose stock seemed to be undervalued and therefore was a solid investment.

A cynic would lament that Argus Corporation produced nothing and made money by tapping into or taking advantage of the success of existing companies—activities that did not offer much benefit to the stock market, ordinary investors, or society. However, a true believer in the merits of free enterprise would counter that notion by pointing out that Taylor and his partners were making money by depending on their own initiative and by investing in the stock market—activities that were both laudatory.

Regardless, Argus Corporation was hugely profitable. The founding partners—E.P. Taylor, Colonel Eric Phillips, and Wallace McCutcheon—all grew wealthy beyond their wildest expectations. That was especially true of Taylor, who was the company's majority shareholder. And Bud McDougald, who had declined to invest in Argus Corporation, did all right, too.

McDougald worked with Taylor and with Argus on various business deals, and in 1963 he would succeed his friend and business partner as head of the corporation. At the still-young age of sixty-two, Taylor retired to live the good life in the tax-free Bahamas and to devote his time to managing his stable of race horses, which beginning in 1969 were running under Windfields Farm colours.

Argus and its founding partners never looked back after the company began doing business in 1945. Prudent investments in the development companies building houses in the new suburban communities that were springing up all around Toronto during the post-war building boom proved to be highly profitable. Argus also continued to invest in established corporations that were making money. How much—if anything—the success of these companies had to do with Argus's involvement is difficult to say since all were successful businesses to begin with. As for those individual investors who purchased shares in Argus, they didn't fare nearly as well as the company's principals. Pierre Berton pointed out that "A speculator buying one share of each [company Argus invested in] at their lowest price in 1949 would have got about eight per cent on his money in dividends

. . . but Argus, which sold to the public at $10 a share in 1945, [in 1950 was] selling at only $7.50. And an investor buying one share of each Argus Company at its high in 1949 would have lost $5."[23]

Regardless, the corporation that was E.P. Taylor's brainchild would come to dominate the world of Canadian business like no other company ever had or likely ever will again. By 1964, Argus Corporation's power and influence would become so pervasive that it was said to control fully ten per cent of all the shares traded on the Toronto Stock Exchange. In 1972, the company's holdings would be worth more than $2.1 billion, with its major investments being in just six blue-chip Canadian companies: Massey Ferguson (28.6 per cent), Hollinger Mines (20.4), Standard Broadcasting Corporation (19.6), Domtar (18.2), Dominion Stores (15), and British Columbia Forest Products (5.3). The total value of Argus's investments in those stocks in today's dollars would be more than $12.8 billion, a jaw-dropping 6,900 per cent return on the partners' original investment. Not a bad return.

It is a measure of how much the Canadian economy has changed since 1972 that of the six companies at the heart of the Argus investment portfolio, only Hollinger Mines, Standard Broadcasting, and Domtar are still in business, albeit in name only, for their corporate structures and core businesses have changed dramatically. Massey Ferguson is now a brand that is owned by another company, while British Columbia Forest Products and Dominion have disappeared, as has Argus Corporation.[24]

When E.P. Taylor retired from the board of directors in 1971, his friend Bud McDougald succeeded him as company chairman. It was a post he would hold until his death in 1978. Not long afterward, his widow and sister sold their shares to the young Conrad Black—the son of George Montegu Black, who had managed Canadian Breweries for E.P. Taylor from 1950 to 1958. He would eventually sell off Argus's assets so he could invest in media properties, a venture that did not end well for Conrad Black.

In 2008, Argus went bankrupt, when Black was doing time in an

American prison after receiving a forty-two-month sentence for felony fraud and obstruction of justice.

Today, the company E.P. Taylor founded in 1945 is all but forgotten, remembered only by those rare people who know anything about Canadian corporate history and the lessons it offers. At the same time, the notion of growing an investment company through unrelated diversification is no longer considered to be smart—or even acceptable—business practice. Michael Porter, a professor at the Harvard School of Business, had discredited it as a corporate strategy, having shown it really does nothing to grow the companies or shareholders' dividends when those corporations become the targets of investors who buy in only to take out.[25]

E.P. Taylor's reputation hasn't fared much better. By the time of his death at age eighty-eight in 1989, he was a forgotten figure. Mention Taylor's name today, and most people's reaction will be to ask, "Wasn't he the guy who owned the racehorse Northern Dancer?" Fair enough. However, it's ironic, isn't it, that the memory of the man who was one of Canada's most powerful and successful business tycoons in the transformative years after WWII and who had such a profound impact on the Canadian corporate world—and collaterally on the zeitgeist of this country—has been eclipsed by the enduring fame of one of his four-legged investments?

My interest has been and still is—and will, I think, remain—the people least able to look out for themselves. I've never been interested in the powerful and the rich because I think they get more than their fair share anyway, so I see no reason why I should bother about them.
—Agnes Macphail, 1949

CHAPTER 11

Rebel without a Pause

N O POLITICIAN EVER WANTS TO LOSE AN ELECTION, AND Miss Agnes Macphail was a born politician. While her defeat in the June 1945 provincial election in Ontario wasn't her first—she had lost twice before—it was especially devastating for several reasons.

First and foremost was that the election losses by Macphail and another female Co-operative Commonwealth Federation (CCF) member of the Ontario legislature, the only women in that ninety-member assembly, were a frustrating reminder of the realities of life in post-war Canada. Hundreds of thousands of returning male veterans were demanding to reclaim jobs they had left when they joined the military, and federal law required employers to rehire them. The women who had held those jobs during the war were expected to revert to being stay-at-home mothers and housewives.

"Your defeat emphasizes the present landslide in women's public life everywhere," a friend lamented in a letter to Macphail. "I never knew a time when . . . women were more needed in public bodies, and when there was a more determined stand to oust them."[1]

The letter writer was correct. Agnes Macphail found herself adrift in a world in which the rights of and life possibilities for women were being called into question in 1945, as many of the economic and social gains that Canadian women had posted during the six years of war, which had always been taken for granted, were now being rolled back.[2]

Compounding Macphail's disappointment were her own unfortunate circumstances. Here she was, a fifty-five-year-old woman who was in failing health after having suffered an attack of cerebral thrombosis, a relatively rare form of stroke. The affliction would plague her the rest of her life. Post-election, Macphail contemplated the very real and sobering possibility that her political career was finished. If so, she feared this could be the end of her struggle to improve the lives of Canadian women and to advance the socialist agenda of "the movement" that was the CCF. Both had been life-long crusades. Macphail was determined to do her utmost to see her efforts hadn't been in vain. She had always been a fighter and a rebel without pause.

The eldest child of a poor farming family from Grey County, Ontario, Macphail had grown up as a tomboy who hated housework. Her talents lay elsewhere—she was a gifted speaker with a quick mind. Both were traits she had inherited from her father. Dougald McPhail[3] raised cattle and was a part-time auctioneer with a ready wit and feisty spirit. Like father, like daughter. On one memorable occasion, a heckler who was taunting Agnes at a political rally called out, "Don't you wish you were a man?" Without missing a breath, she put the man in his place. "Yes, don't *you*?" she demanded.[4]

Agnes Macphail began her working life as a teacher in rural schools before getting involved in politics. In December 1921, at the age of thirty-one, she had bubbled with zeal to spread the progressive gospel and to sing the virtues of freer trade with the United States for agricultural goods. Macphail rode both causes to earn a spot in Canadian history books when she became the first woman to win a seat in Parliament. As such, she was the subject of intense media and public attention. "Her picture gives the impression of a mature woman with heavy features," reported a writer for *Maclean's*—a female writer, it's worth noting. "In reality [Agnes Macphail] looks no more than her [age] and has regular features, her forehead being decidedly of an intellectual type, her skin clear. Fine, and colorless. She is serious-looking—possibly because her life has been one of stern realities—inclined to be brusque, and so far has not been known for any remarkable graciousness of manner."[5]

Whether having a forehead that was "decidedly of an intellectual type" was a good thing or a bad thing was open to debate. What was not was that being a single woman who was earnest by nature, she had found life on Parliament Hill lonely and difficult. Macphail's male colleagues from all parties were condescending. So were other women; some were downright hostile. As one biographer put it, "female members of the press gallery wrote malicious references to her plain navy serge dress and criticized the fledgling politician for not wearing a hat in the House."[6] The badgering and snide comments became so troubling that Macphail stopped dining in the House of Commons cafeteria, losing thirteen pounds (six kilograms) during her first month on the job.

Such travails aside, Macphail represented her constituents' interests with passion, intelligence, and a surprising amount of good humour. In addition to her time in the House, Macphail went on to serve Canada in a variety of important roles, one of which was a stint in the autumn of 1929 as Canada's first female representative to the League of Nations in Geneva.

"What I really admire about her is that she took no guff from the men, and she was quite funny," humorist Will Ferguson has pointed out. "But most importantly, she had an immense impact."[7]

I N MANY WAYS, AGNES Macphail's fortunes, both personal and political, were bound to those of Canada's social-democratic political parties—first to the Prairie-grown Progressive Party, then the United Farmers of Ontario, and then the CCF, of which she was a founding member. While the party's own successes were relatively limited—like those of its intellectual heir, the New Democratic Party—the CCF was to have a profound and enduring impact on Canadian politics and on society. Macphail played an integral role in all of that and in the ideas that would drive the CCF and reshape Canada going forward from 1945.

Founded in Calgary in 1932 as a political coalition of labour, socialist, and progressive groups, the CCF had pushed for economic reforms that its members were convinced would relieve the suffering of the Great Depression. The following July, Macphail and 130 like-minded social activists had gathered in Regina. They arrived by train, by bus, and in "Bennett buggies"—the horse-drawn automobiles that came to symbolize the Great Depression on the prairies. Some even came on foot. Together they had chosen a leader and drafted a manifesto that called for the eradication of capitalism, and the creation of a mixed economy in Canada, one in which a CCF-led federal government would nationalize banks and key industries while weaving together a comprehensive social safety net that would include a universal health and welfare program, employment insurance, old-age pensions, and children's allowances.

Agnes Macphail, Canada's first female MP (1921–40) and one of the first women elected to the Ontario legislature (1945). (LAC, MIKAN no. 3193101)

Fiscal conservatives were aghast; to them, such pronouncements seemed radical, utopian even. Where, they demanded, would the money come from to pay for such grand schemes? Predictably, the CCF's answer to that question lay in a redistribution of wealth that would come by nationalizing key industries and by raising taxes on corporations and on those who were well-off, what today's left-leaning activists refer to as "the One Percent."

Radical though the CCF's collectivist proposals seemed to some people, they had resonated with many Canadians in the darkest days of the Great Depression, at least in principle. Under the leadership of James Shaver (J.S.) Woodsworth, the slight, bearded "saintly socialist" (who, incidentally, was the spitting image of the late British actor Alec Guinness, who played Jedi knight Obi-Wan Kenobi in the original *Star Wars* movie), the CCF had captured seven seats in Parliament in the 1935 general election. The Force evidently was with "the movement"—as its members always referred to it—for the CCF had succeeded in establishing national awareness of its presence, doing so almost in spite of itself. All too often, party members were their own worst enemies.

In 1935, a frustrated Agnes Macphail had withdrawn from the CCF, which was roiled by bitter infighting between hardcore communists, zealous socialists, and moderate social democrats such as her. Sitting in Parliament as the lone representative of the United Farmers of Ontario, Macphail had continued to be sympathetic to the CCF, and in the House she usually voted with that party even though she was no longer a member.

Macphail had been dismayed when in September 1939, the CCF embroiled itself in another one of the seemingly endless internecine battles that are endemic to political parties of the left whenever ideologues butt heads with pragmatists; the CCF was no exception. J.S. Woodsworth, a former Methodist minister who was a staunch pacifist and a starry-eyed idealist, opposed Canadian involvement in the war in Europe. Initially, the CCF's national executive had agreed with that stand; however, when it became clear there was no alternative to war, CCF members sided with English-born Major James W. Coldwell—"Major" was his given name, not a military rank—who argued in favour of Canadian involvement in the fight against the Nazis. "M.J."—who, like Agnes Macphail, was a teacher by vocation—would become party leader following Woodsworth's 1942 death at age sixty-eight. But by that time, the damage had been done; many people were skeptical about the CCF's commitment to the war effort.

What's intriguing and ironic about this is that in 1939, the Canadian population had no great enthusiasm for being involved in "yet another of Europe's endless conflicts." The country's political leaders shared this ambivalence. Prime Minister Mackenzie King thought Poland was as much to blame as Germany, even after the Nazis invaded on September 1, 1939. He also naively continued to believe Hitler couldn't possibly be as evil as his critics insisted. Despite this, once the inevitable decision to fight was made and Canada declared war on Germany for the second time in a quarter century, nationalist fervour flared, at least in English Canada, where Mackenzie King, ever the wily political campaigner, took full advantage.

In the March 1940 general election, the prime minister had portrayed himself as a reluctant warrior who would lead Canada into battle in support of Britain but would never resort to conscription to field an army. Canada's military was to be an all-volunteer force, he pledged. Canadians believed him, and so when the election votes were tallied, the Liberals had won the largest majority in Canadian history to that time; they took 179 seats to the Tories' 39. The CCF managed to hang onto its seven seats and even to add one.

But Agnes Macphail failed to win re-election, finishing a distant third, almost 1,700 votes behind the victorious Liberal who was the husband of one of her closest friends. Macphail had alienated moderate voters and incurred the wrath of the prime minister when she criticized some of the federal government's wartime policies. "I confess

I could not restrain a shout when I heard that Miss Macphail had been beaten," King informed his diary. She had been "nasty at times in the House as she could possibly be."[8]

1945 AND CANADA'S FLAG

From 1867 until 1965, the Red Ensign—the long-time standard of the British merchant marine—served as Canada's de facto flag. It was in 1892 that a warrant of the British Admiralty authorized Canadian ships to fly a Canadianized version of the Red Ensign, one adorned with the provincial coats of arms. Canadian troops fought under this flag at Vimy Ridge in 1917.

In 1921, the Royal Coat of Arms of Canada replaced the provincial coats of arms on this country's version of the Red Ensign. Then in 1924, Prime Minister King asserted national identity when he ordered that the Canadianized "Red Duster" fly above federal government buildings, alongside the Union Jack.

During VE day celebrations, the Red Ensign—Canada's flag during WWII—fluttered atop the Peace Tower flagpole as a salute to the men and women of Canada's military. In September 1945, the King government passed an order-in-council decreeing that the Red Ensign continue to fly above federal buildings until Canadians could agree on a national flag of their own design. That finally happened in February 1965 when the Liberal government of Lester B. Pearson adopted the now-iconic red-and-white Maple Leaf flag (l'Unifolié in French) of today.

Adding insult to injury, Macphail had spent $2,500 of her own money on her re-election campaign. "I told the people the truth at all times, and they say the truth will make you free. Well, it certainly made me free," she said. "I have no idea what I'm going to do [now]."⁹

Then, urged on by pioneer suffragette Nellie McClung and other political allies and friends, Macphail declared herself to be a candidate in a late-summer federal by-election in Saskatoon. That hasty bid to return to Parliament in a riding to which she had few ties also failed. Shunted to the sidelines, Macphail spent the next three years in the political wilderness. What's more, her efforts to reinvent herself by finding suitable full-time work away from politics were difficult. While Mackenzie King made a show of being sympathetic to her plight and helped her get interviews for federal civil service jobs, she landed none of them. This left her biding her time and struggling to pay her bills. She did so by doing some work for the CCF and by writing a triweekly *Globe and Mail* column on farming matters, for which she earned $50 a week; that relatively generous payment was a reflection of her celebrity as much as it was a testament to her journalistic skills.

BY 1943, AFTER THREE lost years, Agnes Macphail had been as restless as the Georgian Bay winds that often buffeted her family's old wood-frame house in Grey County, where she was living. Despite her tenuous health—she had suffered another one of her recurring attacks of cerebral thrombosis—she was itching to return to politics. Macphail, who was nothing if not stubborn, ignored doctors' suggestions that she take life easy. "So, I don't live long," she announced. "I'll live what's left doing what I want to do."¹⁰

She also drew motivation from the perception that the CCF's fortunes had never looked brighter, nationally or provincially. Buoyed by this, Macphail accepted an overture from Ontario CCF leader Ted Jolliffe, who invited her to stand in the August 4 election as the party's candidate in the Toronto riding of York East. This predominantly blue-collar area was home to many factories that were producing war materials, and as Macphail was a star candidate with a high name recognition, her pro-labour campaign messages found a receptive audience. She and another female CCF candidate from a neighbouring Toronto riding, Rae Luckock, became the first women elected to the Ontario legislature.

The CCF surged from having no members in the ninety-seat house to having thirty-four. That was enough to win the party status as the official opposition, just four seats fewer than the governing George Drew–led Conservatives. Drew, a fifty-one-year-old Upper Canada College alumnus was a veteran of World War I (he liked to be addressed as "Colonel"), a staunch monarchist, and a champion of free enterprise. Tall, lean, and habitually attired in a natty navy blue or grey double-breasted suit, he was the very model of a Conservative politician.

Drew was also either very arrogant or shy, depending on the perspective of the observer who was assessing his personality; he could be charming or cold as ice and ruthless as a mob boss. Media wags, having pronounced Drew to be "the handsomest man in Canadian politics," prompted Liberal leader Mitch Hepburn to taunt the Conservative leader, labelling him "Miss Canada of the [Ontario] legislature." Agnes Macphail held a similarly disdainful opinion of the premier, albeit one that was less chauvinistic. "I don't like George," she once admitted, "but that shouldn't bother him. He likes himself so much."[11]

Drew had campaigned in 1943 on a promise to introduce programs of free dental care and universal medicare for Ontario residents. However, once elected—unbelievable though it might seem for a politician to do so—Drew promptly forgot his campaign promises and amended his priorities. In September 1944, he had introduced "the Drew Regulation," a measure that made it compulsory for Ontario schools to provide one hour of religious instruction each week.[12] Not that any of this perfidy mattered in the long run. Unbeknownst to Drew or anyone else at that time, fate would decree that the Conservatives had launched what would be one of the most remarkable and unprecedented political dynasties in Canadian history—a forty-two-year run as Ontario's governing party.

Drew's disingenuousness irked her, but Agnes Macphail had her own priorities. She was tired of being treated as a curiosity because of her gender, and she resented the predictable media fuss about her being one of the first women elected to the Ontario provincial assembly. What's more, as she confided to friends, although she was hailed as a star in the CCF caucus, she regarded her presence at Queen's Park as a political comedown. As Macphail biographers Doris French and Margaret Stewart put it, "Agnes was rather like a world-famous actress who had slipped back into playing summer stock. Everything seemed very small and rather dingy."[13]

Despite this, she was happy to be back in the political fray at a time when the CCF's fortunes were surging. The results of a public opinion poll taken a few weeks after the Ontario election had given her and other party faithful ample reason to be optimistic. That snapshot of voters' preferences suggested the CCF had leapt ahead of the Liberals and Conservatives in popular support. This revelation stunned many people—none more than Prime Minister Mackenzie King. In the west, forty-one per cent of decided voters said they supported the CCF federally, and just twenty-three per cent the Liberals. In Ontario, the CCF led the Liberals by six percentage points: thirty-two to twenty-six.

All politicians—especially those who are trailing in opinion polls—are fond of insisting that the only poll that counts is the one on election day. While that is ultimately true, for Liberal and Conservative supporters alike, the 1943 Ontario election results and the findings of that public opinion poll seemed to portend the coming of an even bigger political storm. Those fears had become reality in June 1944 when the CCF swept to power in Saskatchewan. Under the leadership of spunky socialist T.C. "Tommy" Douglas, a silver-tongued young Baptist minister, the party won forty-seven of fifty-two seats in the provincial legislature to oust a tired Liberal government.

The Saskatchewan election result sent political shockwaves reverberating across the country. "The fact that a so-called socialist government is now governing anywhere in this country—a fact inconceivable a few years ago—alters the structure and balance of national politics, marks, if it did not create, a permanent change in the course of our history," a writer for *Maclean's* magazine reported.[14]

In 1961, Tommy Douglas was destined to become the first leader of the federal New Democratic Party (NDP), which succeeded the CCF as Canada's party of the left. Today, he is remembered for two things. One is that he was the grandfather of popular television and film actor Kiefer Sutherland. The other is that in his time as premier of Saskatchewan, he became the father of medicare, which since its creation in 1962 has become one of the sacred pillars among Canada's social welfare programs.[15] As it has turned out, that latter distinction (medicare) has proved definitive. Viewers of a 2004 CBC television series on "the greatest Canadian of all time"—which was more fun than scholarship—would accord Douglas that honour ahead of such home-grown luminaries as Terry Fox, Wayne Gretzky, and Pierre Trudeau.

In passing, it's also worth noting that "the greatest Canadian of all time" was, in fact, Scottish born, and despite his piety, he was no saint. During his student days, Douglas had considered eugenics as a possible solution to some of society's troubles. In 1933, while earning a master of arts degree in sociology from McMaster University, Douglas had written a thesis in which he made the case for sterilizing "mental defectives and those incurably diseased." To be fair, in a day when so many people rush to view events, people, and ideas through the lens of modern sensibilities, the views Douglas touted were widely held at that time. Two Canadian provinces and thirty-two American states had passed sexual sterilization legislation in the 1920s and 1930s. But the Douglas governments in Saskatchewan never did, despite being urged to do so by two official reviews of the province's mental health care system; by putting eugenics theories into practice, the Nazis caused much reconsideration of this pseudoscience as a way to "uplift society."[16]

What's significant here is that Douglas's electoral success in Saskatchewan gave CCF supporters high hopes that the movement was due for a major breakthrough in Ontario. When Premier George Drew called a snap election for June 4, 1945, in hopes of winning a Conservative majority, Agnes Macphail and her CCF comrades were eager and ready for the fight. Confident that the righteousness of its cause ensured it was bound for victory, the CCF hit the hustings running.

The Allies had declared victory in the war in Europe a month earlier, and hundreds of thousands of veterans were returning home, many of them scornful of Mackenzie King because of his reluctance to institute conscription for overseas service. They were keen to reap the rewards for the sacrifices they had made in Canada's war effort—even though those rewards came from a prime minister they reviled.

Joe Levitt, a young Jewish communist from Montreal who joined the Canadian army to fight Hitler and won a Military Medal for his bravery, summarized the feeling of many veterans. "The propaganda of the 1930s had always been that the government had no money, couldn't do anything about it, and that's the way things were," he said. "But the war taught people a lot. It was a matter of common sense and simple to understand that if the government could find money for war, then they could find it for peace."[17] The CCF understood this and promised to see that it happened. But there was a problem, at least in Ontario.

Premier Drew and many of his corporate supporters had spent the previous two years red-baiting, attacking the CCF as "closet communists." Much of the political muck that Drew hurled the CCF's way had been secretly provided by a police officer in the Special Investigations Unit of the Ontario Provincial Police (OPP). That man was supposed to have been sniffing out wartime German spies and would-be saboteurs. Instead, he devoted his time and energies to digging into the backgrounds of Ontario opposition MPPs, paying special attention to members of the CCF caucus. When Agnes Macphail got wind of this from an OPP contact, she alerted CCF party leader Ted Jolliffe. With just nine days to go before the election, he reacted quickly, sounding the alarm in a May 24 radio address. He alleged the OPP were engaged in "Gestapo-like" behaviour, spying at the behest of Premier George Drew on 16,000 left-leaning Ontario residents. This was "the most infamous story in the history of Ontario," a breathless Jolliffe declared.[18]

Ontario voters chose to believe their dapper premier when he denied all wrongdoing. Amid a rising tide of suspicion and fear of communists here in Canada and south of the border, public opinion turned against Ted Jolliffe and the CCF. Drew's Conservatives triumphed, winning a solid majority in the June 4 election. They increased their seat count in the Ontario legislature from thirty-eight to sixty-six. The CCF, which had entered the election campaign with thirty-four caucus members, was reduced to just eight.

Not willing to let the allegations against him drop, Drew convened a Royal Commission to be chaired by Ontario Supreme Court judge A.M. LeBel. On July 6, 1945, Drew appeared as a witness on the twelfth day of the commission's hearings. Public interest in the premier's testimony was intense, and members of the public, civil servants, politicians, and reporters packed the Toronto City Hall courtroom where the hearings were being held. Responding to questions about what he knew about OPP surveillance activities and why government documents of possible relevance were nowhere to be found, Drew shook his well-coiffured noggin. After clearing his throat and straightening his tie, the premier flashed a toothy smile and insisted he knew nothing about any of these allegations. In fact, Drew hastened to add, like all Canadians, he was shocked by any suggestion of possible OPP wrongdoing. Shocked.[19]

"Honest George" got away with perjuring himself. It would be three decades before the truth came out, and by then the wily former premier, who went on to lead the federal Conservative party to election defeats in 1949 and 1953, was dead and gone.[20]

The Royal Commission debacle and the CCF's disappointing showing in the June 4, 1945, Ontario election and in the federal vote that was held a week later left Agnes Macphail feeling disillusioned and spent. It had been a dismal year in every regard for her, for her party, and for the socialist movement in Canada. David Lewis, the labour lawyer who served as the long-time national secretary of the CCF and was one of the architects of the NDP in 1961, said it succinctly when he wrote that "1945 was the year that decided the fate of the CCF."[21]

After the Great Depression, a collectivist mindset had prompted Canadian men and women to volunteer for the military by the hundreds of thousands. However, a renewed individualism and acquisitiveness were quickly eroding and muscling aside that shared sense of purpose. Both were reactions to the long years of hardship that had preceded the war. Now suddenly, the country was awash in a plenty that was intoxicating. The result was a tsunami of consumerism and a "nesting" urge—to borrow a term from today's lexicon—the likes of which the country had never seen before.

For Agnes Macphail, adding insult to the sting of electoral defeat and the pain of her own chronic health issues, the landlord of her rental home in Toronto sold the property out from under her (and a troubled niece for whom she was caring). Macphail had no choice but to find another place to live. All this was too much for her just then. With the support of a sympathetic benefactor, Macphail retreated to Mexico, where she spent several weeks recuperating physically and emotionally. Then, with nowhere else to go, she returned to her family home in Grey County. The next three years were bleak, unproductive ones for Agnes Macphail.

I N JUNE 1948, UNABLE to resist the urge and having few other options, Macphail would re-enter the political fray when she accepted yet another invitation from CCF organizers in Ontario to make yet another bid for election in her old York East riding. To the surprise of most pundits, Macphail won her old seat again, and the CCF recovered from its 1945 electoral defeat, at least temporarily, winning twenty-one seats and reclaiming its status as the official opposition. Making the victory extra sweet was the fact George Drew went down to defeat in his own riding. To his chagrin, the premier was beaten by a temperance advocate.[22]

Agnes Macphail would serve three years in the Ontario legislature. There she resumed her fight for the rights of farmers, industrial workers, women, and prison inmates. Among her many career accomplishments, one of which she was most proud was her role in reforming Canada's penal system. For many years, Macphail had championed the idea of change, arguing that prisoners—male and female—should be reformed and provided with educational opportunities, rather than merely being punished. To this end, in the late 1940s, Macphail was instrumental in helping to establish the Elizabeth Fry Society in Canada, serving as the honorary president of its newly formed Toronto chapter.[23]

Despite her dedication to her work as a member of the Ontario legislature, her devotion to the CCF movement, and her spirited advocacy of progressive causes, in 1951 Macphail would suffer another electoral defeat. The CCF would be all but wiped out, winning just two seats in the legislature. This ended Macphail's political career. There were rumours she would be appointed to the Senate, but nothing came of it. That's probably just as well because, as she quipped, "The Senate, as at present constituted, to me is a huge joke. I couldn't sit in it and spend time laughing at myself."[24] Agnes Macphail would never have the time or the chance to do that. On February 13, 1954, a few weeks short of her sixty-fourth birthday, she suffered a fatal heart attack.

Tributes to Macphail poured in. Few public figures in Canada had a wider swath of friends and acquaintances across the political spectrum. Interestingly, although Macphail had involved herself in a dizzying variety of progressive causes, she had always insisted she was a *person* first, a woman second. If she is remembered today, it is primarily as the first woman elected to Parliament and as a pioneer in the struggle for women's rights and gender equality. A farmer who was one of her long-time Grey County supporters spoke the words many people were thinking when he observed, "She plowed the road for women today."[25]

There's no question Agnes Macphail did that, and so much more. In retrospect, her legacy—like that of the CCF itself—would prove to be greater and more pervasive than is readily apparent. Macphail was a powerful voice within the CCF for more than two decades. If not for the party's impact on public opinion and on the Mackenzie King government, it's doubtful Canadians today would enjoy the same extensive social safety net that is so integral to this country's national identity and to what it means to be Canadian.

The war had demonstrated that Canada could produce goods in profusion and that billions of dollars worth could be given away to our allies. Could the country not do as much for its own citizens?

—J.L. Granatstein et al., *Nation: Canada Since Confederation* (1983)

CHAPTER 12

"A Fair Shake" for Veterans

THE LATE JAMES GRAY WAS ONE OF WESTERN CANADA'S favourite historians. He was also an unabashed optimist. Recalling the hardships of prairie life during the Great Depression, Gray mused that the experience "brought out more of the best than it did the worst in people ... [and] that if left alone, [they] tend to work out their own problems."[1]

When he died in 1998, the Manitoba-born-and-bred writer was ninety-two. Gray had grown up and come of age during the pioneer era on the prairies. That was a time when the prevailing ethos was that any homesteader could build a good life for himself and his family simply through hard work, self-reliance, and a dash of luck. That may have been a recipe for success in the 1880s, but the cruel economic realities of the Great Depression shattered that myth. They also prompted many Canadians to question the values of an economic system that exalted the individual and put the pursuit of profits ahead of the welfare of its citizens.

In the United States, President Franklin D. Roosevelt's New Deal had fundamentally altered the social fabric of the nation by expanding the role of big government. Meanwhile, across the Atlantic, the jack-booted legions that marched in support of Hitler, Mussolini, Stalin, and the other dictators who "made the trains run on time" insisted that might was right, and that hating (and eliminating) "others"—Jews, Slavs, homosexuals, gypsies, people with mental or physical challenges, and more—would make the world a better place. Simple solutions to complex problems have always appealed to simple minds. Those frustrated, embittered souls who fear they are being left behind too often tend to care only about the bread-and-butter issues of their own lives.

In Canada in the 1930s, Liberal and Conservative governments alike were loath to emulate what Mackenzie King referred to as Roosevelt's "experiment." To follow the American president's lead would have plunged Canada into deficit spending, and that was something this country's leaders abhorred.

King justified his inertia by pointing to the limits of federal power, insisting that the kind of measures at the core of the New Deal were unconstitutional in this country because they probably would intrude on provincial powers. Most Canadians begrudgingly accepted that explanation for a while. How patient or accepting would people have been if they had known that between 1930 and 1936, Ottawa spent more money servicing the debt of publicly owned Canadian National Railways than on providing unemployment relief?[2]

As the misery had continued year after year, the choruses of opposition voices at both ends of the political spectrum had grown ever louder and more impatient with Ottawa's failure to take decisive action to lessen the effects of the economic malaise. Some of these voices were radical; others remained reasoned and patient—being responsible. That's a credo most Canadians live by.

On the political right, the most prominent group was the Prairie-based, evangelically hued populist Social Credit Party, "the Socreds." On the left, it had been the CCF, which had its roots in the agrarian west but also aspired to appeal to urban voters.

One thing the Socreds, the CCF, and swing progressives such as Agnes Macphail had in common was a willingness to work within "the

KEN CUTHBERTSON

system." All had continued to believe that peaceful fundamental change was possible if only they could win power by way of the ballot box.

Where the CCF was concerned, the faith "the movement's" true believers had in the electoral process was rooted in the fact that so many of their leaders—Tommy Douglas, J.S. Woodsworth, and M.J. Coldwell, in particular—hailed from the United Kingdom. There, politicians right and left tended to be sympathetic, if not downright receptive, to the need for the government to guarantee a basic level of social security. As a 1937 *Maclean's* magazine editorial pointed out, in the U.K., "Unemployment and sickness insurance, provision of medical attention, old-age pensions have long been established, and experience is correcting what faults the system had in the beginning."[3]

Things were a tad different in Canada where self-sufficiency was a cherished virtue. In frontier times, when most people lived in isolated rural areas, it was a necessity. Friends helped friends. Neighbours helped neighbours. There was a strong element of shame in accepting handouts from strangers or in being beholden to them. Churches, local governments, well-off individuals, and civic groups provided what little public charity there was available. And because health care and other public welfare needs were "close to home," they were regarded as being matters for provincial or local governments to deal with. That was an underlying principle in the division of powers in the British North America Act, the 1867 playbook for Canadian federalism.

All that began to change post-Confederation, as industrialization and urbanization picked up steam. Then in response to the carnage of World War I, Ottawa started offering pensions to needy veterans, while the provinces provided financial aid to the widows and children of fallen soldiers. With eligibility investigations being "by necessity slow and careful,"[4] the number of widows who received government cheques each month wasn't large. In Ontario in 1920, just 400 women were doing so, and the amounts were a pittance. A widow with two dependent children received $40 per month; each additional child brought an extra $5. At a time when the average monthly industrial

204

wage was $125, a widow's pension didn't go far. About all that can be said is it was only slightly better than nothing.

Apart from modest payouts—sometimes in the form of land grants or scrip—that veterans collected, publicly funded pensions were a novelty in Canada. The idea of anyone receiving "money for doing nothing" took some getting used to, especially for those who had been reared to respect the Calvinist work ethic.

It didn't help that there were the inevitable bureaucratic anomalies and screw-ups as pensions were rolled out. Consider, for example, the case of one Florence Leach of Ottawa. She qualified for not one but two widow's pensions after having lost two husbands in World War I. The first one died on the battlefield in France. The unfortunate Mrs. Leach remarried, only to have hubby number two fall victim to tuberculosis he'd contracted while serving king and country. Mrs. Leach's sad situation was "[one] for which there is no precedent in the Dominion," as the *Toronto Daily Star* reported.[5] (In case you're wondering, there is no record of whether or not the star-crossed Mrs. Leach married a third World War I veteran and eventually qualified to triple-dip for another monthly pension cheque.)

By 1927, the feds were providing provincial governments with three-quarters of the funding for the old-age pension cheques that "worthy" seniors—those who were at least age seventy and destitute— were collecting. That largesse was partially extended to the blind a decade later when the government rolled out pensions for those who were over the age of forty. Of course, such limited measures did nothing to relieve the suffering of the millions of people who were in dire straits in the 1930s.

There was no end to horror stories of how tough times were— of children who were too hungry to go to school because at home it wasn't their day to eat breakfast, of starving men and women who collapsed on the streets, and of babies in their cribs who froze to death on cold winter nights in their unheated homes.

Barbara (née Robson) Fitsell grew up in Sydney, Nova Scotia, where her father worked at the local steel mill. "My family was fortunate because my dad had a job at 'the plant;' that's what we called it. Money was scarce, but we always had enough to eat." Not every family did, and many of Barbara's schoolmates were hungry, desperately so. "I remember one day when my mother gave me some money to run to the butcher shop to buy sausages. On the way home, three or four girls I recognized from school waylaid me. They snatched away the sausages I was carrying and started eating them right there. Raw sausages!

"I was crying when I got home and told my mother what had happened. All she said was, 'Oh my, those poor girls must have been starving.' I suppose they were."[6]

Patience has its limits in the face of such misery and suffering, even among Canadians. The longer the economic woes of the Great Depression dragged on, the louder were the demands for Ottawa to "*do something.*" Federal politicians and bureaucrats slowly began to listen. When some senior civil servants became converts to the principles of Keynesian economics, it was a game changer.

Simply put, what British economist John Maynard Keynes had suggested was that when the free market economy falters, the government should step in to prime the pump with increased spending on social programs and public works initiatives while also cutting taxes. The theory was that doing so would stimulate consumer demand for goods and services and encourage businesses to use borrowed money to expand their operations.

The nub of Keynesian economic theory was acceptance of the notion that government should spend money it didn't have. The thought of borrowing to fund social programs or public works projects set alarm bells ringing in Mackenzie King's cranial vault. "It was clear that the members [of the Liberal caucus] were all wanting to have things done for others; whole families to have pensions now, etc.," he told his diary as late as September 1943. "More and more of expenditures though less and less of taxation."[7]

Deficit spending was—and remains—anathema to fiscal conservatives. It gave William Lyon Mackenzie King the willies (pun intended!).
Yet in 1918, when he was forty-four and still idealistic, King had mused
in his book, *Industry and Humanity*, about the value of government
social welfare programs. The gap between theory and action can be
daunting, however. When the time finally came that he was in a position to implement some of his ideas, he had second thoughts. By then,
King was a fusty sexagenarian who was content to sacrifice the social
democratic ideals of his youth on the altar of political expediency.
Although in conversations with his diary, King still professed his belief
in the value of social welfare, he wasn't willing to take bold, decisive
action to make it a reality—especially if it involved spending public dollars or risking political support. As they say, "Practical politics
ignores the facts."

The shift in thinking that prompted King to review his own beliefs
and to reconsider the need for a government-created social safety
net was evolutionary, not revolutionary. The impetus came from two
sources. One was the advice King was receiving from his political
aides and senior Ottawa mandarins, many of whom were converts to
Keynes's economic theories; the other was Canada's wartime drift to
the political left. It was this latter imperative and the growing electoral
threat posed by the emboldened CCF that would prove decisive for
King. His first priority was always doing whatever it took to win the
next election and hold onto power; at least, it was until King sensed the
end of his own political career was in sight.

T HE UPPER TIER OF Canada's civil service during the Second World
War "was dominated by a coterie of men of undisputed ability and
great power."[8] These bureaucrats—what the British often referred to as
"statesman administrators"—were white males, most of whom were
young, well educated, Protestant, and middle class. They also tended
to be relatively progressive politically and more culturally attuned than

was the prime minister, who lived in his own cloistered world. This made senior federal civil servants, specifically those whose opinions carried the most weight, sensitive to the changing tides of public opinion and the issues that were of concern to ordinary Canadians.

It was Queen's University economics-professor-turned-civil-servant Oscar D. Skelton—dubbed "O.D." by friends and colleagues—who was responsible for hiring several of these bright young civil servants and for creating a hothouse culture in which they could thrive.

Skelton had been a friend and biographer of Wilfrid Laurier, and so it was not at all surprising that he got along well with Mackenzie King or that in 1926 King had appointed him as the Under-Secretary of State for External Affairs. Skelton would fill that all-important position, serving Liberal and Conservative governments alike until 1941, when a heart attack ended his life at age sixty-three. It's with good reason that history remembers O.D. Skelton as an architect of the Canadian public service. He changed civil service hiring policies, instituted examinations for potential employees, and started the practice of hiring on merit rather than partisan connections or nepotism. These measures changed the civil service forever and for the better.

Among Skelton's brightest young recruits was Clifford Clark, a former student who had become a colleague in Queen's University's economics department. Civil servants tend not to be sexy, colourful, outspoken, or interesting to anyone other than policy wonks and political insiders. But Clark merits attention because he played such a vital behind-the-scenes role in shaping post-war Canada.

A native of the Ottawa Valley community of Martintown, Clark was chubby-cheeked, mild-mannered, and insatiably curious. Yet journalists who interviewed him invariably came away convinced he was as dull as a county squire. At the same time, it was clear he was brilliant—he had earned degrees from Queen's and Harvard—and he was a workaholic. Clark put in long hours, often eating meals at his desk as he worked late into the night. His only leisure activities were playing bridge and fishing.

Clifford Clark. (Queen's University Archives)

Clark's politics were difficult to discern. The consummate civil servant, he seldom voiced his personal opinions, and he shunned the spotlight. His biographer described him as being "a new Liberal."[9] He was that because he believed in capitalism and the free market system, but he also recognized that the state had important roles to play in society and the economy. In both regards, he was progressive to a point. As a Conservative friend said of him in 1945, "[Clark] is too much of a realist, too hard-headedly specific, to be taken in by the pious hopes and clichés of the starry-eyed reformers, yet too much of a practical idealist to not be, in sentiment at any rate, on the side of the underdog."[10]

It was at O.D. Skelton's urging that Prime Minister R.B. Bennett invited Clark to be one of his aides at the 1932 Imperial Economic Conference. Clark made such a strong impression there that the prime minister offered him a job. The story goes that when Bennett asked Charlotte Whitton, another Queen's grad who was a staunchly partisan Conservative, about this idea, Whitton praised Clark's abilities but cautioned that he was a Grit. "But I need him!" Bennett insisted. His decision to offer Clark the job of Deputy Minister of the Department of Finance would prove to be a wise one.

Over the course of the next twenty years, Clark would put an indelible stamp on the federal civil service while quietly becoming one of Ottawa's most powerful and influential unelected officials. He was an *éminence grise* if ever there was one.

It was Clark who helped establish the Bank of Canada in 1934 and who was responsible for making Finance one of the most powerful of federal government departments. And if O.D. Skelton was the architect of Canada's modern civil service, it was Clark who actually built it when he persuaded other bright young economists to enter the public service. Because his approach to work was collegial, he wisely listened to and heeded some of the advice his recruits offered.

Not surprisingly, Clifford Clark and Mackenzie King hit it off. Being cautious by nature, the two saw eye to eye on many issues. And "because King was not particularly at home in financial matters, and his Ministers of Finance were strongly conservative,"[11] Clark emerged as one of the prime minister's most trusted advisors where money matters were concerned. He became a power behind the throne. At the same time, unlike the prime minister, Clark remained open to fresh ideas and was flexible in his thinking. It was typical of Clark that while he had argued against wage controls at the end of the Great War, he would help implement them during World War II. His views on government involvement in the economy were constantly evolving.

It was also Clark who in 1940 helped sway Mackenzie King toward establishing a contributory unemployment insurance plan. This was something a Royal Commission on Industrial Relations had recommended in 1919; however, the idea was shelved until 1935 when Conservative prime minister R.B. Bennett tried to act on it. He was stymied when the courts ruled the enabling legislation infringed on provincial authority and was unconstitutional. Ironically, it wasn't until August 1940, when the economy was humming and unemployment was no longer a pressing concern, that Mackenzie King resurrected the idea. As always, King thought strategically. He did so at a time when all those who had jobs could pay into the plan and build a surplus that would be a hedge against future needs. This was possible only after negotiations with the provinces that led to a constitutional amendment. Fundamental change *is* possible in the Canadian federal system, but it's never easy.

Mackenzie King was all too aware of that when in the waning months of the war in Europe, he realized he'd have to focus on reconstruction and the needs of the more than a million veterans who fully expected to be rewarded, given "a fair shake," for the sacrifices they and their families had made during the war. By mid-1944, the government had demobilized a third of the men and women in the Canadian military, and these people were growing restive. This prompted the Liberal government to set to work in earnest developing plans for possible government programming that would ensure a smooth transition to peace and a continuation of the wartime prosperity that Canadians had gotten used to. Doing so would be a tall order.

A T THE OUTBREAK OF war in September 1939, most people assumed the conflict would be over quickly. Clifford Clark wasn't convinced, and so he struck a committee of senior civil servants who set about drawing up plans for the export of food and war supplies to Great Britain. As the fighting intensified, the mandate of this group, the Economic Advisory Committee (EAC), evolved and grew to include planning for post-war reconstruction and transitioning the economy from one that made things that blow up and kill people to one that made toasters, toys, and sundry consumer goods.

Politicians love committees as much as bureaucrats do, and so in December 1939, the federal Cabinet followed the lead of the bureaucrats when it created its own Committee on Demobilization and

Re-Establishment under the chairmanship of Minister of Pensions and National Health Ian Mackenzie. It was Mackenzie who in March 1941 had established a blue-ribbon advisory committee of business leaders, labour heads, and academics.

The Scottish-born Mackenzie, being a strong social democrat, had tasked this group with a mission that was near and dear to his heart: come up with recommendations on steps the government might take to ensure that Canada didn't slip back into an economic depression at war's end. The person Mackenzie had chosen to chair his committee was left-leaning economist F. Cyril James. At thirty-seven, he was—as *Maclean's* magazine described him—McGill University's "boy principal."[12]

James, English-born and a graduate of the London School of Economics (LSE), believed what Canada needed most was a robust government-backed social safety net of pensions and health and employment insurance programs. He wasn't alone in his thinking, not after what transpired in London in December 1942.

Nowadays, any mention of the British capital in the war years summons up clichéd scenes of Blitz-ravaged London streets, derby-hatted Winston Churchill with cigar clenched in his teeth as he flashes two fingers in a "V for victory" sign, and Spitfire fighter planes duelling with their Luftwaffe enemies high in the English skies. While those images are well founded, it's equally true that even in those dark days, there were government officials and academics who—like Clifford Clark—had already started to plan for the post-war era. With that in mind, the British government had invited Oxford University professor William Beveridge to chair an interdepartmental committee that would evaluate the United Kingdom's social service programs and recommend improvements.

Sir William, a tweedy sixty-nine-year-old economist—who in photos looks like a jovial version of British actor Terence Stamp—was England's leading authority on labour and social security issues. Like then-Saskatchewan CCF premier Tommy Douglas, Beveridge was a believer in eugenics. While this belief did not affect the professor's views on social safety nets, it does reveal, yet again, how widespread interest in "controlled human breeding" was as a way to build a better world.

Also, Beveridge was a Fabian socialist. That's a descriptor you don't hear much anymore; however, it was a hugely influential school of political thought in *fin de siècle* London and in the early decades of the twentieth century. The Fabian Society's proponents, who included such luminaries as George Bernard Shaw and Sidney and Beatrice Webb, believed in "evolutionary socialism." Nice and easy does it. The society's name honoured the Roman general Fabius Cunctator, who relied on patience and the avoidance of pitched battles as the best way to outlast and triumph over his enemies. Agnes Macphail, Tommy Douglas, and other CCF leaders subscribed to many of the same ideas, only under a different name.

That 300-page report that William Beveridge delivered to the British government created a sensation when it appeared in December 1942. Understandably so. The visionary ideas on social welfare reform that Beveridge and his committee put forward offered the promise of freedom from want for all those who lacked the means of healthy subsistence.

Media interest in the *Report on Social Insurance and Allied Services* was so intense and there was such a demand for copies that the line-up outside the government printing office in London was more than half a mile (one kilometre) long. Despite the report's soporific title, it became a runaway bestseller, with more than half a million copies sold.

News of the Beveridge Report appeared on page one of many Canadian newspapers. The *Globe and Mail* described it as revolutionary, opining that "in the variety of benefits it envisages and the range of population it would shelter from birth to death, it is the outline of the most sweeping plan for government sponsored social security ever set forth."[13]

Mackenzie King was in Washington on December 5, 1942, for meetings with President Roosevelt when news of the Beveridge Report broke. King informed his diary that "at dinner, we had quite a talk about [it]. The President said the Beveridge Report had made a real impression in this country. The thought of insurance from cradle to grave. That seems to be a line that will appeal."[14]

Although King found FDR's suggestion intriguing, what really grabbed his attention was a smug assumption that the formula for "industrial peace and order in democracies" he had touted in his 1918 book, *Industry and Humanity*—namely "the fundamental doctrines of Jesus [which were] love to God and thy neighbor and the brotherhood of man"—had influenced and inspired Beveridge. Without mentioning or even explaining any of this, King suddenly reminded Roosevelt over the dinner table that a few years earlier, he had presented the president with an inscribed copy of *Industry and Humanity*. Even if Roosevelt had kept that tome in his pile of bedtime reading (which in all likelihood he hadn't) or used it as a doorstop (which was more likely), the president surely must have wondered why King had mentioned this over mashed potatoes.

This wasn't the end of King's interest in the Beveridge Report, which he reportedly never actually got around to reading. That wouldn't stop the prime minister from making sure an oblique reference to the report appeared in the Speech from the Throne, which the Governor General read to open the new session of Parliament in January 1943. "My ministers believe that a comprehensive national scheme of social insurance should be worked out at once which will constitute a charter of social security for the whole of Canada," the Earl of Athlone announced as he outlined the government's agenda.[15]

King knew the Ian Mackenzie–sponsored James Committee was busy striking various subcommittees, doing research, and gathering information for a report that well might outline some possible options for a suite of enhanced or new federal social security programs. King didn't have much faith in James—whom he had dismissed as "an ass of a fellow"[16]—but he nonetheless hoped the committee's recommendations might offer useful homegrown answers to some of the same questions William Beveridge had considered. That seemed like a logical approach. After all, the person to whom Cyril James had entrusted the all-important task of writing his committee's report was one of Beveridge's former students.

Social insurance is a floor to alleviate poverty and prevent people from becoming destitute. But it is only one of the many elements for a successful post-war reconstruction.
—Leonard Marsh, 1943

CHAPTER 13

The Marsh Report

THE ODDS ARE HIGH THAT YOU'VE NEVER HEARD OF Leonard Marsh. To go even farther out on a limb, it's a safe bet that if you asked a hundred Canadians on the street who he was, not one person could identify him. Marsh is unheralded, but he was an important figure in the story of modern Canada. More than one historian has described him as a chief architect of the distinctly Canadian social welfare system that helps define this country.

Born in London, England, in 1906, Marsh was the son of a railway porter. Despite his working-class background, he grew up with dreams of becoming a musician. That all changed when he was seventeen. "I became so keenly interested in economics and social questions [that] I dropped all other ambitions," Marsh recalled.[1] His heart was set on becoming an economist. Now, that's not a goal of many young people coming out of the gate. But it was for Marsh, and he was serious about it.

A gifted student, Marsh won scholarship offers from both Oxford University and the University of London. However, he opted to attend the London School of Economics, an institution that Fabian socialists had founded in 1895. There Marsh continued to excel academically when he came under the tutelage of William Beveridge. Marsh graduated in 1928 with first-class honours and at the top of his class.

With his round wire-rimmed glasses, chiselled features, high cheek bones, and swept-back hair, the lanky Marsh looked every inch the young leftist intellectual that he was. He was comfortable with that, for he described himself as "obviously radical, [but] . . . fundamentally a social scientist, passionately devoted to education."[2] That self-analysis was bang on.

After working in London for a couple of years, Marsh immigrated to Montreal in 1930. On the strength of a recommendation from Beveridge, he was hired to head a McGill University social science research study on employment. That initiative, funded by a $110,000 grant from the Rockefeller Foundation of New York, was one for which Marsh was well suited. He was bright, dedicated, and meticulous. He was also zealous about teaching and writing, especially when it came to spreading the socialist gospel. Having rejected Marxism as being too dogmatic, Marsh succeeded because he was never strident. As historian Michael Horn emphasized, "He acknowledged a Fabian influence early in his intellectual development and believed that it helped shape his faith in social reform. But [Marsh] insisted that his researches into and analyses of Canadian conditions were fundamentally empirical."[3]

During the decade he spent at McGill, in the winter of 1931–32, Marsh was a co-founder of a group called the League for Social Reconstruction. As one of Canada's first left-oriented intellectual groups, it developed a Canadian riff on socialism that historians who study such things describe as "reformist and constitutional while being basically committed to thorough-going changes in the distribution of income, wealth, and power."[4]

Marsh would write several influential academic papers, and in 1940 he would produce a ground-breaking study titled *Employment Research*. "In a decade when unemployment rarely fell below ten per cent, and when it and unemployment relief were subjects of intense public concerns," Horn explained, Marsh's study was "the first attempt to provide a comprehensive statistical analysis of unemployment in Canada."[5] Marsh also delved into Montreal's unemployment situation, which during the Great Depression was among the grimmest in the country. At the time—after a decade of economic hardship—some of Marsh's analysis of the relationship between class and unemployment was provocative, too much so for some people, it seems. When the Rockefeller Foundation funding for the McGill social science research study was not renewed, Marsh found himself out of work, but he had caught the eye of McGill principal Cyril James.

It was James who offered Marsh the job of researching and writing the final report of the federal government's Advisory Committee on Reconstruction, which he was heading. Marsh's challenge was to devise recommendations on some ways Canada in the post-war era might create "adequate employment opportunities for the returning soldiers, as well as for the men and women who will no longer be required in the municipal factories."[6]

With the outcome of the war in Europe becoming increasingly clear, those issues were coming into focus. In Ottawa, it was a preoccupation for bureaucrats and politicians, especially for Mackenzie King, and there was no time to waste in preparing for peace. A federal election was pending in mid-1945, and the prime minister was concerned about a recurrence of the post-war labour unrest that had rocked Canada in 1919. In addition, the prospect of hundreds of thousands of resentful, angry veterans returning home just in time to vote was unsettling.

Mackenzie King knew his refusal to introduce overseas conscription had made him unpopular with many Canadians in uniform. This was just one of the many concerns King wrestled with as he puzzled over how to ensure both a peaceful transition to post-war life and a re-election for his Liberal government. There were two schools of thought about how to achieve these goals. One was that the proverbial glass was half full for Canada; the other was that the glass was half empty.

C.D. Howe was a leading proponent of the glass-half-full view. Howe, who became the Minister of Reconstruction in late 1944, was certain that Canada would experience a post-war economic boom.

His logic was simple: all those veterans who were returning home and re-entering the labour market would become consumers again, and so the resulting demand for consumer goods would drive the Canadian economy.

As Howe saw it, the key to meeting that pent-up demand in a renewed free market economy would be the smooth and rapid "reconversion" of wartime industries to peacetime production. The initial evidence seemed to suggest his concerns about impending shortages were well founded. In late 1944, the government was obliged to redouble its efforts to ration meat consumption; already it was soaring. When Mackenzie King saw this uptick in demand, it gave him something to chew on. Regardless, "his preferences did not go immediately to Howe or his program."[7] As always, the prime minister hedged his political bets.

Among Liberals, there was another very different school of thought on what Canada's post-war priorities should be. This glass-half-empty view was favoured by Ian Mackenzie, the Minister of Pensions and National Health. Scottish-born, gregarious, and full of collectivist zeal, Mackenzie was the most vocal of the various voices in Cabinet who were urging the prime minister to ramp up the federal government's involvement in the economy. Part and parcel with that, Mackenzie urged King to provide Canadians with a comprehensive social welfare safety net—one that would include enhanced pensions, employment insurance, and a system of universal health care. Doing so, Mackenzie argued, would help ensure that if the economy tanked again, the adverse effects would be reduced.

Ian Mackenzie had fought in World War I, and he was popular with veterans, but he was a lacklustre politician who in 1939 had been demoted from the Veterans Affairs portfolio following a scandal. In the prime minister's eyes, he had two saving graces: Mackenzie was British Columbia's representative in Cabinet, and—more importantly—he was a King loyalist, to the point of being obsequious. He remained part of the prime minister's inner circle, despite his shortcomings. When in September 1949 the then-senator Mackenzie died suddenly at the age of fifty-nine, King would spend half a day struggling to write a tribute. "Trying to be sincere," King told his diary, "overlooking as one does of those who have passed away, all I knew and felt of his wrong to himself and others, & giving such praises as I honestly could."[8]

H OT ON THE HEELS of the December 1942 release of the Beveridge Report in England, Leonard Marsh set to work in earnest on the report that Cyril James had hired him to write. If Marsh had any inkling that senior civil servants in Ottawa were already intent on derailing any policy proposals that didn't include them as key players in post-war reconstruction, he didn't let on. Marsh forged ahead; he was little concerned with the political realities of the Byzantine world of the Ottawa bureaucracy. This would prove to be his undoing.

Clifford Clark and his EAC (Economic Advisory Committee) colleagues were less concerned about Leonard Marsh's politics or anything he might write than they were about the makeup of the James Committee. What rankled the mandarins was the fact it was made up of non-government "experts"—business executives, union people, and academics—with nary a top bureaucrat involved. And if that were not bad enough, the committee had set alarm bells ringing with an interim report in which it recommended that politicians, not bureaucrats, should be in charge of government post-war reconstruction programs. That would never do. After all, Canada's civil servants were familiar with how the machinery of government worked, and it was their job to advise and guide politicians on how to get things done. And there was also the reality that when it came to post-war planning, as an American observer noted, "the Canadian government probably had devoted less of its energies and expert personnel than Britain, the United States, or Australia."[9]

Those were valid concerns, but what was left unsaid and what was pivotal in Ottawa was that the mandarins were intent on protecting their turf. With that as one of their goals, Clifford Clark and his colleagues set to work convincing Mackenzie King of the need to make changes that would effectively rein in or even neuter the James Committee. Because Clark had the prime minister's ear, those efforts succeeded.

In early February 1943, the government announced that going forward the James Committee would report directly to the prime minister, and all documents the committee prepared would be subject to review by the fourteen civil-service members of the EAC before they could be made public. Predictably, an outraged Ian Mackenzie threatened to resign from Cabinet. But he did not; he stayed while Leonard Marsh set to work on the report he had been hired to write.

Leonard Marsh. (McGill University Archives, PR041511)

Marsh and a couple of support staff got down to it, closeting themselves in a suite at Ottawa's Château Laurier hotel and working a month of ten-hour days to write a 75,000-word draft report. When the final version was ready in early March, Cyril James ignored the Cabinet directive and the political wisdom that says, "If you're going to sin, do it against God, not the bureaucracy; God forgives, the bureaucracy does not."

James thumbed his nose at the EAC when he presented the *Report on Social Security for Canada* to a House of Commons committee that was also studying the problems associated with post-war reconstruction. That gesture of defiance earned James—and Ian Mackenzie—no friends in the Cabinet or among the ranks of the senior bureaucracy.

The Marsh Report, as it inevitably became known, received a lot of media attention; rightly so, for it presented some bold ideas. The comprehensive recommendations made a case for the federal government to provide a wide range of social welfare programming: health insurance, children's allowances, unemployment insurance, family allowances, and workers' compensation. "Social insurance is a floor to alleviate poverty and prevent people from becoming destitute," Marsh insisted. "But it's only one of many elements essential for a successful post-war reconstruction. For one thing, it must be fitted in with a twin program of employment to take care of the dislocation of those who have been engaged in war work. Successful world reconstruction is going to be as difficult as the war itself."[10]

Marsh described his report as being "a straightforward statement on what a social security plan in Canada should be like."[11] It was impossible to predict the full cost of the programs that Marsh had suggested, but most initial "guesstimates" put the figure in the billions. Marsh was undaunted. He insisted that money would be there once the war ended. The billions of dollars that were being spent on bombs and guns would become available for peaceful needs; it all boiled down to priorities. If Canada could fund a war effort, it surely could fund post-war social welfare programs. After all, the country's gross national product (GNP) had grown from $5.6 billion in 1939 to $11.84 billion in 1945; today, Canada's GNP is almost $1.7 *trillion*.

At a time when a billion dollars was still an unfathomable amount of money for most people, the media predictably focused on the dollar amounts being bandied about in the discussions of the Marsh Report. Ironically, when Conservative Members of Parliament questioned Ian Mackenzie on how much it cost to produce the report itself, his answer surprised them. Not counting the staff salaries of Marsh and the government employees who had helped him with his research, the document cost just $445.[12]

Stunning though that figure was, the overall cost of what Marsh was proposing became the focus of public attention. "Billion Dollar Program Urged for Employment," trumpeted the headline above the page one *Globe and Mail* news article about the report.[13] Meanwhile, the *Toronto Daily Star* announced, "[Billion Dollar] Program Would Banish Spectre of Privation in Canada."[14]

A *Maclean's* magazine editorial dismissed the Marsh Report as politically unworkable without significant changes to the balance of federal–provincial powers in Canada. That concern aside, the editorial continued, "the best long-term channel for job creation and the best guarantee for success of a social security plan is a responsible free enterprise system, expanding industry and business, both domestic and export."[15]

The *Canadian Forum*, the defunct left-wing journal that allied itself with the CCF, offered faint praise that was tinged with cynicism. The editors commented that the Marsh Report was "the price that Liberalism is willing to pay in order to prevent socialism."[16]

For his part, Leonard Marsh continued to hope his recommendations would serve as the basis for a discussion of reconstruction issues and of the kind of post-war society in which Canadians would live. In that regard at least, his report was a success, for it did spark a lively public debate. However, the reception his recommendations received from those in Ottawa whose opinions mattered was less than enthusiastic. Among them were two of the Cabinet's most important ministers: C.D. Howe and Finance Minister J.L. Ilsley.

Howe objected to Marsh's ideas for political reasons; Ilsley dismissed them as being unworkable and too expensive. He reiterated those concerns in his conversations with the prime minister.

The members of the Clifford Clark–led EAC were no less skeptical of the Marsh Report's recommendations. Prominent among the cynics was William A. Mackintosh, another Queen's University economics professor. After signing on as Clark's special assistant in 1942, Mackintosh had quickly proven himself to be an astute, no-nonsense policy analyst who had a knack for getting to the core of any issue, and so Clark installed him as his successor as chair of the Economic Advisory Committee. He was the ideal person for the job. As historian Jack Granatstein has stressed, "To Mackintosh, it was fitting and proper for economists to remain aloof from the political passions of the day, for their discipline 'prescribes no policy and enunciates no doctrine apart from the analysis of the particular facts of the moment.'"[17]

Mackintosh agreed with C.D. Howe's assessment of the Marsh Report. He felt that many of its recommendations were too expensive, while others were beyond the constitutional powers of the federal government. Mackintosh, who was an academic at heart, scoffed at the price tag. For every week Marsh had spent writing his "pie-in-the-sky" report, he had figured out a way to spend a billion dollars of taxpayers' money.

In the end, the Marsh Report went nowhere, as did most of the other sixteen reports produced by the various James Committee subcommittees. Among them was a 1944 study of the treatment of Canadian women. It was shelved because "as one embittered critic remarked, there was a general tendency to say to women: 'Well, girls, you have done a nice job; you looked very cute in your overalls and we appreciate what you have done for us; but just run along; go home; we can get along without you very nicely.'"[18] Those were certainly the sentiments in the ranks of business leaders, union heads, and Canadian military commanders; with demobilization, all three of the women's wartime services were quickly and unceremoniously abolished at war's end. "Communal uniformed life does not appeal to most women," Commander Adelaide Sinclair of the Women's Royal Canadian Naval Service explained.[19]

Where the Marsh Report was concerned, its fate was sealed as much by the jaw-dropping dollar estimates involved in acting on its proposed programs as by committee chair Cyril James's temerity in releasing the document to a parliamentary committee rather than through the EAC. Eventually, the Marsh Report would be consigned to that big bottomless drawer where over the decades so many government reports have gone to collect dust. However, as more than one political commentator has noted, "the spirit [the Marsh Report] represented had a long and profound effect on government thinking."[20]

But what about the public? What, if anything, did the average Canadian think of the Marsh Report? The answers to those questions would be made clear in the results of the 1945 general election.

1945 GOVERNOR GENERAL'S LITERARY AWARD WINNERS

The 1945 Governor General's Awards for Literary Merit were the tenth iteration of these annual honours, which recognize Canadian writers for new English-language books. (The first French-language awards were given in 1959.) There were no cash prizes in those early days. The 1945 winners were as follows:

Fiction: Hugh MacLennan, *Two Solitudes*
Poetry or drama: Earle Birney, *Now Is Time*
Non-fiction (creative): Evelyn M. Richardson, *We Keep a Light*
Non-fiction (academic): Ross Munro, *Gauntlet to Overlord*

PUBLIC OPINION POLLING BEGAN in Canada in 1941. That was the year that American pollster Dr. George Gallup launched the Canadian Institute of Public Opinion (CIPO). That agency surveyed the public each week on myriad topics, everything from conscription to support for social welfare programs, and then sold its findings to newspapers across the country. The English writer J.B. Priestley once observed that "public opinion polls are rather like children in a garden, digging things up all the time to see how they're growing."[21] He was right, and this observation goes a long way toward explaining why politicians and bureaucrats have always been so enamoured with polls.

The federal government had also gotten into the polling business in 1942 when it secretly directed the Wartime Information Board (WIB), Canada's propaganda agency, to sound out public opinion on various topics. Mackenzie King suspected that much of the opposition to his position on conscription was the result of misinformation the media were spreading. (And here you thought mistrust of the media by politicians and charges of "fake news" were relatively new phenomena.)

From 1942 on, the findings of almost every public opinion poll done by the CIPO and WIB confirmed that Canadians' greatest fear was that the country would slip back into depression once the war ended and government spending was slashed. That fear fuelled voter support for the CCF and prompted even the Conservative party to take a marked turn to the left.

In the wake of a dismal showing in the 1940 election, the Tories had resurrected former prime minister Arthur Meighen as their leader, and they championed the idea of Canada waging "total war." That would have included the formation of an all-party national government (as in World War I) and overseas conscription. However, that push had fallen as flat as a tombstone. Meighen lost a February 1942 by-election to a CCF candidate in York South, a supposedly "safe" Conservative riding in Toronto. The Liberals had even declined to field a candidate, observing the convention that called for extending a courtesy by allowing the leader of the opposition to win a seat uncontested in any by-election. However, the reality was that King disliked Meighen personally, and he feared the Conservative leader's pro-conscription pronouncements would inflame French–English tensions. King's decision not to contest York South was also a shrewd move politically in that it killed any possibility of a centre-left vote split that might benefit Meighen. That savvy strategy and the rising tide of CCF popularity were enough to ensure the Conservative leader's electoral defeat while also effectively snuffing out his political comeback and his career.

Youthful Conservatives had been frustrated and angry at the party brass when they met in Port Hope, Ontario, in the summer of 1942. There they had passed a series of policy resolutions that steered the Conservatives to the left. In December, they followed up at a national conference where they orchestrated the election of the progressive-minded former Manitoba premier John Bracken as party leader and the changing of the national party's name to the Progressive Conservatives, an oxymoron if ever there was one.

All of this jockeying for political support had prompted Mackenzie King to reassess his personal priorities and those of his government. As historian Donald Creighton noted, "King, whose ear was always attentively cocked to the slightest tremors in the body politic, was quickly conscious of the expanding social expectations of wartime and of the popular interest in the Beveridge Report."[22] As a result, in the wake of the CCF's unexpectedly strong showing in the August 1943 provincial election in Ontario and the stunning results of a public opinion poll a few weeks later that indicated the CCF had surged ahead of the Liberals in popular support, King resolved to act decisively.

In a bid to undermine support for the CCF, King shepherded the Liberal party executive through a September 1943 meeting where it adopted fourteen resolutions that promised a generous package of social welfare benefits. Among them were a Veterans Charter that was the most generous and comprehensive in the world, and a parcel of new social welfare programs that included an enhanced federal unemployment insurance plan, improved old-age security benefits, workers' compensation, expanded and improved pensions for the blind, a public works program, and family allowance payments that were intended to supplement the monthly children's allowance payments King had introduced in 1940.

It was no coincidence that this latter initiative was part of the Liberal plan; the CCF had passed a similar resolution at its 1942 convention, and the Marsh Report echoed it. Mackenzie King knew an idea whose time had come when he saw it—especially after a public opinion poll confirmed that a monthly "baby bonus" would be a vote getter. King was never averse to poaching policy ideas that were politically popular.

The intriguing thing about this approach to policy-making, which was typical of Mackenzie King, is how it has endured to become a cornerstone of Liberal strategy. As political scientists Janet Ajzenstat and Peter Smith pointed out in a perceptive 1997 essay, the Liberals have never been a party that has led the way by forging ahead with new policy initiatives. Instead, Liberals long have been content to co-opt and repurpose ideas that originated with the CCF and its successor, the New Democratic Party; this uniquely Canadian phenomenon has served the Liberals well. (There is no similar situation in either the United States or Britain, with the result that politics in both countries has become polarized to a degree not seen in Canada.)

Ajzenstat and Smith described the Liberal–NDP relationship as "antagonistic symbiosis." Pointy-headed though that label sounds, it's apt. "As a centre party [the Liberals] have allowed the CCF-NDP to introduce innovations," Ajzenstat and Smith noted. "They have then waited for signs of substantial acceptance by all strata of the population and for signs of reassurance against possible electoral reprisals before actually proceeding to implement the innovations."[23]

MACKENZIE KING WAS CERTAIN his vision for what he began referring to as a "new social order" not only was the right thing to do morally but would pay dividends politically. He adopted the slogan as the basis of the Liberal party's campaign platform in the upcoming 1945 election. There was one big "if" in all this, of course. King hastened to remind Canadians that the new initiatives he proposed could be launched only if the provinces opted to play ball and cooperate with Ottawa. That was something they eventually did to varying degrees. However, the allocation of federal–provincial powers as set out in the BNA Act of 1867 would continue to bedevil relations between the two levels of government, as it does to this day.

Mackenzie King rolled out his grand package of social welfare programs in a January 27, 1944, Speech from the Throne. That initiative committed the Liberals to establishing minimum levels of social security and human welfare nationally. Three new departments would bring this about: Veterans Affairs, Reconstruction, and Social Welfare. The Department of Pensions and National Health, Ian Mackenzie's portfolio, was redundant and would disappear.

In his mind, the prime minister was convinced that not only would his program of social legislation ensure him re-election in that spring's vote, it would also stand as his political legacy. King had assumed ownership of many of the saleable ideas in the Beveridge and Marsh Reports, both of which he was convinced had been inspired by his own writings. He made no public reference to either, yet their influences are undeniable. As historians Desmond Morton and J.L. Granatstein explained, "In almost the sole departure from the Marsh Report, industry would be given substantial tax credits to ensure it invested large sums in the immediate postwar period."[24]

Once the prime minister had committed his government to moving ahead, there could be no turning back. He once famously quipped, "The politician's promises of yesterday are the taxes of today." That message was now forgotten; King had convinced himself the initiatives he was championing in 1944–45 were straight out of his 1918 tome, *Industry and Humanity*. This notion buttressed his determination to proceed despite protests coming from fiscal conservatives within his own Cabinet—with C.D. Howe and Ilsley being the most prominent of the naysayers. The finance minister had not initially recognized the extent or full impact of the proposals King had in mind, nor had he appreciated how far left they were nudging

---

him. By the time these realities became clear, Ilsley had no choice but to go along or resign.

King was determined to proceed regardless, and it was a source of reassurance for him that he had the full support of Clifford Clark and his EAC colleagues. The fact that Canada's senior civil servants had bought into what King was proposing and were eager to manage the necessary changes was evidence of the depth of acceptance in Ottawa for the guiding principles of Keynesian economics. The April 1945 publication of the *White Paper on Employment and Income*—the first such document ever issued by the federal government—underscored that reality. Written by W.A. Mackintosh, it outlined the Liberals' post-war fiscal and employment policies, which were meant to assist private enterprise by establishing optimum conditions for carrying on business. Doing so included a willingness on the part of Ottawa, as Keynesian economic theory recommended, to engage in deficit spending when needed to maintain a "high level" of employment and income for all Canadians. The white paper's original wording had referred to "full" employment," but Mackintosh made the change as a sop to C.D. Howe, who, as Minister of Reconstruction, was tasked with presenting the document to Parliament. Howe remained a reluctant passenger on the Keynesian bandwagon. He still wasn't sold on the need for peacetime government intervention in the economy.

As it turned out, Mackenzie King's political instincts were sound. The old campaigner had sniffed the political winds and staked his own future and that of his Liberal government on a program of post-war reconstruction and renewal the likes of which Canadians had never seen. In addition, leaving as little to chance as possible, in a bid to curry favour with Canada's growing and increasingly vocal union movement, the Cabinet had passed a February 1944 order-in-council that guaranteed workers the right to organize, bargain collectively, present their grievances, and strike.

All of these issues were up for debate and public consideration in the June 1945 general election. Conservatives attacked many of the Liberals' proposed social welfare programs, at times bitterly so. (If you thought negative election campaign advertising was new, think again. It isn't; it is only the frequency and intensity of the pronouncements that have changed today.) At other times, the Tories appeared to be divided and unsure of how to proceed.

When Parliament had considered the Family Allowance Act in late July 1944, the enabling legislation passed second reading by a resounding vote of 139–0; Tory leader John Bracken had voted in favour, while most of his caucus absented themselves from the chamber when the vote was called so that they didn't seem against providing money to feed and clothe children. Many Conservatives continued objecting to the cost of the monthly payments to the program—about $250 million per year, an amount that was almost half of what Canada's total spending had been before the war. Critics charged that the initiative was intended to win votes from Roman Catholics, especially in Quebec. They were right about that. However, polling numbers assured Mackenzie King that the program was popular Canada-wide. Understandably so. At a time when the average factory worker made about $25 a week, a family with three or four school-age children stood to receive the equivalent of an extra week's pay each month. That money was hard to turn down.[25]

The Conservatives miscalculated badly in other ways, too, handing forty-seven of Quebec's sixty-five seats to the Liberals (the Conservatives took just one) when they trumpeted their intention, if elected, to send the zombie draft dodgers off to fight in the Pacific. Polls showed that most Canadians felt that was the Americans' war; it was far away and of little consequence other than to people living on the west coast (not to mention the hundreds of Japanese Canadians who remained confined to internment camps and the thousands more who had been shipped to towns and cities inland for the duration of the war). Mackenzie King wisely had announced in May that while Canada would send an all-volunteer contingent of troops, a couple of ships, and some aircraft to the Pacific, this country would not become heavily involved there when fighting ended in Europe.

Conservative leader Bracken railed against this decision and foolishly talked about the urgent need for a post-war return to the pre-Depression days of small government and renewed deification of free enterprise. Those ideas were non-starters. A CIPO poll done early in 1945 suggested that forty per cent of Canadians had no idea what the term "free enterprise" entailed or even what it meant.[26]

The Liberals' election campaign advertising emphasized bread-and-butter issues, offering hope with a platform that promised Prime Minister King's new social order. In an era when issues were still paramount in any election campaign and negative attack ads were virtually unknown, that strategy paid off.

After six years of war and sacrifice, in 1945 Canadians were tired. Most simply wanted peace so they could get on with life. Many of the 350,000 veterans who were ready to return home from Europe reviled Mackenzie King, but they were less than inspired by Tory leader John Bracken, and they didn't trust M.J. Coldwell of the CCF or Solon Low and his Socreds. Mackenzie King seemed to be the best of a bad lot, and he had promised Canadians a huge bounty of election goodies and a better life going forward. Who could resist? The war had shown that Canada could be a rich country, and people—especially veterans, who had given so much of themselves—were keen to have their fair share of the wealth.

The Liberals won re-election in the June 11 vote, taking 125 of the 245 seats in the House of Commons (and winning thirty-five per cent of the army vote, while the CCF got thirty-two per cent and the Tories just twenty-eight). The Liberal seat total was fifty-six fewer than the party had won in 1940, but with support of independents, it was still good enough for a slim majority. Despite this, it was not all good news for Mackenzie King.

The prime minister had lost his own seat. Just as Winston Churchill, who had so ably led Britain through the war, would be unceremoniously voted out of office a few weeks later, King suffered electoral defeat. In retrospect, this outcome wasn't all that surprising.

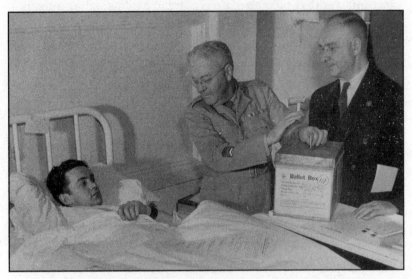

A wounded veteran voting in Winnipeg's Deer Lodge Hospital, June 1945. (Archives of Manitoba, Canadian Army Photo Collection, negative 131)

King had been so preoccupied with his involvement at the founding conference of the United Nations in San Francisco that he'd neglected his re-election campaign. He had spent two months in California, from April 25 to June 26, after having resolved to attend the conference before the election call and before the April 12 death of President Franklin Roosevelt. Once he had committed to doing so, King forged ahead. He felt he was "gaining more political capital" by playing the role of statesman on the international stage than he would by campaigning across Canada.[27] That would be part of his legacy. He also naively believed he would be called upon to play a leadership role in San Francisco. "I felt I should bring in thoughts of my own from *Industry and Humanity*," King told his diary. "After all, that book contains the foundational principles of which the whole work of the United Nations organization is based."[28]

Things didn't work out as King had expected. The Soviet delegation led by Foreign Minister Vyacheslav Molotov pointedly had minimal contact with the representatives of other nations at the conference, and on VE day Molotov promptly packed up and went home. When the Soviet delegates did take part in meetings, it was mostly to object and insist on having things their own way. The wartime cooperation between the Soviet Union and the Allies was clearly finished. Stalin had his own post-war agenda and was now intent on achieving it.

Mackenzie King had addressed the conference, attended plenary sessions, and met with leaders and diplomats from various countries. He was in all his glory, heading an official seven-member Canadian delegation that was "composite and non-partisan in character";[29] in addition, the Canadian delegation was supported by key King advisors from the Department of External Affairs—Norman Robertson, Hume Wrong, and Lester B. Pearson being among them.

Despite his best efforts, King ultimately found the proceedings of the San Francisco conference frustrating and tiring. Canada was a key player behind the scenes, acting as an advocate for the middle powers, yet this country's representatives were consigned to the background when the United States, Russia, Britain, France, and China set about jockeying for position in the post-war world. The irony, of course, was that without Canadian food, war materials, and financial aid, which included $2 billion in forgivable loans, Britain might well have suffered defeat in the war. All of that was quickly forgotten in the euphoria of victory.

King's attentions were divided for most of the nine weeks he spent in San Francisco. He was suffering from a bad cold, and was keeping one eye on the progress of the war in Europe and the election campaign that was in full swing back home. In addition, he felt out of his element on the world stage, where his mien of "respected elder statesman" rang hollow, and the leaders of some other Commonwealth countries overshadowed him as a speaker. In the end, the only issue for which King showed any real concern was the article in the draft

United Nations charter that authorized the Security Council to call upon member nations to supply military forces to maintain peace. As historian Donald Creighton would note, that was a measure that stoked Mackenzie King's "obsessive fear" of external commitments over which he had no control: "'I did not see how it was possible,' he told the principal Commonwealth delegates earnestly, 'to agree to a step which meant conscription of a nation's forces at the instance of four or five great powers. I doubted if such a charter with such a provision would ever be accepted by our Parliament.'"[30]

W.L. Mackenzie King addressing the United Nations Conference on International Organization, April 1945. (LAC, MIKAN no. 3624069)

The post-conference journey home aboard an RCAF Lancaster bomber was a long, sobering one for Mackenzie King. After arriving back in Ottawa on June 27 after a twelve-hour flight from the west coast, he told his diary, "I felt too tired and worn to be much interested in anything."[31]

King would soon understand that his time would have been better spent campaigning in the June federal election. After nineteen years as the Member of Parliament for the Saskatchewan riding of Prince Albert, he had smugly assumed that a victory in his fifth bid for re-election was a sure thing. He was sadly mistaken. In some measure, at least, it may have been resentment over King's refusal to impose conscription for overseas service that led to his defeat. He had incurred the enmity of many returning veterans. "King's refusal to send conscripts—the zombies—overseas cost lives," recalls A. Britton Smith, a captain in the "C" Company of the Fusiliers Mont-Royal. "Units were so short of men that cooks and drivers were being given a couple of weeks training and then put into the field. They weren't properly trained for combat, and so many of them were killed. Veterans didn't soon forget or forgive that."[32]

There were rumours that scores of army men listed their hometown as being Prince Albert just so they could vote against King in the overseas polls. Whether or not that's true is impossible to say, but when all the votes were counted, King went down to defeat. He had 6,287 votes on election night, while the CCF runner-up in the four-person contest finished with 6,007. However, when the "army vote" was tallied a week later, King's 280-vote margin disappeared; he lost the election by 129 votes. The surprise victor was a political neophyte named Edward Bowerman. A Toronto-born Mormon missionary-turned-farmer and father of six, he told reporters he was as surprised as anyone when he became a giant killer.

King's embarrassing Prince Albert election defeat would prove to be the fourth and final one of his political career. Mind you, he didn't remain long without a seat in Parliament. Liberal incumbent W.B. MacDiarmid resigned as Member of Parliament for the eastern Ontario riding of Glengarry, as safe a Liberal seat as there was in the country. King won an August by-election there, which by coincidence was held only a few days after the first "baby bonus" cheques began arriving in mailboxes across the country. If there were any lingering doubts about the public's support for that program and for the others on which the Liberals had campaigned in June, they were erased. King returned to the House of Commons after racking up the largest majority in the long history of the Glengarry riding; in seven polls, the only other candidate on the ballot failed to win a single vote.

The statement King issued after the votes were counted speaks volumes about the man's ego and his feelings about the indignity he had suffered in his Prince Albert election loss. "I regret that the country should have been put to the expense and the people of Glengarry subjected to the inconvenience of a wholly unnecessary by-election contest," he said. "It is to be hoped that the result of today's polling may serve to avoid in other constituencies futile contests born of a love of notoriety and publicity."[33]

THE 1945 ELECTION WOULD be Mackenzie King's electoral swan song. He was seventy-one and felt it. He was tired and in failing health. King would remain as prime minister and as Liberal leader three more years, before finally stepping down in the autumn of 1948. By then, he had spent twenty-two consecutive and eventful years as Canada's prime minister. However, nothing among King's many accomplishments is more meaningful or had greater impact on Canada and the everyday lives of Canadians than the social safety net he stitched together in 1945.

That initiative was integral to the golden era of post-war prosperity in this country. Some additional wrangling was needed to iron out federal–provincial jurisdictional issues, and there are still routine flare-ups. Despite this, Canada today has an extensive and well-developed program of social welfare benefits that may not be perfect, but it works. It is distinctly Canadian, and it is the envy of people in many other nations. The imperatives that inspired Mackenzie King to push for its creation were rooted in the Fabian socialism that galvanized the CCF movement's true believers—people such as Agnes Macphail,

M.J. Coldwell, and J.S. Woodsworth—and that drove Leonard Marsh to write his seminal 1943 *Report on Social Security for Canada*.

Mackenzie King was nothing if not a political pragmatist. For most of his career, he willingly shelved his youthful idealism for the sake of political gain. However, as the curtain was coming down on him politically and personally, it also seems that finally he sensed the time had come to act on the beliefs that had once fired his passions. King's decision to do so wasn't fuelled by political desperation or by an epiphany—not in the way that R.B. Bennett's strange, ill-fated decision in 1935 to launch a Canadian New Deal had been. King believed he was doing what was right, moral, and preordained.

While reading a book about the life of French microbiologist Louis Pasteur, he had chanced upon a quotation that struck a chord with him: "Blessed is he who carries within himself a God, an ideal, and who obeys it."[34] King was convinced his reading these words at that moment in his life was a message from his late parents, Pasteur, and others in the "great beyond." They were directing him to continue his "service to humanity." The impact of that decision would be as profound as it has been enduring.

The new social order that Mackenzie King played a pivotal role in creating and launching at war's end in many ways continues to define what Canada is all about.

PART III

COMING HOME AND "THE BOMB"

By the fall of 1945, ships were bringing thousands of jubilant Canadian troops home from overseas. (LAC, MIKAN no. 4233505)

When you've seen your friends blown to bits around you, it
makes you think that the post-war world . . . better be good.
—Canadian soldier's letter home from Italy, 1943

CHAPTER 14

Waiting to Go Home

AFTER TEN LONG, GRUELLING MONTHS ON THE FRONT
lines of the war in Europe, Captain Hal MacDonald of the North
Shore (New Brunswick) Regiment was awash in mixed emotions
on VE day. Sadness and anger tempered the sense of relief he felt
on May 8, 1945.

The men of the North Shore Regiment had stormed ashore at Juno
Beach on D-Day. Ten months later, after clawing their way across western Europe, the New Brunswickers were still in the thick of the fighting. They were front and centre among the five First Canadian Army
divisions who, with the help of British and Polish troops, were battling
to liberate the Netherlands. The fighting was hard, and it was bloody.

About a third of the Dutch countryside lies below sea level, and
in the final weeks of the war, the retreating Germans had opened and
destroyed sluice gates on the massive dikes that held back the North Sea.
The water rushed in, flooding vast sections of the lowland countryside
to a depth of several feet. But this desperate last-gasp German effort
to stave off defeat hadn't worked; the relentless Canadian-led Allied
advance had continued. And now, with the outcome of the war all but
certain, apart from the last of the crazed, diehard Nazis who were ready
to give their lives for their führer, soldiers on both sides of the lines
were "scared stiff" of "catching one" in the final fearsome days of the
fighting. No one wanted to be the last man to die at war's end.

Hal MacDonald certainly felt that way. The war had been a marathon ordeal for him. The Saint John native had been just twenty-two when he enlisted in September 1939. He had done a lot of growing up over the course of his six years in uniform. By 1945, MacDonald had spent more than a fifth of his life in the army, the last three years on the battlefields of France, Belgium, and the Netherlands. His wartime experiences would colour the rest of his life; memories of the eventful final days in Europe were forever etched on his mind, as they were for all veterans of the First Canadian Army.

They would never forget how the Dutch people poured into the streets to welcome the Canadian troops who liberated them from the horrors of the German occupation. The victory celebrations were loud, joyous, and unrestrained. Fifteen-year-old Cornelia Fuykschot was among the throng of Dutch civilians who lined the roadway and waited patiently on the morning of May 5, 1945, for the Canadians to come marching into her village.

A murmur went through the crowd the moment people heard the distant skirl of bagpipes and the roaring engines of the approaching Canadian Jeeps, trucks, and tanks. "And then we suddenly saw the soldiers themselves who had come this far, fighting up from the beach in Normandy, through France and Germany . . . fighting all the way to liberate us," Fuykschot would recall many years later. "We saw [the soldiers] passing by, more and more of them, and finally it was too much. A cry went up, a shout of pent-up anguish and jubilation and sheer love after all the hatred of five years. We could not stop ourselves, we had to be nearer, closer, with those men . . . and what our voices would not be able to tell them, our arms had to do."[1] The crowd surged forward onto the road, swarming the Canadian soldiers and showering them with hugs, kisses, and flowers.

That joyful scene was repeated time and time again, along every road and in every town in the Netherlands. And with good reason. Despite the fact their country had officially been neutral in the war, the Dutch people had endured the highest per capita death rate of all the Nazi-occupied countries in western Europe. On top of that, in early 1945 hundreds of thousands of Dutch people were starving, especially the children, some of whom were surviving by eating tulip bulbs. "We found huts filled with . . . all kinds of food that the Germans had stored, yet the Dutch had nothing to eat, absolutely nothing. Many of them were in pretty bad shape," one Canadian veteran would recall in an interview with CBC radio many years later.[2]

In late April and the first week of May, the German military commanders had agreed to a series of ceasefires, during which relief flights by RCAF and RAF bombers carried out Operation Manna, dropping thousands of tons of food to Dutch civilians. Perhaps the Germans were tacitly accepting their guilt for the situation. Or perhaps they were hoping for a quid pro quo in which the Canadians and their Allied partners would protect from Dutch payback the surrendered Germans who had been responsible for this humanitarian disaster and for so many other war crimes—especially the concentration camp mass murder of six million Jews and countless thousands of other people the Nazis had earmarked for extermination. As the details and the extent of German barbarities became known, the disgust and anger on the Allied side of the lines were palpable. Despite an alarming and disgraceful willingness to allow German officers to continue commanding their troops,[3] showing mercy to the vanquished Nazi enemy did not come easily.

One Canadian army officer, a lieutenant, would forever recall what happened when, in fighting near the Dutch–German border, the men of his unit captured a German officer who was "a vest-pocket Hitler." The man, a rabid Nazi, remained unrepentant and uncooperative, and when the Canadian major who was in charge had finally had a belly full of trying to question him, the major told the lieutenant, "Take two good men and walk this man to the edge of the trees. Give him a running start. Five yards. He'll be shot for attempting to escape."

Hearing and understanding this death sentence, the German cried out that he had "expected more" of a Canadian army officer because he insisted he'd always respected Canadians as "fair and worthy opponents."

The lieutenant who had been ordered to carry out the major's order to kill was in a quandary. What to do? After considering the matter for a few moments, he balked. Executing a prisoner of war was against the Geneva Convention, he protested. The major who had issued the order listened and then nodded. Yes, he agreed, killing the German would reduce the Canadians to "playing the Germans' own game."

Left to make his own decision on the fate of the Nazi zealot, the lieutenant opted to turn him over to Canadian military police, with orders to take the man to a detention area. As the German prisoner was climbing into the Jeep that would be used to transport him to the rear, he thanked the lieutenant for saving his life.

Many years later, the Canadian would recall, "Then he said, 'Would you consider, sir, that I was lucky?' and I said, 'If you live to be a hundred and five years old . . . you'll never be so lucky again.' Then [the German] stuck out his hand. And what the hell, what could I do? I shook it."[4] How Canadian is that?

THE DAY THE WAR in Europe officially ended, Hal MacDonald found himself in the hamlet of Holtrop, twelve miles (twenty kilometres) inside the northwestern corner of Germany and within shelling distance of the front lines. As the official diary of the North Shore Regiment recorded, "We were not in the best of places for any kind of celebration"[5] on VE day. MacDonald and his mates could only look skyward and thank heaven they had been among the lucky ones who had survived the war. Despite this, the joy and relief they felt were tempered by a sobering awareness.

More than 45,000 of their fellow Canadians were buried in the graveyards of Allied soldiers who had fallen on the battlefields of western Europe. At the same time, 55,000 other Canadian servicemen and servicewomen had suffered wounds, more than half of which were disabling and would be life-altering. And untold numbers of other Canadian veterans would carry the psychological scars of war with them for the rest of their lives. No matter. For now, like every other Allied soldier in Europe, Hal MacDonald could think of only one thing: with the war over, it was finally time to go home. "Expect to be here for a few weeks and then after that, oh, I daren't think of it. It can't be long now, after all these years," he wrote in a letter to his wife.[6]

Marjorie and Hal MacDonald had married on June 15, 1942, just ten days before Hal shipped out for Europe. What a grim way to start off a marriage. For the next three years, Marjorie MacDonald could only pray for her husband's safe return as she read each and every one of the steady stream of letters—three or more missives each week—that he sent home to Saint John. In them, he had recounted many of his experiences and shared his emotions as best he had been able to given the restrictions of wartime censorship.

From afar, Hal MacDonald had marvelled at the wondrous developments on the home front that his wife recounted in some of her letters. All things considered, in the wake of the worst economic depression of the twentieth century, life in Canada had never been better during the war years. Despite this, in the final months of war in Europe, many people in English Canada sympathized and agreed with those in the military who were angry with the federal government's stand on conscription. Mackenzie King understood this and was intent on doing what he could to make amends. Central to his efforts to do so was the parcel of veteran-friendly legislation that Parliament had enacted in 1944–45. In mid-1945, as officials in Ottawa were dismantling much of the wartime bureaucracy, they were rolling out a package of veterans' benefits, the most generous and wide-ranging of any of the Allied powers, enacted "in the same high spirit of service which inspired Canadians to fulfill their obligations in the crucible of war,"[7] as Minister of Veterans Affairs Ian Mackenzie put it.

The 750,000 veterans who had already returned home and resumed civilian life were grateful. Not so the 350,000 Canadian soldiers and support people who weren't as fortunate. They were frustrated and, in many cases, angry. First there had been the conscription debate; now they found themselves stuck in Europe because the government had no timely way to repatriate them. They wanted to be home with their loved ones, and they resented that they might be missing out on jobs, benefits, and other opportunities.

The nub of the problem was that in a world in which there was a shortage of passenger ships, the logistics of repatriation were daunting and challenging. "The business of getting the Canadians home will not be speedily accomplished, though I have hopes that more than half of them will be back before the end of the year," General Harry Crerar, the man in command of the First Canadian Army, confided in a letter he sent to his wife a few days before the war ended.[8]

Crerar had first-hand memories of the transportation problems that had occurred at the end of WWI. He also understood that while Canada's navy had grown immeasurably during the war, the fleet did not include vessels that could carry large numbers of passengers.

Compounding the difficulties Canada faced was a decision by the American military to prioritize its own needs when it came to the deployment of the passenger ships at its disposal.[9] Relations between Canada and its erstwhile allies changed in the wake of President Roosevelt's death on April 12, 1945. Just as Mackenzie King and Canada were shunted aside at the founding conference of the United Nations in San Francisco and at the Nuremberg War Crimes trials—where there were no Canadian judges or prosecutors—at war's end this country's needs reverted to being an afterthought for officials in Britain and the United States. During the war, Canada had been a key member of the Allied coalition and had punched well above its weight militarily and economically. Now suddenly, this country was just another middle power that found itself consigned to the spectators' gallery as the representatives of the major powers set about redrawing the world's geopolitical map.

None of these lofty concerns mattered much to Hal MacDonald or to the thousands of other Canadian soldiers who were left cooling their heels in Europe. The only thing they wanted now that the war was over was to go home. When they couldn't do that, they grew increasingly impatient. Writing in a May 21 letter to his wife, MacDonald stated a common frustration when he reported feeling "in the dumps." He then hastened to add, "This just waiting to get back to you is getting me down—it's becoming difficult to be patient."[10]

Officers did their best to keep the men under their command active and out of trouble, but the distractions of physical training, sports, watching movies, or playing cards have their limits. Even relations with the Dutch people were becoming strained at times. With so many young Dutch men having been displaced or killed in the war, there was a surplus of women in the country. And human nature being what it is, it was inevitable that some Canadian soldiers struck up relationships with local women. Almost 1,900 Canadian soldiers would marry Dutch brides and eventually bring them to Canada. Not surprisingly, such fraternization stirred the resentments of Dutch men and occasionally got them fighting mad. In the town of Utrecht, when Canadian soldiers and locals brawled, the mayor explained, "It was a matter of girls."[11]

Marjorie and Hal MacDonald. (Catharine MacDonald)

Fisticuffs weren't the only problem. The number of unwanted pregnancies in Holland soared, as did the incidence of sexually transmitted diseases. "There's a hell of a lot of VD amongst the troops. We've started a drive against it," Hal MacDonald mentioned in yet another of his letters home.[12]

MacDonald passed his days socializing with Dutch, British, and Polish military officers, and he attended civilian events where he sometimes danced with local women. However, for him that was as far as he allowed things to go. When on June 8 he left a lively social gathering that he and other Canadians were attending, MacDonald explained to his puzzled pals that this day was his wedding anniversary. "I'm with my wife," he said.[13] In spirit at least, he was.

B ACK IN CANADA, CANADA's senior military commanders, bureaucrats, and politicians were struggling to decide the best and fairest criteria for demobilizing and repatriating from Europe the 350,000 men and women in uniform who were still "over there" Canada had actually been planning for demobilization since the war's beginning in 1939, but somehow all the issues still hadn't been sorted out.

General Harry Crerar remembered how at the end of WWI, General Arthur Currie had argued that the best way "to bring the boys home" was by regiment rather than by individual. Crerar was of the same opinion in 1945; however, his superiors at Canadian Military Headquarters in London and back in Ottawa had other ideas. They preferred a simple "points-based" system in which the guiding principle was "first in, first out." Each soldier, sailor, or flier earned two points for every month served in Canada and three for every month served overseas. That sounds straightforward, but as the Scottish poet Robbie Burns once observed, "The best laid schemes o' mice an' men / Gang aft a-gley." And go awry, they did.

Individual needs had to take a back seat to military ones, a necessity that complicated the Canadian repatriation plans. This country was obligated to leave some troops and aircraft in Europe in a Canadian Occupation Force that would help see to it that Germany complied with the terms of the surrender agreement. In addition, Canadian soldiers who were wounded, who had been prisoners of war, who had volunteered to serve in the Pacific, or who had urgent family responsibilities back home were entitled to jump the queue. Then there were those men who received priority status when their employers successfully appealed to the Industrial Selection and Release Board for early release from service. This government agency had the power to prioritize homecoming transportation for anyone with special skills that were in high demand.

Unfortunately for Hal MacDonald, he didn't qualify for priority repatriation. As a result, he grew more and more frustrated and embittered as he saw others with lower "point scores" going home before he did. "The army HQ admits [repatriation] is buggered up," MacDonald complained in a June 24 letter home. "Guys going home with 70 & 80 pts—cripes, the whole thing is bogging down."[14] He wasn't alone in feeling that way or in making his feelings known.

Some soldiers complained to DVA minister Ian Mackenzie when he travelled to Europe in July to look into the situation for himself; other soldiers in Europe sent home letters of complaint. *Maclean's* magazine reported having heard from disgruntled Canadian troops— officers and enlisted men alike—who were "good and mad"[15] that so many men with high point totals were left waiting while others with less service time were on homeward-bound ships. Then there were some Canadian soldiers who did more than sound off or write letters. They took to the streets in violent protests.

On the nights of July 4 and 5, 1945, hundreds of angry Canucks rioted in Aldershot, the garrison town in southern England that has long been known as "the home of the British Army." Incensed by the glacial pace of their homecoming, pay grievances, the poor quality of the food they were being served, and the perceived hostility of the local people, in scenes that echoed the VE day Halifax riots and similar trouble back in 1918, the men smashed shop windows, set fires, and damaged property. Senior military commanders and politicians in Ottawa were aghast, and they condemned the outburst. But Hal MacDonald saw things differently. "The men had every reason to vent their frustration, though it's unfortunate they destroyed civilian property," he mused in a July 9 letter to his wife.[16]

MacDonald's own discontent continued to simmer until August 24, the day he finally received orders to depart for England. He did that, and three weeks later was delighted at long last to be homeward bound. MacDonald sailed aboard an impossibly crowded Halifax-bound troop ship. "We have been warned of the possibility of sleeping on troop decks in hammocks or paillasses," Hal MacDonald reported on September 14 in the last of the 463 letters he mailed home during his three years overseas. "Gosh, if needs be, I'll sleep in the boiler room or the hold. The main thing is, I'm on my way back . . . still find it hard to believe."[17]

MacDonald and his compatriots were eager to get home, but one and all wondered whether Canada would be ready for them. The country they were returning to was very different from the one they had left years earlier.

The Ontario Regiment march through the streets of Oshawa, Ontario, to celebrate their November 1945 return home. (City of Toronto Archives, *Globe and Mail* fonds, fond 1266, item 100525)

CHAPTER 15

Polka-Dot Bandanas and Sten Guns

NTIL THE MOMENT THE MASKED MEN DASHED THROUGH
the front doors of the bank, it had been a routine day. The branch
of the Canadian Bank of Commerce on King Street West in downtown Toronto was open just three days a week, and it was seldom
busy. Perhaps that was the reason these two thugs chose it as their target
on this sunlit autumn day, October 17, 1945. The pair, dressed in work
overalls, covered the lower half of their faces with red-and-white polka-
dot bandanas. The swatches of fabric were as much a brand statement
as a disguise. The taller of the two men sported a stylish fedora, the
other a peaked cap. Each carried a gleaming nickel-plated handgun.

One of them shouted at the five female customers in the bank,
"Face the wall and shut up!" A moment later, the fedora-wearing rob-
ber tried the door of the four-foot-high wrought-iron grill behind
which the tellers worked. Finding it locked, he clambered up and over
the barrier, landing with a thud among the startled tellers.

"You too! Turn around and face the wall!" he commanded, bran-
dishing his weapon as if to add an exclamation point to his words.
Teller Margaret Ramsay, who worked part time at two banks to make
ends meet, had no desire to be a heroine or a martyr. She immediately
did as she was told. Her two female co-workers followed suit. They
looked on in stunned silence as bank manager Hilliard Bryan struggled

251

to open the vault with hands that quivered like leaves in the autumn breeze. He was desperately hoping one of his staff had sounded the alarm that would bring police running. "One gunman ordered me not to look at him. [But] I glanced at him occasionally and saw that he wore a white shirt with a striped tie," Bryan would later tell a newspaper reporter. The robbers, who were "polite, but forceful, . . . showed they meant business."[1]

The bank manager was correct in that. The men did mean business. Police would later conclude that the gun-toting bank robbers most likely were members of the notorious gang of stick-up men that legendary *Toronto Daily Star* police reporter Gwyn "Jocko" Thomas had dubbed "the Polka-Dot Machine Gun Gang"—a moniker parsimonious editors soon shortened to "the Polka Dot Gang." It rolled off the tongue more easily and made for a snappier headline. The leader of this image-conscious quintet of felons was a baby-faced thug with a rap sheet longer than film star Betty Grable's legs.[2] At the still young age of twenty-one, Kenneth "Budger" Green had already spent more than six years behind bars for a variety of crimes, enough time for him to avoid wartime military service.

Green and his accomplices weren't pacifists, nor were they averse to using guns. They never shied away from violence when it suited their needs. The gang had pulled off at least eight armed robberies during a five-month spree that netted them more than $38,000—more than half a million dollars in today's inflated currency—in heists in the Toronto area and in smaller southwestern Ontario cities and towns. Green and his mates had beaten up and seriously injured a half-dozen people, and they'd fired their guns on several occasions. It was more by luck than by design—or was it poor aim?—that they hadn't killed anyone. Not yet, anyway.

If the two masked men in the Canadian Bank of Commerce on this day really were Green and one of his sidekicks, it was their experience that cautioned them after just a few minutes that they'd already been inside the bank too long. In their haste to be gone before police arrived, the pair stuffed their pockets with $2,000 in cash; however, they left behind a stack of savings bonds big enough to choke a goat. Then, after herding the staff into the vault and securing the door with only a chair propped against it (so no one would suffocate in the airless chamber), the two robbers calmly exited the bank, got into their car, and drove off. (Toronto was a very different city in 1945. Imagine finding a parking spot at King and Bay Streets today. Fat chance.) "They didn't seem to be in any big hurry," said a woman who happened to enter the bank just as the pair were making their getaway.[3]

Welcome to Kingston Penitentiary—Budger Green's prison mug shot.
(Canadian Penitentiary Research Service)

Police had no way to confirm whether the two robbers were members of the Polka Dot Gang. They had sported the gang's trademark bandanas, but imitation has always been the sincerest form of flattery. A daylight robbery in which no one was pistol-whipped or roughed up would have been atypical for Budger Green and his crew. About all the police knew for certain was that although the gang had been busy as bees in the weeks leading up to that Bank of Commerce heist, they had dropped out of sight for several weeks, most likely because they now topped the "most wanted" felons list.

I T SEEMS THAT HISTORY really *does* repeat itself, at least sometimes. In 1919, Canada had experienced a mini crime wave when hundreds of thousands of veterans returned home from "over there." In the wake of the Second World War, a similar scenario began playing out, but "on a little larger scale," as one veteran police officer observed.[4] The criminal justice data suggest he was right. Adult offenders committed 41,965 indictable offences in Canada in 1945; in 1946, that number rose to 46,935.

Across the country, the number of break-ins spiked, as did the incidence of petty crimes, especially shoplifting. Businesses reported that most of the offenders were young people. This revelation prompted the *Globe and Mail* to issue a front-page call for police and the courts to "get tough" with offenders. Mayor Robert Saunders agreed. "I believe in the lash . . . there should be an increase in [its use]," he said.[5] The lash's cutting thrust was an immediate, no-nonsense, one-size-fits-all response to whatever social or economic issues might have been fuelling the urge to steal; however, the root causes of the malaise, as is always the case, ran much deeper, were far more complex, and beggared such an easy solution.

When rationing was in effect, shoplifting had become a problem, and that continued in the months immediately after the war. Grocery stores were the main targets for those with sticky fingers and empty stomachs. "Novelty shops. Five-and-ten stores and hard wares are also heavy losers," journalist Gordon Sinclair reported. "While the annual loss obtained by large metropolitan department stores may run into a cool $100,000 or more."[6] Today that figure may sound like small potatoes, but it was big money in 1945.

However, the rates of such petty crimes were less concerning to police and the general public than what the media trumpeted as being an alarming increase in the incidence of murder and mayhem. Canada's murder rate jumped forty-three per cent in 1945—up to 152 from 106 in 1944. As a consequence, Canadian courts meted out seventeen death sentences in 1945 and nineteen the following year.

The country's increased murder rate was alarming at first glance, but the actual numbers were small in relation to the total population, 11.5 million. Despite this, tough-on-crime politicians and police suspected it was veterans returning home from overseas who were and would be responsible for any crime wave. Those fears seemed to be justified.

Halifax experienced a wave of stick-ups. So did Montreal, which was also dealing with a growing dual threat from organized crime and police corruption. In the summer of 1945, "*barbotte houses*"—hole-in-the-wall venues where the illegal craps-like dice game called *barbotte* was played—were said to be raking in $75,000 an hour. On September 28, morality squad police officers raided and padlocked the doors of thirty-one of these establishments. Five days later, twenty-one of them were operating again, and business was as brisk as ever.

Cities across Canada experienced similar upticks in criminal activity. The number of armed robberies doubled—up from 106 in 1944 to 229 in 1945. That figure reflected itself in the crime statistics from Winnipeg and Vancouver; and like Montreal, Vancouver also had a burgeoning problem with gangs.

Nowhere in Canada was the increase in criminal activity more noticeable nor more covered by the media than in Ontario, which then, as now, was the country's most populous province. As one journalist told readers, "The insurance companies noticed it first. Between V-E and V-J Days the daily stream of claims for theft and holdup losses began to climb."[7] The media were filled with stories of daring robberies and the wild police chases that often followed.

For example, one hot summer day in August 1945, two young

thugs who were on the run after hacksawing their way out of Waterloo County jail—a twenty-two-year-old Windsor-born criminal with the memorable name of Ulysses Lauzon and his baby-faced nineteen-year-old accomplice, Joe Peltier from Ottawa—waltzed into the bank on the main street of the village of Bath, Ontario (pop. 297). With guns drawn, the "nerveless, gun-happy" pair made off with $10,000 in cash and more than $300,000 in bonds. It was said to be the largest bank robbery in Canadian history to that point, and the newspapers reported every aspect of the crime in sensational detail, including the allegation the pair's getaway car was driven by "Lauzon's pretty blond sister." The woman driving the stolen getaway car turned out to be Lauzon's wife, who was either eighteen or twenty. But what did it matter how old she was? News stories about the robbery sold newspapers.

It was headline news two weeks later when Peltier died after being shot in the back by a teller at a Montreal bank when he tried to cash $25,000 in bonds stolen in the Bath heist and another in Ayr, Ontario. Some bank tellers in 1945 carried guns, and they used them to thwart robberies. "It was him or I [sic]," said teller Hatton Longshaw, who evidently was a better marksman than a grammarian.[8]

Peltier staggered out of the bank after being mortally wounded, only to have Lauzon and his wife leave him lying on the sidewalk in a pool of blood when they sped off in their car. Police nabbed Lauzon, his wife, and another man in Charlottetown a week later. The thirty-five-year sentence to Kingston Penitentiary that Lauzon received for his crimes derailed his wanderings and his criminal career, but only briefly.[9]

Around the same time that Mr. Lauzon was busy robbing banks, police in Windsor, Ontario, were frantically trying to track down a serial killer who was targeting gay men. Police and the media downplayed that aspect of the case, but the crimes still received extensive coverage. The Windsor area was on edge, and rumours swirled as people compared the savage "Slasher Killer" knife attacks to those of Jack the Ripper.

At one point that autumn, as many as a hundred police officers were tracking the Slasher. Despite that, he continued his reign of terror for almost a year. It wasn't until July 1946 that police finally nabbed him. That happened only because his fifth victim managed to fend off his attacker, and the *Windsor Star* newspaper published a photo of the knife that had been left embedded in the man's back. When the killer's sister-in-law recognized the weapon, she turned in eighteen-year-old Ronald Sears and pocketed the $3,000 reward.[10]

It was such a high-profile case that it prompted *Maclean's* magazine to investigate the reasons "serious crime is increasing four times faster than the population." An investigation by writer A.S. Marshall came up with a surprising conclusion: despite all the speculation, it wasn't entirely veterans who were responsible for the crime wave. It was teen-agers—mostly young men from working-class families in which one of the few things there was no shortage of was social problems.[11]

Regardless of the ages of the criminals, media reports stoked the public's anxieties and helped create the impression that a tsunami of crime was sweeping the nation. An October 1946 Gallup public opinion poll found that Canadians believed the number one problem facing the country was a soaring crime rate.[12]

Not surprisingly, police held the same view. There were widespread demands for tougher laws to deal with criminals, and police chiefs pleaded for better and more firearms. Even in North Bay, a sleepy northern Ontario city of 15,000 residents, the police chief petitioned city council for money to buy tear gas and to arm his officers with Thompson submachine guns—the "Tommy guns" that were the weapon of choice for police and gangsters during Prohibition.[13]

I N HINDSIGHT, ANY RISE in the crime or murder rates shouldn't have come as a surprise to anyone. After all, post-war society was very much in flux. More than a million Canadian men and women had been in uniform during the war, and the first of the more than

350,000 of them who were overseas on VE day began arriving back in the weeks that followed. For them, as military historian Tim Cook has noted, "the war lingered on in the mind, replayed at the conscious and subconscious levels."[14] It did all that and much more.

The vast majority of veterans were law-abiding and wanted only to get back to civilian life and reap benefits they felt they'd earned. There can be no doubt that some of them had paid a high price. A significant number of veterans returned as walking wounded; for them, life would never be the same, nor would it be easy. Their pain was unrelenting, and sometimes it was life-altering. More than 55,000 Canadian veterans were physically broken; many others were scarred mentally. The exact number will never be known.

Some were racked with survivor's guilt. Others struggled to deal with marital discord, alcoholism, depression, and all manner of psychiatric disorders, none of which were easily diagnosed or effectively treated. Demobilization and a return to "normalcy" dominated all aspects of life in 1945 and for at least the next decade. The movie *The Best Years of Our Lives*, the Academy Award winner for Best Picture of 1946, was as popular in Canada as it was in the United States since veterans' issues resonated in both countries. Harold Russell, who won an Oscar as best supporting actor for his portrayal of an army veteran who'd lost both hands in the war, was a native of Sydney, Nova Scotia. He had seen wartime service in the U.S. Army.[15]

The reasons Russell's performance and the movie struck such a chord with audiences aren't hard to fathom. *The Best Years of Our Lives* caught the zeitgeist of the day. It wasn't alone in that regard.

There was no shortage of veterans' accounts of the post-war travails and—in many cases—the personal hells these men and women endured. Library shelves are overflowing with books that tell their stories; most make for sober reading. The sad story of Montreal native Ronald "Ronnie" Pyves is typical.

Pyves, an RCAF veteran, was a teenager when he flew as tail gunner aboard a Halifax bomber. One of the "lucky ones," he survived thirty-five missions over Germany in the final months of the war. Among the most memorable of those missions was a nighttime bombing run in February 1945 over the German city of Dresden. As many as 25,000 civilians died in a series of four fire-bombing raids, the military need for which some historians now question. Pyves evidently did, too.

His experiences had such a profound effect on him that whenever the media and academics discussed the Dresden raids and second-guessed the need for them, Pyves fell to drinking heavily and grew depressed.[16] His alcohol abuse and the mental trauma he endured—a casebook example of what today is recognized as post-traumatic stress disorder (PTSD)—took a terrible toll on him and his family. His ordeal ended in August 1987 when his liver gave out and he died. He was just sixty-two at the time.[17] Sadly, Ronnie Pyves wasn't the only veteran to suffer from the long-term effects of WWII combat horrors. Many veterans clung to life while never fully recovering from the PTSD that neither they nor their loved ones or care providers understood or were prepared to deal with.

That was certainly so for Ted Patrick, who saw action in Europe with the Irish Regiment of Canada. Following his return home, Patrick struggled to cope with nightmares. Sometimes he dreamed about being engaged in hand-to-hand combat with Germans, and when he did, more than once he was horrified to wake up with his hands on his wife's throat. Patrick was by no means the only veteran to suffer through years of mental trauma that went undiagnosed and untreated.[18]

In 1945, the term *PTSD* hadn't been coined; it didn't appear in medical journals until the 1980s when the American Psychiatric Association added the term to its diagnostic manual. Not surprisingly, it took many years for doctors to tab Ted Patrick as a PTSD victim, something for which he would eventually receive a small government pension.[19]

The idea that the kind of stress endured by combatants in war and by those innocents who suffer collateral damage has its roots in antiquity. The Greeks and Romans were aware that war does bad things to the minds of otherwise good people, although they didn't understand why or how the trauma affects people or sears their psyches. Fortunately, modern medicine has a somewhat better idea. We know now that the hormones the human body produces in times of stress ramp up activity in that area of the brain called the amygdala— pronounced "ahh-MIG-da-la."

The word may sound like the name of a flower, but it's a walnut-sized bundle of neurons where our fears and emotions reside. The kind of long-term stress a person endures in combat upsets the chemistry of the amygdala. It also messes with the hippocampus, that part of your brain where memories are formed and stored.

There were myriad examples in the American Civil War (1861–65) and in the First World War (1914–18) of the terrible toll that combat stress exacts on the human body. As doctors became aware of the phenomenon and studied it, they coined the descriptor *combat stress reaction*—"combat fatigue" in Second World War vernacular.

To their credit, many of Canada's senior military commanders recognized early in the war that not all combat wounds were physical, and so they launched a number of initiatives to treat mental traumas. Most of the Canadians who suffered such injuries were infantrymen, and that service opened a 200-bed psychiatric facility near Basingstoke, England. Doctors at the No. 1 Neurological Hospital treated psychiatric disorders and performed plastic surgery.

Psychiatrists had started to recognize that some of the men who suffered from combat fatigue should never have been sent to the front in the first place; mentally, they simply weren't capable of coping with the trauma of intense or prolonged periods of front-line combat where it was "kill or be killed" day after day, for weeks on end. Not surprisingly, some senior commanders in the field, who were increasingly desperate for reinforcements as the war dragged on, were hostile to that notion. Nowhere was that truer than in the RCAF. Any air crew who suffered from battle-related traumatic stress were labelled as "lacking in moral fibre." The treatment for that wasn't hospitalization; it was harsh discipline.[20]

No amount of discipline or medical treatment would have made a difference to those veterans who returned home unwilling or unable to settle down to a nine-to-five routine, a spouse and kids, bills, and a mortgage. Some of them took to self-destructive behaviour; others—a much smaller number—were drawn by the lure of quick money and turned to crime for their livelihoods. That was the Polka Dot Gang's motivation. At least two of the gang members were army veterans; one was Hubert Hiscox, a man who knew all there was to know about weapons and killing.

Hiscox's life had gone off the rails early. Born in Toronto in 1920, he was, in the words of his mother, "the black sheep" in a family of eight children.[21] While coming of age during the Great Depression, he fell in with the proverbial bad crowd. His teenage involvement in an escalating cycle of petty crime inevitably landed him in jail, and he was doing time in Kingston Penitentiary in September 1939 when war broke out in Europe. For Hiscox, volunteering for the army was his "get out of jail free" card. Even better, he suddenly found himself in his element.

Because he already was familiar with and loved guns, Hiscox proved himself to be a crack shot—the best in his army training group—with a pistol and a machine gun. He went on to see combat action in Italy in 1943 where he fought as a member of the legendary Devil's Brigade. That elite American–Canadian commando unit was a forerunner of today's Joint Task Force 2 of the Canadian military and the United States Navy's SEAL special-ops teams. Dark-haired, with chiselled features and an icy, piercing gaze, Hubert Hiscox was twenty-three years old, wily, and ruthless. As the *Globe and Mail* reported, "Fellow soldiers had described him as tough, capable and 'able to lick his weight in wildcats.'"[22]

SENSATIONAL MEDIA REPORTS ABOUT bank robberies, heists, gun battles, and police chases in the Toronto area in the late summer and autumn of 1945 fanned the flames of public fears of a jump in the country's crime rate. "It's the number of firearms around that alarms me. We didn't have as much gunplay after the last war," a retired police officer said. "I can't understand how those fellows are getting hold of machine-guns."[23]

The answer to that question should not have been hard to fathom. A Toronto factory had produced tens of thousands of Sten guns during the war, and at the end not all of them went to the scrap bin or were accounted for. They were, the media reported, "circulating throughout Canada in increasing numbers."[24] These British-designed automatic weapons, which were of relatively simple design, lightweight, and inexpensive to make—$10 each, it was said—were good only at close range and were prone to jamming. Despite this, they were widely used by Canadian, British, and other Commonwealth troops during the war. In automatic mode, a Sten gun could spray out its thirty-two-bullet clip in about four seconds, making it a formidable weapon in the hands of a determined criminal such as Hubert Hiscox. However, the Sten gun wasn't the Polka Dot Gang's weapon of choice. They preferred their nickel-plated handguns, which along with their bandanas were their calling cards.

Why Budger Green decided these two accessories should carve out a distinctive identity for himself and his gang isn't clear. It became their "brand," even though it originated with another gang of hoodlums who were active in Chicago in 1942. Then in 1943, a popular movie musical directed by Busby Berkeley called *The Gang's All Here* featured a lavish song-and-dance number called the "Polka-Dot Polka." Budger Green no doubt read the newspaper and went to the movies; in those days, both were popular pastimes.

What *is* known for certain is that Green, who was born in 1924 in Toronto, fit the stereotype of the young hoodlum of the day: he came from a troubled single-parent home and had limited education.

His American-born father, Herbert Green, was an alcoholic who frequently crawled inside a bottle and disappeared for weeks. It was a struggle for his wife to raise their four children, and on at least one occasion, Budger Green and his siblings ended up in foster care. Not surprisingly, Green didn't progress past grade school. Hot-headed and prone to violence, he was still a teenager when he turned to crime to pay for the expensive clothes he loved.

Green was partial to bespoke suits, colourful ties, and stylish fedoras. Six-feet tall, he was a lean 175 pounds (183 centimetres and 79 kilograms), with brown eyes, bushy brows, a broad nose, a strong chin, and a full head of dark brown hair that he combed straight back. Green cut a stylish figure, and so he seldom wanted for female company. He had the look of a young man who knew what he wanted and wasted no time grabbing it.

Green's criminal activities ramped up until 1944. He was just nineteen when a judge sentenced him to fourteen years in prison on five criminal charges, one of which was resisting arrest. He had shot at police when they nabbed him during a break-and-enter attempt. In prison, Green was smart enough to stay out of trouble and won early release after just three years, but he wasn't reformed; far from it. Green and four pals formed the Polka Dot Gang, and their first heist was at the Wellington Packers meat-packing plant in Guelph, Ontario, on the night of June 25, 1945.

After breaking into the building, the gang surprised a night watchman named J. Forestell. After roughing up the sixty-eight-year-old man and knocking him unconscious, the gang tied poor Mr. Forestell to a chair. When he began to stir, they smacked him senseless twice more.

The Polka Dot Gang made up in muscle for whatever they lacked in finesse. They used sledgehammers to smash open the safe and pocket $1,000. Then, having worked up an appetite with all their hard labour, they took off their bandanas long enough to enjoy soft drinks they found in the lunchroom icebox and some smoked-meat cold cuts they retrieved from a storage locker. It later took the night watchman a couple of hours to regain his senses, free himself, and call the police to report the break-in. He then went to hospital, where doctors stitched the cuts on his head and wired his broken jaw back into place.

Budger Green and his pals used the modus operandi they adopted for that Guelph heist in similar nocturnal robberies of packing plants, dairies, and flour mills they pulled off in Hamilton, Stratford, and elsewhere in southwestern Ontario.

The alarming upward spiral of robberies and violence continued on October 8 when the Polka Dot Gang hit the Roselawn Farms Dairy on Dufferin Street in what in 1945 was Toronto's west end. After breaking into the business in the wee hours of the morning, the gang roughed up a couple of dairy employees, one of whom was night watchman William Bartie. The gang member who knocked him out relieved the watchman's wallet of $150 after slugging Bartie so hard it broke his false teeth. The night's violence didn't end there.

When two more employees showed up while the gang were pounding at the safe with sledgehammers, the robbers herded the frightened men at gunpoint into the business office, where Bartie and his fellow employee were lying unconscious in a pool of their blood.

It was the abrupt ringing of the office telephone that ended the dairy workers' ordeal. When another early arriving employee, shipping clerk Lew Ireland, called the office, the bandits panicked. They prepared to flee just as Ireland, curious why no one was answering the phone in the main office, hopped into a delivery truck and raced around to the front entrance to see if there was any trouble. He arrived just as Green and his crew were leaving the parking lot. The two vehicles screeched to a halt just inches from a collision.

Ireland, mouth agape, was still wondering what was happening when he spotted the barrel of a Sten gun poking out a window of the strange car. Instantly throwing his vehicle into reverse, he backed out of the way just as the gunman fired off a quick burst of eight shots, likely meant to serve as a warning. Ireland's split-second decision to retreat may well have saved his life. "There was a steady flame from the barrel of the gun, but none of the shots hit me," he later said. "It must have been my lucky day."[25]

Frustrated that their latest heist had been a bust, Green and his crew struck again the following night. On October 9, they robbed the business office of a bus line. As usual, they roughed up the lone employee they encountered. But rather than wasting time trying to hammer open the safe, this time they just hauled it away on a stolen truck. This turned out to be a lot of heavy lifting for not much loot. The safe contained just $400, a single Victory Bond worth $100, and $350 in bus tickets.

The Polka Dot Gang's run of unsuccessful robberies continued two nights later when they tried to knock off another Toronto dairy. Again, they attempted to make off with the safe, this one with $4,000 locked inside. All five of the gang members were straining to push the heavy coffer onto the back of a truck when one of them noticed the dairy company's stableman—Jim Morgan—had disappeared. He had slipped out of the ropes that bound him and run off. Having suffered a broken nose when one of the robbers punched him in the face, Morgan was trailing blood as he sprinted to the nearest business that had a telephone. Unfortunately, an army veteran in a wheelchair was using the phone, and he refused to surrender it for ten long minutes. The absurd scene was a Monty Python skit. By the time Morgan was able to call the police and they went racing to the dairy, the robbers were long gone. Again, they'd left empty-handed and frustrated.

Police and the media were on high alert, waiting for the gang's next robbery attempt in Toronto. That would be more than two weeks later. In the meantime, Budger Green and his henchmen, with bills to pay, returned to small-town Ontario. They found what they figured would be a quick, easy score on October 12 in bucolic Stratford, ninety-three miles (150 kilometres) west of Toronto. The Swift Canadian meat-packing plant seemed like an easy target; the safe contained a little over $3,200, but once again the gang were thwarted in their efforts to get at the money and fled the scene mere minutes before police arrived with guns drawn. The robbers were starting to make mistakes, and those slip-ups were about to matter.

For one thing, the cleaner at the Swift Canadian plant had her three young sons with her when the gang burst in. They tied up the boys and the company's nighttime engineer but didn't harm or even restrain the woman. One of the robbers informed her that in the army he and his pals had been trained to kill only "the enemy." That meant as long as she kept quiet, no harm would come to her or anyone else. That bit of information about the gang members' backgrounds helped police narrow the list of suspects. So, too, did the detailed descriptions of the gang's nattily dressed six-foot ringleader, which the Swift Canadian cleaner and several other robbery witnesses provided. When police figured out that Budger Green was their target, their informants on the street soon helped pinpoint the Polka Dot Gang's hideout. It was somewhere in the northeast Toronto suburb of Richmond Hill, which in 1945 was still largely a sleepy rural area.[26] The authorities figured it was only a matter of time until the gang resurfaced, and when they did, the police would be ready for them. They were right on both counts.

FRIDAY, OCTOBER 26, WAS a clear, crisp autumn day. To Green and his associates, it probably seemed like a perfect day to scope out potential robbery targets. When all five members of the Polka Dot Gang took a drive to do just that, police spotted their vehicle parked outside a Spadina Road dairy; Toronto had a lot of dairies in 1945. In a wink, the chase was on. Seven police cars, sirens blaring, pursued the gang's vehicle on a high-speed chase through Toronto streets. The dragnet ended abruptly when police patrol cars blocked a busy Dufferin Street intersection. A shotgun-wielding officer covered Green and his men until a small army of police officers arrived and arrested the suspects.

Initially, the men were held on vagrancy charges, but it didn't take long for police to identify them all as being members of the Polka Dot Gang, or to gather enough evidence to put together a solid case against them. Police were chagrined to discover that Budger Green was out of jail on bail at the time of his latest arrest. Police in the Toronto suburb of Markham had detained him two days earlier, October 23, for being drunk in public. In the scuffle to arrest him, Green had broken the nose and blackened an eye of one cop and threatened to kill another. Small wonder that when Green and his co-accused appeared in a Toronto courtroom on November 2 to face arraignment on six charges, presiding magistrate R.J. Brown was in no mood to be lenient. "Don't take up my time talking about bail," he cautioned the gang's lawyer.[27]

Budger Green was never one to hide his emotions, and he didn't take well the news that he'd been refused bail. Guards jumped to restrain him on the way out of court when he charged newspaper photographers. Undeterred by Green's threats, the cameramen continued snapping away, flashbulbs popping. A photo that appeared in that day's late edition of the *Toronto Daily Star* showed an accused gang member hunched over, shielding his face behind his overcoat, as he was hustled into a police paddy wagon.

Predictably, when Green and his co-defendants next appeared in court on December 10, they pleaded not guilty to all charges against them. Court officials set a January trial date. However, the proceedings were delayed after two of the gang—George Dobbie, twenty-nine, and Bruce Kay, twenty-five—took off after their lawyer convinced a judge to grant them bail, Kay's mother and two other women having posted the $10,000 fee. The pair slipped across the border into the United States, where police in Detroit arrested them and a companion. They were nabbed for driving the wrong direction on a one-way street and making an illegal turn against a red light.[28] It seems safe to assume that Dobbie and Kay weren't the brains behind the Polka Dot Gang.

A Michigan court would sentence the pair to "between four and ten years" in prison.[29] Even so, they still fared better than Budger Green and his co-accused, twenty-two-year-old George Constantine. When the pair stood trial in June 1946, the evidence against them was so overwhelming that the presiding judge sentenced both men to fourteen-year terms in prison.

However, Green wasn't ready to go away quietly. Not yet. A few weeks later, he masterminded a daring attempt to break out of Toronto's Don Jail, where he and Constantine were being held as their appeals were pending. Like many of Green's capers, his escape attempt was nothing if not inventive. After overcoming two guards and using strips of torn bedsheets to tie them up, Green and Constantine tried to scale the twenty-foot (six metre) jail wall by clambering up a human pyramid of thirty inmates who'd gathered in the jail's exercise yard. Their Cirque du Soleil–like climb to possible freedom ended abruptly when armed guards arrived on the scene.[30] Green and Constantine meekly returned to their cells, and by February 1947, both were among the inmates at the infamous Kingston Penitentiary, the closest thing Canada had to an Alcatraz.[31]

That was game over for Budger Green. He was just twenty-three and was destined to spend the rest of what would be an abbreviated life behind bars, where he kept busy learning to be a tailor—what else?—when he wasn't busy plotting another escape. Unfortunately for Green, he would never enjoy the opportunity to use his newly acquired sewing skills on the outside. On the morning of July 4, 1954, he died in the prison hospital. The exact cause of death wasn't recorded; however, a newspaper report indicated that at age thirty, Green had died of viral meningitis, which he had contracted in prison.[32]

Although Budger Green was dead, and three of his gang were serving long sentences, police remained on the lookout for the last member of the Polka Dot Gang. Hubert Hiscox had walked out of court a free man after beating the rap for his alleged role in the Lake of the Woods Milling Company heist. Although Hiscox had been lying low for more than two years, Toronto police suspected he was involved in a series of robberies in which thieves had blasted open safes. It seemed likely it would be only a matter of time until he would try to pull off another heist. They were right about that. When Hiscox resurfaced, he would do so with a bang, a very loud one.

A snowstorm was raging early on the morning of February 28, 1948, when police responded to a burglar alarm at the offices of a construction company in Toronto's north end. Three officers who entered the building surprised Hiscox, who was using explosives to open the company safe. Its door was half off the hinges, and Hiscox was about to set off another blast when police interrupted him. A brief, frantic foot chase through the darkened building ended abruptly when Hiscox tried to hurl a bottle of nitroglycerine at his pursuers and it detonated in his hand. The blast blew three fingers off his left hand, tore out both his eyes, and collapsed his lungs. He died three hours later in hospital.[33] It was an abrupt, inglorious end for the last member of the infamous Polka Dot Gang. They were gone from the streets, but they were not soon forgotten.

Police in the Toronto area were kept busy dealing with the gang's legacy, which included would-be treasure hunters who turned up at the gang's old Richmond Hill hideout seeking missing loot, and with chasing down other high-profile criminal gangs. Among the most notable of them was the Boyd Gang, four felons who in the late 1940s and early 1950s were responsible for a string of sensational bank robberies, jail breaks, and gun battles with police in and around Toronto. Alonzo Boyd, the leader, took a page out of Budger Green's playbook. He was colourful, had a flair for the dramatic, wore expensive bespoke suits, and loved the limelight. Unlike Green, Boyd was a veteran, one of that small—but not insignificant—number of returning soldiers who had trouble settling into civilian life when the war ended and turned to crime in a country that had changed irrevocably.

====

CAPTURING THE LOOK AND SOUL OF CANADA IN THE '40S

George Franklin Arbuckle
(Neville Quinlan)

No artist better captured the essence of everyday life in Canada during the war years than did George Franklin Arbuckle (1909–2001). Among the more than one hundred covers he created for Maclean's magazine beginning in 1944 (including those seen on pages 113 and 273), are many images that are pure Canadiana.

It's been said Arbuckle was "Canada's Norman Rockwell." While that comparison is fair, it's not entirely accurate. Rockwell was primarily an illustrator; Arbuckle was that and so much more. He was also a serious artist whose paintings now hang in major museums, galleries, and private collections far and wide.

Toronto-born "Archie" Arbuckle was eighteen when he enrolled at the Ontario College of Art in 1927. Three decades years later, in 1958, he returned there to teach, and from 1960 to 1964 served as president of the Royal Canadian Academy of Arts. Throughout his career, Arbuckle—whose wife was fellow artist Frances-Anne Johnston, the daughter of Group of Seven member Frank Johnston—travelled widely and painted prolifically. Canadian artists in the 1940s never got rich, and so in addition to his "serious art," Arbuckle earned his living as a commercial artist, painting commissioned works for CP Railway, CP Air, the Hudson's Bay Company, and Maclean's at a time when that magazine was helping to forge a more nationalist identity for Canada.

If the present rate of production can be maintained after
the war, the absorption into civilian life of the men and women
of the Armed Services and in the war industry presents no
serious problems.
—C.D. Howe, Minister of Munitions and Supply, 1943

CHAPTER 16

The Post-War Boom Begins

D OROTHY GALE SAID IT WELL. WHEN THE CHARACTER
played by actress Judy Garland in the iconic 1939 film *The Wizard
of Oz* gushed, "There's no place like home," she was giving voice
to the thoughts of Hal MacDonald and every other man and
woman who wore the uniforms of the Canadian military during
WWII. It was true; there was no place like home.

In MacDonald's case, that was Saint John, New Brunswick.
The city joined other cities, towns, and communities all across the
country in staging joyous welcome-home parades and receptions
for their local regiments. Cheering crowds and bands met the troop
trains that arrived at local stations, and the Department of Veterans
Affairs, with help from provincial governments, the Red Cross, and
Bell Telephone, set up discharge depots. Staff at these facilities were
themselves veterans. That helped smooth the way and eased the anxieties of the veterans who came into the depots, but it did not make
the wheels of bureaucracy turn any faster. "To the veteran, [the]
rehabilitation machinery moves with maddening slowness . . . but it
gets things done," Blair Fraser of *Maclean's* reported after visiting the
Montreal Veterans' Rehabilitation Centre in June 1945.[1]

Demobilization was a massive, complex, and costly undertaking.

Prior to VE day on May 8, more than 250,000 members of the armed forces had already been discharged. Another 145,000 returned to "civvy street" by year's end, and a further 381,031 in 1946. Once they were back on Canadian soil, returning veterans remained in uniform and on the military payroll for the thirty days it took to process demobilization papers, and then they received a tax-free gratuity that was based on the length and circumstances of their service time. The basic payout was $7.50 for each month of service, $7.75 for those who had served overseas. Many veterans also got a $100 clothing allowance to help them in their return to civilian life. Corporal Havelyn Chiasson, the radio operator in the North Shore (New Brunswick) Regiment—the same unit Hal MacDonald served with—recalled receiving his clothing allowance; the experience was less than satisfying. "When I got back to New Brunswick, I had to go to pay my own way to get to Fredericton, where I received my discharge," he said. "I also got a $100 voucher to buy clothing, but it didn't go very far. I went into a shop in Bathurst that catered to veterans, and I bought some clothes—socks, underwear and such—but I had no money to buy work clothes, so I ended up borrowing some from friends. I wasn't very happy about that."[2]

A. Britton Smith, an army veteran who was gravely wounded and won a Military Cross for his battlefield bravery in July 1944, returned to Canada on a hospital ship that autumn. He resumed his life in Kingston, Ontario, and married Edith "Sally" Carruthers, the sweetheart who had waited for him. After recovering his health, Smith attended Osgoode Hall Law School in Toronto courtesy of an educational program that allowed veterans to attend university tuition-free and receive a living allowance.

"I used my $100 clothing chit to buy a nice grey suit that I planned to wear to my first day of law school classes in Toronto; I thought I'd be the sharpest-looking guy at the law school," Smith recalled. "When I turned up for class, I saw that three-quarters of the guys in my class were wearing what looked to be the same grey suit I had on. It must have been some kind of standard government issue."[3]

Artist Franklin Arbuckle's wonderful cover of the June 1, 1945, issue of *Maclean's*.
(Thomas Fisher Rare Book Library, University of Toronto)

Hal MacDonald had no similar post-war experiences with his clothing allowance or with other government programs for veterans. He was atypical in that he steered clear of the demobilization depot at

Saint John. Nor did he join the Canadian Legion, a veterans' organization whose membership ballooned in the late 1940s. MacDonald did his best to move on in his life and seldom bothered to speak about his wartime experiences. "The old saying still holds good, we who have seen a bit of the real thing, dislike and refuse to talk about it—only when some of us who were together then, get together, do we discuss the funnier side of it," he explained.[4]

Captain R.B. Menzies, Highland Light Infantry of Canada, and Miss Pamela van der Jagt, wed in the town hall of Naarden, Netherlands, October 18, 1945. (LAC, MIKAN no. 3200840)

Once he was safely back home, MacDonald wanted only to settle into post-war civilian life. He and his wife, Marjorie, would have two children—a son and a daughter—and Hal would work at a local firm of manufacturers' agents and food brokers, eventually becoming a partner in Leonard and MacDonald Limited. Like many veterans who continued to believe in the idea of public service, he involved himself in his community and also stood as president of the New Brunswick chapter of the Canadian Red Cross for three years, 1964–67, and as national president of the Canadian Food Wholesalers in 1977–78.[5]

It's fair to say that for Havelyn Chiasson, A. Britton Smith, and most other Canadian veterans of WWII—and even for independent-minded veterans such as Hal MacDonald—the Veterans Charter proved to be one of the most ambitious and far-reaching legislative packages ever enacted by a Canadian government. Its effects were myriad, and they were transformative.

One of the most popular individual initiatives was the Department of Veterans Affairs program that allowed vets to return to school; a single man received $65 per month while attending classes full time, while a married man got $85. Tuition was free for all veterans. Such an offer was too good to pass up for all those who felt their wartime service to Canada had earned them the opportunity to better themselves.

Among them was John Wolpe, a young Jewish man who had escaped Nazi persecution by fleeing Germany early in the war. He lay low in France until 1944 and then joined the Royal Winnipeg Rifles upon their post–D-Day arrival there. Wolpe served as a corporal for the duration of the war in the Canadian army, doing so without pay. He had vengeance on his mind and was unflinching in battle. Wolpe killed twenty-eight German soldiers, persuaded twenty others to surrender, and ended up in a military hospital with wounds he suffered in combat. After the war, he immigrated to Winnipeg with help from the Canadian Legion and then enrolled at the University of Manitoba. "Twenty-eight Dead Nazis His Tuition Fee for Diploma at Canadian U," the Canadian Press news service reported.[6]

Wolpe joined the almost 175,000 Canadian veterans who returned to school post-war. Between 1944 and 1951, 53,000 of them enrolled at universities across the country. Admission standards were relaxed to allow those who might not have qualified otherwise to enroll and to benefit from special tutoring. Prior to this time, attending any of Canada's twenty-nine universities was something few Canadians did— less than three per cent in the 1930s—and usually those who did so were the sons and daughters of the well-to-do. Now suddenly, anyone with the desire and the intellectual ability to study at university could and did. "It was this great influx of veterans, men and women, in the first post-war years, which began a completely new era in the history of Canadian higher education,"[7] noted historian Donald Creighton.

University enrollments swelled when the first great wave of veterans arrived on campuses in the summer of 1945.[8] And when that happened, the demand for humanities fell as students who were veterans opted to study in applied science programs. This put enormous strain on engineering facilities, libraries, teaching staffs, and housing, especially at smaller schools. The situation was typical at Queen's University, located in the sleepy eastern Ontario city of Kingston.

There, an influx of almost 700 students grew enrollment to about 4,200, a number that created a huge student housing problem in a city of 32,000. Until more suitable accommodations were found, veteran students who were single found themselves sleeping in gymnasiums, cafeterias, storerooms, and just about any other available space. Some veteran students were housed in a vacant dormitory at Royal Military College, while others bunked in temporary buildings that had been built for war workers on the grounds of the local aluminum plant.

Housing problems were even greater for those married veterans who arrived in Kingston with wives and children in tow. Some set up housekeeping in house trailers that were parked on vacant campus lots; others lived in tents and assorted temporary shelters, while still others scrounged for whatever accommodation they could find. "If you want to see how anxious to obtain quarters these young people really are," the editor of the *Kingston Whig-Standard* newspaper reported one day in October 1945, "visit [our] office nearly any day as the paper rolls off the press. You will see young couples, the husband often still wearing the trench coat of the army or the blue raincoat of the RCAF, buying the papers and quickly turning to the classified ads. The few 'To Let' are spotted, and the daily quest begins."[9]

The severe student housing crunch at Queen's and at many other schools lasted into the 1950s. Some veteran students who discovered they simply weren't cut out for student life inevitably became frustrated and dropped out. However, the majority hung in there and graduated. Having grown up during the Great Depression and then spending as much as six years in the military, these were men and women who were used to "making do."

Those veterans who earned their university degrees in the late 1940s and early 1950s would go on to be some of the most product- ive, energetic, and successful graduates in the history of Canadian post-secondary education. They were also among the most loyal and generous when it came to giving back in support of their alma mater. For example, at Queen's the engineering grads of the Class of Science '48½—who had started an accelerated four-year program in the middle of an academic year and graduated in three-and-a-half years—would donate unstintingly to the university, and in 1998 they would launch a mature student entrance bursary that paid more than $60,000 over four years, one of the most generous awards of its kind in Canada and possibly even in North America. There are myriad examples of similar acts of selfless generosity on the part of alumni veterans at many of Canada's universities.

Other post-war government initiatives were similarly successful, and their effects were no less significant or enduring. A prime example is the program that enabled veterans to buy their own homes with money provided by low-cost, government-backed mortgages.

Home ownership was a dream come true for an entire genera- tion that probably would otherwise never have been able to purchase a house. The ripple effects of such a massive infusion of money into the economy sparked a boom that literally transformed Canada, cata- pulting it into the most prosperous era in its history.

Prior to the war, much of this country's housing was old, over- crowded, and in need of repair or modernization.[10] The 1941 census had revealed that just sixty per cent of homes had plumbing, while fifty-six per cent had an indoor toilet, and forty-five per cent had a bathtub or shower. The numbers were far lower in rural areas than in cities and towns.

There had been little new housing built during the ten years of the Great Depression and during the war—apart from the rental housing units erected by a federal Crown corporation called Wartime Housing Limited (WHL), that is. Between 1941 and 1945, the WHL had erected 26,000 rental units for war-industry workers and veterans, mostly in the Toronto area. The entire town of Ajax, Ontario, was just one of the WHL housing projects that consisted of street after street filled with modest wood-frame bungalows.

At war's end, the federal government exited the rental housing business—and according to some critics, abandoned its nascent leadership role in providing Canadians with affordable housing. Ottawa did this on January 1, 1946, when it turned over the administration of its housing legislation and most WHL properties to a new Crown agency. The Central Mortgage and Housing Corporation (CMHC) was capitalized with $25 million in public money. "Possibly the most important piece of legislation the corporation will administer," the *Globe and Mail* reported, "is the National Housing Act of 1944, aimed at promoting the construction of new houses and the repair and modernization of existing homes."[11]

Canada's financial institutions took the creation of the CMHC as their cue to jump into the mortgage business. And when they did so, business was brisk and profitable.

Federal bureaucrats had set a goal of 50,000 new homes to be built in the first year after VE day, May 8, 1945, to May 8, 1946. Despite the shortages of building materials and skilled tradespeople, that number proved to be more than doable; by the end of 1945, the goal had already been surpassed. Then in 1946, builders constructed 67,200 new homes, and the following year 79,300, with a total value of more than $526 million; in today's dollars, that would be more than $7.1 billion. Any way you look at it, that was an enormous boost for the Canadian economy.

Those hundreds of thousands of veterans who had returned home eager to find work, buy a house, get married, and have children drove the red-hot housing market. And why not? These were men and women who by virtue of their wartime service and what they had sacrificed felt they were entitled to live "the life of Reilly."[12] They say that most good fortune is earned, and in the case of Canada's veterans, it clearly was. The Veterans Charter provided all those who fought for their country with educational opportunities, home ownership programs, free medical care for a year, and lifetime care for service-related wounds or conditions. It all added up.

Maclean's journalist Douglas MacFarlane travelled to Windsor, Ontario, in March of 1946 to interview sixteen veterans of the Essex South Regiment. He wanted to find out how the men were faring in their return to civilian life. There were, of course, the inevitable bureaucratic snafus that affected life for veterans in Windsor and everywhere else in Canada. The Pension Commission was inundated with applications, resulting in a three-month backlog in processing claims. That was government in action.

Each of the Canadian veterans who came home with serious wounds and disabilities faced a unique set of problems, and then there were those men whose marriages had crumbled during the long years they had been away. MacFarlane heard about all those problems and more, yet his conclusion was sanguine. "Out of it all comes confirmation that no matter what pains a government may take in planning rehabilitation, Human Nature still wields a big stick," he concluded. "Some veterans are lining their sights a bit too high; others aren't bothering to aim at all. Some employers aren't pulling their weight. There are faults on both sides and the Government's system isn't foolproof. But in the main, it is sincere."[13]

Fate smiled most broadly on those veterans who had set their sights sensibly and well. It also smiled on Canada as a country. As historian Douglas Orwam explained, "Everything thus came together— low unemployment, low down-payments, and availability of credit. Canadians built and bought houses at a greater rate than at any time in their history."[14] This led to what has been aptly described as "the great phenomenon of the mid-twentieth century"[15]—the growth of suburbia and the sprawling subdivisions that sprang up around cities all across Canada.

The chief attraction of suburban life, especially for WWII veterans who had been born in the 1920s and came of age during the hungry years of the 1930s, was the prospect of owning a detached single-family home, one with a grassy backyard and a garage in a nice neighbourhood. With the affordability issue resolved, "the Canadian dream" of home ownership became achievable and affordable for an entire generation. Interest rates were low, and mortgage amortization rates were spread over twenty-five or thirty years. Even as prices rose, the monthly cost of home ownership remained manageable and wise. A popular refrain of the day summarized that sentiment: "It's better to make a monthly mortgage payment on your own place than it is to waste the money on rent." Those words are still heard today, although regrettably much less often—especially coming from the lips of young people in Canada's big cities.

In 1945, $12,000 bought you a comfortable bungalow in the north Toronto suburb of Don Mills, one of the communities being built by a development company that savvy entrepreneurs such as E.P. Taylor and his Argus Corporation partners had invested in. On the outskirts of cities from coast to coast, suburbs sprouted up like dandelions after a spring rain. Farmland was relatively inexpensive, and developers snapped up vast acreages. And as cities sprawled and the pace of Canada's urbanization quickened, the demand for utilities and services grew—an ever-spreading electrical grid, roads and sewers, expanded public transit, and new schools, hospitals, and shopping centres.

Owning a new home in suburbia also required buying furnishings, appliances, and fixtures to fill the rooms and possibly a shiny new North American–made automobile. That seemed like the thing to do. Wages were rising; the middle class was prospering, and labour unions were thriving. A January 1944 emergency order-in-council, PC 1003, had protected the rights of workers to join a union while imposing a legal duty on employers to recognize any union that was chosen by their employees. These provisions were destined to become a corner-stone of post-war industrial relations in this country.

New housing developments, many consisting of pre-fab structures, were springing up all across Canada at war's end. (City of Toronto Archives, *Globe and Mail* fonds, fond 1266, item 100525)

Unions flexed their muscles in the last half of 1945 when they staged a series of high-profile strikes across the country. Workers felt they were now in the driver's seat, and it seemed they were when they won major wage hikes, reduced work hours, improved fringe benefits, and other concessions that enabled the unions themselves to keep growing. A bitter ninety-nine-day strike by 17,000 United Auto Workers members at the Ford automotive plant in Windsor, Ontario, ended on December 19 after a landmark arbitration decision made by Supreme Court justice Ivan C. Rand. The judge's ruling gave unions the right to collect "closed shop" compulsory dues from all employees in a workplace. This ruling was pivotal because it gave unions financial security and enabled them to build huge war chests.

Canadian workers and their unions were doing very well post-war, thank you. But so were many employers. The feverish housing market and the rising wage levels powered a robust, pent-up demand for consumer goods of all kinds.

In 1941, barely a quarter of Canadian homes had a refrigerator, while most of the rest still relied on an icebox to keep food from spoiling. Now, suddenly, the owners of every new home in the country wanted refrigerators and other new appliances. The Canadian economy was firing on all cylinders at war's end. Between 1946 and 1976, Canada's economic growth was phenomenal. It averaged 9.4 per cent annually, split evenly between real growth of 4.7 per cent and inflation at 4.3 per cent.

Veterans had money in their pockets. Jobs were plentiful, and all signs pointed toward a rosy future. A majority of the men who had volunteered for Canada's armed forces were young, between the ages of eighteen and twenty-four. Many of them had hastily wed before going overseas, and so in 1941 and 1942 there had been a spike in the number of weddings. Many of the bachelors who returned to "civvy street" in 1945 did so eager to find a wife and then settle down. From coast to coast, wedding bells began ringing in earnest.

GREY CUP CHAMPIONS

Football returned to relative normalcy in 1945 following the end of the war. Two long-time rivals from the pre-war years met in the thirty-third annual Grey Cup game. However, on this occasion, the Winnipeg Blue Bombers were no match for the Toronto Argonauts, losing by a score of 35–0 in the game, which was played at Varsity Stadium in Toronto. Winnipeg's loss was the worst by a western team in the Grey Cup since 1923 when Queen's University routed the Regina Roughriders 54–0.

Upon arrival in Canada, women travelling beyond Nova
Scotia continued by train, still escorted by the Red Cross.
It was nerve-wracking, coming to a new country to join
husbands whom they barely knew and whose families
they had never met.
— *The Canadian Encyclopedia*

CHAPTER 17

War Brides and the Baby Boom

THERE WERE 108,031 WEDDINGS IN CANADA IN 1945, AND that number jumped to 138,088 in 1946.[1] Each year for the next two decades, more than 123,000 couples tied the knot; in 1964, Canada reached a post-war high-water mark when 138,135 marriages were recorded. Nowadays, in a typical year, there are about 160,000 marriages in Canada (with about four per cent of them being same-sex unions). In 1945, the country's population was twelve million; today, it's about thirty-seven million, more than three times as large. If Canadians were still marrying at the same rate they were in 1945, the annual total of weddings would be about 480,000. That, of course, is impossible in a world in which the very concept of "marriage" has evolved and it's no longer *de rigueur* to include a religious ceremony, let alone one that legally unites a man and a woman.

A 2018 Angus Reid poll found that a slim majority of Canadians— fifty-three per cent—thought a formal marriage ceremony is "no longer necessary,"[2] and about forty per cent of marriages end in divorce. Attitudes and social mores have changed dramatically since 1945.

The vast majority of Canadian veterans who married in the post-war years wed brides who were Canadian born—high school sweethearts or partners the men had met while they were in uniform and stationed in bases around Canada, especially on the east coast. That was so for navy veteran Bill Fitsell, who had been the ship scribe on HMCS *St. Francis*. The Barrie, Ontario, native was twenty-three on the night in February 1945 that he and some of his shipmates attended a dance in Sydney, Nova Scotia. "I met a beautiful young lady on the dance floor named Barbara Robson," Fitsell recalled. "She wanted to jitterbug, but I did a version of the foxtrot. As the story goes, she said: 'Don't tell me I'm stuck with *this* guy all night.' So I learned the jitterbug, and the rest is history."[3]

Barbara Robson and Bill Fitsell wed six months later, in an October 12 ceremony at an Anglican church in Sydney. More than seven decades later, the still happily married couple are the parents of five grown daughters and the grandparents of seventeen grandchildren. Said Bill, "I guess you could say it all turned out pretty well for both of us."[4]

The Fitsells' story is typical; however, another aspect of the story of Canada's post-war marriage boom that's no less striking is the number of brides who were foreign born. Human nature being what it is, love happens in the most unlikely of situations. And so it was that more than 48,000 women whom members of the Canadian military— mostly army men—met while serving overseas crossed the Atlantic as war brides.

Barbara (née Robson) and Bill Fitsell on their October 1945 wedding day and on their seventieth anniversary in 2015. (Bill Fitsell)

Given that so many Canadian servicemen spent long months, years even, based in the United Kingdom, it is not surprising that 45,000 of those imported brides were English, Scottish, Irish, or Welsh. (Another 3,000 came from the Netherlands, Belgium, and France.) There are as many stories of how the flames of romance were kindled as there are couples who met and fell in love. Calgary writer Jacqueline Chartier, who has delved into this aspect of the wartime experiences of Canadian soldiers in Britain, explained it well when she noted, "Although it has become a cliché, the terror and destruction of war itself have traditionally provided a powerful catalyst for young love."[5]

Young love sometimes came with its pitfalls, at least one of which is timeless and predictable. The "guesstimate" is that Canadian servicemen in the United Kingdom—enlisted men and officers—fathered some 22,000 children out of wedlock during the war. Among them is someone whose name any fan of rock music will recognize. The legendary guitarist Eric Clapton, born in March 1945, was the son of one Eric Fryer, a Canadian soldier from Montreal. Fryer shipped out of England before the arrival of his baby son, and so the lad was raised by his grandparents. Clapton's mother was just sixteen when she gave birth, and her son grew up believing she was his older sister. Strange and sad, but true.

Unplanned pregnancies were just one of the concerns for Canadian servicemen and their new-found loves. Many a soldier who was single and eligible was dismayed to discover that falling in love was easier than getting married. Any soldier below the rank of officer who wished to wed needed the approval of his commanding officer, had to swear a declaration attesting to his marital status as a single man who was eligible to marry, and had to prove he had saved at least $200. Those would-be grooms who were under the age of twenty-one were required to have a note of permission from their parents back in Canada. Marriages happened regardless—1,221 of them in 1940 alone, and the number grew each year. So did the number of babies.

Members of the RCAF and the RCN weren't subject to the same restrictions as their army comrades. Commander Peter Chance (Ret'd), who was twenty-four years old in 1944, was serving aboard the destroyer HMCS *Skeena* when he met his future wife. "I was involved with the D-Day landings. Afterward, our ship and many others returned to port in the United Kingdom. We went to Londonderry, Northern Ireland, which was our home port," the Ottawa-born Chance recalled.

"A bunch of us jumped into a Jeep and off we went to a town called Portrush. There was a little restaurant there called the Trocadero. We were seated at our table when across the room we saw a group of young women sitting together. One of the fellows in our group who wasn't as shy as the rest of us sent over a note asking if there were any Irish girls who might like to join us for supper. A note came back that read, 'We're *not* Irish girls, we're English Wrens, and yes, we're hungry.' When the girls came over, the Wren who sat down beside me introduced herself as Margaret Parker. 'But you can call me Peggy.'

"It was love at first sight. I took one look at her, and I said, 'By God, you're beautiful! I'm going to marry you!' Six weeks later, we *were* married, and we even had our wedding reception in the mess aboard *Skeena*. We stayed married for fifty-five years [until Peggy passed away in 1999], and we had four children together—two boys and two girls."[6]

Peggy and Peter Chance (*centre*) celebrating their 1944 wedding at a reception aboard HMCS *Skeena*. (Tim Chance)

Peter Chance today. (Tim Chance)

It was also love at first sight when Isabella Neilson met Gordon French, a young Canadian soldier from North Vancouver. Lean, dark-haired, and bubbling with life, Neilson worked in a Johnny Walker distillery; she and her two younger siblings lived with their mother in a Glasgow working-class neighbourhood. One evening in the spring of 1945, Neilson and two girlfriends were waiting at a bus stop when they heard a male voice behind them announce, "See that one in the middle? I'm going to marry her,"[7] Neilson recalled in a 1995 reminiscence.

She was standing between her two friends, and so naturally she looked around. There were two Canadian soldiers standing there. "They're drunk, don't bother with them," Neilson whispered. Her chums followed Neilson's advice, but as the three young women were boarding their bus, Neilson turned and waved goodbye to the soldiers. That cheeky spur-of-the-moment gesture would change her life.

Next morning, Neilson was late for work, and while racing along the street, she chanced to spot the same two Canadian soldiers to whom she had waved the previous night. (Cue the violins and fast forward eight hours.) That afternoon, when Neilson was leaving work after her shift, she found two young men waiting for her at the distillery gates. One was her fiancé, a young Scotsman. The other was that lovestruck Canadian soldier. Neilson would recall many years later: "I said to one of my friends, 'Go see the Canadian and take him around the corner for an ice cream or something while I talk to my fiancé.' I knew right away I wanted to be with Gordon, so I said to the Scotch boy, 'The engagement is off.'"[8] And it was.

On January 28, 1946, Isabella Neilson and her Canadian suitor became Mr. and Mrs. Gordon French. With VE day now eight months in the past, the couple needed no blessings or permissions other than those given by Neilson's mother and her husband, from whom she was estranged. The wedding ceremony itself was as basic and austere as post-war life in the United Kingdom. A couple of the Neilsons' neighbours who owned an accordion and a saxophone provided the musical soundtrack; other neighbours pitched in to make sandwiches for the wedding meal, and the bride wore a wedding dress she bought "on-time," paying for it over three months.

Gordon French returned home to Canada with his army unit in March 1946, while Isabella, as so many other war brides did, followed when transport ships became available a few months later. The day Isabella French left Glasgow forever, her mother accompanied her to the train station. The scene was heartbreaking. While Isabella looked out the window of the passenger car and waved goodbye as the train was leaving, she was horrified to see her mother collapse on the platform. All the way to London, a tearful daughter worried and agonized about turning back.

Isabella's fears were not quelled until a sympathetic Red Cross worker in the British capital telephoned the police station in the Glasgow neighbourhood of the Neilsons' home. A policeman who went to check on Mrs. Neilson found that although she had fainted at the train station, she was all right and wished her daughter a safe journey. A few days later, a relieved and reassured Isabella French joined 350 other war brides—many of them doubtless with similar haunting memories—on a ship bound for Canada and their new lives.[9]

From January 1942 to August 1944, the London office of the

Immigration Branch of the Canadian Department of Mines and Resources (strange, but true!) had arranged transatlantic transportation to Canada for the war brides and children of servicemen who were serving overseas. In December 1944, Beverley Baxter of *Maclean's* reported in his "London Letter" column that Canadian soldiers "have married British girls at the rate of fifteen a day."[10]

With the number of such marriages ever growing, it was apparent that a more efficient and solicitous system of transit was urgently needed. Alice Massey, wife of the Canadian High Commissioner in London, responded. She established the Canadian Wives' Bureau, an agency that arranged their passage to Canada and prepared the women for their new lives in a distant land. Most of them knew nothing about Canada and in many cases had been told or read information that was untrue or downright fanciful. As one war bride explained, "In England, Canada [was] the back of the beyond."[11]

For most war brides, their first glimpse of Canada was Pier 21 in Halifax, the iconic venue that is now the site of the Canadian Museum of Immigration. In 1945, the pier was the bare-bones passenger landing terminal where hundreds of thousands of immigrants set foot on Canadian soil for the first time and where almost as many military personnel departed for Europe or returned home during WWII. When the war brides arrived in Canada, often with a child or two, and almost always on their own, they were adrift in a strange new country, and many of them faced long journeys before they reached their new homes.

That was certainly so for twenty-two-year-old Betty Harper, who hailed from Yorkshire county in northern England. Home for her Canadian husband was Cromarty, a rural community near Mitchell, twelve miles (twenty kilometres) as the Canada geese fly northwest of Stratford—not Stratford-upon-Avon, William Shakespeare's hometown in England, but that *other* Stratford, in far-off Ontario.

David Mervin ("Merv") Dow had joined the RCAF in WWII intent on becoming a pilot, but his colour-blindness prevented him from achieving his dream. Instead, he became a leading air craftsman—the military term for an airplane engine mechanic—with 432 Squadron, based at East Moor airfield in Yorkshire. That wasn't far from the village where Betty Harper lived with her parents and two sisters.

During the war years, morale-building dances were held in the Grey Village Hall, Sutton-on-Forest. As Betty Dow would recall many years later, it was there one cool evening in January 1944 that she met the "handsome, blond, blue-eyed Canadian airman"[12] who warmed her heart. Twenty-four-year-old Merv Dow had grown up on a farm, and he and Betty hit it off. The couple had a few dances, and afterward Merv walked Betty home. That led to a dinner invitation from the Harper family, and you can probably guess the rest of the happy story: true love blossomed. Betty Harper and Merv Dow married in All Hallows Church in Sutton-on-Forest on October 28, 1944.

Reflecting on her wartime courtship and wedding from a vantage point three-quarters of a century later, at age ninety-six, Betty remembered those days as if they were only yesterday. "I knew Merv would be going back to Canada after the war and that I'd be leaving England to go with him," she said. "Fortunately, my parents liked Merv, and they approved of us getting married. My dad told him, 'You're a great guy,' and he was."[13]

It was June 1945, a month after VE day, when the men of the RCAF contingent at East Moor returned to Canada; Merv Dow was among them. However, with space on passenger ships being scarce at the time, it wasn't until nine long months later, in mid-March 1946, that his bride was able to follow him. "I'd never been very far from home before that, certainly not on a ship," Betty noted. "The day I left home, my family took me to the train station in York to catch the train to London. I was sad to say goodbye to my parents and sisters, but I was also excited. Travelling to Canada was a great adventure for me. I wasn't homesick. Not much, anyway. When you're in love, lots of new and strange things happen in your life."[14]

The Department of National Defence, which had assumed postwar responsibility for transporting the British war brides and children of Canadian servicemen to Canada, had made all the arrangements for Betty Dow's travel. In 1946 alone, 31,250 war brides and 14,070 children made the voyage.[15]

Betty and Merv Dow on their wedding day and in 1994. (Carol Ann Scott)

Betty did so in the company of 1,360 other Halifax-bound war brides and their children who sailed from Southampton aboard the aging Cunard liner RMS *Aquitania*. Five days of rough seas left Betty and many of the other passengers feeling seasick, but there was at least one consolation. "I met some wonderful people aboard the ship," said Betty. "One of them was a girl who was on her way to London, Ontario. I was going to Cromarty, and when we learned we'd be living near one another, we became lifelong friends."[16]

Upon her arrival in Halifax, Betty boarded one of the passenger trains that departed from Pier 21 each day bound for points west; it was a two-day, 1,100-mile (1,800 kilometre) journey to Toronto. At railway stations all along the route—and all across Canada—the federal government with help from the Red Cross had set up reception depots to welcome war brides. Betty also had her own welcoming celebration at Union Station in Toronto. Merv had made the drive from Cromarty to the big city in his Ford Model A coupe, bought with wartime military pay he had sent home from overseas. "There was an early spring that year, and it had rained a lot. I'd never seen a gravel road before, and the ones we travelled on were filled with potholes, some of which were so big you could have lost a cow in them," Betty recalled with a laugh.[17]

Potholed roads weren't the only aspect of life in Canada that took some getting used to. The cold, snowy winters, the expansiveness of the landscape, the strange customs, and the idiomatic quirks of the English language that's spoken in Canada were sources of confusion, some of it amusing. More than one British war bride evoked puzzled looks when she advised someone to "knock me up." While that may have been a common expression back home in the United Kingdom, it was seldom heard in Canada, where "knock on my door" or "knock to wake me in the morning" is more common and less suggestive.

Even more puzzling—not to mention inadvertently cheeky—was the British informal advice to "keep your pecker up." In the United Kingdom, "pecker" is a word for a person's mouth or nose. Of course, in North America the same word is vulgar slang for a male body part that's several degrees lower on the anatomical chart. In Canada, it's more common and socially acceptable to bid someone, "Have a nice day." Those British war brides who advised a male acquaintance to "keep your pecker up" doubtless elicited a wink or a laugh in response.

Despite the strangeness of some aspects of life in Canada, there was one thing all war brides savoured: the relative plenty that Canadians enjoyed. "What a supper I found waiting for me when we got to the home of Merv's family. What a supper, such food as I hadn't seen in six years," Betty Dow recalled. "Oranges and bananas weren't available in England during the war, but I found both waiting for me!"[18]

She and Merv would go on to run a farm in Cromarty for forty years, have two children (a daughter who was born in 1948 and a son who came along in 1953), and lead a full, happy life together until 2000, when Merv died three weeks short of his eightieth birthday. "I know there were some British war brides who weren't happy here, and some went back home. But I never knew any of them. I never had any regrets about marrying Merv or about coming to Canada. I built a wonderful life here," said Betty Dow.[19]

Happily, that was generally the case. Despite the many challenges they faced, it all somehow worked out for most of the war brides. Of course, not all these marriages were happy and some of the women returned home, but the majority of them stuck it out. The remarkable thing is that only about ten per cent of war-bride marriages ended in divorce. Contrast that with the situation today, when Canada's divorce rate hovers around forty per cent. Admittedly, the world now is much different than it was in the immediate post-war years. Divorce was less common then, and it was harder to arrange, but even so, that ten per cent figure is still surprising. Life wasn't easy for many war brides.

THERE WAS ONE OTHER big difference between marriage in post-war Canada and marriage today that merits mention: between 1945 and 1964, newlyweds produced babies at a record rate. The post-war baby boom is now a fading memory.

We live in a time when birth rates in this country have fallen to record-low levels. In 1945, Canada's birth rate was 24.3 babies per thousand of population. That number lingered between 27 and 28.5 until 1959, when it began a long, slow decline. Today, Canada's birth rate languishes at just 10.3. That isn't enough to keep the economy functioning at an optimum level, let alone to continue meeting the fiscal needs of a federal government with myriad spending priorities that continue to grow, especially in the wake of the COVID-19 pandemic that began in 2020. Apart from that, more than 6.5 million Canadians are seniors—age sixty-five and older—who are collecting pensions. Today they represent about seventeen per cent of Canada's population. By 2030, it's estimated that 9.5 million Canadians will be in this age bracket, almost one-quarter of the population.

Some demographers have made the case that Canada should accept enough immigrants to increase the national population to fifty million. Humorist Stephen Leacock went even further—with tongue in cheek, as usual—when he opined that to realize the country's true potential, Canada needs a population of a hundred million. "And below that, I will not go," he quipped.[20] There doubtless are some observers today who would agree with Leacock, *sans* tongue in cheek.

Sadly, the story of Canadian immigration policies both pre- and post-1945 is nothing to be proud of. In the years immediately after the war, the attitude of the Mackenzie King government toward immigration can be charitably described as laissez-faire. To be more blunt and truthful, this country's "selective" approach to immigration was unabashedly racist. That was clear even at the time. Jack Pickersgill, one of King's most trusted aides, admitted the prime minister feared that too much immigration would alter "the *fundamental character* of the Canadian people." That was really "a euphemism for a white Canadian policy, only we were too polite to put it that way."[21]

Ottawa maintained immigration quotas for Black people and for those from Southeast Asia and China. (A 1923 law that had barred Chinese immigration was repealed in 1947.) Despite this, more than a million immigrants came to Canada in the decade after the war, and this country experienced what one historian termed "the collapse of the intellectual underpinning of Anglo-Saxon superiority" at the same time the world was witnessing the decline of Britain as a great imperial power.[22] The United States now stood as a world superpower and the ever-increasing focus of Canada's trade, military alliances, cultural preferences, and much more. At the same time, immigration was already on its way to replacing live births as the source of Canada's population growth.

In the post-war era, ninety-two per cent of women of child-bearing age had children, usually two or three. The result was what demographers aptly dubbed the "baby boom." The same phenomenon that happened in Canada occurred in the United States, in Britain, and even in most of the war-ravaged nations of western Europe. The numbers tell the tale.

A total of 288,730 babies were born in this country in 1945. In 1948, that number jumped to 347,307, and by 1952, it soared to 402,527. That demographic tsunami swept over Canada in two waves; the first occurred between 1944 and 1955, while the second happened between 1956 and 1964. All told, this resulted in about 1.5 million more births (there were about 8.6 million overall) than would have occurred normally, an increase of more than eighteen per cent.

Worldwide, the baby boom generation was the largest in history. In Canada and the United States, by virtue of sheer numbers alone, it was also the best fed, most pampered, and most culturally influential. As stand-up comedian Scott Harris has pointed out, "If you've ever played with a Slinky, or played Twister, or sat in a bean bag chair, or wore something tie-dyed, or hated your parents, or were told to cut your hair and get a job, you're a baby boomer."[23]

So, too, are you if you remember Howdy Doody, the hula hoop, Bobby Gimby and Expo '67, the Cuban missile crisis, Woodstock, rotary-dial telephones, transistor radios, the Beatles craze, the assassination of John F. Kennedy, the Vietnam war, the Toronto Maple Leafs winning the Stanley Cup (1967), cigarette advertising, cheese fondues, or *The Sound of Music* winning the Oscar for best picture (1966); all were cultural touchstones of the baby boom era.

Dr. Benjamin Spock, the American child psychologist, wrote a hugely influential 1946 book called *Baby and Child Care*. This how-to manual for child rearing stands as one of the bestselling books of all time. Spock advised new parents to instill in their children a sense of self-esteem and independence. They did so, following the good doctor's advice to a T. As a result, baby boomers matured to earn another sobriquet that was less than flattering, but well deserved: "the Me Generation."

In the 1960s, millions of young people followed the advice of American LSD guru Timothy Leary, who counselled them to "tune in, turn on, and drop out." Even those boomers who did not experiment with hallucinogens rebelled against the materialism of their parents and instead embraced the counterculture—with its long hair, pot smoking, sexual liberation, and anti-war mantra.

Baby boomers have distorted Canada's demographic profile in the last half of the twentieth century and into the first three decades of this one. Demographers have used the metaphor of a snake swallowing a rabbit. As the rabbit moves along the snake's digestive tract, the once-fat bunny eventually grows ever smaller. The analogy isn't pretty, but it's apt. "Within 20 years after the end of the boom in 1966, the 'rabbit' reached ages twenty to thirty-nine, and its members had moved into the labour force." *The Canadian Encyclopedia* reminds us, "In 2011, the oldest members of the 'rabbit' had reached sixty-five, the traditional retirement age. Until 2031, large further additions to age groups in retirement are expected."[24]

It's ironic that boomers, who were blessed to be born during the golden age of post-war prosperity, came of age at a time when all things seemed possible. They bubbled with idealism and preached love and understanding in their youthful years, and now—at a time when sixty is the new forty—seem utterly intent on "doing their own thing" while refusing to go gently into that good night. Boomers have given demographers, social scientists, and doctoral students no end of material to study and expound upon.

Perhaps we can chalk up—or is it blame?—the baby boomer mindset on human nature, which dictates that as the years fly by, most people hunker down, grow more conservative, cling to whatever it is they've acquired, and puzzle over their legacy in this world.

That said, we shouldn't forget or underestimate the corrosive effects of the negatives that shaped the attitudes of baby boomers as they were coming of age. Think of the Vietnam War and the cynicism the Watergate scandal in the United States bred in an entire generation. Then, too, there was the overarching dread of nuclear apocalypse that hung like a dark cloud over life in Canada and the world for almost forty-five years after the end of the war—until the fall of the Berlin Wall in November 1991. The Cold War competition between the Western world and the old Union of Soviet Socialist Republics (USSR) was the proverbial elephant in the room for all those years.

Many Canadians have forgotten, if they ever knew, that it was events in Ottawa in the autumn of 1945 that marked the start of the Cold War. That conflict exerted a profound impact on life in the last half of the twentieth century and to this day.

The growing threat of a new Cold War being waged by a new cast of characters who are motivated by a whole new set of geopolitical dynamics threatens to lead us to repeat the mistakes and insanities of yesteryear.

Seldom, if ever, has a war ended leaving the victors with
such a sense of uncertainty and fear, with such a realization
that the future is obscure.
—American newsman Edward R. Murrow, 1945

CHAPTER 18

The Bomb

I T'S RARE THAT A SINGLE EVENT STANDS OUT AS ONE OF HIS-
tory's turning points. Yet there were two such events in the late summer of 1945, that most extraordinary of years. Canada played a role
in both. One was a mere bit part in the epochal, earth-shattering
American bombing of the Japanese city of Hiroshima that took place
on August 6. The other was a lead role in a cloak-and-dagger espionage
drama that played out in Ottawa a month later.

The former event occurred against the backdrop of the increasingly
bloody war with Japan that had continued to grind on after VE day in
May. It is difficult today to imagine, let alone understand, the extent to
which racist hatred had infected all the combatants in the Pacific war.
As the sage English cleric Charles Caleb Colton once pointed out, "We
hate some persons because we do not know them, and we will not know
them because we hate them." That pretty much summarizes the attitude
of all sides in the war in the Pacific.

With each new day of the war, passions deepened and fears grew.
More and more, it looked as if the only action that would bring the
fighting in the Pacific to a close would be an Allied invasion of the
islands of Japan. That prospect was a terrifying one to the Americans
and their Allied partners. Certainly, Canadians wanted revenge for
December 1941—the loss of 293 soldiers of the Royal Rifles of Canada,

the Winnipeg Grenadiers, and the Royal Canadian Corps of Signals; the barbaric treatment of wounded soldiers and POWs; and the brutal rape and murder of Canadian nurses by the victorious Japanese when Hong Kong fell to them. But most people in this country had little enthusiasm for any deep involvement in a war so far away that was seen as being America's to fight; the results of the 1945 general election in Canada had made that abundantly clear.

Worrisome, too, was the realization that if the only way to end the war was to invade Japan, it would be "the rat-in-the-corner" scenario— Allied soldiers would face a desperate enemy. Japanese military and civilians alike would fight to the death rather than surrender. If that happened, there would be a staggering number of military casualties on both sides, and millions of innocent civilians would be condemned to be what we now call "collateral damage."

Those were the concerns that United States president Harry Truman agonized over in July 1945. A high-level advisory committee of American government officials, military leaders, and scientists recommended to Truman that if he wanted to end the war quickly and with as little loss of lives as possible, it would be necessary to use the atomic bomb against Japan itself; issuing a warning by exploding a bomb in a remote location simply would not work.

Truman alone had to decide where and when to drop the atomic bomb. Although the president had worked as a bank clerk, a judge, a farmer, and a haberdasher prior to becoming a politician, he had been vice-president for only three months before vaulting into the Oval Office. As such, he had minimal understanding of the destructive power of the atomic bomb; Truman could not even be sure the weapon would actually detonate in uncontrolled conditions. Despite this, he insisted that whatever target was chosen, it had to have military significance. Given that dictate, his Pentagon advisors came up with a short-list of Japanese cities for the president's consideration: Hiroshima, Kokura, Niigata, and Nagasaki. Logistical concerns—weather conditions, primarily—would be the final determinant.

In the end, Hiroshima, a port city of 350,000 on Honshu, Japan's main island, was chosen. Thus, early on the morning of Monday, August 6, 1945, a Japan-bound United States Air Force B-29 Superfortress bomber and two support aircraft took off from their base in the Northern Mariana Islands. In the weapons bay of the lead aircraft, the *Enola Gay* (named for the mother of pilot Colonel Paul W. Tibbets), was an atomic bomb carrying the code name "Little Boy." The weapon, ten feet (three metres) long and twenty-eight inches (seventy-one centimetres) across, weighed 9,700 pounds (4,400 kilograms). It looked very much like a cartoonist's stock rendering of a bomb with its little tail fins. But Little Boy was no laughing matter. Nor was it like any other bomb to that point in history. Although its explosive power had been partially determined in test blasts conducted in the New Mexico desert, the bomb's full potential as a weapon of mass destruction was still unknown. As the world was about to learn, it was horrifying.

The Little Boy atomic bomb dropped on Hiroshima, August 6, 1945, contained Canadian-mined and -refined uranium.
(United States National Archives and Records Administration)

After a six-hour flight, the *Enola Gay* reached Hiroshima just as a typical workday was beginning. The day was warm, and although the sky was clear, no Japanese fighter planes appeared to challenge the American aircraft. Conditions were nearly perfect as *Enola Gay* bombardier Colonel Thomas Wilson Ferebee set about his work. At 8:15 a.m., Ferebee pressed the button that released Little Boy from the belly of the *Enola Gay*. The plane was cruising at a height of 31,060 feet (9,470 metres) at that moment. The bomb had forty-four seconds to fall to its predetermined detonation height of 1,968 feet (600 metres) above ground zero, and then ...

A heartbeat later, temperatures as hot as the sun's core seared a three-square-mile (seven square kilometre) patch of earth beneath the rapidly receding plane.

The *Enola Gay* was already more than eleven miles (almost eighteen kilometres) away when a huge portion of the city of Hiroshima disappeared in a blinding incendiary flash. Eighty thousand people who had been going about their daily lives that morning were vaporized instantly. In the coming months, another 65,000 residents of Hiroshima would die slow, painful deaths as a result of acute radiation poisoning, burns, and other injuries. The nature of warfare—and of life on this planet—was forever changed in that momentous split second. Captain Robert Lewis, the *Enola Gay*'s co-pilot, sensed this, for he wrote in his logbook, "My God, what have we done?" What, indeed.

THE ATOMIC BOMB THAT levelled Hiroshima on that fateful August morning threw up a mushroom cloud of fire, smoke, debris, and radioactive waste that billowed nine miles (fifteen kilometres) high, turning day into hellish night.

Remnants of the blast cloud lingered high above the charred landscape for several hours. It's likely the radioactive debris was still drifting there when news of the blast reached President Truman half a world away. He was somewhere in the mid-Atlantic, travelling aboard the

USS *Augusta*, the battle cruiser that served as the American presidential flagship during the war. Truman was returning to Washington after having met with Churchill and Stalin in the German city of Potsdam; he had just sat down to lunch when the message he'd been anxiously waiting for arrived. "This is the greatest thing in history!" Truman blurted to the naval officers who were seated at his table.[1]

In Ottawa, Prime Minister Mackenzie King's reaction to news of the Hiroshima attack a few hours later was no less sanguine. Unlike Truman, King was not waiting to hear that an atomic bomb had been dropped on Japan. He had other, more immediate concerns. It was by-election day in the eastern Ontario riding of Glengarry; King fully expected to regain a seat in Parliament after his embarrassing election loss in Prince Albert two months earlier. Glengarry was such a safe Liberal seat that King had barely bothered to campaign there, and on voting day he remained on Parliament Hill for the opening of a pivotal four-day Dominion–Provincial Conference on Reconstruction. All nine of Canada's provincial premiers had assembled with King in the chamber of the House of Commons to thrash out the issues of post-war reconstruction. There were many to deal with. Ottawa had usurped many provincial powers during the six years of war. But now, with growing fears of a return to the economic hard times of the 1930s, all the familiar federal–provincial antagonisms and tensions began to resurface. They did so in the wake of the April 1945 publication of the King government's *White Paper on Employment and Income*.

That policy document had committed Ottawa to providing Canadians with stable levels of employment and income. In order to achieve those ends, the federal government needed provincial cooperation—specifically for premiers to abandon their direct taxation powers over individuals and corporations and their collection of succession duties. In return, Ottawa was offering to pay each province a per capita allowance ($12 a head), plus additional money to support various programs. Not surprisingly, this proposal, like the very idea of the federal government seizing control of the post-war reconstruction agenda, appealed to the premiers about as much as cold gruel; Conservative George Drew of Ontario, in particular, was opposed.

The prime minister was about to begin stating his case when Minister of Munitions and Supply C.D. Howe slipped him a note with details of that morning's dramatic developments in far-off Hiroshima, but King was so absorbed in the matters at hand that at first he misinterpreted the meaning of the message. In some measure, that also may well have been due to his limited knowledge of the details of the American efforts to build an atomic bomb. In spite of this, Canada's involvement in the project, while small, had been significant.

A football-sized package of Canadian uranium—mined at Port Radium in the Northwest Territories and processed at the Eldorado refinery in Port Hope, Ontario—was at the heart of the atomic bomb dropped on Hiroshima Given the Nazis' frenzied efforts to build a nuclear weapon of their own, it's ironic that it was German machinery that originally had gotten the Port Radium mine up and running in 1934 and that had kept it operational in the harsh sub-Arctic conditions.

Few of the Canadian politicians and government officials who were gathered in Ottawa on August 6 for the Dominion–Provincial Conference knew anything about any of this, and even less about the Manhattan Project, the code name for the American push to build an atomic weapon. Equally, few Canadians had any inkling of the secret research into the peaceful uses of atomic energy that was going on at a national research facility at Chalk River, a two-hour drive northwest of Ottawa. And so King was correct when shortly before the lunch break, he rose to his feet to make "a world-shaking announcement" about what he described as the "most amazing of scientific discoveries."[2] For the first time that morning, the chamber fell deathly quiet. King had everyone's attention as he solemnly read statements issued by President Truman and Prime Minister Winston Churchill providing details about a powerful new American bomb that had "at a single stroke destroyed a large part of the great Japanese Army base at Hiroshima."[3]

A stunned silence greeted King's announcement. Exactly what was meant by the dawn of "the Atomic Age"—as some commentators were already calling it—was still unclear. But whatever the meaning, it was clarified once and for all by the stark and horrifying reality of what happened three days later. On August 9, another American bomber dropped a second atomic bomb, this one on the Japanese city of Nagasaki. "Fat Man," as this one was called, was fuelled by plutonium and was even more powerful than Little Boy. This bomb killed another 40,000 people instantly and drove Japan to its knees.

Truman's decision to use the atomic bomb to bring the war in the Pacific to a screeching halt touched off a vigorous and emotional moral debate. Was using the atomic bomb as a weapon of war the "right" thing to do? Historians are still arguing this question.

For his part, Mackenzie King had no doubts at all about the wisdom of the American actions, nor did he second-guess them. "We now see what might have come to the British race had German scientists won the race," King told his diary. "It is fortunate that the use of the atomic bomb should have been upon the Japanese rather than upon the white races of Europe."[4]

Such a view was consistent with King's attitudes about race. A product of his time and also white, Anglo-Saxon, and protestant (WASP) to the core, he was unabashedly racist. King's views were reflected both in his own actions and in those of his government. In the years before the war, officials at Canadian ports had turned away boatloads of desperate Jewish and East Indian refugees. As mentioned earlier, during the war government officials had rounded up and forcibly resettled or interned Japanese Canadians in British Columbia. Government officials had maintained the now-infamous residential schools for Aboriginal people. And even in the decade after the war, when a million immigrants came to Canada, the government would enforce strict quotas on Blacks, Jews, and other racial groups, as well as an outright ban on Chinese immigration (until 1947).

From a modern perspective, such state-sanctioned bigotry, including a willingness to categorize would-be immigrants as "preferred" (a euphemism for WASP) or "non-preferred" (almost everyone else, especially persons of colour) is abhorrent; however, in 1945, not only were such measures tolerated, they were generally accepted by the public. Such prejudices were in line with the thinking of a majority of Canadians—English and French alike. And, in turn, these two "founding peoples" had little use or affection for each other. It's fair to say that for much of the twentieth century, Canada was a racist country. In the post-war era, the proof was in the CIPO polls.

In 1946, these polls suggested that while Canadians were in favour of increasing the national population through immigration, "It was well established . . . that the Canadian public regards British and Scandinavian people as the most desirable immigrant stock."[5] At the same time, when Canadians were asked if there were people they wanted to keep out of this country, sixty per cent of poll respondents cited the Japanese. Forty-nine per cent named Jews, thirty-four per cent Germans, thirty-one per cent "Negroes," and twenty-four per cent Chinese.

To be fair, Canada wasn't alone in its racial prejudices. Xenophobia had always been "an international syndrome" and despite the lessons of the 1930s and World War II, nothing changed post-war. Historian Jean Bruce was right when she noted that "Immigration policies in the United States and Australia reflected the same prejudices, the same fierce hostilities and anxieties."[6]

THE DROPPING OF THAT second atomic bomb, on Nagasaki, proved to be the knockout blow in the Pacific war. Emperor Hirohito emerged from the shadows to overrule the nation's political and military leaders when he appealed to Washington for terms in an unconditional surrender. Despite having incurred the wrath of fanatics in the Japanese military, he forged ahead, and on Wednesday, August 15 (August 14 in North America), the war ended when the emperor announced his country's surrender on Japanese radio. In the United States, Canada, and their Allies, jubilation reigned as people celebrated victory over Japan, VJ day. As it happened, some Canadians did so twice.

Banner newspaper headlines trumpeted VJ day in Montreal.
(Archives de la Ville de Montréal, P500-T-1_022-017)

The first time was on August 12, two days early; the second was on the actual day. The mix-up was due to an error committed by a CBC technician. Mackenzie King had prepared a pre-recorded address to be aired at war's end, but unfortunately, Canada's national radio network somehow mistakenly broadcast it on August 12. The premature news of Japan's surrender spread with lightning speed all across North America. Church bells pealed, sirens wailed, and crowds began celebrating in cities and towns all across Canada, just as they had on VE day. In Vancouver, on the periphery of the Pacific theatre of war, the city's eight air-raid sirens sounded simultaneously, and jubilant crowds filled Pender Street and other downtown thoroughfares. Then, word got around that the war wasn't really over yet, not officially, anyway.

VJ day parade in the streets of Vancouver's Chinatown. (City of Vancouver Archives, James Crookall fonds, AM1545-S3:CVA 586-3964)

VJ day celebrations in Vancouver. (City of Vancouver Archives, CVA 586-3836)

That was not the only bizarre situation involving Canadians that occurred as the war with Japan was coming to an end. There were a couple of others. One of them, which happened aboard the only Canadian warship to see action in the war in the Pacific, was an embarrassment to military brass in Ottawa.

On May 7, the day the war in Europe ended, the crew of HMCS *Uganda* voted on whether or not to "volunteer" to continue fighting. When the ballots were counted, 605 of 907 members of the crew opted to return home. They were as keen to do so as other Canadian servicemen and servicewomen were. The ship's captain insisted there had been "no mutiny on the *Uganda*."[7] It was true, there hadn't been, but there was no denying that many of the crew were done with war and wanted nothing more to do with it. Before they could all go home, their ship needed to refuel and undergo boiler repairs. When *Uganda* limped into the United States naval base at Pearl Harbor on August 4, it received a frosty reception; the Americans were angry that the Canadians had "quit" the war. Undeterred, *Uganda* and her crew took on fuel and then departed for Canada. En route, news that atomic bombs had been dropped on Japan reached the ship. *Uganda* arrived in Esquimalt, its home port, on August 10, the same day Japan announced its acceptance of the instrument of surrender.

Apart from the *Uganda* incident, there was another Monty Python–like episode at war's end that involved the Canadian military. This one happened at the historic September 2, 1945, ceremony that took place in Tokyo Bay. There, on the deck of the American battleship USS *Missouri*, nine representatives of the Japanese military and government met with Supreme Allied Commander General Douglas MacArthur, Admiral Chester Nimitz, and other high-ranking Allied military officials. They were there to sign surrender documents that officially ended the war in the Pacific.

The Canadian signatory was Colonel Lawrence M. Cosgrave, this country's military liaison officer in Australia. The fifty-five-year-old Toronto native was a veteran of World War I and a good friend of

Lieutenant-Colonel John McCrae, author of the renowned poem "In Flanders Fields." In fact, Cosgrave claimed McCrae wrote the verse on a scrap of paper while using Cosgrave's back as a desk. That makes for a wonderful human-interest story, but there is no way to confirm if it's true. More verifiable is Cosgrave's role in the signing of the Japanese surrender.

Colonel Lawrence Cosgrave, Canada's representative, signed the Japanese instrument of surrender aboard the battleship USS *Missouri* in Tokyo Bay, September 2, 1945. (Australian War Memorial, photo 040970)

Newsman Richard Malone, who was among the throng that observed the surrender ceremony, would recall the awkward moment that occurred when it was Cosgrave's turn to sign the documents. "[He] was a bit short-sighted, but did not wish to wear his glasses while appearing in uniform," Malone wrote. "He had signed one of the documents on the wrong line, placing his signature under the word

'Canada' instead of *above* it. This threw the entire sequence out of kilter. Subsequently one of MacArthur's aides had to correct the mistake, which mucked the document up a bit. The Japanese were given a copy, which had to be corrected."[8]

And so it was that Canada's military involvement in WWII came to a decidedly anti-climactic—and mildly amusing—end.

CHAPTER 19

The Little Cipher Clerk

I T WAS A FATEFUL DECISION THAT WOULD FOREVER CHANGE life for him, his family, Canada, and the world. On September 5, 1945, Igor Sergeievitch Gouzenko, the twenty-six-year-old cipher clerk at the Soviet Union's legation in Ottawa, cast his fate to the wind when he decided to defect to the West.

When Gouzenko stepped out of his office that warm autumn evening, he did so with a ream of documents tucked inside his shirt. These weren't just *any* documents. They were top-secret papers that revealed the details of Soviet spying activities in Ottawa, Washington, and London. This revelatory information, Gouzenko's insurance policy that he would receive favourable treatment in the West, would tear the last frayed threads of the uneasy wartime anti-Nazi alliance between Stalinist Russia and the Allied powers. It would also inadvertently set in motion a chain of events that would change the course of history. In the words of historian Jack Granatstein, Gouzenko's defection "made the public aware of the fact for the first time that the Russians are not entirely our friends."[1]

The Cold War chill that ensued would define and shape world events through much of the latter half of the twentieth century. Time and time again over the course of the forty-six years bookended by the 1945 end of the war and the 1991 fall of the Berlin Wall, the protracted rivalry between the USSR and its erstwhile wartime allies in the West would threaten to erupt into a full-blown hot war. Had it done so, the conflict could easily have ended in a *Dr. Strangelove* scenario: shrouded by the mushroom-shaped clouds of nuclear apocalypse.[2]

In his 1948 autobiography, *This Was My Choice*, Gouzenko explained that his decision to defect was a personal one that had its roots in his memory of an incident he had witnessed during his teenage years in the *Komsomol*, the Young Communist League. Gouzenko recounted how he had looked on helplessly and in dismay as party zealots persecuted one of his young female comrades; in the process, they unknowingly planted the seed of Gouzenko's disillusionment with life in Stalinist Russia. "That miserable memory, more perhaps than any other, influenced me . . . when I made my big decision," he wrote.[3]

Maybe it did. However, other evidence suggests Gouzenko's motives were less idealistic and more self-serving than that. As one of the Mounties who guarded him after his defection put it, "I firmly believe [Igor] defected because he wanted to eat regularly."[4] No one's actions get more basic than that.

That explanation, like Gouzenko's, seems a tad simplistic. However, there's no question he was someone who grew up hungry amid the horrors of Stalinist Russia in the 1930s. It is also true that Gouzenko was astounded by the cornucopia of food available to one and all on the shelves of Canadian supermarkets, even with wartime rationing in effect.

Some Canadians who got to know Gouzenko suspected he had an even more compelling reason to defect: fear. Gouzenko dreaded what was in store for him after he received a sudden and unexpected summons to return to Moscow. His apprehension was understandable; many a Russian citizen who was merely suspected of loosely defined anti-Soviet activities or who ran afoul of someone higher up in the Communist Party pecking order had ended up in a Siberian prison camp or had fallen victim to lead poisoning—the kind that's caused by nine grams of lead in an executioner's bullet being fired into the back of the head.

Still other people who spent time with Gouzenko came to recognize him as a bright, savvy man who was a survivor, adept at manipulating events and people to get what he wanted. And in 1945, what "[Igor] wanted [was] to be Gouzenko the Great, the fellow who sprung the trap on the [Russian] spies," as one Canadian journalist mused.[5]

William Kelly, a former deputy commissioner of the RCMP, had a similar impression of the little cipher clerk: "I can tell you that there was a time when [he] thought that only two men in the world mattered: Winston Churchill and himself. And probably *he* took priority."[6] At the same time, Gouzenko was painfully aware of the perils of defecting and of basking in the limelight. He confided to his wife that he didn't expect to live longer than a year after his defection. He knew the Soviet secret police, the dreaded NKVD,[7] had a long arm and an even longer memory. Its agents were very good at finding and punishing defectors and other traitors; murder was the NKVD's favourite tool for that. There was no better example than Leon Trotsky, one of the leaders of the Bolshevik revolution that had toppled the tsar.

Following the 1924 death of Soviet leader Vladimir Lenin, Joseph Stalin became the new leader of the Soviet Union. Because Stalin viewed Trotsky as both trouble and a leadership rival who had to be eliminated, Trotsky's days were numbered. After several botched assassination attempts, an NKVD hit man took another stab at killing Trotsky, literally. After finally tracking him to Mexico, where he was living in exile, an assassin crept up behind the old Bolshevik one day in August 1940 and smashed an ice axe into the top of his head, with predictable results.

Gouzenko understood his defection ensured that he, too, would be a marked man, but it was a risk he was willing to take. As he saw it, he had two choices: sure death if he returned to Moscow, or possible assassination by the NKVD if he defected. Gouzenko also knew if he betrayed the Soviet Union, his fate was sealed; he could never go home again, and his mother and other family members there would likely suffer dire consequences because of his actions. If that happened, he said, it was the price that had to be paid to end the misery he and other Russians were forced to endure under Stalin. Life in the USSR was not something he would miss, even if it was all he had ever known.

Igor Gouzenko. (LAC, photo e002282934)

IGOR GOUZENKO WAS BORN in 1919 in a village called Rogachev, which he described in his autobiography as being "not far distant from Moscow."[8] It was here, in that same year, that some wealthier peasants—the *kulaks*—staged one of the many failed uprisings against the property seizures and forced collectivization that was being imposed by the fledgling Bolshevik regime. Times were tough in this corner of the Soviet Union, and life was cheap.[9]

Two things about Gouzenko's childhood speak volumes about conditions in the country then. One is that baby Igor was named in memory of an older brother who had died in infancy of malnutrition. The other is that Igor and his two sisters were raised by their mother and their maternal grandmother, their *babushka*. Gouzenko's father, a soldier in the Red Army, had disappeared during the brutal three-year civil war that ravaged Russia from early March 1918 to October 1922.

Fortunately for young Igor, he was blessed with his mother's sharp mind; she was a teacher of advanced mathematics. And because he was a gifted student, Gouzenko quickly mastered the "lessons" being taught in the young communist groups he was obliged to join. This put him in a privileged position, and in 1937, he gained admission to a Moscow art studio where he worked off his tuition by teaching literacy skills to workers at a nearby iron foundry.

When Gouzenko continued to excel academically, he won acceptance into studies at the prestigious Moscow Architectural Institute. Here he met a fellow student who became his wife, fair-haired Svetlana "Anna" Gouseva. The common Russian term of endearment for Svetlana is "Sveta." It may have been that the Gouzenkos opted for "Anna" post-defection on the assumption that Canadians could have a difficult time getting their tongues around Svetlana.

The couple married in November 1942, about the same time that Gouzenko was drafted into the army. His academic prowess saved him from being sent to the front as cannon fodder. Instead, he found himself studying first at the Military Engineering Academy in Moscow and then at the Red Army's Higher Intelligence School. It was in this latter institution that he received training as a cipher clerk with the Soviet Union's military intelligence service, the GRU.[10]

In June 1943, Gouzenko left Moscow on his first—and as it would turn out, his only—overseas posting. He accompanied his new boss, military attaché Colonel Nikolai Zabotin, and his aide, Major Alexander Romanov, when they took up postings at the GRU *rezidentura* (field station) housed in the Soviet legation in Ottawa. The Canadian and Soviet governments had not established diplomatic relations until June 1942, following the German invasion of Russia earlier that month. The

GRU didn't waste time. Thanks to Zabotin, Canada quickly became a hotbed of Soviet espionage activity.

Tall, wavy-haired, handsome, personable, and a veteran of the Battle of Stalingrad, Zabotin had a touch of aristocratic mien. The fact he was the son of a tsarist-era military officer may help explain his social refinement and his fondness for the arts, gourmet food, and good drink. Zabotin also had a keen eye for the ladies. He made himself at home in Ottawa (where he reportedly seduced the wives of various leading citizens) and soon found himself a mistress in Montreal. Both Zabotin and Romanov were socially active, cultivating relationships with Canadian senior bureaucrats, military brass, politicians, and left-leaning academics. All the while, of course, they were busy seeking out whatever useful information they could gather. Zabotin and his agents were busy as squirrels in a wheel. In less than two years, they had recruited contacts "in the Royal Canadian Navy, the Department of Munitions and Supply, the National Research Council, and the Foreign Exchange Board."[11]

The Soviets regarded Canada as a soft target, an easy place to sniff out Allied war secrets, especially information about the United States military's ultra-secret Manhattan Project and the new superbomb the Americans were rumoured to be rushing to build before the Germans could do so.

Igor Gouzenko's job was to encode and send to Moscow the top-secret GRU telegrams and reports that Zabotin, Romanov, and their network of spies prepared. The Soviet mission's cipher clerk knew almost everything there was to know about the army intelligence service's spying operations in Canada. He also had some inklings about the parallel spying operation run by the Soviet secret police in this country, and he had a general sense of the mischief Soviet agents in Washington and London were engaged in. Gouzenko was good at his job and was savvy enough to keep a low profile. That wasn't difficult for him to do.

Igor Gouzenko wasn't someone who stood out in a crowd. Brown-haired, five-foot-six (168 centimetres) with a square, stocky build, he was by nature quiet and reserved; one of his Ottawa neighbours described him as being "a very quiet chap, a mousy type of fellow."[12] It's understandable that Gouzenko projected that image; he spoke little English, and growing up in Stalinist times, he'd had no end of practice being suspicious of strangers. Paranoia was a constant in his life. The same was true for Anna, who was seven months pregnant when she arrived in Ottawa in October 1943.

Not long after the birth of their first child, the Gouzenkos moved into an apartment at 511 Somerset Street, a boxy two-storey, red-brick building in Ottawa's Centretown area. Neighbours there would recall often seeing the couple and their infant son in his stroller sitting in Dundonald Park, just across the street. The Gouzenkos went there whenever they wanted to talk candidly; they feared the NKVD might have bugged their apartment.

One of the Gouzenkos' downstairs neighbours would remember something else different about them: when little Andrei Gouzenko was a toddler, he had an unusual way of amusing himself. Instead of using the toilet, he sometimes "used to stand on the balcony upstairs and take a leak over the side. He would just stand at the edge and let it go."[13]

Residents of Somerset Street weren't the only ones to take note of the Gouzenkos. It was usual for all employees of the Soviet Embassy (it achieved that elevated status in November 1943) to live in the same apartment building, where they could keep an eye on one another. Colonel Zabotin made an exception to this practice when he suggested the Gouzenkos find another place to live; their son's crying kept him and his wife awake at night. This seemingly innocuous "suggestion" would prove to be significant.

When a GRU big shot visited Ottawa and happened to meet Gouzenko, he was suspicious of the cipher clerk's different living arrangements. Neither Gouzenko nor his boss had ever given them much thought or considered them problematic. But the GRU spy chief thought differently. The devil, as they say, is in the details.

For the first year or so that he lived in Ottawa, Gouzenko was the very model of the dutiful Soviet comrade, although both he and his wife secretly marvelled at life in Canada. People were friendly. Food was relatively plentiful. Housing was luxurious by Soviet standards. Even more surprising was the openness of Canadian society. Back home in Russia, any criticism of the regime was strictly taboo; even a wrong word could lead to dire consequences. In Canada, elections were open, and they were free, without coercion. Even more astounding was that the media and ordinary citizens openly and without fear criticized the government and government officials. This was all a wonder to the Gouzenkos. They lived quietly, kept to themselves, and observed all that was going on around them. In the summer of 1945, there was a lot to see and much to think about.

THE SEVENTEENTH ACADEMY AWARDS

Movies were one of the most popular and affordable forms of entertainment in Canada in 1945. The country's 1,323 theatres sold more than 215 million tickets that year, raking in $69.4 million. A double bill—two feature films, a cartoon, trailers, and a Movietone news reel—typically cost twenty-five cents per person, sometimes more for evening screenings on Friday and Saturday, date nights. Virtually all the films shown in Canadian theatres in 1945 were American-made; this was the golden age of Hollywood. When the Academy Awards were handed out on March 15 at Grauman's Chinese Theatre in Hollywood, the big winners were as follows:

Best picture: *Going My Way*
Best actor: Bing Crosby
Best actress: Ingrid Bergman
Best director: Leo McCarey

A s CANADIANS WERE CELEBRATING VJ day and wondering what lay ahead for them and their country, Igor Gouzenko had his own worries.

Several months earlier, he had received a sudden, quite unexpected message from Moscow: he was being recalled. No reason was given. Colonel Zabotin liked his cipher clerk, and so he had done his best to string out the process. However, by September 1945, Gouzenko's time to return to Russia was almost at hand. He wasn't keen to go for a couple of compelling reasons.

For one, the Gouzenkos and their son had settled into a comfortable life in Ottawa. They had a spacious apartment and plenty to eat; both were luxuries they would not enjoy if they returned home. For another, being recalled to Moscow was cause for worry. Gouzenko was certain the recall meant he had fallen out of favour for some unknown reason, and if that was indeed the case, his fate would be a long term in a Siberian prison camp or even execution. Gouzenko had no way of knowing the actual reason for his recall, which was less sinister than he imagined.

The reality was that Gouzenko had been summoned for what were purely bureaucratic reasons. That GRU spy chief who had visited Ottawa and wondered about Gouzenko's unusual housing arrangements had recommended recalling Gouzenko. He cited no specific reason other than the vague suspicion that if the young cipher clerk stayed in Ottawa, he *might* fall prey to the lures of decadent capitalism.

Gouzenko knew none of this, of course. Fearing he was a dead man walking if he returned to the USSR, his only hope, he had reasoned, was to defect. But there were a couple of huge problems with that strategy. Things had not ended well for a couple of Soviet officials who had defected in the United States. These men had no way to corroborate the information they offered American counter-intelligence officials in return for the protection and financial rewards that were vital for their survival. Gouzenko was smart enough to understand that for him to be taken seriously and to find safe haven, he needed to carry with him documents that would prove the truth of any information he might offer to Western intelligence officials in return for physical protection and financial support.

In his autobiography, Gouzenko claimed that on the day he chose to defect—September 5, 1945—he went to the Soviet Embassy in the evening and snuck out with 109 secret documents crammed inside his shirt. However, American historian Amy Knight, whom the *New York Times* has hailed as "the West's foremost scholar" of Russian spying activities, has determined that at least some of the details in the story Gouzenko spun in *This Was My Choice* were enhanced for dramatic effect. Knight concluded that what Gouzenko made off with and that "ended up in the hands of the RCMP, including telegrams, letters, reports, dossiers on agents, and handwritten notes, was around 250 [pieces of paper], because, as Gouzenko said, some of the documents contained several pages."[14] He subsequently revealed he had been stealthily stockpiling individual documents for several weeks before his actual defection.

Gouzenko took a huge risk when he made off with that cache of documents. "He had to hold his stomach in not to be too bulgy," his wife would recall many years later. "You know, otherwise he would have [looked] like a pregnant elephant."[15]

The paper count aside, much of Gouzenko's story of what happened to him after he left the Soviet Embassy on the night he defected rings true, although there were—and still are—unanswered questions about the events of the next few days. The story of the Gouzenko defection unfolded like a Coen brothers' movie. Much of what transpired would have been amusing had the situation not been one of life or death for the Gouzenkos.

Igor was deathly afraid, and because he distrusted police—in the Soviet Union, local police invariably were in league with the NKVD— he instead made a beeline for the offices of the now-defunct *Ottawa Journal* newspaper. Gouzenko had sometimes read the newspaper and had developed an inflated idea of how much power the press in Canada actually had to effect change, expose corruption, and right wrongs. What exactly Gouzenko hoped the *Journal* could do for a Soviet defector on the run is unclear, but he wasn't exactly thinking clearly.

It was about nine o'clock in the evening when Gouzenko appeared in the bustling, noisy *Journal* newsroom. Teletypes and typewriters were clattering away, and people were scurrying about in all directions in the fog of cigarette smoke that filled the vast room. The staff were preoccupied with getting out the next morning's edition of the newspaper, and nobody paid much attention to the dishevelled-looking little man who stood in the reception area, near the elevator, repeating over and over in broken English, "It's war. It's war. It's Russia!"

After a few minutes of this, an office boy escorted the agitated visitor to the copy desk. Night editor George Paterson interrupted his work to listen as Gouzenko rambled on in broken English. Paterson couldn't make head or tail of what this strange little man was saying, and so he dismissed him. Lots of "crazies" wandered into the *Journal* newsroom in those days, as they did at most newspapers. A second editor who listened to Gouzenko's tale and glanced at some of the documents he was carrying advised him to go to the RCMP. Or to just go away.

Gouzenko desperately didn't want to do either. Instead, he beetled over to the nearby Justice Building in hopes of gaining an audience with Justice Minister Louis St. Laurent. By now, it was almost ten o'clock, and a security guard waved Gouzenko away, telling him to come back in the morning. Having no other option, Gouzenko obeyed. He rushed home to recount his misadventures to his wife.

THE GOUZENKOS MADE IT through a sleepless, fraught night. First thing next morning, with their toddler in tow, they made a hasty return to the Justice Building. The day was unseasonably hot, and with Anna Gouzenko eight months pregnant with baby number two, it wasn't easy for the couple and their son to make that trek or to sit there waiting and hoping to meet with the justice minister.

After two anxious hours, the Gouzenkos decided a better option was to return to the *Ottawa Journal*, where they hoped the editor-in-chief might agree to see them. However, in what became a frustrating rehash of the events of the previous evening, the reporter who interviewed Igor Gouzenko and listened to his breathless pleas decided parts of his story were unbelievable. After conferring with an editor, Elizabeth Fraser advised Gouzenko to go to the police. "We had no one who could read Russian. We simply saw the potential for damage being far too great," she would recall. "He had to go to the police for protection. We thought, they'll protect him one way or another, whether it's in a mental hospital or whatever."[16]

By this time, the Gouzenkos realized they were running in circles. After another fruitless visit to an RCMP office, they changed tack completely. Mistakenly believing they could save themselves from being forced to return to Russia, early on the afternoon of September 6 they visited the offices of the local Crown attorney in hopes of being allowed to apply for Canadian citizenship. The Gouzenkos explained this to a puzzled but sympathetic secretary named Fernande Coulson. As she listened to this short, stocky man with his very pregnant wife and toddler son in tow, it occurred to her that the Gouzenkos looked like the stock image of a family of Russian peasants. It was evident they were at their wits' end, and so Coulson decided to do her best to help them. After making a few phone calls, she learned two relevant bits of information.

One was that the Gouzenkos could expect no help from senior government officials. When she called the prime minister's office, King's private secretary, a man named Sam Gobeil, curtly advised her, "Get rid of him."[17] The other thing Coulson learned was that if the Gouzenkos wanted to apply for landed immigrant status, they would have to wait a year before filling out a citizenship application. The whole process would take five years. Hearing this, Gouzenko went into a full-blown panic. "Nobody will listen to me!" he shouted as his wife began taking out some of the secret documents she was carrying in her purse. "I said to myself that this man can't be lying," Coulson would recall.[18]

Now that she understood why the Gouzenkos were so agitated, Coulson hurriedly made still more phone calls on their behalf. Finally, she succeeded in convincing an RCMP intelligence officer to meet with Gouzenko; however, the man said he could not do so until the next morning. To say that the Gouzenkos were disappointed would be an understatement. Having no other option open to them and with a soaring sense of dread, they returned to their Somerset Street apartment. Gouzenko knew that by now Colonel Zabotin would be wondering why his cipher clerk hadn't shown up for work or called in. Even more worrisome was the possibility that one of Gouzenko's co-workers might have discovered that secret documents were missing. If so, Gouzenko knew his life would be on the line. Suicide would be preferable to what would happen to him if the embassy's NKVD chief got hold of him.

BACK AT THEIR APARTMENT, the Gouzenkos huddled in their bedroom and did their best to stay calm. They froze when there came a loud knock on their door. Colonel Zabotin had sent the embassy's driver to check on Gouzenko. The man, an army captain named Gorskov, was persistent. He pounded on the door and shouted Gouzenko's name for several minutes. All the while, Anna Gouzenko struggled to keep little Andrei quiet. She did not entirely succeed, but Gorskov grew frustrated and finally left. When he did, Igor Gouzenko knew the next visitor to arrive at the apartment door would be the Soviet Embassy's resident NKVD man.

Gouzenko's anxiety level took yet another quantum leap when he peeked out a window and spotted two suspicious-looking men sitting on a bench in the park across the street. Convinced his every move was now being watched and with nowhere else to turn, Gouzenko appealed to the next-door neighbour for help. The man, an RCAF veteran, feared the phone lines in the building might be tapped, and so he hopped on his bicycle and raced off to fetch the city police.

It would later come out that the RCMP had already alerted them. Exactly how and why the Mounties knew what was happening isn't clear, but they were already keeping an eye on the Gouzenkos and may have told the city police to back off. Those two men Gouzenko saw sitting in the park across from his apartment building weren't NKVD thugs; they were RCMP counter-intelligence officers.

While the Gouzenkos were waiting for the police to arrive, the neighbour who lived across the hall had heard the uproar, and she invited the Gouzenkos to spend the night in her apartment. It was a good thing she did. When city police got there and found that all was quiet, they promptly left. The next callers were the Soviet Embassy's NKVD chief and three of his henchmen. It was around midnight when they arrived at the Gouzenkos' apartment. After forcing open the door and finding no one home, the men began ransacking the place to find the documents Gouzenko had taken. Peeking through his neighbour's keyhole, Igor watched with bated breath.

Several minutes passed before Ottawa city police officers returned to the scene and confronted the Russians. The NKVD chief snarled that he had diplomatic immunity and he and his men had every right to be in the apartment since they were searching for a Soviet citizen who had stolen money from the embassy. The brief, tense standoff ended when the Russians finally departed, followed by one of the city police officers. The other stayed behind, and when Gouzenko revealed himself, the cop spent the night standing guard in the neighbour's apartment. The next morning, September 7, several Mounties showed up to escort Gouzenko to RCMP headquarters, where he was relieved to find himself placed in protective custody, though Anna and Andrei stayed put. The full shocking story that Gouzenko wanted to tell was finally about to come out.

IGOR GOUZENKO'S DECISION TO defect posed a huge headache for Prime Minister Mackenzie King. He had learned of the defection on

September 6, when the Gouzenkos were cooling their heels in the waiting room at Justice Minister St. Laurent's office. Two of King's aides, Under-Secretary of State for External Affairs Norman Robertson and his assistant, Hume Wrong, had rushed to alert the prime minister to the developing, potentially explosive situation. They advised him that a would-be defector from the Soviet Embassy claimed to have proof that the Soviet Union was operating an extensive network of spies in Canada, the United States, and England, and that these agents were intent on stealing military secrets about American troop movements in Europe, Canadian air defences, and more—especially vital secrets of the atomic bomb and about any atomic research that was under way in Canada.

The news was problematic for King. Robertson and Wrong had interrupted his preparations for that afternoon's opening of the fall session of Parliament and bothered him. Wearing two hats as he did—those of prime minister and Minister of External Affairs—"the Gouzenko situation" was King's to deal with, and he felt rattled. At age seventy-one, Canada's prime minister was bone-weary after ten stressful years in office. He was also out of his depth in the cloak-and-dagger world of espionage and counter-intelligence, even if that wasn't something he ever would have admitted.

King, ever cautious, feared this Russian defector might be a "crank." Even worse, what if he wasn't? What would that do to Canada–USSR relations? What impact would the defection of a cipher clerk from the Soviet Embassy in Ottawa have on delicate negotiations that were under way to persuade the Russians to become fully engaged in the work of the newly created United Nations? And what would happen if the media learned about the defection and made a big deal out of it? King weighed all these questions and many more. "I was strongly against any step of the kind [that was] certain to create an issue between Russia and Canada," he advised his diary that evening.[19]

The prime minister's knee-jerk reaction was to do whatever he had to do to make the problem quickly go away. The easiest way to do that was to comply with Soviet demands and hand over this defector along with any "stolen documents" he possessed. Fortunately for Igor Gouzenko and the Western Allies, although the prime minister may have been in charge, Norman Robertson also had a hand on the levers of decision making in Ottawa. He had already been in touch on an unrelated intelligence matter with William Stephenson, the Winnipeg-born head of British Security Coordination (BSC) who was known by the code name "Intrepid." The New York–based BSC was Britain's wartime counter-espionage agency in the Western Hemisphere. Serendipitously, Stephenson happened to be visiting Ottawa as the Gouzenko affair was unfolding.[20] It was purely by chance that he was in the Canadian capital, but his presence would prove to be pivotal.

Stephenson advised Robertson that under no circumstances should Gouzenko be turned over to the Soviets; he was adamant. The spy chief realized the cipher clerk's defection was a game changer in relations between the Soviet Union and the wartime Western Allies. Stephenson also saw it as "an argument for BSC's indispensability in the post-war world and for promoting Anglo-American-Canadian intelligence cooperation."[21]

As events were swirling and the crisis deepened, Canada's ever-cautious prime minister was growing increasingly dismayed that Gouzenko's defection seemed to defy easy or quick resolution. He was concerned that the RCMP's interrogation of the Soviet cipher clerk was prolonging the crisis. The possible implications of this development weighed heavily on King's mind when he attended a garden party at the British High Commissioner's residence on the afternoon of September 7. King was resentful and complained to his diary that night, "It is always the way—the moment I take an hour or two off for social events, most important events come up."[22] About that much, at least, he was correct: Gouzenko's defection was important.

The more the defector talked, the more the intentions and shocking extent of Soviet espionage operations became apparent. The details of the infiltration that were coming to light revealed that Soviet agents were engaged in espionage to a degree that no one in the King government could ever have believed possible. The top-secret documents Gouzenko had removed from the Soviet Embassy revealed that Stalin's spies were active everywhere. In Canada alone, there were more than twenty agents at work quietly stealing classified information and sniffing out information about the atomic bomb. Among them were civil servants, university academics, and even a Member of Parliament. Gouzenko had pointed a finger at Polish-born Fred Rose, the Labour Progressive representative for the heavily Jewish Montreal riding of Cartier—and the only communist ever elected to the House of Commons. Rose's disloyalty should not have surprised anyone; he had served a year in jail after being convicted of sedition in 1931. Despite this, Rose won election in 1943 and re-election in 1945, largely because he had for many years roundly denounced Hitler in a riding with many Jewish voters.

Farther afield, Gouzenko provided evidence that proved Alan Nunn May, one of Britain's top atomic scientists, was selling secrets to the Soviet Union, supposedly doing his utmost to stop Hitler. And in Washington, a Soviet mole had been on the staff of an assistant to United States Secretary of State Edward Stettinius, who had resigned in June 1945 to become his country's first ambassador to the United Nations. That wasn't the full extent of the spying. Gouzenko did not know their names, but he claimed other spies were at work inside the U.S. State Department. Nonetheless, Gouzenko wasn't aware of one vital fact: a double agent was working at the very highest level of the British counter-intelligence operations. The mole's treachery would have profound implications going forward.

What Gouzenko had revealed was too much to ignore, even for Mackenzie King. The prime minister now understood he could not simply sweep things under the proverbial rug and hope they would go away. In this case, events were moving too quickly. The Soviets were also in a panic; Ambassador Georgi Zarubin was demanding that Igor Gouzenko be handed over immediately. Canadian officials were stalling for time, insisting that Gouzenko was on the lam; RCMP commissioner Stuart Wood assured Zarubin that as soon as Gouzenko was caught he would be returned to Soviet officials.

With a fog of intrigue now enveloping Ottawa, Mackenzie King reluctantly conceded that he had no choice but to alert both the Americans and the British to what was happening. In fact, Norman Robertson had already done that. He was also aware that at William Stephenson's urging, Igor Gouzenko, his wife, and their son had been spirited out of Ottawa for their own safety. RCMP officers had escorted them first to secluded cottages in the eastern Ontario countryside and then to Camp X, the top-secret wartime spy training school on the shore of Lake Ontario, near the town of Whitby. The Gouzenkos would remain there for several months while officials from the RCMP, the FBI, and British intelligence agencies continued questioning Igor, whom they were now referring to by the code name "Corby." He had acquired that moniker because Norman Robertson was storing his growing file of Gouzenko paperwork in an old Corby Spirit and Wine box.

O N SEPTEMBER 29, 1945, Mackenzie King flew to Washington for what was supposedly a "get acquainted" session with President Truman, who had come to office in mid-April when President Roosevelt died. The real purpose of the visit was to discuss the implications of the revelations Gouzenko had divulged. The more Igor talked, the more issues and concerns there were to be sorted out and dealt with.

Immediately after leaving the White House, King departed for London for planned meetings with Prime Minister Clement Attlee and the heads of the British intelligence agencies. When reporters pressed King for more details on the purpose of his overseas trip, he waved them off, but not before obligingly posing for photos showing him boarding the *Queen Mary* in New York harbour.[23]

The outcome of all these discussions was that King, Truman, and Attlee decided to proceed cautiously and hush-up the story of Igor

Gouzenko's defection for the time being. They would say nothing about the secrets he had revealed. The politicians had a couple of reasons for doing so. First of all, suspicions about Soviet post-war intentions were growing—particularly in the United States where another Red Scare was already gaining momentum—and the Allied powers feared that if the full extent of Soviet espionage activities became known, the news would poison international relations, cripple the fledgling United Nations, and in a worst-case scenario even lead to another world war. Generals Douglas MacArthur and George S. Patton and other hawks within the United States armed forces were keen to use the military to "solve the Russian problem" and deal with the threat of communism.

The other reason the Allies were reluctant to reveal any of the details of Gouzenko's defection was the belief that doing so would end the secret surveillance of Soviet spies and sympathizers by Allied agents. They needn't have worried about that; the head of counter-intelligence for Britain's MI6, Kim Philby, was a Soviet double agent. He was privy to all the secret information about Igor Gouzenko that Canadian and American officials were providing to Britain, and he was passing it along to Moscow. Soviet spies and agents were already on alert.

It would be 1963 before knowledge of Philby's treachery finally began to leak out, and although he was working as a journalist by then and no longer engaged in intelligence work, he defected to the Soviet Union. In the closing weeks of 1945, the pivotal question for Mackenzie King was how to deal with the embarrassment of his government's uncertain handling of the situation and the potential damage caused by the Soviet spying that had been going on in Canada. King's solution was to make use of emergency powers still available to him under the War Measures Act, which were due to expire at year's end.

On October 6, King signed a top-secret order-in-council (PC 6444) authorizing the RCMP to detain and interrogate anyone who was suspected of having supplied secret information to a foreign government, and to do so "in such place and under such conditions as [the Minister of Justice] may from time to time determine."[24]

Once they had made the decision to launch a sweeping wave of police investigations, King and his key advisors puzzled over their next step. After much discussion, they decided to enlist the help of a prominent Winnipeg lawyer and legal scholar named Esten (E.K.) Williams, the head of the Canadian Bar Association. He would consider "the Corby case" and offer recommendations on a possible course of action for the federal government.

Williams crafted a nine-page "top-secret" memo. In it, he opined that until more facts were known, it would be premature to begin criminal proceedings against the almost two dozen individuals whose names appeared in the papers Gouzenko had given to the RCMP. Instead, Williams's advice was that Ottawa should convene a Royal Commission. This body could hold private hearings at which anyone who was suspected of being involved in a Soviet spy ring would be questioned. "[The commission] need not be bound by the ordinary rules of evidence if it considers it desirable to disregard them. It need not permit counsel to appear for those to be interrogated by or before it," Williams wrote.[25]

It might seem surprising, even shocking, that such a principled and reputable lawyer as E.K. Williams—after whom the library at the University of Manitoba law school is named—would recommend the government shelve due process on what would be, for all intents and purposes, a fishing expedition. In retrospect, it seems likely he did so because he regarded the Gouzenko allegations as being of great importance for national security, and because he thought any Royal Commission hearings would be just the first step in a two-stage process. Where the evidence warranted it, criminal prosecution should and would follow.

The prime minister accepted Williams's advice and began making plans to convene a Royal Commission. He was still pondering logistical details when developments in Washington forced his hand. By now, too many people with loose lips in too many government agencies and police forces in three countries had knowledge of Gouzenko's defection and its implications. The inevitable happened on February 3, 1946: American journalist Drew Pearson broke the story on his Sunday night program on the NBC radio network.

Mackenzie King and Norman Robertson suspected an official or government agency in Washington had spilled the beans, and they were right. According to espionage historian Amy Knight, Pearson's informant "almost certainly" was FBI director J. Edgar Hoover, who was eager to stir up anti-Soviet animus, which would give him a good excuse to intensify the hunt for communists and their sympathizers in public life in America.[26]

Pearson got many of the details of the Gouzenko story wrong, and because his report was short on specifics, reactions on both sides of the border were initially muted. Despite this, Mackenzie King felt he now had no choice but to be proactive and get out in front of the story while there was still time to do so; this was public relations 101.

King set to work on February 5 when he informed his Cabinet about what had happened and signed another secret order-in-council. This one, PC411, appointed Supreme Court judges Robert Taschereau and Roy L. Kellock to head a Royal Commission that would delve into the facts of the Soviet spying activities in Canada and determine if there had been any breaches of the Official Secrets Act.

Having two of the judges from Canada's highest court of appeal presiding over the proceedings was intended to lend an air of legitimacy to them. Despite this, the government remained intent on secrecy, and so only the sketchiest of details about the security breaches that had happened, who was involved, and what steps Ottawa had taken to limit the damage were revealed to the media and the Canadian public. King and Justice Minister Louis St. Laurent hoped to maintain the element of surprise as Canadian police set about rounding up as many Soviet spies and their enablers and sympathizers as possible before they could disappear.

There was no longer much doubt about the veracity of the information Gouzenko was providing, for at least partial corroboration had been provided by none other than a staff member of the Soviet Embassy in Ottawa. The man got into a drunken brawl in the wee hours of February 2, 1946, while he was out on the town in Toronto. When police arrested him, in addition to the loaded revolver they found in his coat pocket, they found a receipt for money he had paid to one of the people Gouzenko had identified as a Soviet spy. Even spies keep financial records. How else would they be reimbursed for their expenses?

T HE RCMP LAUNCHED A series of raids on the morning of February 15, 1946, and rounded up eleven of the people Igor Gouzenko had named as being involved in the Soviet spy rings.[27] A couple more suspects were scooped up the following day. As is the case in most such hastily organized police sweeps, mistakes were made.

In one such incident, an Ottawa civil servant who was identified in a newspaper report only as J.W. Simpson, a late riser evidently, was roused from his bed at eight o'clock by someone pounding on his apartment door. When Simpson, still in his pyjamas, opened the door, four burly Mounties burst into his living room. A struggle ensued. "I couldn't hold them off, and not knowing what the score was, I stood there slugging," Simpson later told a reporter.[28]

When his wife came rushing out of the bedroom and saw what was happening, she tried to call the police. However, one of the intruders saw her and snatched the phone out of her hand. "We were battling all over the living room floor, and my wife and [our] girls were screaming their heads off," Simpson said.

Once the posse of Mounties had subdued the now breathless Simpson, one of them advised him he was under arrest, and the officers were about to search his apartment. Mrs. Simpson had the good sense to demand to be told what crime her husband was supposed to have committed. This prompted one of the Mounties to ask poor Mr. Simpson, who was pinned to the floor, "You're [*name deleted in news-paper story*], aren't you?" Simpson shook his head. "That man lives next door," he said.

With that, the Mounties released Simpson and raced off in search of the right man. D'oh! (Sorry about that, Homer!)

The Simpson family's neighbour, like most of those who were rounded up that winter morning, found himself jailed at the RCMP barracks in the Rockcliffe area of Ottawa. Police held them here incommunicado, some for as long as five weeks, with no access to legal counsel or visitors, and without any formal charges being laid against them. One by one, they were paraded before the Royal Commission, where they were questioned on the pretext that they were "witnesses." Those who cooperated were told they would be allowed to go. Those who didn't risked being imprisoned for contempt of the commission, and they remained behind bars.

Judges Kellock and Taschereau went about their work for twenty-nine days, from February 15 until March 15, 1946. During that time, they accumulated hundreds of pages of transcripts of testimony, much of which was chronicled in three interim reports. A 162-page final summary detailed allegations of suspected violations of the Official Secrets Act by each of the accused. As espionage historian Amy Knight has noted, that document "read like a spy thriller, with code names and Russian documents and testimony from Gouzenko."[29]

Mackenzie King had followed the proceedings of the Royal Commission with keen interest and no small measure of self-congratulatory zeal. "It can be honestly say [*sic*] that few more cour-ageous acts have been performed by leaders of the government than my own in the Russian intrigue against the Christian world and the manner in which I have fearlessly taken up and have begun to expose the whole of it,"[30] he told his diary. A few weeks later, when the com-mission had gathered the last of its evidence, the prime minister mused, "It is a rather extraordinary thing that most of those caught in this present net are Jewish or have Jewish wives or [are] of Jewish descent."[31] King's comment wasn't indicative of his mindset alone: it was common thinking in both the federal government and Canadian society in general in 1945.

Civil libertarians, many members of the legal community, and some media critics had a markedly different view of the proceedings of the espionage commission. They condemned its secrecy and slammed police and the two Supreme Court judges involved for failing to observe due legal process. However, for the most part the Canadian public had little sympathy for any of those who were accused of being communist spies. Ten of the twenty-three people who stood as defendants in the "spy trials" were found guilty and went to jail, in no small measure because of testimony provided by Igor Gouzenko, who was a very convincing star Crown witness.

The most high-profile defendant to go to prison was Fred Rose, the thirty-eight-year-old Labour Progressive MP from the Montreal riding of Cartier. The jury at his trial deliberated for barely half an hour before they found him guilty. Rose would spend six years in prison, and after his release, his life in Canada ruined, he had no choice but to return to his native Poland, although he had left it as a young teen.

Five of Rose's co-accused, who refused to testify against him, also went to jail.[32] Even those individuals who were acquitted in criminal court suffered in the court of public opinion. Many of them lost their jobs. Their reputations were ruined and their lives shattered.

Mackenzie King cared nothing about any of this. He was relieved that the uproar over the Gouzenko affair had begun to die down, even if the Soviet government had singled out Canada as the object of its scorn and an instigator of the Cold War that was destroying relations between the Soviet Union and its erstwhile wartime allies. Amy Knight correctly observed that "there were no winners in the Gouzenko affair, except perhaps for Gouzenko himself, who seemed to be enjoying the limelight."[33]

It is true that, all things considered, Igor Gouzenko not only survived his defection, he prospered from it. In addition to serving as a witness at Canada's spy trials, he gave evidence at two government hearings in the United States and was treated as a hero by the media and officials in the Canadian government. Mackenzie King himself praised Gouzenko when the two met on July 16, 1946, after police escorted Gouzenko to the prime minister's office on the second floor of the Centre Block on Parliament Hill. King's initial impressions of the Soviet defector were positive. The Russian was "youthful in appearance. Fair-haired. Clean cut. Steady eyes. Keen intellect," King told his diary.

For many years after his defection, whenever Igor Gouzenko appeared in public, he wore a hood, as he did in this 1954 appearance. (LAC, MIKAN no. 3239912)

Gouzenko seemed to be at ease and self-assured during the meeting, although King noticed when he shook Gouzenko's hand afterward that it was dewy with perspiration. "I told [Gouzenko] I was very pleased at the way in which he had conducted himself throughout the period of great anxiety," King reported to his diary. He also suggested that Gouzenko should write about his experiences. "He said that he was writing something bit by bit."[34]

It turned out that Gouzenko would make a lot of money telling his story. His 1948 autobiography, *This Was My Choice* (written with help from a ghostwriter, Montreal sportswriter Andy O'Brien, an odd choice),[35] achieved bestseller status and earned him $150,000. In addition, the American magazine *Cosmopolitan* paid $50,000 (U.S.) for serial rights, while 20th Century Fox anted up $75,000 (U.S.) for the movie rights. Then in 1954, Gouzenko's first and only novel, *The Fall of a Titan*, which was based on the final years of Russian author and social activist Maxim Gorky, also became a bestseller and won a Governor General's Literary Award as the year's best English-language work of fiction.

These literary successes further inflated Gouzenko's already sizeable ego. He was no less proud of his landscape paintings—one of which he tried to convince Mackenzie King to accept as a Christmas gift. Others he arranged to display in the window of a Montreal department store. Gouzenko granted numerous interviews to journalists and even appeared on various television programs while wearing a pillowcase over his head. Then in 1964, nearly two decades after his defection, he would sue *Maclean's* after the magazine published an article that dared to downplay his role in exposing and breaking the Soviet spy rings that were operating in Canada in the 1940s. In the end, *Maclean's* paid Gouzenko $7,501 in an out-of-court settlement.[36]

By most accounts, Igor Gouzenko wasn't a sympathetic person, nor was he likeable. At least, that was how most of his RCMP bodyguards regarded him. Gouzenko didn't get along well with them, and at one point in early 1948, RCMP commissioner Stuart Wood was so fed up with Gouzenko's behaviour that he wanted to end the security arrangements that protected Igor from Soviet retaliation. Government officials wisely refused that request.

Anna Gouzenko and the couple's two small children could also be a handful at times for their RCMP guards. After "Mrs. G." gave birth to the couple's second child, a daughter who arrived in late 1945, and Igor was done testifying at the many spy trials that were held, the Gouzenkos were given new identities. The couple had no idea that the name 'Krysac,' which government officials had assigned to them, means 'rat' or 'snitch' in the Czech language. (Someone in the RCMP or in Ottawa had a dark sense of humour.) The family was also granted Canadian citizenship, and Igor Gouzenko received a monthly government pension. For several years after his defection, he and his family moved to a new address every few months. However, as time passed and the spotlight faded, they settled down in a suburban neighbourhood of Mississauga, west of Toronto. That is where Gouzenko, his wife, and their eight children were living on June 27, 1982, when at age sixty-three, Igor suffered a fatal heart attack. The little cipher clerk's final five years of life had been trying; he had gone blind as a complication of diabetes.

Svetlana Gouzenko outlived her husband by nineteen years, and in the late 1990s—crazy though it seems—she appealed to Russian president Vladimir Putin for a pardon for her husband's defection. Putin, a former KGB officer, was predictably unsympathetic.[37] Following Svetlana's 2001 death at age seventy-seven, the grave marker she and Igor share was finally inscribed with the particulars of the Gouzenkos' lives and with these words: "On September 5th, 1945 in Ottawa, Canada, Igor, Svetlana and their young son Andrei escaped from the Soviet Embassy and tyranny." Escaped, not defected.

A similar message is conveyed on commemorative plaques that the City of Ottawa and the Department of Canadian Heritage erected in 2003 in Dundonald Park, directly across from the building on Somerset Street West in which the Gouzenkos lived in 1945. Ottawa amateur historian Andrew Kavchak lobbied long and hard for the plaques. "To me, Igor and Svetlana Gouzenko have come to represent and symbolize many things, including the victory of the individual over tribal ethnic nationalism, as well as the victory of the individual over totalitarian communism," Kavchak said.[38]

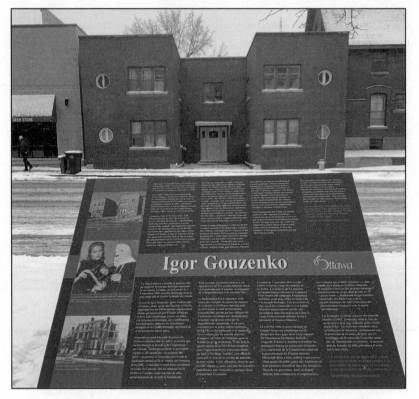

Commemorative plaques now mark the apartment building where the Gouzenkos lived on Somerset Street in Ottawa. (Hayley Cuthbertson)

IN RETROSPECT, THERE CAN be no doubt that Igor Gouzenko did Canada—and the West—a service when he made the momentous decision to defect and blow the whistle on Soviet spy activities in this country, the United States, and Britain. In a quirky kind of way, the mere fact that the Soviet Union was interested enough to bother deploying and maintaining an espionage network in Canada was a vivid reminder of this country's new-found status as a middle power in the post-1945 world. The secret atomic energy research being conducted at Chalk River was vivid proof of that reality.

"The Gouzenko affair," as it has come to be known, served as an eye-opener for Canadian government officials, the military, and the public. As Professor Wesley Wark, one of Canada's leading experts on national security, intelligence, and terrorism, has pointed out, "[It] caused the Canadian government, for the first time, to institute security screening measures for federal civil servants and to beef up security practices in general ... and forced the RCMP to embark on the creation of a genuine counter-intelligence capability, which operated after 1945 in uneasy relationship with the more favoured—and pernicious—counter-subversion capabilities of the RCMP security service."[39]

Wark also notes that the Gouzenko affair occurred less than a month after the United States brought the war in the Pacific to a sudden and dramatic end when it dropped two atomic bombs on Japan. "Gouzenko's revelations made the link between atomic warfare and atomic espionage ... and there can be no doubt that it was the atomic underlining of the affair that boosted the impact of the Gouzenko story," said Wark.[40]

That point is worth bearing in mind, for it goes a long way toward explaining why this country has continued to be an espionage target for a variety of foreign powers. Canada's proximity to the United States, our military's close ties to the American military, and our role as an important player in Western defence alliances have ensured that this is so.

In 1945 Canadians had relatively little, hoped for much, but did not really expect it. Surely they never expected what they got.
—Robert Bothwell, Ian Drummond, and John English,
Canada Since 1945 (1981)

CONCLUSION

The New Canada

BY THE FINAL DAY OF 1945, THE WAR HAD BEEN OVER FOR more than six months. But many Canadians were still struggling to come to grips with their emotions, to make sense of all that had happened, or to cope with their losses.

It had been a momentous year, one like none other in the history of Canada or of the world. Of that, people were certain. "The world of a year ago exists no longer. . . . We have passed through one of the most momentous years in the whole of history," a December 31 editorial in the *Montreal Gazette* announced.[1]

An editorial in the *Calgary Herald* on that same day echoed that sentiment. "Historians of the future will view this passing year against the vast background of events—those which went before and those which came after," the article predicted. "Certainly, it will be looked upon as a year of destiny."[2]

Across the country, editorial writers, politicians, and clergymen echoed that notion. Canadians felt an overwhelming sense of relief that the war was over, and while there were those who would remember those six years as the best of their lives, most people were looking to the future with a keen sense of expectation. But all felt numbed by the horrors they had lived through and awed by how much life had changed for them and for Canada.

One of the few constants going into the war and ending it was Mackenzie King. Like Ol' Man River, this country's septuagenarian prime minister just kept rolling along. In 1946, at the age of seventy-two, he continued to lead the country, although doing so was becoming increasingly difficult for him.

King was tired; he looked worn down and felt it. He was plagued by a nagging array of old-man minor health issues. Even worse from his perspective was the realization that he had become a divisive figure politically, and his popularity was slipping. The loss of his Prince Albert seat in the June general election had been a jolting reminder of that. King had never been a dynamic or charismatic leader; it wasn't in him to be one. That was just as well, for during the war, United States president Franklin D. Roosevelt and British prime minister Winston Churchill had overshadowed him for all the obvious reasons.

None of this bothered King much, if at all. One thing that did, however, was the changing mood of the electorate. Canada was no longer the inward-looking former British colony it had been in the years before the war; the country's bustling economy, the return home from overseas of hundreds of thousands of veterans, the arrival of tens of thousands of foreign-born war brides, and the Gouzenko affair all had underscored that new reality. In 1945, more than thirty per cent of Canadians had never travelled outside their home province, and yet in July of 1946, a CIPO poll found that fifty-nine per cent of "a national cross-section of voters"—with Quebec being the lone exception—said they'd be happy to have Canada surrender control of its armed forces and all munitions to "a World Parliament."[3]

Any such possibility made Mackenzie King uneasy. Despite feeling comfortable in his dealings with government officials in London and Washington, he was too cautious to ever be truly comfortable on the international stage or to see Canada more engaged there. King's experiences as leader of the Canadian delegation that attended the founding conference of the United Nations had been a sobering experience for him. He'd returned home from that lengthy sojourn feeling bone-weary and with a much better sense of the pecking order in the new post-war world.

Increasingly in the wake of the Liberals' victory in the June general election—the same one in which he lost his own seat—King began looking to the future and his personal legacy. He assumed his colleagues and supporters would erect a memorial in his honour once he retired. And when they did that, he hoped it would be in a prominent Ottawa location, across the street from Parliament Hill. "I would like to have it on the little triangle between the War Memorial [which King had built in 1939], the Langevin Block, and Parliament Hill," King confided to his diary. "Perhaps a sort of reproduction of the standing one with little Pat [King's dog], which was given to me on my 25th anniversary as leader of the Party."[4]

In January 1948, Mackenzie King would formally announce a decision he had made prior to the 1945 election: that would be his last election campaign. He was planning to retire. By 1948, King had been Liberal leader for twenty-nine years—the last twenty-two as prime minister—and he was finally ready to devote himself to personal pursuits, one of which was the memoir he intended to write.

In August 1948, the Liberals held their first national leadership convention since 1919. There they chose Louis St. Laurent, King's preferred successor, as the new leader of the party. The sixty-year-old Quebec-born lawyer had served as justice minister before King gave him the Secretary of State for External Affairs portfolio in September 1946.

King had no way of knowing he had less than two years to live. He would never get around to writing that planned memoir. His health and willpower deteriorated, and on July 20, 1950, he died at the age of seventy-five. It wasn't until 1967 that the Liberal government of Lester B. Pearson got around to erecting a Mackenzie King statue on Parliament Hill, doing so as part of its centennial year celebrations.

After King's death, a team of four literary executors faced the task of deciding what to do with the massive corpus of his diaries, those 50,000 pages he had written over the course of fifty-seven years—from

1893 when he was an undergraduate at the University of Toronto, until three days before his death. King stipulated in his will, dated February 28, 1950, that he wanted his literary executors "to destroy all of my diaries except those parts which I have indicated are and shall be available for publication and use."[5]

Unfortunately for King, but fortunately for posterity and for his biographers, he hadn't gotten around to marking any passages in the diaries. That left to his literary executors any decisions on what to keep and what to dispose of. Uncertain of how to proceed, they sought the expert advice of Dominion Archivist W. Kaye Lamb. Unable or unwilling to offer an opinion, Lamb consulted with lawyers, but the legal advice he received wasn't as definitive as he had hoped for. The lawyers felt it wasn't necessary for the literary executors to destroy the King diaries; they could do with them as they saw fit. And so they opted to keep them for posterity's sake.

Historian C.P. Stacey, who would be one of King's biographers, has called the diaries "the most important single political document in twentieth-century Canadian history."[6] He was right about that. Reading King's words provides us with valuable insights into events in this country's history during the first half of the twentieth century. The diaries also provide a window into the life of "Weird Willie," a man who is one of the strangest and most complex, contradictory, and endlessly interesting figures in Canadian history. More than anyone else, it was King who shaped modern Canada.

Reading his diary entries during the war years helps explain how and why in the twilight of his lengthy final term as prime minister—and especially in 1944–45—King rediscovered his idealism and resurrected some of the ideas that inspired his 1918 book, *Industry and Humanity*. There were two important results. One was PC 1003, that January 1944 labour-friendly order-in-council that guaranteed a union's right to organize. The other was that wide-ranging package of social welfare legislation that led to the creation of the safety net that's so much a part of life in Canada today—unemployment insurance, old-age pensions, and family allowance payments—and to the package of veterans' benefits that fundamentally altered and bettered life in this country in the post-war years.

M ACKENZIE KING MAY HAVE become more socially conscious as he neared the end of his political career and his life, but he remained very much a solitary man. It was so typical of him that while most Canadians were celebrating the final night of 1945 in the convivial company of family and friends, King marked New Year's Eve as he generally always had: he stayed home alone. The final volume of his diaries for 1945 has gone missing, despite searches by his literary executors, former aides, and in more recent years, the Canadian Security Intelligence Service.

However, King's diary entry for January 1, 1946, provides a recap of how he spent New Year's Eve, and elsewhere in his diaries, he commented that he had enjoyed his "usual practice" for that celebratory occasion, which was a crisp, cold winter night. King attended the watch night service at historic St. Andrew's Presbyterian Church on Kent Street, a ten-minute drive from his home. Afterward, he passed the rest of the evening on his own, speaking via telephone with a few friends, writing letters, poring over the scriptures, conversing with dead relatives, enjoying the annual concert put on by the Peace Tower carillonneur, and communing with his beloved Irish terrier, Pat. "[He] went to his little basket and I to bed in the first hour of the New Year," King told his diary. "I shall always feel that 1945 was the best year of my life. I hope and pray that the new year may, in an equally significant way, afford opportunities for service to the world as great, if not greater, than those of 1945."[7]

King needn't have worried about that. There would be plenty of such opportunities, though never again as challenging or fraught as those Canada had battled through in the six years of World War II. The country had emerged from that conflict with a robust, thriving economy and a whole new outlook on its place in the world. In 1939, Canada's annual budget had been $553 million; by 1945, it had grown to $5.1 billion, a tenfold increase. In the years after the war, consumer and investment spending took off, and they didn't slow for more than a decade. The baby boom echoed across all aspects of everyday life, and a frenetic flurry of investment that was fuelled by the insatiable demand for new housing, consumer goods, public infrastructure, and institutional construction powered the economy.

As it became apparent that there would be no post-war return to the grim economic conditions of the 1930s, and as Canada needed more workers, the federal government loosened the immigration laws. But only somewhat. Between January 1946 and December 31, 1953, more than 750,000 immigrants came to Canada. The government gave top priority to applicants from the United Kingdom, the United States, and France. Between 1947 and 1949, people from other countries and specific areas of the world were admitted on an ad hoc basis. More than 16,000 Dutch farming families were among them. At the same time, the numbers of immigrants from the Caribbean, Southeast Asia, Africa, and other developing areas of the world where whites weren't in the majority were so minuscule as to be insignificant. The total ban on Chinese immigration that had been in place for more than two decades was finally lifted in 1947, but then only because of pressure from the United Nations.

Canada's new-found affluence moderated Canadians' attitudes toward "others"—non-whites and members of other ethnic minorities that a certain blustery hockey commentator with a high collar famously termed "you people." As a result, the Canada of today is infinitely more diverse, in all regards, than it was in the 1940s. Canadians are now more open-minded toward newcomers; prosperity has that effect on people. There's no shortage of examples of this new-found tolerance. In the late 1970s, Canada would open its doors to 50,000 Vietnamese "boat people," and more recently to more than 40,000 Syrian refugees. Despite this, there remains a chronic undercurrent of systemic racism in Canadian society. Like mould in the shower, it's stubbornly resistant and difficult to remove.

Such concerns aside, going forward from 1945, Canada's economic and political indicators were generally favourable, even when there were storm clouds forming on the horizon or passing overhead. Like death and taxes, some things are constants in life. For example, as Ottawa began to loosen wartime wage and price controls, inflation became a problem, as did shortages of some high-demand consumer foods, especially meat. Adding to Mackenzie King's concerns, with the war over, provincial premiers were eager to reclaim the constitutional powers that Ottawa had usurped in the name of the war effort. The results were predictable: the old federal–provincial political tensions began to flare anew. Small wonder the prime minister was ready to retire.

Even more problematic were some of the difficulties that were part and parcel of Canada's renewed focus on international trade. In the post-Confederation era, up to 1914 at the start of World War I, Canada's main trading partner and its most enthusiastic foreign investor was Britain. That all changed by the 1920s when the United States usurped that role. The relationship languished during the lean years of the Great Depression, but it resumed and regained momentum during World War II. In the wake of the April 1941 Hyde Park Declaration, the Canadian and American economies were integrated to an extent that was unprecedented.

Canada had prospered in this new arrangement, and some business leaders and federal government officials were eager to see a postwar continuation—and even an expansion—of the wartime economic integration. A small but vocal coterie of diplomats in the United States State Department were of like mind; for a while, there was talk of another round of negotiations to hammer out a comprehensive free trade agreement between Canada and the United States. Although Mackenzie King found the idea attractive, he ultimately vetoed it for fear it could open the door to American annexation of this country.

IT FELL TO PRIME Minister Louis St. Laurent, who was King's successor, to continue broadening Canada's perspectives in the post-war era
by upping this country's international involvements—most notably
ones that regulated global trade, monetary policies, and financial matters. When in October 1947, Canada joined twenty-two other nations
in signing a new General Agreement on Tariffs and Trade, it put an end
to the crippling protectionism of the 1930s. That, in turn, promoted
liberalization of the global trading environment, which began ticking
along with a healthy seven per cent annual growth rate.

The Canada that emerged from the war was once again a great
trading nation. This country had also come of age and now stood as
one of the world's foremost middle powers at the United Nations, an
organization that Canada supported and would continue to support.
However, in the cutthroat world of Cold War geopolitics, Canadian
diplomats increasingly found themselves shunted aside or ignored
whenever the major powers made decisions on big-picture issues. This
was both humbling and frustrating for Canada.

During the war, this country had punched well above its weight
economically and militarily. As a result, many of the "Ottawa men"—
the senior bureaucrats who were among King's closest advisors—
prodded the prime minister to be more assertive in his dealings with
the great powers. They argued that Ottawa deserved to be consulted
in proportion to its mighty wartime contributions, especially in significant 'functional areas,' such as the production of war materials
and food. As historian Jack Granatstein has stressed, "The functional
principle involved an equation of capacity and responsibility, power,
and influence, and was eminently suited to Canada. It was also, in its
appropriate good sense, typically Canadian."[8] Fair though that idea
was, the world isn't always a fair place, and none of this counted for
much in the new post-war world.

However, Canada was invited to be a charter member of the various Western defence and intelligence networks that were being formed.
Where Mackenzie King might have demurred, his successor, Louis

St. Laurent, was enthusiastic about such engagements. Among the most important of them was the North Atlantic Treaty Organization (NATO), the mutual-defence bloc that was established in April 1949 to serve as a Cold War bulwark against the threat of an attack by the Soviet Union and its East European allies. However, when the Soviet Union–dominated Warsaw Pact crumbled in 1991, that threat ended and NATO lost its main sparring partner. Since then, NATO has grown a tad long in the tooth. No matter. It continues to exist even if its reason for being and its role in the world are much less certain. Despite this, Canada remains a committed member.

It was also in 1949 that Canada entered into an intelligence-sharing agreement with the United States. The details of this top-secret pact—dubbed CANUSA by those who negotiated it—did not come to light until July 2019 and then only because of the efforts of Canadian Press journalist Jim Bronskill and Professor Wesley Wark, the historian who had spent four years (1998–2002) writing a secret Privy Council Office–commissioned history of the Canadian intelligence operations.

Where the post-war emergence of modern Canada is concerned, what is important about CANUSA is that in many ways it reflected a new-found sense of national identity that had taken root among some key civil servants and military brass in Ottawa. "Fuelling all of this was a groundswell of feeling about a new exercise of Canadian power on the global stage, rooted in the expansion of Canadian capabilities during the Second World War," Wark has written. "In the minds of that small cadre of Canadian officials who had experience in intelligence in wartime, the connection between the looked-for exercise of greater global power in future and the need for an intelligence capacity was clear."[9]

During six years of conflict, when Canada and the United States had been in lockstep economically and militarily, Uncle Sam had acted like a big brother to Canada, sharing a vast amount of intelligence information, most of it related to Allied military operations. As for other kinds of intelligence, the kind spy novelists Alan Furst and John le Carré write about, Canada didn't have much, if any, capability. That fact was highlighted when Igor Gouzenko defected in September 1945 and the country's meagre counter-intelligence service was unprepared to deal with the crisis. As one of Britain's former colonies, Canada had never really been involved in the world of cloak-and-dagger espionage. It was this lack of sophistication combined with the country's close ties to the United States that made Canada such an inviting target for Soviet spies in 1945.

Canada began developing its own intelligence capabilities during the war, and the military and the Department of External Affairs personnel who had been involved in these efforts were eager to see them continue post-war. They also wanted Canada to interact as an equal in a post-war tripartite relationship with the United States and Britain

Those who subscribed to this notion feared that as the King government demobilized and pared military spending, Canada's fledgling intelligence operation—a secret that didn't exist on paper—would lose funding and die. One of the people who were intent on seeing that didn't happen was Gordon ("Bill") Crean, a thirty-four-year-old Toronto native who'd served in the British army during the war and then became involved in secret intelligence, rising to become a lieutenant-colonel in MI5, the British security service.[10]

Crean and a small group of other Canadians had worked to develop a Canadian signals intelligence (SIGINT) capability that intercepted and decoded enemy messages; the information gathered was shared with American and British allies. Crean's involvement in this highly secretive activity prompted him to fight to see to it that these operations continued post-1945. With that in mind, he took the lead in quietly beginning negotiations on a cooperation agreement with the Americans, who'd already formalized their wartime arrangements with the British when they signed an agreement in March 1946. However, Canada wasn't included in BRUSA, as it was called; the assumption in London seems to have been that Britain still spoke for Canada where security issues were concerned. Canadians didn't agree.

Gordon "Bill" Crean. (Courtesy of the Estate of Yousuf Karsh)

Bill Crean had a plan firmly in mind to assert this country's independence in the intelligence game, and he stuck to his guns in negotiating with the Americans. One of his key demands was that any agreement should not involve high-level political sign-off. His fear was that it would complicate and delay things when time was of the essence.

Conspiracy theorists might insist this kind of secretive activity is an example of the "deep state" apparatus that exists in Ottawa (and Washington). Other observers, those with a more sanguine view of the world, would counter that such direct action was a tool that enabled negotiators to get things done quickly at a time when the Cold War was intensifying. In the end, Canadian and American intelligence officers signed the CANUSA agreement, a model of compromise that gave each side much of what it wanted.

Faced with what in effect was a *fait accompli*, the British accepted that CANUSA made sense for pragmatic reasons and because of the geographical proximity of Canada and the United States. Canada's Liberal government also supported the agreement since it marked another subtle, but crucial, milestone for Canada on the road to achieving total independence from this country's colonial history.

The precedent of Canada standing as a full partner in intelligence-sharing operations having been set, in the 1950s this country joined with the United States and Britain in welcoming Australia and New Zealand into a loosely structured intelligence operation that became known as the Five Eyes; it is often described as "the most exclusive intelligence-sharing club in the world." A great deal of intelligence now circulates among the Five Eyes partners, along with technology and decisions of what adversaries to target and when. That's about as much as is known. Five Eyes doesn't advertise, and you won't learn much about it by Googling the name.

T HAT IS THE STORY of the "modern Canada" that emerged in 1945 from the crucible of war. There's no question that ours is a country with its share of faults and problems—regional divides, constitutional disputes, unresolved issues with First Nations peoples, recurring French–English squabbles, the struggle to adapt to the challenges of climate change while continuing to tap the country's natural resources, and the widening disparity between rich and poor, to name just some of them. But no country is perfect. And on balance, Canada is better than most, much better. And unlike too many other countries, where political, ethnic, or religious differences spark violence and bloodshed, Canada remains relatively peaceful, tolerant, and reasonable. That goes a long way toward explaining why this country consistently places in the top three of annual lists of best countries in the world to live.

IBM chairman Thomas Watson Sr. was onto something in November 1938 when he predicted that Canada was poised "for just about the greatest expansion of any country in the world." If he could visit Canada today, Watson would be stunned to see how right he was and how far this country has come since those dark days during the Great Depression.

The Second World War forever changed the nation, and in so very many ways it was the year 1945 that marked the birth of modern Canada.

Companies aimed their post-war advertising at all those veterans who came home, married, bought homes, and started families in what was Canada's golden age of consumerism. (Thomas Fisher Rare Book Library, University of Toronto)

Acknowledgements

THEY SAY THAT WRITING IS A SOLITARY ART FORM. THAT may be true for novelists and poets, but anyone who has ever written a non-fiction book—especially one that's about historical events—can tell you it would be impossible to do so without help from others; it's very much a group effort. The writing of 1945: *The Year That Made Modern Canada* certainly was. This book is the product of more than two years of research, reading, and emailing, talking to, and meeting with scores of people who were kind enough to provide me with information and to share their ideas, memories, and time with me. I'm forever in their debt.

I owe special thanks to Patrick Crean at HarperCollins Canada, the best editor any writer could ever have, or hope to have—he's patient beyond measure, knowledgeable, supportive, and ever-ready with insightful suggestions and words of encouragement when they're needed. Special thanks also to my agent, Richard Curtis of Richard Curtis Associates in New York; and to my wife, Marianne Hunter, who's the pillar in my life and keeps me on the right path.

I also owe a huge thank you to the many other people who were kind enough to provide me with information and help as I researched and wrote this book. They include Deborah Aldcorn, Toronto, ON; author Ted Barris, Uxbridge, ON; Prof. Robert Bothwell, University of Toronto, Toronto, ON; Marjorie Bousfield, Wolfe Island, ON;

353

Cmdr. (Ret'd) Peter Chance, Sidney-by-the-Sea, BC; Tim Chance, Kingston, ON; the late Havelyn Chiasson, Dartmouth, NS; military historian Tim Cook, Canadian War Museum, Ottawa, ON; F. Stuart Crawford, Kingston, ON; Elizabeth M. Crean, Framlingham, Suffolk, UK; Nicole Crescenzi, multimedia journalist, *Victoria News*, Victoria, BC; Netisha Currie, archives specialist, National Archives of Australia, Canberra, Australia; naval historian Alec Douglas, Toronto, ON; Betty Dow, Stratford, ON; Patrick Fahy, archives technician, Franklin D. Roosevelt Library and Museum, Hyde Park, NY; Bill and Barbara Fitsell, Kingston, ON; Jillian Forsyth, research analyst, City of Toronto Archives, Toronto, ON; Ingrid Gagnon, Kingston, ON; Alice M. Gibb, London, ON; Prof. Emeritus J.L. Granatstein, Toronto, ON; Capt. D.A.W. Gullachsen, assistant professor, Royal Military College History Department, Kingston, ON; Larry Harris, Kingston, ON; Julia Holland, archives technician, York University Libraries, Toronto, ON; Heather Home, public services/private records archivist, Queen's University Archives, Kingston, ON; Jeannie Hounslow, City of Vancouver Archives, Vancouver, BC; Elis Ing, liaison librarian, Rare Books and Special Collections, McGill University Library, Montreal, QC; Alan Klinkhoff, Alan Klinkhoff Gallery, Toronto, ON; Jennifer Longon, Archives & Research Library, New Brunswick Museum, Saint John, NB; Catharine MacDonald, Saint John, NB; Gina Martin, *National Geographic* image collection, Washington, D.C.; Prof. Emeritus Joe Martin, Rotman School of Business, University of Toronto, Toronto, ON; Susan McClure, municipal archivist, Halifax Municipal Archives, Halifax, NS; Prof. Duncan McDowell, Kingston, ON; Prof. J. Marc Milner, director of the Gregg Centre, University of New Brunswick, Fredericton, NB; historian David More, Kingston, ON; Allan Moscovitch, Department of Social Work, Carleton University, Ottawa, ON; Dominic (Don) Petrie, Yarker, ON; Mike Postovit, CKWS television (Global), Kingston, ON; Agnieszka Prycik, archives technician, City of Montreal Archives, Montreal, QC; Robin Quinlan, Montreal, QC; Garry D. Shutlak, Nova Scotia Archives,

Halifax, NS; Prof. Roger Sarty, Department of History, Wilfrid Laurier University, Waterloo, ON; Carol Ann Scott, Stratford, ON; A.B. Smith, Kingston, ON; nautical historian *par excellence* B.C. Smith, Kingston, ON; Patricia M. Smith, Kingston, ON; Jacqueline Vincent, Brechin Imaging, Kanata, ON; Heldegard Von Derheiden, Kingston, ON; Sharon Walker, library manager, Vancouver Island Regional Library, Sidney/North Saanich, BC; Prof. Wesley Wark, visiting professor, University of Ottawa, Ottawa, ON; and Cameron Willis, chief researcher, Canada's Penitentiary Museum, Kingston, ON.

Notes

INTRODUCTION

1. Broadfoot, Barry, *Six War Years, 1939–45: Memories of Canadians at Home and Abroad* (Doubleday, 1974), p. ix.
2. Morton, Desmond, and Granatstein, J.L. "1945: Canada Comes of Age," *Maclean's*, May 1, 1995, p. 64.
3. Laurier's actual words have been the subject of much discussion. According to John Robert Colombo, Laurier reportedly said in a January 18, 1904, speech to the Canadian Club of Ottawa that "Canada shall fill the twentieth century." However, those words soon took on a life of their own and became the aphorism "The twentieth century belongs to Canada." *John Robert Colombo's Famous Lasting Words: Great Canadian Quotations* (Douglas & McIntyre, 2000), p. 535.
4. *Toronto Daily Star*, November 28, 1938, p. 1.
5. *Toronto Daily Star*, June 30, 1939, p. 28.
6. www150.statscan.gc.ca.
7. Most countries use gross domestic product (GDP) to measure national production, and so Statistics Canada switched from calculating gross national product (GNP) to calculating GDP in 1986 in order to make comparisons easier. However, this has had the opposite effect on historical comparisons.
8. *Regina Leader-Post*, December 31, 1945, p. 11.

CHAPTER 1

1. Almost half of the 50,656 Canadian women who served in the military during the war—21,624—did so in the Canadian Women's Army Corps, while 17,467 wore the blue uniforms of the Royal Canadian Air Force. The rest were navy Wrens.

2. Cook, Tim, *Fight to the Finish: Canadians in the Second World War, 1944–45,* Vol II (Allen Lane, 2015), p. 389.
3. Broadfoot, Barry, *Six War Years, 1939–45: Memories of Canadians at Home and Abroad* (Doubleday, 1974), p. 338.
4. Duhamel, Roger, "A French Canadian Speaks," *Maclean's,* January 1, 1945, p. 25.
5. MacDonald, Marjorie, with Captain Harold MacDonald, "In the Heat of Battle: Letters from the Normandy Campaign, 1944," *Canadian Military History,* Vol. 12, No. 3/4 (2003), p. 2. This article and four others about Hal MacDonald's wartime correspondence can be accessed online at https://scholars.wlu.ca/cmh.
6. Ibid., p. 4.
7. Ibid.
8. Ibid.

Chapter 2

1. Ritchie, Charles, *Diplomatic Passport: More Undiplomatic Diaries, 1947–1962* (Macmillan, 1981), entry for January 18, 1950.
2. Bothwell, Robert, Drummond, Ian, and English, John, *Canada Since 1945: Power, Politics, and Provincialism* (University of Toronto Press, 1981), p. 71.
3. *Maclean's,* May 15, 1941, p. 18.
4. Ritchie, op. cit.
5. Bothwell, Robert, and Killbourn, William, *C.D. Howe: A Biography* (McClelland & Stewart, 1979), p. 77.
6. Hillmer, Norman, and Granetstein, J.L., *Maclean's,* "Historians Rank the Best and Worst Canadian Prime Ministers," April 21, 1997, p. 37.
7. Ibid.
8. Stacey, C.P., *A Very Double Life: The Private World of Mackenzie King* (Macmillan, 1976).
9. Brown, E.K., "Mackenzie King of Canada," *Harper's,* January 1, 1943, p. 196.
10. Hillmer and Granatstein, op. cit.
11. Berton, Pierre, *The Great Depression: 1929–1939* (McClelland & Stewart, 1990), p. 352.
12. Laurier House National Historic site home page, "Servants at Laurier House."
13. Mackenzie King diaries, Library and Archives Canada, www.bac-lac.gc.ca, October 20, 1897.
14. King diaries, op. cit., October 30, 1897.
15. Ibid., February 13, 1898.
16. *Maclean's,* "Forecast for 1945," January 1, 1945, p. 11.
17. *Toronto Daily Star,* December 30, 1944, p. 3.

18. Cook, Tim, *Warlords: Borden, Mackenzie King, and Canada's World Wars* (Allen Lane, 2012), p. 270.
19. Malone, Richard S., *A World in Flames, 1944–45* (Collins, 1984), p. 143.
20. King diaries, op. cit., December 31, 1944.
21. "Watch night" services are held on New Year's Eve, particularly in African-American churches, to celebrate and remember the Emancipation Proclamation of January 1, 1863. A similar tradition can also be traced to John Wesley, the eighteenth-century English cleric, who adopted the idea of holding a New Year's Eve vigil during which participants reflected on events of the year past and thought about the year ahead.
22. King diaries, op. cit., December 31, 1944.

CHAPTER 3

1. Author interview with Barbara Fitsell (née Robson), Kingston, ON, December 9, 2019.
2. *Toronto Daily Star*, November 21, 1940, p. 32.
3. Gouzenko, Igor, *This Was My Choice: Gouzenko's Story* (J.M. Dent and Sons, 1948), p. 213.
4. Abella, Irving, Acheson, T.W., Bercuson, David, Brown, R. Craig, Granatstein, J.L., and Neatby, Blair (eds.), *Nation: Canada Since Confederation* (3rd ed.) (McGraw-Hill Ryerson, 1990), p. 381.
5. Berton, Pierre, *The Great Depression: 1929–1939* (McClelland & Stewart, 1990), p. 435.
6. Schull, Joseph, *The Great Scot: A Biography of Donald Gordon* (McGill-Queen's University Press, 1979), p. 53.
7. A Japanese submarine did fire some shells at Estevan Point on Vancouver Island, and Japanese soldiers occupied the Aleutian Islands off Alaska, but that was pretty much the extent of Japanese attacks on the west coast. In 1979, American film director Stephen Spielberg's big-budget comedy film *1941* poked fun at the hysteria in California over a possible Japanese invasion in the weeks after Pearl Harbor.
8. Suzuki, David, *David Suzuki: The Autobiography* (Greystone Press, 2006), p. 15.
9. On September 22, 1988, Prime Minister Brian Mulroney acknowledged that fact when he delivered an apology to Canada's Japanese community, and the Canadian government announced that the descendants of those whose property had been unjustly seized and sold would receive compensation. Interestingly, Mulroney's announcement came one month after President Ronald Reagan made similar gestures in the United States.
10. Edugyan, Esi, *Dreaming of Elsewhere: Observations on Home* (University of Alberta Press, 2014), p. 28.
11. Suzuki, op. cit., p. 14.
12. *Globe and Mail*, October 22, 1943, p. 16.

13. *Globe and Mail*, August 20, 1914, p. 13.
14. Bothwell, Robert, Drummond, Ian, and English, John, *Canada Since 1945: Power, Politics, and Provincialism* (University of Toronto Press, 1981), p. 71.
15. Chapman, Christopher, in *Too Young to Fight*, edited by Priscilla Galloway (Stoddart, 1999), pp. 103–104.

CHAPTER 4

1. Gossage, Carolyn, *Greatcoats and Glamour Boots: Canadian Women at War (1939–1945)* (Dundurn, 2001), p. 24.
2. www.veterans.gc.ca/eng/remembrance/those-who-served/women-and-war/fallen ?filterYr=1945.
3. *Globe and Mail*, August 18, 1941, p. 11.
4. *Maclean's*, September 1, 1943, p. 24.
5. The Royal Navy adopted the practice of commissioning its land bases as ships because the British government prohibited it from engaging in activities on land, which was the army's turf.
6. *Globe and Mail*, June 28, 1943, p. 11.
7. Allan, Laura, "The Women's Royal Canadian Naval Service," *Canadian Naval Review*, Vol. 3, No. 3 (2007), p. 18.
8. Broadfoot, Barry, *Six War Years, 1939–45: Memories of Canadians at Home and Abroad* (Doubleday, 1974), pp. 140–141.
9. Author interview with Geraldine Bagnall (née Gorman), Kingston, ON, April 16, 2019.
10. *Kingston Whig-Standard*, June 4, 1994, p. 6.
11. To view a Historica Canada video on Marion Orr, please visit https://www.historicacanada.ca/content/heritage-minutes/marion-orr. To view a 1994 CBC archival video report on Orr and Violet Milstead Warren, please visit www.cbc.ca/archives/entry/women-of-WWII-spitfires-in-the-rhododendrons.
12. Carter, David, *Behind Canadian Barbed Wire* (Eagle Butte Press, 1998), p. 5.
13. Broadfoot, op. cit., p. 353.
14. Jaques, Edna, "We Are the Workers," *Maclean's*, May 15, 1942, p. 7.
15. "Queen of the Hurricanes," Elsie MacGill profile posted on www.cbc.ca/history.

CHAPTER 5

1. Jackson, Gilbert, "Can We All Get Jobs?," *Maclean's*, August 1, 1945, pp. 5–6, 44–46.
2. *Globe and Mail*, December 24, 1942, p. 8.
3. Granatstein, J.L. "Arming the Nation: Canada's Industrial War Effort, 1939–45," paper written for the Canadian Council of Chief Executives, 2005. p. 9.

4. *Globe and Mail*, January 10, 1944, p. 5.
5. Ibid.
6. Tupper, Janet, "Little Women—What Now?," *Maclean's*, November 1, 1944, p. 33.
7. *Toronto Daily Star*, October 17, 1945, p. 9.
8. *The Canadian Encyclopedia*, "Royal Commission on Dominion–Provincial Relations."
9. Newman, Peter C., "Taking a Page from Howe's Book," *Maclean's*, October 18, 1982, p. 62.
10. Howe was American-born, but his extended family had historic Canadian roots. Howe's distant cousin was Joseph Howe, Nova Scotia's most famous Confederation statesman.
11. McDowall, Duncan, *The Sum of All Satisfactions: Canada in the Age of National Accounting* (McGill-Queen's University Press, 2008), p. 58.
12. *Toronto Daily Star*, May 5, 1941, p. 6.
13. Bothwell, Robert, and Killbourn, William, *C.D. Howe: A Biography* (McClelland & Stewart, 1979), p. 66.
14. Ibid., p. 181.
15. *Toronto Daily Star*, November 28, 1938, p. 3.
16. Dexter, Grant, "Minister of Supply," *Maclean's*, May 15, 1942, p. 9.
17. *C.D. Howe*, op. cit., p. 49.
18. Ibid., p. 23.
19. Port Arthur amalgamated with nearby Fort William in 1961 to form the city of Thunder Bay. Located at the western end—"the head"—of Lake Superior, Thunder Bay (pop. 121,000) is a key port for the export of Canadian grain crops.
20. *Maclean's*, May 15, 1942, p. 58.
21. The idea of working for a dollar a day for patriotic reasons was born and took root in the United States during WWI. The American-born Howe brought the idea north when he came, and it was used to great effect during WWII.
22. *C.D. Howe*, op. cit., p. 10.
23. Mackenzie King diaries, Library and Archives Canada, www.bac-lac.gc.ca, December 14, 1940, p. 3.
24. Ibid.
25. Harbron, John, *C.D. Howe* (Fitzhenry and Whiteside, 1980), pp. 44–45.
26. Newman, op. cit.

CHAPTER 6

1. All figures are in Canadian dollars. According to the Canadian Inflation Calculator, posted online by Statistics Canada, $3,500 in 1945 dollars would amount to about $50,750 today. That is livable, but just barely, being slightly less than today's average income of $55,808.

2. *Montreal Gazette*, February 15, 1943, p. 16.

3. Single men between the ages of twenty and forty-five were the first wave of military recruits. That included many NHL players, but others were able to continue playing when they joined the reserves or earned a deferral by working at jobs in war-related industries.

4. www.si.com/nhl/2017/02/09/montreal-arena-fire-wanderers.

5. *New York Times*, December 10, 1881, p. 2.

6. Fischler, Stan, and Richard, Maurice, *The Flying Frenchmen: Hockey's Greatest Dynasty* (Hawthorn Books, 1971), p. 97.

7. The age limit for minor hockey in Quebec in the 1930s was nineteen, but in Ontario and many other provinces it was eighteen.

8. The first NHL player to regularly wear a hockey helmet was defenceman George Owen of the Boston Bruins. The Harvard graduate donned his protective headgear in 1928–29.

9. Faulkner, William, "An Innocent at Rinkside," *Sports Illustrated*, January 24, 1955.

10. O'Brien, Andy, *Rocket Richard* (Ryerson Press, 1961), p. 17.

11. Ibid., p. 13.

12. Foran, Charles, *Rocket Richard* (Penguin Canada, 2011), p. 4.

13. Fitken, Ed, *Hockey's Rocket* (Castle Publications, 1951), p. 50.

14. O'Brien, op. cit., p. 13.

15. Callwood, June, "The Maurice Richards," *Maclean's*, May 1959, p. 48.

16. *Globe and Mail*, June 20, 2008, p. S8.

17. Carrier, Roch, *Our Life with the Rocket: The Maurice Richard Story* (Viking, 2001), p. 76.

18. Carrier, Roch, in *Too Young to Fight*, edited by Priscilla Galloway (Stoddart, 1999), p. 70.

19. Cameron, Elspeth, *Hugh MacLennan: A Writer's Life* (University of Toronto Press, 1981), p. 177.

20. Ibid.

21. Vanasse, André, *Gabrielle Roy: A Passion for Writing* (XYZ Publishing, 2007), p. 93.

22. Ibid., p. 90.

23. https://www150.statcan.gc.ca.

24. Atwood, Margaret, "Gabrielle Roy, in Nine Parts," in *Legacy: How French Canadians Shaped North America*, Andre Pratt and Jonathan Kay (eds.) (McClelland & Stewart, 2016).

25. Carrier, op. cit., p. 2.

26. Young, Scott, *Hello Canada! The Life and Times of Foster Hewitt* (Seal Books, 1985), p. 3.

27. Ibid., p. 88.

28. *Globe and Mail*, February 19, 1945, p. 14.

29. *Globe and Mail*, February 26, 1945, p. 17.

30. Carrier, op. cit., p. 85.
31. Fitken, op. cit., p. 50.
32. According to the HockeyZone Plus online database, Maurice Richard earned $82,220 U.S. during his career. www.hockeyzoneplus.com/salaries/33158-Maurice-Richard.
33. *Montreal Gazette*, May 31, 2000, p. B2.

CHAPTER 7

1. Dickson, Paul, *A Thoroughly Canadian General* (University of Toronto Press, 2007), pp. 423–424.
2. Blumenson, Martin, *The Patton Papers, 1940–1945* (Houghton Mifflin, 1974), p. 462.
3. Dickson, op. cit., p. 262.
4. Broadfoot, Barry, *Six War Years, 1939–45: Memories of Canadians at Home and Abroad* (Doubleday, 1974), p. 381.
5. MacDonald, Marjorie, and Captain Harold MacDonald, "Striking into Germany: From the Scheldt to the German surrender," *Canadian Military History*, Vol. 12, No. 3 (2003), p. 17.
6. The IJsselmeer (known as Lake IJssel in English) is a 425-mile-square (1,100 kilometre square) closed-off inland bay in the central Netherlands. It borders on the provinces of Flevoland, North Holland, and Friesland.
7. *Time*, September 18, 1944, pp. 33–36.
8. Oliver, Dean, "In the Shadow of the Corps: Historiography, Generalship, and Harry Crerar," in *Warrior Chiefs*, Stephen Harris and Bernd Horn (eds.) (Dundurn Press, 2001), p. 92.
9. Dickson, op. cit.
10. Granatstein, Jack, *The Best Little Army in the World: The Canadians in Northwest Europe, 1944–45* (HarperCollins Canada, 2015), p. 134.
11. *Time*, September 18, 1944, pp. 33–36.
12. Dickson, op. cit.
13. *Warrior Chiefs*, op. cit., p. 92.
14. *The Best Little Army in the World*, op. cit. pp. 151–152.
15. Stacey, C.P., *A Date with History: Memoirs of a Canadian Historian* (Deneau, 1982), pp. 165–166.
16. Dickson, op. cit., p. 252
17. Dickson, op. cit., p. 423.
18. Stacey, C.P., *Official History of the Canadian Army in the Second World War*, Vol. III, p. 611. Accessed online on June 20, 2019, at www.canada.ca/en/department-national-defence/services/military-history/history-heritage/official-military-history-lineages/official-histories/book-1960-army-ww2-3.html.

19. There was a series of surrender ceremonies in the days after the German surrender. The official documents, which formally ended the war and the Nazi regime, were signed in Berlin on the night of May 8, 1945. Representatives of the German military, the Allied Expeditionary Force, and the Supreme High Command of the Soviet Red Army inked the document while other French and American representatives signed as witnesses. Surprisingly, there were no Canadian or British signatories to the document. An earlier version of the text had been signed in a ceremony in Reims on May 7.
20. *The Best Little Army in the World*, op. cit., p. 227.
21. *Globe and Mail*, May 7, 1945, p. 1.
22. Ibid.
23. Ibid.
24. Roberts, James, *The Canadian Summer* (University of Toronto Bookroom, 1981), pp. 145–146.
25. *The Best Little Army in the World*, op. cit., pp. 229–230.
26. Dickson, op. cit., p. 422.
27. *Maclean's*, September 15, 1945, p. 6.
28. Dickson, op. cit., p. 443.
29. *Toronto Daily Star*, August 8, 1945, p. 15.
30. *Toronto Daily Star*, April 2, 1945, p. 6.
31. Dickson, op. cit., p. 443.

CHAPTER 8

1. Mackenzie King diaries, Library and Archives Canada, www.bac-lac.gc.ca, May 7, 1945.
2. CBC Radio archives, https://www.cbc.ca/archives.
3. Author interview with F. Stuart Crawford, Kingston, ON, January 7, 2020.
4. CBC Archives, May 6, 1945, www.cbc.ca/archives/topic/reports-from-abroad-matthew-halton.
5. CBC Archives, May 8, 1945, Matthew Halton, www.cbc.ca/archives.
6. Author telephone interview with George Henderson, Wilton, ON, June 8, 2019.
7. *Montreal Gazette*, May 9, 1945, p. 17.
8. *Toronto Daily Star*, May 7, 1945, p. 8.
9. *Edmonton Journal*, May 8, 1945, p. 1.
10. *Vancouver Sun*, May 7, 1945, p. 1.
11. *Vancouver Province*, May 7, 1945, p. 2.
12. CBC Radio archives, www.cbc.ca/archives/the-nightmare-is-over-ve-day-as-seen-at-home-and-abroad-1.5110746.

CHAPTER 9

1. Of this total, 78,000 were members of the Royal Canadian Navy Volunteer Reserves (RCNVR), 5,300 were reservists (RCNR), while just 4,384 were full-time naval personnel (RCN).

2. Redman, Stanley, *Open Gangway: An Account of the Halifax Riots, 1945* (Lancelot Press, 1991), p. 13.

3. On the evening of July 18, 1945, a fire broke out on a barge that was moored at the pier at the Bedford Magazine, now Canadian Forces Ammunition Dump (CFAD) Bedford, just north of Dartmouth. When the fire spread, some ammunition that was being temporarily stored on the pier exploded. The ensuing fire and more explosions went on for twenty-four hours. Fortunately, local officials had learned the hard lessons of the 1917 disaster, and they had emergency plans in place. Police, fire, and the military organized an orderly evacuation of Halifax's north end. As a result, the 1946 explosions shattered windows, damaged roofs, and shifted some structures on their foundations, but no Haligonians suffered serious injuries, and there were no deaths.

4. Author telephone interview with Cmdr. Peter Chance (Ret'd), Victoria, BC, February 18, 2019.

5. Author telephone interview with naval historian Alec Douglas, Toronto, ON, July 11, 2019.

6. Juno Beach Centre home page, www.junobeach.org/canada-in-WWII/articles/admiral-l-w-murray-2/.

7. Douglas interview, op. cit.

8. *Halifax Herald*, May 10, 1945.

9. *Maclean's*, March 26, 1960, p. 26.

10. Redman, op. cit., p. 11.

11. Barris, Ted, *Days of Victory: Canadians Remember, 1939–45* (Thomas Allen, 2005), p. 309.

12. Broadfoot, Barry, *Six War Years, 1939–45: Memories of Canadians at Home and Abroad* (Doubleday, 1974), p. 389.

13. Redman, op. cit., p. 14.

14. Kellock, Justice R.L., Report on the Halifax Disorders, May 7–8, 1945, p. 51.

15. *Globe and Mail*, May 9, 1945, p. 2.

16. Author interview with Bill Fitsell, Kingston, ON, February 18, 2019.

17. Author interview with Dominic Petrie, Yarker, ON, July 13, 2019.

18. *Halifax Herald*, May 9, 1945, p. 3.

19. Redman, op. cit., p. 63.

20. *Halifax Herald*, May 9, 1945, p. 1.

21. Redman, op. cit., p. 147.

22. Milner, Marc, *The Admirals: Canada's Senior Naval Leadership in the Twentieth Century* (Dundurn Press, 2006), p. 118.
23. Douglas interview, op. cit.
24. Milner, op. cit., p. 97.

CHAPTER 10

---

1. Newman, Peter C., *The Canadian Establishment*, Vol. I (McClelland & Stewart, 1975), p. 278.
2. Berton, Pierre, "E.P. Taylor and His Empire," *Maclean's*, March 1, 1950, p. 12. (Cited hereafter as Berton.)
3. Moon, Barbara, "The Last Chapter of the Great E.P. Taylor Myth," *Maclean's*, July 6, 1963, p. 10.
4. Ibid.
5. *New York Times*, May 16, 1989, p. B6.
6. *Toronto Daily Star*, September 3, 1941, p. 2.
7. The Hyde Park Declaration, which derived its name from the Roosevelt estate at Hyde Park, New York (where King and the president met), provided for American war purchases in Canada. American-produced war materials that were made here for British use were to be included in the Lend-Lease Act, an arrangement that reduced Canada's trade deficit and made it easier for this country to fill British orders for war materials and to guarantee payment for them. While Lend-Lease was vital to the Allied war effort, Canada enjoyed only indirect benefits from the initiative.
8. *New York Times*, April 21, 1941, p. 1.
9. Mackenzie King diaries, Library and Archives Canada, www.bac-lac.gc.ca, 1941.
10. *Ottawa Journal*, February 11, 1943, p. 8.
11. When the annual list of honours bestowed by King George was announced on January 1, 1944, Taylor's name was conspicuously absent when other "dollar-a-year" men were included. The prime minister had struck Taylor's name from the list of recommended award recipients. Mackenzie King attempted to do the same thing in 1945 but relented when C.D. Howe threatened to resign unless Taylor was honoured.
12. Brown, E.K., "Mackenzie King of Canada," *Harper's*, January 1943, pp. 192–200.
13. Ibid., p. 193.
14. Rohmer, Richard, *E.P. Taylor: The Biography of Edward Plunket Taylor* (McClelland & Stewart, 1978), p. 150.
15. Ibid., p. 62.
16. *The Canadian Encyclopedia*, www.thecanadianencyclopedia.ca/en/article/brewing-industry.

17. A closed-end fund is a collective investment model based on issuing a fixed number of shares that are not redeemable from the fund itself. Unlike in open-end funds, new shares in a closed-end fund are not created by managers to meet demand from investors.
18. Rohmer, op. cit., p. 168.
19. Berton, op. cit., p. 48.
20. Ibid.
21. Ibid.
22. Newman, op. cit., p. 32.
23. Berton, op. cit., p. 48.
24. BC Forest Products ceased operations in 1986, while Dominion Stores—now owned by the Great Atlantic and Pacific Tea Company (A&P)—was rebranded as Metro Incorporated. Massey Ferguson was purchased in 1997 by AGCO, the owner of its former competitor Allis-Chalmers. Massey Ferguson is one of several brands produced by agricultural conglomerate AGCO and remains a major seller around the world.
25. Porter, Michael, "From Competitive Advantage to Corporate Strategy," *Harvard Business Review*, May 1987, found online at hbr.org/1987/05/from-competitive-advantage-to-corporate-strategy.

CHAPTER 11

1. Pennington, Doris, *Agnes Macphail: Reformer* (Simon and Pierre, 1990), p. 229.
2. An example of this was the lack of media and public attention accorded the news of the March 2, 1945, death of artist Emily Carr. "The genius we loved to laugh at," as one critic dubbed her, was seventy-three when she died in Victoria. Her obituary in the *Globe and Mail* was a brief eight paragraphs, while the *Toronto Daily Star* devoted just two paragraphs, a total of sixty-four words, to the news.
3. Agnes was born with the surname "McPhail." However, when she discovered on a trip to Scotland that the family surname originally had been spelled "Macphail," she promptly changed the spelling of her own surname to reflect this reality.
4. *Maclean's*, September 15, 1949, p. 16.
5. Ibid., p. 47.
6. Gibb, Alice, "Agnes Campbell Macphail: 'I'm No Lady,'" *High Profile*, March/April 1988, p. 14.
7. *Canada's History*, September 30, 2010, www.canadashistory.ca/.
8. Mackenzie King diaries, Library and Archives Canada, www.bac-lac.gc.ca, March 26, 1940.
9. Pennington, op. cit., p. 229.

10. Crowley, Terry, *Agnes Macphail and the Politics of Equality* (James Lorimer & Company, 1990), p. 187.
11. Ibid., p. 186.
12. *Globe and Mail*, September 15, 1944, p. 18.
13. French, Doris, and Stewart, Margaret, *Ask No Quarter: A Biography of Agnes Macphail* (Longman, Green and Company, 1959), p. 269.
14. *Maclean's*, August 1, 1944, p. 7.
15. While Douglas is widely regarded as the founder of free universal health care in this country, he had stepped down as premier of Saskatchewan in November 1961. It was his successor, Woodrow Lloyd, who ended up shepherding the enabling legislation through the legislature and dealing with a bitter strike by Saskatchewan doctors in the summer of 1962.
16. For more on Tommy Douglas's early flirtation with eugenics, see *The Canadian Encyclopedia* at www.thecanadianencyclopedia.ca.
17. Morton, Desmond, and Granatstein, J.L., *Victory 1945: Canadians from War to Peace* (HarperCollins Canada, 1995), p. 114.
18. *Toronto Daily Star*, May 25, 1945, p. 3.
19. *Globe and Mail*, July 7, 1945, p. 3.
20. Crowley, op. cit., p. 188.
21. Lewis, David, *The Good Fight: Political Memoirs, 1909–1958* (Macmillan of Canada, 1981), p. 261.
22. Rather than seeking to re-enter the Ontario legislature in a by-election, George Drew entered federal politics. He won the leadership of the federal Progressive Conservative party at a 1948 party convention, defeating John Diefenbaker on the first ballot. Drew then led the party to defeat in two elections before resigning as leader in 1956. He died in 1973.
23. For more information on Agnes Macphail's efforts on behalf of prison reform, watch the Canadian Heritage Minute on the topic, which can be found online at www.historicacanada.ca/content/heritage-minutes/agnes-macphail.
24. *Globe and Mail*, February 15, 1954, p. 4.
25. Gibb, op. cit., p. 17.

CHAPTER 12

1. Gray, James H., *The Winter Years: The Depression on the Prairies* (Macmillan Canada, 1966), p. 7.
2. Berton, Pierre, *The Great Depression: 1929–1939* (McClelland & Stewart, 1990), p. 10.
3. *Maclean's*, December 15, 1937, p. 4.
4. *Globe and Mail*, December 28, 1920, p. 7.
5. *Toronto Daily Star*, March 3, 1919, p. 4.

6. Author interview with Bill Fitsell, Kingston, ON, February 18, 2019.
7. Mackenzie King diaries, Library and Archives Canada, www.bac-lac.gc.ca, p. 2.
8. Granatstein, J.L., *The Ottawa Men: The Civil Service Mandarins, 1935–1957* (Oxford University Press, 1982), p. 1.
9. Wardhaugh, Robert, *Behind the Scenes: The Life and Work of William Clifford Clark* (University of Toronto Press, 2010), p. 381.
10. O'Leary, M. Gratton, "The Man Behind Ilsley," *Maclean's*, May 1, 1945, p. 12.
11. Wardhaugh, op. cit., p. 35.
12. *Maclean's*, January 15, 1940, p. 15.
13. *Globe and Mail*, December 2, 1942, p. 1.
14. King diaries, op. cit., December 5, 1942, p. 13.
15. Speech from the Throne, 19th Parliament, January 28, 1943, found online at lop.parl.ca/staticfiles/ParlInfo/Documents/ThroneSpeech/En/19-04-e.pdf.
16. Morton, Desmond, and Granatstein, J.L., *Victory 1945: Canadians from War to Peace* (HarperCollins Canada, 1995), p. 121.

CHAPTER 13

1. *Toronto Daily Star*, March 17, 1943, p. 17.
2. Horn, Michael, "Leonard Marsh and His Ideas: 1967–1982: Some Personal Recollections," *Journal of Canadian Studies*, Vol. 21, No. 2 (1986), p. 70.
3. Ibid., p. 72.
4. Horn, Michael, "Leonard Marsh and the Coming of a Welfare State in Canada," *Histoire Sociale*, Vol. 9, No. 17 (1976), p. 199.
5. Ibid., p. 198.
6. Morton, Desmond, and Granatstein, J.L., *Victory 1945: Canadians from War to Peace* (HarperCollins Canada, 1995), pp. 120–121.
7. Bothwell, Robert, Drummond, Ian, and English, John, *Canada Since 1945: Power, Politics, and Provincialism* (University of Toronto Press, 1981), p. 65.
8. Mackenzie King diaries, Library and Archives Canada, www.bac-lac.gc.ca, September 2, 1949.
9. Maxwell, Eaton, "Canada Looks to the Postwar," *Antioch Review*, December 1, 1943, p. 483.
10. *Toronto Daily Star*, March 16, 1943, p. 17.
11. Ibid.
12. Moscovitch, Allan, *Report on Social Security for Canada* (McGill-Queen's University Press, 2017), p. xxi.
13. *Globe and Mail*, March 17, 1943, p. 1.
14. *Toronto Daily Star*, March 16, 1943, p. 1.
15. *Maclean's*, April 15, 1943, p. 1.

16. *Victory 1945*, op. cit., p. 122.
17. Granatstein, J.L., *The Ottawa Men: The Civil Service Mandarins, 1935–1957* (Oxford University Press, 1982), p. 156.
18. Brandt, Gail Cuthbert, "'Pigeon Holed and Forgotten': The Work of the Subcommittee on the Post-War Problems of Women, 1943," *Social History*, Vol. XV, No. 29 (1982), p. 259.
19. *Victory 1945*, op. cit., p. 170.
20. *Canada Since 1945*, op. cit., p. 68.
21. J.B. Priestley. BrainyQuote.com, www.brainyquote.com/quotes/j_b_priestley _390628.
22. Creighton, Donald, *The Forked Road: Canada 1939–57* (McClelland & Stewart, 1976), pp. 81–82.
23. Ajzenstat, Janet, and Smith, Peter (eds.), *Canada's Origins: Liberal, Tory or Republican?* (McGill-Queen's University Press, 1997), p. 37.
24. *Victory 1945*, op. cit., p. 124.
25. The monthly "baby bonus," as it became known, was $5 for a child up to five years of age, and escalated to $8 a month for children aged thirteen to fifteen.
26. *Maclean's*, June 15, 1945, p. 1.
27. King diaries, op. cit., May 7, 1945.
28. Ibid., June 26, 1945.
29. Creighton, op. cit., p. 99.
30. Creighton, op. cit., p. 100.
31. King diaries, op. cit., June 27, 1945.
32. Author interview with A. Britton Smith, Kingston, ON, December 4, 2019.
33. *Globe and Mail*, August 7, 1945, p. 1.
34. King diaries, op. cit., October 4, 1944, p. 4.

CHAPTER 14

1. Fuykschot, Cornelia, *Hunger in Holland* (CeFar Associates, 1988).
2. CBC Archives, www.cbc.ca/archives.
3. This willingness extended to allowing German officers to order the post-war executions of some soldiers who had laid down their arms in the closing days of the war and refused to fight.
4. Broadfoot, Barry, *Six War Years, 1939–45: Memories of Canadians at Home and Abroad* (Doubleday, 1974), pp. 382–383.
5. Bird, Will L., *North Shore (New Brunswick) Regiment* (Brunswick Press, 1963), p. 558.
6. *Canadian Military History*, Vol. 13, No. 4 (2004), p. 31.
7. Ives, Don, "The Veterans Charter: The Compensation Principle and the Principle of Recognition for Service," in Neary, Peter, and J.L. Granatstein (eds.), *The*

Veterans Charter and Post–World War II Canada (McGill-Queen's University Press, 1998), p. 86.

8. Dickson, Paul, *A Thoroughly Canadian General* (University of Toronto Press, 2007), p. 425.

9. The United States had made full use of Britain's three largest passenger ships—the *Queen Mary*, the *Queen Elizabeth*, and the *Aquitania*—as troop transports. By October 1945, on any given day, these ships and others were carrying 25,000 GIs home from Europe and the Far East.

10. *Canadian Military History*, Vol. 13, No. 4 (2004), p. 31.

11. Morton, Desmond, and Granatstein, J.L., *Victory 1945: Canadians from War to Peace* (HarperCollins Canada, 1995), p. 157.

12. Ibid., p. 34.

13. Ibid.

14. Ibid., p. 36.

15. *Maclean's*, September 1, 1945, p. 1.

16. *Canadian Military History*, Vol. 13, No. 4 (2004), p. 38.

17. Ibid., p. 45.

CHAPTER 15

1. *Toronto Daily Star*, October 17, 1945, p. 1.

2. Betty Grable was one of Hollywood's biggest stars from 1943 to 1951. While she was a talented singer and dancer, her signature attribute was her legs. An iconic pinup of a cheeky-looking Grable in a white bathing suit was a favourite of wartime American GIs—and many Canadian soldiers. Grable reportedly earned $300,000 a year, mostly because of her legs, which she insured for $1 million.

3. *Toronto Daily Star*, October 17, 1945, p. 1.

4. *Toronto Daily Star*, October 18, 1945, p. 2.

5. *Globe and Mail*, December 29, 1945, p. 5.

6. *Maclean's*, August 15, 1945, p. 34.

7. Marshall, A.S. "Crime Wave," *Maclean's*, April 15, 1946, p. 7.

8. *Toronto Daily Star*, August 31, 1945, p. 1.

9. Lauzon and two other inmates would break out of Kingston Penitentiary (KP) in August 1947. Lauzon was better off in prison. Not long after his escape, he and some fellow criminals in Mississippi got into a gun battle over some stolen bank loot. When Lauzon was shot dead, his body was dumped into a swamp. Mickey MacDonald, one of Lauzon's fellow KP escapees, disappeared after slipping through the massive police dragnet and was never seen again. The third escapee was recaptured and returned to KP.

10. *Queer Life: SW Ontario*, found online at cdigs.uwindsor.ca.

11. Marshall, op. cit., p. 8.
12. *Toronto Daily Star*, October 17, 1946, p. 8.
13. Ibid.
14. Cook, Tim, *Fight to the Finish: Canadians in the Second World War, 1939–1945*, Vol. II (Allen Lane, 2015), p. 423.
15. Harold Russell is one of just two non-professional actors to win an Academy Award (the other being Haing S. Ngor, who appeared in the 1984 film *The Killing Fields*). Russell is also said to carry the distinction of being the only actor to sell his own Oscar at auction. He sold it in 1992 for $60,500 and used the money to pay his wife's medical bills.
16. A 1995 report by the CBC television program *The Fifth Estate* stirred up a huge controversy when it made the case the Dresden raids were militarily unnecessary and had been carried out purely to avenge German bombing of British cities. www.cbc.ca/archives/entry/the-bombing-of-dresden.
17. Pyves, Richard, *Night Madness: A Rear Gunner's Story of Love, Courage, and Hope in WWII* (Red Deer Press, 2012), p. 248.
18. *Fight to the Finish*, op. cit., p. 422.
19. Ibid., p. 422.
20. Military historian Terry Copp has written the definitive account of Canadian efforts to deal with the traumatic psychiatric wounds of the Second World War in his book *Battle Exhaustion: Soldiers and Psychiatrists in the Canadian Army, 1939–1945* (McGill-Queen's University Press, 1990).
21. *Toronto Daily Star*, February 28, 1948, p. 2.
22. *Globe and Mail*, March 1, 1948, p. 4.
23. *Toronto Daily Star*, October 18, 1945, p. 2.
24. *Globe and Mail*, October 18, 1945, p. 15.
25. Butts, Edward, *Wrong Side of the Law* (Dundurn Press, 2013), p. 121.
26. The two-room shack the Polka Dot Gang used as their hideout was located at the intersection of Bathurst and Mill Streets in Richmond Hill. The building was demolished many years ago, and the land where it once stood is now the site of Rumble Pond Park.
27. *Toronto Daily Star*, November 2, 1945, p. 1.
28. *Globe and Mail*, January 21, 1946, p. 5.
29. *Toronto Daily Star*, May 30, 1946, p. 7.
30. *Toronto Daily Star*, June 27, 1946, p. 1.
31. The lawyer for Green and Constantine appealed the men's convictions all the way to the Supreme Court of Canada, which dismissed both appeals.
32. *Globe and Mail*, July 5, 1954, p. 5.
33. *Globe and Mail*, March 1, 1948, p. 4.

Chapter 16

1. *Maclean's*, July 1, 1945, p. 12.
2. Author telephone interview with Havelyn Chiasson, Halifax, NS, June 11, 2019.
3. Author interview with A. Britton Smith, Kingston, ON, December 13, 2019.
4. MacDonald, Harold, and MacDonald, M.A., "Striking into Germany: From the Scheldt to the German Surrender," *Canadian Military History*, Vol. 12, No. 3, p. 7.
5. Sadly, Hal MacDonald died in a November 1984 car accident. He was sixty-seven at the time.
6. *Globe and Mail*, October 30, 1946, p. 17.
7. Creighton, Donald, *The Forked Road: Canada 1939-1957* (McClelland & Stewart, 1976), p. 116.
8. When the anticipated return to lower student enrollments didn't happen, Ottawa followed the advice offered by the 1951 Massey Royal Commission on National Development in the Arts, Letters and Sciences and began providing some financial support to Canadian universities, mainly for research. By 1950, university enrollment in Canada was double what it had been in 1940 (growing from 48,000 to 99,000); by 1963, enrollment would double again. With demographers predicting another huge increase in numbers as hundreds of thousands of baby boomers began studying at university, provincial governments jettisoned the idea of trying to meet enrollment increases by expanding existing institutions. The single-university policy in western provinces was abandoned as affiliated colleges became universities. Today, Canada has ninety-eight universities with a total student enrollment of 1.8 million. Post-secondary education is now a multi-billion-dollar business in this country.
9. *Kingston Whig-Standard*, October 10, 1945.
10. Until the early 1950s, wood and coal were the traditional fuels of winter home heating in Canada. All across the country, cleaner and safer furnaces that burned oil and natural gas gained in popularity. For better and worse, Canadians embraced the new products and services of "the oil age"—everything from shiny new automobiles and plastics to air travel. But that is another story for another time.
11. *Globe and Mail*, January 3, 1946, p. 11. In 1979, the Crown corporation's name would be changed to Canada Mortgage and Housing Corporation (CMHC).
12. The expression became popular with servicemen—initially American—during World War II. Its origins are uncertain, but there were references in Irish folk songs to a character named "Reilly" who lived a prosperous and easy life. That is certainly what veterans aspired to when they came home.
13. *Maclean's*, April 1, 1946, p. 53.

14. Orwam, Douglas, *Born at the Right Time: A History of the Baby Boom Generation* (University of Toronto Press, 1996), p. 56.
15. *Maclean's*, September 1, 1954, p. 7.

CHAPTER 17

1. These statistics, found in the Canada Year Books (online at www66.statcan.gc.ca), are for traditional heterosexual marriages only. Prior to 2005, there were no legal same-sex unions in Canada.
2. www.angusreid.org/marriage-trends-canada/.
3. Mitic, Jody (ed.), *Everyday Heroes: Inspirational Stories from Men and Women in the Canadian Armed Forces* (Simon & Schuster, 2017), p. 37.
4. Author interview with Bill Fitsell, Kingston, ON, September 27, 2018.
5. Chartier, Jacqueline, "Canada's Forgotten War Babies," *Esprit de Corps*, Vol. 12, No. 4 (2005), p. 22.
6. Author telephone interview with Cmdr. Peter Chance (Ret'd), Victoria, BC, February 18, 2019.
7. Ladouceur, Barbara, and Spence, Phyllis (eds.), *Blackouts to Bright Lights: Canadian War Bride Stories* (Rosedale Press, 1995), p. 46.
8. Ibid., p. 47.
9. For the full personal stories of the experiences of Isabella (Neilson) French and thirty-five other Canadian war brides, please see *Blackouts to Bright Lights*, op. cit.
10. *Maclean's*, December 15, 1944, p. 12.
11. *Blackouts to Bright Lights*, op. cit., p. 14.
12. *Stratford Beacon Herald*, May 11, 1995.
13. Author telephone interview with Betty Dow, Stratford, ON, December 21, 2019.
14. Ibid.
15. Between August 1944 and January 1947, a total of 41,351 war brides and 19,737 children made the crossing to Canada. http://canadianwarbrides.com/cwbstats1.asp.
16. Dow interview, op. cit.
17. Ibid.
18. Ibid.
19. Ibid.
20. Bruce, Jean, *After the War* (Fitzhenry and Whiteside, 1982), p. 16.
21. Ibid., p. 107.
22. Ibid., p. 189.
23. *The Boomer Revolution*, a CBC archival film, online at www.curio.ca.
24. *The Canadian Encyclopedia*, www.thecanadianencyclopedia.ca/en/article/baby-boom.

CHAPTER 18

1. Truman, Harry, *Memoirs: Year of Decisions*, Vol. I (Doubleday, 1955), p. 421.
2. Mackenzie King diaries, Library and Archives Canada, www.bac-lac.gc.ca, August 6, 1945, p. 3.
3. *Globe and Mail*, August 7, 1945, p. 1.
4. King diaries, op. cit., August 6, 1945, p. 3.
5. *Toronto Daily Star*, October 30, 1946, p. 7.
6. Bruce, Jean, *After the War* (Fitzhenry and Whiteside, 1982), p. 12.
7. *Globe and Mail*, August 11, 1945, p. 3.
8. Malone, Richard S., *A World in Flames, 1944–45* (Collins, 1984), p. 255.

CHAPTER 19

1. Sawatsky, John, *Gouzenko: The Untold Story* (Macmillan of Canada, 1984), p. 277.
2. That is the final scene in British director Stanley Kubrick's brilliant, dark 1964 political satire *Dr. Strangelove: How I Learned to Stop Worrying and Love the Bomb.*
3. Gouzenko, Igor, *This Was My Choice* (J.M. Dent and Sons, 1948), p. 12.
4. Don Fast, as quoted in Sawatsky, op. cit., p 7.
5. Ibid., pp. 9–10.
6. Ibid., p. 10.
7. NKVD was the acronym for the *Narodnyy Komissariat Vnutrennikh Del*, which translates into English as the People's Commissariat of Internal Affairs.
8. Gouzenko, op. cit., p. 15.
9. An alternative spelling of the town's name is Rogachvovo. An online Russian-language article about the town identifies Gouzenko as a "famous native son."
10. GRU is the English version of the Russian acronym ГРУ, which means "main intelligence directorate." Today, the GRU is Russia's chief spy agency and is reportedly behind cyber attacks, computer hacking, political assassinations, and other dirty work in foreign countries.
11. Fischer, Benjamin B., "The Gouzenko Affair, the Beginnings of the Cold War, and American Counterintelligence," in *The Gouzenko Affair*, J.L. Black and Martin Rudner (eds.) (Penumbra Press, 2006), p. 73.
12. Sawatsky, op. cit., p. 3.
13. Ibid., p. 2.
14. Knight, Amy, *How the Cold War Began: The Gouzenko Affair and the Hunt for Soviet Spies* (McClelland & Stewart, 2005), pp. 32–33. This book stands as the definitive account of Gouzenko's defection and on post-war Soviet espionage in Canada.
15. Sawatsky, op. cit., p. 20.

16. Sawatsky, op. cit., p. 31.
17. Communications Security Establishment Twitter feed, https://twitter.com/cse_cst/status/1037789474116304897, accessed November 15, 2019.
18. Sawatsky, op. cit., p. 31.
19. Mackenzie King diaries, Library and Archives Canada, www.bac-lac.gc.ca, op. cit., September 6, 1945, p. 2.
20. Stephenson, who was known by his wartime code name "Intrepid," is said to have inspired author Ian Fleming to create his now-iconic fictional 007 spy, James Bond. Stephenson's presence in Ottawa in September 1945 during the initial stages of the Gouzenko affair was secret at the time and remained unconfirmed until July 2019, when it came to light that Stephenson had indeed been there. This information was made public as a result of an Access to Information and Privacy (ATIP) request by Canadian Press journalist Jim Bronskill that led to the release of large portions of a classified history of the Canadian intelligence community written by Professor Wesley Wark, a retired faculty member of the Munk School of Global Affairs at the University of Toronto, who is one of Canada's leading experts on national security, intelligence, and terrorism. Wark had written the narrative under the sponsorship of the Privy Council Office in the years between 1998 and 2002.
21. Fischer, op. cit., p. 75.
22. Mackenzie King diaries, Library and Archives Canada, www.bac-lac.gc.ca, September 7, 1945.
23. *Globe and Mail*, October 2, 1945, p. 1.
24. PC 6444, found online at http://publications.gc.ca/collections/collection_2014/bcp-pco/CP32-103-1946-5-eng.pdf.
25. Williams's secret memo on the Corby Case, December 7, 1945, is available online at https://historyofrights.ca/wp-content/uploads/documents/williams_memo.pdf.
26. Knight, op. cit., p. 106.
27. Their contacts had not alerted them to the details of Gouzenko's defection; low-level operatives and sympathizers were expendable. The Soviets had decided that shielding Philby's presence in the highest levels of the British counter-intelligence network was of paramount importance.
28. *Toronto Daily Star*, February 16, 1946, p. 3.
29. Knight, op. cit., pp. 184–185.
30. King diaries, op. cit., February 17, 1946.
31. Ibid., March 21, 1946.
32. *Globe and Mail*, June 21, 1946, p. 15.
33. Knight, op. cit., p. 189.
34. King diaries, op. cit., July 26, 1945.
35. Gouzenko decided he could not work with two other journalists whom his publisher had hired. O'Brien was the compromise third candidate.

36. *Globe and Mail*, June 30, 1982, p. 1.
37. Woodside, John, "Seeing Red," *Maisonneuve Quarterly*, April 23, 2019, https://maisonneuve.org/article/2019/04/23/seeing-red-gouzenko/.
38. Kavchak, Andrew, "Remembering Igor Gouzenko," in Fischer, op. cit.
39. Wesley Wark, email to the author, December 30, 2019.
40. Ibid.

Conclusion

1. *Montreal Gazette*, December 31, 1945, p. 8.
2. *Calgary Herald*, December 31, 1945. p. 4.
3. *Toronto Daily Star*, July 13, 1946, p. 14.
4. Mackenzie King diaries, Library and Archives Canada, www.bac-lac.gc.ca, January 1, 1947, p. 1.
5. Stacey, C.P., *A Very Double Life: The Private World of Mackenzie King* (Macmillan, 1976), p. 11.
6. Ibid., p. 9.
7. King diaries, op. cit., January 1, 1946.
8. Granatstein, J.L., *The Ottawa Men: The Civil Service Mandarins, 1935–1957* (Oxford University Press, 1982), p. 92.
9. Wark, Wesley, "The Road to CANUSA: How Canadian Signals Intelligence Won Its Independence and Helped Create the Five Eyes," *Journal of Intelligence and National Security*, Vol. 35, No. 1 (2020). (Accessible online.)
10. MI5 is the acronym for Section 5 of Britain's Military Intelligence operation. It is involved in domestic counter-intelligence and security work alongside the Secret Intelligence Service (MI6), Government Communications Headquarters (GCHQ), and Defence Intelligence (DI).

Selected Bibliography

Abella, Irving, *None Is Too Many: Canada and the Jews of Europe* (University of Toronto Press, 2012).

Abella, Irving, Acheson, T.W., Bercuson, David, Brown, R. Craig, Granatstein, J.L., and Neatby, Blair (eds.), *Nation: Canada Since Confederation* (3rd ed.) (McGraw-Hill Ryerson, 1990).

Ajzenstat, Janet, and Smith, Peter (eds.), *Canada's Origins: Liberal, Tory or Republican?* (McGill-Queen's University Press, 1997).

Balzer, Timothy John, "The Information Front: The Canadian Army, Public Relations, and War News during the Second World War" (University of British Columbia Press, 2011).

Barris, Ted, *Days of Victory: Canadians Remember, 1939–45* (Thomas Allen, 2005).

Béliveau, Jean, *My Life in Hockey* (McClelland & Stewart, 1994).

Berton, Pierre, *The Great Depression: 1929–1939* (McClelland & Stewart, 1990).

Bird, Will, *North Shore (New Brunswick) Regiment* (Brunswick Press, 1963).

Black, J.L., and Rudner, Martin (eds.), *The Gouzenko Affair* (Penumbra Press, 2006).

Blumenson, Martin, *The Patton Papers, 1940–1945* (Houghton Mifflin, 1974).

Bothwell, Robert (ed.), *The Gouzenko Transcripts: The Evidence Presented to the Kellock-Taschereau Royal Commission of 1946* (Breakthrough Publishing, 1982).

Bothwell, Robert, Drummond, Ian, and English, John, *Canada Since 1945: Power, Politics, and Provincialism* (University of Toronto Press, 1981).

Bothwell, Robert, and Granatstein, J.L., *Our Century: The Canadian Journey in the Twentieth Century* (McArthur & Co., 2000).

Bothwell, Robert, and Killbourn, William, *C.D. Howe: A Biography* (McClelland & Stewart, 1979).

Broadfoot, Barry, *Six War Years* (Doubleday, 1974).

Bruce, Jean, *After the War* (Fitzhenry and Whiteside, 1982).

Butts, Edward, *Wrong Side of the Law* (Dundurn Press, 2013).

Cameron, Elspeth, *Hugh MacLennan: A Writer's Life* (University of Toronto Press, 1981).

Cameron, James, *Murray: The Martyred Admiral* (Lancelot Press, 1981).

Carrier, Roch, *Our Life with the Rocket: The Maurice Richard Story* (Viking, 2001).

Carter, David, *Behind Canadian Barbed Wire* (Eagle Butte Press, 1998).

Cook, Tim, *Fight to the Finish: Canadians in the Second World War, 1944–45*, Vol. II (Allen Lane, 2015).

Cook, Tim, *Warlords: Borden, Mackenzie King, and Canada's World Wars* (Allen Lane, 2012).

Copp, Terry, *Battle Exhaustion: Soldiers and Psychiatrists in the Canadian Army, 1939–1945* (McGill-Queen's University Press, 1990).

Creighton, Donald, *The Forked Road: Canada 1939–1957* (McClelland & Stewart, 1976).

Crowley, Terry, *Agnes Macphail and the Politics of Equality* (James Lorimer & Company, 1990).

Cuthbertson, Ken, (ed.), *Queen's Goes to War* (Queen's University Alumni Association, 1995).

Dickson, Paul, *A Thoroughly Canadian General* (University of Toronto Press, 2007).

Edugyan, Esi, *Dreaming of Elsewhere: Observations on Home* (University of Alberta Press, 2014).

Edwards, Kenneth, *Seven Sailors* (Collins, 1945).

English, John, and Stubbs, J.O., *Mackenzie King: Widening the Debate* (Macmillan of Canada, 1977).

Fischler, Stan, and Richard, Maurice, *The Flying Frenchmen: Hockey's Greatest Dynasty* (Hawthorn Books, 1971).

Fitken, Ed, *Hockey's Rocket* (Castle Publications, 1951).

Foran, Charles, *Maurice Richard* (Penguin Canada, 2011).

French, Doris, and Stewart, Margaret, *Ask No Quarter: A Biography of Agnes Macphail* (Longman, Green and Company, 1959).

Fuykschot, Cornelia, *Hunger in Holland* (CeFar Associates, 1988).

Galloway, Priscilla (ed.), *Too Young to Fight* (Stoddart, 1999).

Gossage, Carolyn, *Greatcoats and Glamour Boots: Canadian Women at War (1939–1945)* (Dundurn, 2001).

Gouzenko, Igor, *This Was My Choice: Gouzenko's Story* (J.M. Dent and Sons, 1948).

Granatstein, Jack, *The Best Little Army in the World: The Canadians in Northwest Europe, 1944–1945* (HarperCollins Canada, 2015).

Granatstein, J.L., *A Man of Influence: Norman Robertson and the Canadian Statecraft, 1929–1968* (Deneau Publishers, 1981).

Granatstein, J.L., *The Ottawa Men: The Civil Service Mandarins, 1935–1957* (Oxford University Press, 1982).

Gray, James H., *The Winter Years: The Depression on the Prairies* (Macmillan Canada, 1966).

Gregory, Doris, *How I Won the War for the Allies: One Sassy Canadian Soldier's Story* (Ronsdale Press, 2004).

Harbron, John, *C.D. Howe* (Fitzhenry and Whiteside, 1980).

Harris, Stephen, and Horn, Bernd (eds.), *Warrior Chiefs: Perspectives on Senior Canadian Military Leaders* (Dundurn Press, 2000).

Horn, Michael, *The Great Depression of the 1930s in Canada* (Booklet 39) (Canadian Historical Association, 2004).

Hunter, Douglas, *War Games: Conn Smythe & Hockey's Fighting Men* (Viking, 1996).

Kellock, Justice R.L., *Report on the Halifax Disorders: May 7–8, 1945* (The King's Printer, 1945).

Keshen, A. Jeffrey, *Saints, Sinners, and Soldiers: Canada's Second World War* (University of British Columbia Press, 2007).

Knight, Amy, *How the Cold War Began: The Gouzenko Affair and the Hunt for Soviet Spies* (McClelland & Stewart, 2005).

Ladouceur, Barbara, and Spence, Phyllis (eds.), *Blackouts to Bright Lights: Canadian War Bride Stories* (Rosedale Press, 1995).

Lewis, David, *The Good Fight: Political Memoirs, 1909–1958* (Macmillan of Canada, 1981).

Malone, Richard S., *A World in Flames, 1944–45* (Collins, 1984).

MacLaren, Roy, *Mackenzie King in the Age of Dictators: Canada's Imperial and Foreign Policies* (McGill-Queen's University Press, 2019).

McDowall, Duncan, *The Sum of All Satisfactions: Canada in the Age of National Accounting* (McGill-Queen's University Press, 2008).

Menzies, Robert, *Dark and Hurrying Days: Menzies's 1941 Diary* (National Library of Australia, 1993).

Milner, Marc, *The Admirals: Canada's Senior Naval Leadership in the Twentieth Century* (Dundurn Press, 2006).

Mitic, Jody (ed.), *Everyday Heroes: Inspirational Stories from Men and Women in the Canadian Armed Forces* (Simon & Schuster, 2017).

Morton, Desmond, and Granatstein, J.L., *Victory 1945: Canadians from War to Peace* (HarperCollins Canada, 1995).

Moscovitch, Allan, *Report on Social Security for Canada* (McGill-Queen's University Press, 2017).

Neary, Peter, and Granatstein, J.L. (eds.), *The Veterans Charter and Post–World War II Canada* (McGill-Queen's University Press, 1998).

Newman, Peter C., *The Canadian Establishment*, Vol. I (McClelland & Stewart, 1975).

O'Brien, Andy, *Rocket Richard* (Ryerson Press, 1961).

Ogilvie, Sarah, and Miller, Scott, *Refuge Denied: The* St. Louis *Passengers and the Holocaust* (University of Wisconsin Press, 2010).

Orwam, Douglas, *Born at the Right Time: A History of the Baby Boom Generation* (University of Toronto Press, 1996).

Pennington, Doris, *Agnes Macphail: Reformer* (Simon and Pierre, 1990).

Pratt, Andre, and Kay, Jonathan (eds.), *Legacy: How French Canadians Shaped North America* (McClelland & Stewart, 2016).

Pyves, Richard, *Night Madness: A Rear Gunner's Story of Love, Courage, and Hope in WWII* (Red Deer Press, 2012).

Redman, Stanley, *Open Gangway: An Account of the Halifax Riots, 1945* (Lancelot Press, 1991).

Ritchie, Charles, *Diplomatic Passport: More Undiplomatic Diaries, 1947–1962* (Macmillan, 1981).

Roberts, James, *The Canadian Summer* (University of Toronto Bookroom, 1981).

Robertson, Gordon, *Memoirs of a Very Civil Servant: Mackenzie King to Pierre Trudeau* (University of Toronto Press, 2000).

Rohmer, Richard, *E.P. Taylor: The Biography of Edward Plunket Taylor* (McClelland & Stewart, 1978).

Sawatsky, John, *Gouzenko: The Untold Story* (Macmillan of Canada, 1984).

Schull, Joseph, *The Great Scot: A Biography of Donald Gordon* (McGill-Queen's University Press, 1979).

Stacey, C.P., *A Date with History: Memoirs of a Canadian Historian* (Deneau, 1982).

Stacey, C.P., *Official History of the Canadian Army in the Second World War*, Vol. III (The Queen's Printer, 1960).

Stacey, C.P., *A Very Double Life: The Private World of Mackenzie King* (Macmillan, 1976).

Suzuki, David, *David Suzuki: The Autobiography* (Greystone Press, 2006).

Truman, Harry, *Memoirs: Year of Decisions*, Vol. I (Doubleday, 1955).

Tucker, Gilbert N., *The Naval Service of Canada: Its Official History, Vol. 2: Activities on Shore During the Second World War* (Department of National Defence, 1952).

Vanasse, André, *Gabrielle Roy: A Passion for Writing* (XYZ Publishing, 2007).

Wardhaugh, Robert, *Behind the Scenes: The Life and Work of William Clifford Clark* (University of Toronto Press, 2010).

Whitby, Michael, Gimblett, Richard, and Haydon, Peter, *The Admirals: Canada's Senior Naval Leadership in the Twentieth Century* (Dundurn Press, 2006).

Young, Scott, *Hello Canada! The Life and Times of Foster Hewitt* (Seal Books, 1985).

Selected Newspaper and Magazine/Journal Articles

Allan, Laura, "The Women's Royal Canadian Naval Service," *Canadian Naval Review*, Vol. 3, No. 3 (2007).

Berton, Pierre, "E.P. Taylor and His Empire," *Maclean's*, March 1, 1950.

Brandt, Gail Cuthbert, "'Pigeon Holed and Forgotten': The Work of the Subcommittee on the Post-War Problems of Women, 1943," *Social History*, Vol. XV, No. 29 (1982).

Brown, E.K. "Mackenzie King of Canada," *Harper's*, January 1, 1943.

Callwood, June, "The Maurice Richards," *Maclean's*, May 1959.

Chartier, Jacqueline, "Canada's Forgotten War Babies," *Esprit de Corps*, Vol. 12, No. 4 (2005).

Dufour, Paul, "Eggheads and Espionage: The Gouzenko Affair in Canada," *Journal of Canadian Studies*, Vol. 16, No. 3/4.

Faulkner, William, "An Innocent at Rinkside," *Sports Illustrated*, January 24, 1955.

Fraser, Blair, "Blair Fraser Keeps a Rendezvous with Igor Gouzenko," *Maclean's*, September 1, 1953.

Gibb, Alice, "Agnes Campbell Macphail: 'I'm No Lady,'" *High Profile*, March/April 1988, p. 14.

Granatstein, J.L., "Arming the Nation: Canada's Industrial War Effort, 1939–45," paper written for the Canadian Council of Chief Executives, 2005.

Granatstein, J.L., "Gouzenko: The Defector Who Served the West Well," *Globe and Mail*, July 6, 1982.

Horn, Michael, "Leonard Marsh and His Ideas: 1967–1982: Some Personal Recollections," *Journal of Canadian Studies*, Vol. 21, No. 2 (1986).

Horn, Michael, "Leonard Marsh and the Coming of a Welfare State in Canada," *Histoire sociale*, Vol. 9, No. 17 (1976).

MacDonald, Marjorie, and Captain Harold MacDonald, "Holland Summer: Awaiting Repatriation, May–August 1945," *Canadian Military History*, Vol. 13, No. 45 (2004), pp. 29–45.

MacDonald, Marjorie, and Captain Harold MacDonald, "In the Heat of Battle: Letters from the Normandy Campaign, 1944," *Canadian Military History*, Vol. 11, No. 2 (2003), pp. 29–43.

MacDonald Marjorie, and Captain Harold MacDonald, "The Long Wait (Part I): A Personal Account of Infantry Training in Britain, June 1942–June 1943," *Canadian Military History*, Vol. 15, No. 2 (2006), pp. 35–50.

MacDonald, Marjorie, and Captain Harold MacDonald, "The Long Wait (Part II): A Personal Account of Infantry Training in Britain, June 1942–June 1943," Vol. 15, No. 3/4 (2006), pp. 71–85.

MacDonald, Marjorie, and Captain Harold MacDonald, "Striking into Germany: From the Scheldt to the German Surrender," *Canadian Military History*, Vol. 12, No. 3 (2003), pp. 1–22.

Marshall, A.S., "Crime Wave," *Maclean's*, April 15, 1946.

Maxwell, Eaton, "Canada Looks to the Postwar," *Antioch Review*, December 1, 1943.

Milner, Marc, "The Rise of Leonard Murray: Navy Part 30," *Legion Magazine*, December 12, 2008.

Moon, Barbara, "The Last Chapter of the Great E.P. Taylor Myth," *Maclean's*, July 6, 1963.

O'Leary, M. Gratton, "The Man Behind Ilsley," *Maclean's*, May 1, 1945.

Porter, Michael, "From Competitive Advantage to Corporate Strategy," *Harvard Business Review*, May 1987.

Pringle, Gertrude, "Bake, Churn, Cook, Milk, Sew . . ." *Maclean's*, January 15, 1922, p. 45.

Slide, Anthony, "Lost Gay Novel: John Buchan's *Greenmantle*," *Harrington Gay Men's Literary Quarterly*, May 2007, pp. 147–150.

Wark, Wesley, "The Road to CANUSA: How Canadian Signals Intelligence Won Its Independence and Helped Create the Five Eyes," *Journal of Intelligence and National Security*, Vol. 35, No. 1 (2020).

Woodside, John, "Seeing Red," *Maisonneuve Quarterly*, April 23, 2019.

SELECTED ONLINE RESOURCES

CBC Archives, www.cbc.ca/history.

The Canadian Encyclopedia, www.thecanadianencyclopedia.ca/en.

Canadian naval history, www.canada.ca/en/navy/services/history/naval-service-1910-2010.html.

Canada Year Books online, https://www66.statcan.gc.ca/acyb_000-eng.htm.

Juno Beach Centre home page, www.junobeach.org.

Mackenzie King diaries, Library and Archives Canada, www.bac-lac.gc.ca.

Statistics Canada, www150.statcan.gc.ca.

PERSONAL INTERVIEWS

Geraldine (Gorman) Bagnall, Kingston, ON, April 16, 2019.

Cmdr. Peter Chance (Ret'd), Victoria, BC, February 18, 2019.

Havelyn Chiasson, Halifax, NS, June 11, 2019.

F. Stuart Crawford, Kingston, ON, January 7, 2020.

Hildegard Von Derheiden, Kingston, ON, April 5, 2019.

Alec Douglas, Toronto, ON, July 11, 2019.

Betty Dow, Stratford, ON, December 21, 2019.

Barbara (Robson) Fitsell, Kingston, ON, December 9, 2019.

Bill Fitsell, Kingston, ON, September 27, 2018; February 18, 2019.

George Henderson, Wilton, ON, June 8, 2019.

Catherine MacDonald, Saint John, NB, June 3, 2019.

Dominic Petrie, Yarker, ON, July 13, 2019.

A. Britton Smith, Kingston, ON, December 4, 2019; December 13, 2019.

Index

Note: Page numbers in italics indicate photographs.
Page numbers with an "n" indicate notes.

Japanese Canadians, 40–42, 45, 231, 304, 359n

Japanese fire balloons, 46

Jaques, Edna, 56, 61

Jews, in Canada, 42–43, 304, 305

Joliat, Aurèle, 84–85

Jolliffe, Ted, 193, 197–98

Jones, Admiral George C., 155–56, 167–69

K

Kellock, Justice Roy L., 167, 331, 333

Keynes, John Maynard, 206, 230

King, William Lyon Mackenzie, 5, 13–14, 26, 33–35, 124, 138, 151, 341
appearance, 25
atomic bomb (reaction to), 302–3
baby bonus, 228
Canada's flag, 192
Clifford Clark, relationship with, 210
conscription issue, 13, 33, 96, 226
death, 342
diary, 34–35, 342–43
dog (Irish terrier, Pat), 28, 34, 344
economic policies, 38–39, 64–65, 203, 206
election (1945), 64–65, 218, 228–37
and Gouzenko defection, 326–27, 329–30, 332–33, 336
Halifax riots (reaction to), 166
Hitler, opinion of, 191
Industry and Humanity (book), 207, 214, 229, 233, 343
mother, Isabel (née Mackenzie), 25, 28, 34
political career, 23–24, 31
private life, 30–31, 180
racism, 45, 304

Roosevelt, Franklin D. (relations with), 214

Royal Commission (re Gouzenko) 333–34
sexuality, 29–30
spiritualism, 28, 34–35, 71–72
superstitions, 34, 72–73
temperament, 11, 20, 25–27
and temperance, 171–72, 176
United Nations founding conference (1945), 138–139, 234–35, 246
VE day, 144
veterans' scorn for, 14, 232
VJ day, 306–307
War Measures Act, 45–46

Knight, Amy (American historian and scholar of Russian spying activities), 320, 331, 333, 334, 375n

Knowles, R.E. (*Toronto Daily Star* celebrity reporter), 2

L

Labatt Breweries, 176, 179

Lach, Elmer (hockey centre), 93, 94, 105, 106, 111

Laurier House, 27–29

Laurier, Wilfrid, 1, 23, 24, 27–28, 208, 357n

Laurier, Zoé, 27, 28

Lauzon, Ulysses, 256, 371n

Leach, Florence, 205

League for Social Reconstruction, 217

LeBel, A.M. (Ontario Supreme Court judge), 198

LeSueur, Percy (*Hockey Night in Canada* broadcaster), 103

Levitt, Joe, 197

Lewis, Captain Robert (USAF, co-pilot of the *Enola Gay*), 301